Building Europe

The EU today seeks to forge 'ever-closer union among the peoples of Europe' and to lay the foundations for a new system of government that will supersede the nation-state. But corruption scandals in Brussels and declining public support for European institutions highlight serious deficiencies, and reveal a corrosive lack of democracy and accountability. In the search for solutions, the EU has increasingly turned to 'cultural action'.

Building Europe details the attempts of EU elites to use culture as a tool for forging a sense of cohesion and belonging among Europeans – from invented Euro-symbols and statistics to European citizenship and the single currency. Unprecedented first-hand insights into the working culture of the European Commission are provided, with explanations for its seemingly endemic fraud and corruption. The author asks whether, in the absence of a popular European consciousness, the EU's supranational ideal can ever lead to a 'people's Europe' rather than a centralised and unaccountable nation-state.

Building Europe offers a revelatory anthropological scrutiny and powerful critique of the attempt to create a single Europe. It will be essential reading for anyone with an interest in the culture and politics of the EU, as well as being highly relevant to courses in international relations, politics and social anthropology.

Cris Shore is Head of the Anthropology Department at Goldsmiths College, University of London. He has published and lectured extensively on European integration and EU cultural politics. His co-edited volume *Anthropology of Policy* (with Susan Wright) is published by Routledge (1997).

Building Europe
The Cultural Politics of European Integration

Cris Shore

London and New York

First published 2000
by Routledge
2 Park Square, Milton Park, Abingdon, Oxon, OX14 4RN

Simultaneously published in the USA and Canada
by Routledge
270 Madison Ave, New York, NY 10016

Routledge is an imprint of the Taylor & Francis Group

Transferred to Digital Printing 2006

Typeset in Galliard by RefineCatch Limited, Bungay, Suffolk

British Library Cataloguing in Publication Data
A catalogue record for this book is available from the British Library

Library of Congress Cataloging in Publication Data
Shore, Cris, 1959–
   Building Europe: the cultural politics of European integration /
   Cris Shore.
      p. cm.
   Includes bibliographical references and index.
   1. Europe – Politics and government – 1989–   2. European
   Union.   3. Nationalism – Europe.   I. Title.
   D2009.S54   2000
   306.2′094 – dc21   99–054929

ISBN 0–415–18014–7 (hbk)
ISBN 0–415–18015–5 (pbk)

Printed and bound by CPI Antony Rowe, Eastbourne

To my father, who taught me why politics matter, and to Paul Van Buitenen, whose revelations stimulated a long-overdue debate about democracy and the rule of law inside the European Union.

Contents

List of illustrations

Figures

Tables

Preface

The origins of this book lie in an interest, nurtured over many years, in the anthropology of Europe and in the European Union as a social project. In 1993 I conducted a pilot study, funded by the Nuffield Foundation, into the information policy of the European Parliament and European Commission. That research alerted me to the panoply of cultural devices and techniques being deployed by EU policy professionals to turn the so-called 'European idea' into a reality. The phrase '*Europe on the Move*' – which is also the title of a series of European Commission public information booklets – summed up the feeling of optimism that I encountered in Brussels. At that time, the cultural dimensions of European integration had barely begun to be seriously researched, let alone theorised. A grant from the Economic and Social Research Council in 1995 enabled me to return to Brussels armed with more probing questions about the role of 'culture' in the integration project. I was also interested in studying the EU's institutions themselves and the cultural attitudes of those who staff them. Clifford Geertz (1984: 125) once wrote that the task of anthropology is not merely to study what people do but also 'to figure out what the devil they think they are up to'; to understand social reality 'from the native's point of view'. That principle has guided my approach throughout this study, although I have also tried to con-textualise and critique the norms and assumptions that inform that point of view.

The construction of the EU represents the most exciting and profound de-velopment in European politics and society of the twentieth century. It therefore deserves careful and rigorous analysis. The aim of this book is to provide precisely such a critical commentary on that construction process. It is not, however, a comprehensive account, nor does it seek to introduce the reader to all aspects of EU cultural policy and politics. Rather, the goal is to open up for scrutiny and debate cultural aspects of the integration process that are often taken for granted, as well as some areas that have traditionally been conceived as the domain of economics, politics and law.

The tone of this study is critical and sceptical. To be otherwise would, in my view, be contrary to the principles of good social science. Yet scepticism, as Ian Ward (1996: vii) says, is too readily castigated in European Union studies. Scep-tics are portrayed as somehow small-minded and anti-European. A few are, but for the most part these accusations are unfounded, ignorant and intellectually dishonest. Indeed, they reflect precisely the ideology that sustains the European project that this study seeks to unravel.

The best way to read this book is from beginning to end. However, the two halves of the study can be read separately and most of the chapters, although thematically linked and cumulative, can be read individually without too much difficulty as each deals with a specific and relatively discrete aspect of the integration process, such as citizenship, the single currency, the powers of the Commission and so forth.

There are a great many people to whom I owe a debt of gratitude. Without the encouragement and the unflagging support of Fiona Graham I would not have finished this book. Thank you for living with this book through all its stages of evolution. Several people were also kind enough to comment on chapters of the book. Sue Wright, Simon Duffin, Stephen Roberts, David Powell and Nigel Llewellyn all gave helpful feedback and their conversations have helped to stir my thoughts. I am particularly grateful to colleagues at the universities of Bath, Berlin, Birmingham, Frankfurt, London, Malta, Prague and Stockholm for their critical comments on the various seminar and conference papers where earlier drafts of the book were presented and honed over the past year. Those discussions were particularly helpful in fusing my anthropological concerns with more mainstream political and European debates. I also wish to thank Paul Clough, Jeremy Boissevain, Ulf Hannerz, Ronalde Stade, Don Handleman, Hastings Donnan, Liisa Malki, Seteney Shami, Hugh Gusterson, Annabel Black, Iain Hendry, Peter Niedermüller, John Cole, Jonas Frykman, Klaus Roth, Mike O'Hanlon, Liz Edwards, Irène Bellier and Birgit Muller, all of whom provided valuable feedback. Since I have not accepted all the suggestions made by any of those who have read or heard me deliver papers on parts of the book, and few would accept everything that I argue, the usual disclaimers apply. Finally, I thank my colleagues and Goldsmiths College for granting me a term's sabbatical to finish this manuscript, Anna Whitworth for producing the tables of figures used in Chapter 7, and the students at Goldsmiths College who have followed my course on the Anthropology of European Integration over the years, and with whom I have benefited from innumerable stimulating discussions.

Parts of Chapters 1 and 2 appeared in an article written for the *Journal of Historical Sociology*. I am grateful to the editors of that journal for granting me permission to use that material here.

Introduction

European integration as a cultural project

Over the past fifty years the project for European unification has developed from a 'European Coal and Steel Community' to a Common Market, from a Common Market to the 'European Economic Community' (EEC), from the European Economic Community to the 'European Communities' (EC), and from the European Communities to the 'European Union' (EU) – defined in the 1992 Maastricht Treaty as 'a new stage in the process of creating an ever-closer union among the peoples of Europe'. This evolution has been accompanied by a shift in emphasis from integration, perceived as a rational by-product of economic prosperity and legal harmonisation, to more recent concerns with integration as a cultural process, and 'culture' as a political instrument for furthering that construction process. Despite this profound transformation in the scope and character of the European venture, most people in Britain remain ill-informed and in the dark about the European Union and still perceive integration as a largely technical and economic issue of little serious constitutional or cultural importance. By contrast, what concerns EU officials and politicians is not *whether* a political union can be developed, but how to go beyond this and foster a 'European identity' that will extend integration into the more 'cultural' and psychological domains of everyday life. This concern is driven, as we shall see, largely by political imperatives, particularly the need to endow the EU's institutions and emerging system of transnational governance with legitimacy.

This book is an anthropological study of the cultural politics of European integration.[1] Drawing on ethnographic fieldwork carried out among European Union civil servants and politicians in Brussels between 1993 and 1997, it explores the ways in which EU elites have attempted to further the integration process by forging and diffusing their vision of 'European consciousness' and 'European culture' among the peoples of Europe. It also sets out to identify and examine more closely the key actors and architects responsible for promoting this vision. Three questions permeate this study. First, what role does 'culture' play in the process of European integration and how are EU policy-professionals using this concept in their efforts to create a more coherent sense of identity and belonging among European citizens? Second, can conditions be created to facilitate the transferal of popular loyalty and sovereignty from the nation-states to supranational institutions, as theories of integration claim? Third, what are the implications of this project for state-formation in Europe, or for the prospect of creating a more unified '*nation*-state of Europe'?

The title of the book was suggested by EU officials themselves during the many hours of conversations and interviews among civil servants of the European Commission and Parliament that were carried out during the course of the research.[2] As they saw it, the goal of the EU was to lay the foundations for a new kind of social and political order in Europe, one that would 'go beyond' the existing order based on competitive nation states. As I soon discovered, architectural metaphors featured prominently in the discourse of EU elites and in the project they call 'European construction'.[3] Their image of themselves, sometimes implicit, often explicit, was that of architects and masons engaged in the historical task of designing a new Europe. 'Building Europe' was therefore an important local idiom as well as a powerful political metaphor. Nowhere is this idea expressed more clearly than in the speeches and writings of Yves-Thibault de Silguy, the French Commissioner for Economic and Monetary Affairs and a leading advocate of the single currency. 'Since 1992', he writes (1997: 1–2):

> Community output seems to have expanded constantly, a phenomenon which is usually described – revealingly – as the 'construction' of Europe: architects and masons busying themselves around an edifice, while onlookers must wait until it is completed before they can appreciate its quality. All are laying the stones of a cathedral, the design and majesty of which will only be fully appreciated by our successors. Building Europe undeniably takes time. If on the human scale and in the eyes of its most fervent supporters the process appears to be hopelessly slow, in the eyes of the historians it is surprisingly rapid. After all, what is forty years of living amicably together compared with 1,500 years of rivalries and wars on our continent? Certainly, we cannot immediately break with such a long past. Solidarity among Europeans is not yet fully assured; it is still in the process of being created. This is the secret of the European alchemy initiated by the founding fathers: the 'great work' is achieved in stages.

Exactly how this 'great work' is being conducted provides the main focus for the first half of this study. This entails, among other things, an exploration of elite conceptions of culture and identity and the various ways in which these conceptions have been translated into policy. It also includes an analysis of specific case-studies of EU-sponsored initiatives designed to affect what EU officials call the 'Europeanisation' of the public sector – another Brussels folk idiom that is examined in detail later. As Chapter 1 illustrates, the study of EU cultural politics raises wider issues of public policy and politics, including theories of nationalism and supranationalism, hegemony, the politics of language and changing models of governance in Europe.

From an exploration of the various ways in which EU elites have attempted to Europeanise the masses, Part II ('EU Civil Servants: The New Europeans?') turns to examine the Europeanisation of the EU elites themselves, particularly the civil servants (or *fonctionnaires*) who work for the European Commission in Brussels. The composition and character of this organisation, often described as the 'heart of Europe' and 'motor of integration', raises fundamental questions about the dynamics of European integration. Given its claims about building a new Europe, it seems logical to ask whether the EU's transnational and supranational institutions provide a model of how European nationals might live and work together. Do EU civil servants embody the 'Europeanist' vision proclaimed in official texts and speeches? What sort of political culture(s) has the EU created within its own institutional heartlands? Is there evidence of an embryonic 'European identity' growing up inside the womb of the EU's bureaucracies and, if so, what are its defining features? It is widely claimed – most notably by EU officials and supporters themselves – that the European Commission is a 'supranational' institution; an 'honest broker' independent of external influences that exists to protect the 'European interest'. In the pages that follow we interrogate these assumptions by analysing the organisational culture or *modus vivendi* of the Commission and its implications for European integration and, more specifically, state-formation and democracy in Europe.

Structure and contents

Chapter 1 ('Forging a European *nation*-state? The European Union and questions of culture') draws together the main themes of the book and outlines the scope of the term 'cultural politics' as it applies to the EU and its project for uniting Europe. Taking up contemporary debates in anthropology over the concepts of 'identity', 'nation-building' and 'Europeanisation', it explores why the idea of a 'European identity' and shared 'cultural heritage' have come to feature so prominently in discourses on integration. As the chapter argues, the politicisation of culture in the EU arises from the attempt by European elites to solve the EU's chronic problem of legitimacy. In virtually all political systems, particularly democratic ones, culture is the fundamental bedrock upon which political legitimacy is established. What is often termed the EU's 'democratic deficit' is symptomatic of a deeper 'cultural deficit'; a deficit vividly reflected in the absence of a European public. By tracing the threads that link identity, legitimacy and democracy, the cultural politics of European integration thus provides an ideal site for addressing larger issues of ideology, power and state-formation in the EU.

The final part of Chapter 1 explores the relevance of theories of nation-state-formation for understanding European integration. It asks, can conditions be created for shifting popular loyalties and transcending the nation-state, as some theorists and EU enthusiasts predict? Can love of Europe as a *patria* be engineered? And if so, how might this be achieved? What factors could precipitate the creation of 'Europeanness' as a new category of subjectivity, or self-awareness? It has become fashionable to conceptualise nation-states as 'imagined communities', to use Anderson's (1983) phrase, invented through print capitalism, mass communication, mass education, historiography, conscription and other nation-building technologies. But what insights does the history of nation-state-formation offer for understanding the invention of Europe as a geopolitical category? These are the central questions that the rest of the book attempts to deal with.

Chapter 2 ('Creating the people's Europe: symbols, history and invented traditions') develops the notion of 'imagined communities' to look more closely at the way Europe is being constructed as a symbolic and political entity – and therefore as a more knowable and governable space. It tracks the history of EU cultural policy from the mid-1970s to the present day, focusing on the way 'culture' has been appropriated as a political instrument for the construction of Europe. Following an analysis of the European Commission's 'people's Europe' campaign in the 1980s, the chapter explores the various cultural strategies that are being used to mobilise mass opinion and foster 'European consciousness' among the citizenry. These strategies range from EU information policy and the creation of new Euro-symbols to the invention of Euro-statistics and the rewriting of history.

Chapter 3 ('Citizenship of the Union: the cultural construction of a European citizen') extends this inquiry a step further by analysing the history and politics of EU citizenship as a new legal category. Drawing on parallels with the cultural construction of citizenship in earlier times (notably eighteenth-century France), it focuses on the role of citizenship as a mobilising symbol and as a claim to statehood. It argues that while the specific rights and duties entailed by citizenship of the Union remain vague and limited, the political intent behind this initiative is quite transparent. However, exactly what citizenship might mean in a multicultural, transnational and post-welfare-state Europe is far from clear. While European Citizenship may indeed help to nurture a sense of belonging among fellow EU nationals, the chapter concludes by pointing out some of the negative consequences this has for non-EU nationals.

Chapter 4 ('Symbolising boundaries: the single currency and the art of European governance') assesses the political, constitutional and cultural implications of Europe's new single European currency, the 'euro'. Currencies have long been associated with statehood and national identity. What, therefore, is the relationship between the euro and state-formation in that recently created currency zone commonly referred to as 'Euroland'? Based on extensive interviews with officials and politicians in Brussels responsible for preparing public opinion for the launch of the euro, it examines the way the campaign for introducing the single currency was orchestrated, from its conception to its birth in January 1999. In doing so, it also provides an ethnographic analysis of elite attitudes to public opinion and a critical assessment of the arguments for and against Economic and Monetary Union (EMU). We end with a structural or 'semiotic' analysis of the designs for the euro banknotes and coins themselves and how these might be 'read' as icons and symbols of the new Europe.

Taken together, the chapters in Part I present a comprehensive picture of the different strategies and techniques used by Europe's *classe politique* to shape public opinion and advance the project for European political integration. More importantly, they show the cultural assumptions and instrumental logic underlying these initiatives. That, in turn, raises questions about the EU's image of itself and its claims to be promoting 'subsidiarity' and 'unity in diversity' in its approach to culture. Part II pushes the enquiry further by probing into the 'culture' of EU bureaucracy itself. The European Commission occupies a uniquely strategic position in the process of European construction, yet its role and powers are still much debated. Technically a bureaucracy and impartial executive whose independence is 'beyond doubt', it is also a political broker and diplomatic body that sees itself as 'custodian of the European idea' and 'conscience of Europe'. The civil servants appointed to administer the domains of governance ceded to Brussels are therefore a key element in the integration process. However, the character of EU institutions is itself indicative of the problems of trying to forge an ever-closer union among the peoples of Europe.

Despite the proliferation in recent years of books dealing with the EU's institutions and developing 'political culture', very little attention has been paid to everyday life within those institutions. We still know surprisingly little about the men and women who staff the EU offices, and still less about the social relations and cultural practices that shape their working environment. The second half of the book, therefore, is an anthropological study of part of the EU's growing web of transnational bodies and agents: the European Commission and its staff. Who are these officials and where do they come from? What exactly is the role of the Commission in the integration process, and how do staff perceive that role? What does *construction européenne* mean from the point of view of EU officials? And what does the Commission's 'organisational culture' indicate about the trajectory or nature of the European idea at the level of practice?

Chapter 5 ('A "supranational" civil service? The role of the Commission in the integration process') begins by examining the peculiar powers and functions of the Commission and the way these influence the character and identity of the organisation and its personnel. It also analyses the key terminology and idioms used by the Commission to describe itself and its objectives. Foremost among these is the concept of 'supranationalism', a legal term that has an ambiguous set of meanings. As I show, the meanings and uses of this concept have shifted as it has migrated from the domain of law to the field of politics. The result is that the term 'supranationalism' as a descriptive category has come to be imbued with the norms and assumptions typical of the ideology of European construction. The Commission's complex role as bureaucracy and public administration on the one hand and political broker and policy initiator on the other is yet another factor that shapes its unusual hybrid character. However, as we shall see, these complicated and sometimes contradictory roles lead to problems within the institution.

Chapter 6 ('The Brussels context: Integration and *engrenage* among EU elites') considers the political geography of the Commission and the Brussels environment in which its offices are located. It asks, what effect does the Brussels factor have on life within the EU institutions? In addressing this question, it examines a further key idiom used by officials in Brussels to describe European integration: '*engrenage*'. This term, which translates as 'enmeshing', is particularly important to debates about identity-formation among EU elites. Conventional theories of integration hold that EU officials, once appointed, will become progressively more 'European' in orientation as the process of '*engrenage*', the effect of working together in a 'European' environment, gradually shifts their loyalties towards the supranational ideals and institutions they serve. This theory is put to the test in the final chapters when we analyse the Commission's administration. The evidence presented in this chapter, however, suggests that the institutional lifestyle and rarefied environment in which most expatriate officials inhabit tend to isolate them from ordinary Belgians. The resulting insularity undoubtedly contributes to the formation of a strong *esprit de corps* among staff. However, the relationship between the Commission and its local setting is more complex than this and, while the Europeanisation of Brussels is incontestable, the 'Brusselsisation' of the EU is a more subtle process that is also occurring.

Chapter 7 ('Transnational, supranational or post-national? The organisational culture of the Commission') analyses the Commission's political culture. As a multinational and multicultural bureaucracy charged with a supranational mission, its task has always been to forge a distinctly 'European' system of public administration. How far has it succeeded in its attempt to create a new model of administration and an independent civil service of dedicated and professional Europeans? This chapter reviews the evidence by assessing the Commission's administrative regime, including its ethos and working methods, its management structure and recruitment practices, and its social composition. Finally, it explores the informal politics and practices that shape staffing and personnel policy within the Commission, including what officials call the 'parallel' or pragmatic system of administration. This parallel system includes patronage, nepotism, the employment of non-statutory staff, the use of informal networks and backdoor recruitment practices (including *parachutage* and *piston*). Taking up Spence's (1994a) argument that these practices undermine the EU's supranational quest, the chapter asks whether these practices might not be, instead, a necessary consequence of that quest.

Chapter 8 ('Conclusions: European construction, democracy and the politics of culture') draws together the conclusions of this study. Taking up questions posed by the tension between the Commission's formal and informal systems of administration, it turns to consider in detail the Committee of Independent Experts' report on fraud and mismanagement in the Commission, whose findings led to the mass resignation of the College of Commissioners in March 1999. Evidence of endemic corruption within the Commission, from the most senior levels downwards, have led to allegations that a 'culture of collusion and secrecy' was allowed to flourish within the EU's transnational bureaucracy. This has prompted a renewed and urgent debate about accountability and the lack of democracy in the EU. Reviewing the evidence, this chapter goes beyond the conclusions of the Committee of Independent Experts and asks, what lessons can be drawn from the Commission's organisational culture regarding supranational institutions and transnational governance in Europe, and what implications does all this have for the future of Europe? In the light of these debates we probe further into the EU's claim to be 'transcending the nation-state' and ask whether the trajectory of European construction might not instead be leading towards the creation of a European superstate. From here the chapter returns to the questions posed at the outset concerning the Europeanisation of Europe and its peoples. Drawing on recent research on consumer cultures and public opinion it asks, is there evidence of a European identity emerging among European consumers and citizens? If so, what likelihood is there of transforming that identity into a body-politic?

Fieldwork in the Commission: a note on methods

Before turning to address these issues, it is important to say something about the anthropological approach used in this study and how it differs from that of other disciplines. What follows is an account of EU politics from a critical cultural perspective based on ethnographic research carried out among EU officials and politicians in Brussels. This included two extended periods of four and six months' intensive fieldwork, in 1993 and 1996 respectively. 'Fieldwork', as Donnan and McFarlane (1997: 262) point out, 'is a gloss for a blend of all sorts of quantitative and qualitative research styles, none of which are the exclusive property of anthropology'. Ethnographic fieldwork is, therefore, a broad approach that incorporates a variety of methods besides participant-observation. These range from the use of statistical data, survey research, historical archives and the use of textual analysis, to biographies, oral histories, recorded interviews and informal conversations. At the risk of simplification, the heart of the anthropological endeavour and its objectives could be characterised as twofold. First, to study social action *in situ* and from a personal yet cultural perspective. That requires a commitment to 'being there' in the presence of the people one is studying in order to evaluate what they actually do, as opposed to what they say they do. In this respect, the 'subjective' dimension of the fieldwork encounter (including one's own emotional and intellectual engagement) constitutes a major part of the research data. Second, to attempt a cultural understanding (and from there, an explanation) of the social, semantic and cognitive worlds inhabited by those who constitute the subjects of our study. The aim here is to bring together whichever techniques are appropriate for understanding the social life and cultural predisposition of those we study. Both of these broad and ambitious aims necessarily entail a flexible approach and a large degree of subjective interpretation based on empirical analysis. I emphasise this point particularly for the non-anthropological reader and for those of a more 'scientific' disposition for whom, perhaps, any attempt to express the feelings of informants in their own language might be dismissed as 'merely anecdotal' or 'statistically unsound' and therefore inadmissible as evidence of anything substantive. To these critics I would say simply that quantitative approaches alone can never succeed in grasping the subtleties or complexities of social reality. Indeed, part of the project of critical anthropology is precisely to question received wisdom and those unquestioned 'facts' which so often mask ideological claims to the 'truth'.

All of the eclectic methods described above have informed the present study.

However, given the nature of this enquiry, the most frequently used strategy was that of the in-depth interview combined with cross-check or follow-up interviews. The bulk of the fieldwork was carried out between January and July of 1996. During that period my family and I lived in Brussels, close to the 'European quarter', and had an office in Rue de la Loi, a few minutes' walk away from the main headquarters of the European Council, Parliament and Commission. For the next six months I immersed myself in a daily round of EU-related activities. As well as the many valuable informal conversations, meetings and exchanges, these included over a hundred formal interviews with officials across a wide spectrum of Services and Directorates-General (DGs). My initial research focus drew me naturally to the activities of officials in the Directorate-General for Culture and Information (DG X), where most of the cultural actions and initiatives described in this book were devised. DG X was also responsible for orchestrating the information and publicity campaign for the introduction of the single currency, which began to take shape in early 1996. It therefore seemed appropriate to extend my research focus to cover this key episode in the history of European integration as I witnessed it unfolding. To study the Commission's organisational culture meant a shift of focus towards DG IX (Administration and Personnel) and those staff within the various Commission *cabinets* with responsibility for human resource management. During the this phase of the research I also benefited from having a Belgian research assistant who conducted further interviews (particularly among recent recruits), as well as attending an 'induction course' for new *fonctionnaires*. To corroborate these findings and to gain alternative perspectives on the views being expressed from the Commission, I also held interviews with journalists, MEPs, officials in the European Parliament and European Council, professional lobbyists and Belgian local government officers. In some cases this meant meeting staff after work and outside of an office context: and in one case this included joining striking staff on an official picket line outside the European Parliament in protest against nepotism and alleged cronyism in the Committee of the Regions.[4]

For many people, the enduring stereotype of the European Commission is that of a massive, closed, secretive and above all alien bureaucracy whose only pleasure is derived from inventing rules and regulations to harmonise laws and standards, create a 'level playing field' and prevent people from doing things. In reality, the Commission is a small organisation (barely 18,300 people in 1997), particularly with respect to the scope of its tasks and the size of the Euro 80 billion budget for which it is responsible. Far from being 'closed', it is worryingly open to journalists, researchers, pressure groups and professional lobbyists (thousands of whom have established offices in Brussels). I therefore found contacting officials remarkably easy – although certain areas of discussion were out of bounds and one sensed a considerable degree of self-censorship operating. Nevertheless, most were surprisingly generous with their time – far more so than most national civil servants. As one seasoned Brussels correspondent summed it up:

> A call to the British government's bureaucracy produces a press officer who grudgingly agrees to try to find a civil servant who might agree to be talked

to, but certainly not this week. In Brussels, you telephone a bureaucrat direct: he returns your call, makes an appointment, sees you in his office, shows you files, argues well and makes jokes he will doubtless regret later.[5]

This description concurred with my own experience, although getting past a protective secretary was often a formidable hurdle and many asked to have a list of questions faxed through to them before consenting to allow the interview to proceed. Few interviews lasted less than one hour, the average being of one and a half or two hours; some even three and half hours. I quickly discovered that officials were most at ease and likely to talk longer if the interviews were scheduled for late afternoon: in general, I also found that officials tend to have long lunches but work late, and that the best time to catch someone at their desk was after 6.00pm. Officials were evidently keen to talk about their work; indeed, in some cases it seemed almost therapeutic and a twenty-minute interview would sometimes stretch into the late evening. What I found particularly striking in the individuals that I met was their candour, good humour, depth of thinking and the sense of engagement with the topics under discussion. Only in DG IX and among some officials involved in the campaign to promote the 'euro' were staff deliberately obtuse and cagey about disclosing details of their work. In most cases, this was for obvious political reasons (see Chapter 4). In the case of personnel and administration, the issues of internal working practices, recruitment and national quotas proved particularly sensitive. Even where staff were personally willing to discuss certain subjects, many were apprehensive about doing so because of Article 17 of the Staff Regulations. Commonly referred to as a 'gagging clause', this states that:

> An official shall exercise the greatest discretion with regard to all facts and information coming to his knowledge in the course of or in connection with the performance of his duties; he shall not in any manner whatsoever disclose to any unauthorised person any document or information not already made public.
>
> (Staff Regulations 1993: 13)

The continued existence of Article 17 was cited by many officials as evidence of the Commission's lingering 'culture of secrecy' and as a clear indication that the Commission's new rhetoric about promoting 'openness and transparency' was not always matched by its deeds. This was particularly evident whenever I requested a breakdown of the composition of the Commission's civil service by nationality – which I learned was stored on the Commission's CISPER computer files and apparently available to most staff in DG IX. My requests were usually met with a denial that such information existed or else a straightforward refusal on the grounds that this information was 'confidential'. When challenged on this, the most memorable reply given to me was: 'How do I know, for instance, that you're not working for an MEP? If I gave you the information and it showed, say, that Spain was a deficit country, under-represented in this or that DG, what's to stop a Spanish MEP getting up in the European Parliament to demand more posts for Spain?' The official who said this clearly felt that allowing the public or MEPs to know confidential and delicate details, such as the balance of nationalities in the different Commission services, would be irresponsible and against the 'European interest'. Eventually I did obtain a copy of DG IX's half-yearly statistical report which gave a precise breakdown of the composition of each Service (by grade and nationality) – but only by going through the personnel officer of one of the Permanent Representatives (who also pay keen attention to these issues, I discovered). Carrying away my illicit copy of the report in an unmarked brown envelope, I had to promise to copy and return the original immediately, and not to disclose the identity of my source to anyone.

This excessive secrecy was extraordinary. In November 1995, shortly before the 1996 Intergovernmental Conference, the Commission had responded to its critics by sponsoring a seminar on 'Openness and Transparency in the European Institutions'. However, the following month the head of DG IX sent a memo reminding all staff (in eleven official languages) of their duty to remain silent, and emphasising the closing sentence of Article 17 which states that an official 'shall continue to be bound by this obligation after leaving the service'. This provoked an angry response from staff. Even one of the Commission's own official spokespersons accused the Commission of 'hypocrisy' and 'acting like Big Brother' (Hersom 1996: 2). As a result, many of those interviewed insisted on 'journalist rules' (i.e. non-attributable quotations) as a condition of being interviewed. In the interests of preserving that confidentiality, many of the informants' names and details have been altered or removed.

Finally, a note about my own status and identity as a researcher working in the EU. How was I perceived and positioned by the subjects of this study? The research was funded by the UK's Economic and Social Research Council and I did not have to seek official permission or undergo any vetting procedures to carry out my interviews, which gave me a far greater degree of autonomy than had the research been funded by the EU itself or subject to its own 'house rules'. On the other hand, I did not have *carte blanche* access to meetings, officials or unofficial documents other than those that I was able to negotiate through my own fieldwork encounters. Many informants found the idea of an anthropologist investigating EU bureaucracy rather odd or faintly amusing. 'So you're here to study the tribes of Brussels?' they would often quip. I quickly learned that introducing myself as a 'university researcher' and 'social scientist' was a more acceptable badge of identity, although this was usually accompanied with all sorts of expectations about my research hypothesis and methods (and surprise that I did not have a questionnaire to administer).

On other occasions, however, I found that Commission officials had a very clear and sympathetic understanding of what an anthropological approach entails. Indeed, at the beginning of my fieldwork staff often asked whether I was part of the team of anthropologists (or '*équipe anthropologique*') working for President Delors's think-tank, the *Cellule de Prospective*. This was an intriguing discovery.

Senior Commission officials were so interested in the culture and character of the Commission's internal bureaucracy that they had hired a group of anthropologists (two French and one Brtitish) to carry out a one-year investigation into the 'cultures' emerging within its services and departments. Why had it done this? The answer, according to one senior official, was because 'unlike the British civil service, the Commission is interested in studying itself and a lot of money is earmarked for intellectual research'. This was part of what he called 'the Commission's "sense of mission"'. Officials in the staff unions, by contrast, saw this as part of Delors's attempt 'to spy on the House' in order to learn how to control it more effectively. Whatever the motive, this fact reflected the extraordinary interest now being displayed towards questions of culture in understanding the dynamics of European integration. Many officials suggested that I might find the report written by the anthropological team interesting.[6] However, when I requested a copy and asked what use had been made of the report, the answers I received were equally revealing of the contradictory mixture of intellectual openness and bureaucratic secrecy that characterises much of the Commission's administrative culture. The report was never published: I was told that the Commission was disappointed with the results ('too anecdotal' and 'not sociological enough') and that it had found the report something of an embarassment and that its publication would only damage the credibility of those who had commissioned it. As a result, senior Commission officials had decided 'to bury it'. In a note accompanying the report written in 1994, Jerôme Vignon, the head of the *Cellule de Prospective*, had suggested that the report could be used for training middle management, but that plan was also dropped. On two separate occasions officials told me that they were not sure whether they were allowed to let me have a copy as the report was 'classified' and 'confidential'. When I suggested that I would wait to read the published version I was told that the Commission had 'bought the copyright' and therefore 'effectively owned the report' so 'the authors cannot use it without permission from the Commission' – which the Commission was unlikely to grant. This confirmed for me a key point raised by this book: namely that the ability to define one's identity and to control the way an organisation such as the European Commission is represented to the world at large are central components and key considerations in the cultural politics of European integration.

Notes

1 See Chapter 1 for a definition of the term 'cultural politics' as used in this study.
2 'Building Europe Together' is also the title of a 1996 European Commission's information sheet.
3 For a discussion of the strategic importance in metaphors in shaping the European political agenda, see Shore (1997a).
4 The scandal in 1996 which led to several strike actions and a legal challenge by unions representing staff in the Economic and Social Committee involved allegations of favouritism and 'rigged exams' in the appointment of staff to the newly constituted Committee of the Regions. The events surrounding this incident bore

Part I
Inventing Europe

1 Forging a European *nation-state?* The European Union and questions of culture

> The world of culture clearly cannot remain outside the process of completion of the big European internal market: that process demands the formation of a true European culture area.
>
> (European Commission (CEC) 1988a, 4)

Introduction: transcending the nation-state in Europe?

In his introduction to the European Commission's mass-circulation booklet entitled *A Citizen's Europe*, Pascal Fontaine[1] sets out what he sees as the rationale and moral foundation for the European Union (EU).[2] 'It is an experiment whose results are of universal significance, an attempt to establish between States the same rules and codes of behaviour that enabled primitive societies to become peaceful and civilised' (Fontaine 1993: 6). According to the Commission, the EU exists first and foremost 'to build peace'. This objective, together with the idea of creating a new kind of 'supranational' political order in Europe, is enshrined in the founding Treaties of the European Economic Community (EEC). As the preambles to the 1957 Treaty of Rome and 1951 ECSC Treaty state, the aim is 'to lay the foundations for an ever closer union among the peoples of Europe', and even

> to substitute for age-old rivalries the merging of their essential interests; to create, by establishing an economic community, the basis of a broader and deeper community among peoples long divided by bloody conflicts; and to lay the foundations for institutions which will give direction to a destiny henceforward shared.
>
> (CEC 1983a: 113 and 15)

From the outset, these goals have embodied a supranational and federalist logic, however controversial these terms may be in some EU member states. Subsequent treaties may have removed or disguised the emotive word 'federalism' from their final texts, as was the case in 1991 with the Maastricht Treaty,[3] but a federalist vision of Europe has been implicit in the ethos and organisational

structures of the European Community ever since its creation. As Konrad Adenauer, chancellor of the Federal Republic of Germany and one of the signatories
to the Treaty of Rome, wrote of the 1950 Schuman plan: 'I was in full agreement
with the French government that the significance of the Schuman proposal was
first and foremost political, not economic. This plan was to be the beginning of a
federal structure of Europe.'[4] The aim in 1951, as today, was to bind Europe's
nation-states into a federal political system.

Underlying this objective were a series of political and cultural assumptions
about the causes of war and the future of European societies that are intrinsic to
the EU's conception of history. According to the European Commission, the
antithesis of peace and the major obstacle to European integration is the continuing presence of the nation-state and its allied ideology of nationalism. 'What
alternative is there for the citizens of the new greater Europe', Fontaine asks
rhetorically, 'but a return to nationalism, insecurity and instability, if they opt for
any course other than union and solidarity?' Quoting Jean Monnet, one of the
Community's 'founding fathers' and 'visionary statesmen', he declares: 'We are
not forming coalitions between States but union among peoples'. For the Commission, integration is not simply about the elimination of barriers to trade or the
free movement of capital, goods and labour. Rather, it is primarily a 'humanistic'
enterprise involving a 'coming together' among peoples of different national
cultures. This is the reason, Fontaine claims, that the creation of a 'people's
Europe' became the Commission's 'avowed political objective in the 1970s'
(Fontaine 1993: 7).

These comments highlight an issue of major importance not only for EU officials and supporters concerned with furthering European integration, but also for
historians and social scientists interested in the future of the nation-state. According to EU policy-makers, the European Union has created an institutional
framework for what is, in effect, a new kind of pan-European political architecture
that will transcend the old international order based on competitive nation-states.
While the ideal of a Europe close to its well-informed citizens united by shared
cultural values and a sense of belonging to a 'common European homeland' has
long been part of the *raison d'être* and moral foundation of the European Union,
the idea of creating a pan-national 'People's Europe' emerged only relatively
recently as a political issue. However, this raises the fundamental question of
whether a 'supranational community' or 'European *nation*-state' is possible.
Anthony Smith (1991; 1992a; 1992b) has argued that most previous pan-
national movements failed to achieve their political goal of unification largely
because of deficiencies in the cultural field, which in turn stemmed from the poor
state of their communications technologies. But given the nature of mass communications today the opportunities for superseding the nation-state and creating
cultural pan-nationalism in Europe are immeasurably greater than in the past. If
there is a basis for transcending the nation-state, Smith adds, it is located in
the 'patterns of European culture' and 'in traditions like Roman law, Greek
philosophy and science, Hebraic ethics and Christian theology, as well as their
Renaissance and Enlightenment successors'. These traditions have permeated the

European continent to produce a 'European culture-area' or 'family of cultures' (Smith 1993: 133).[5]

What is striking about these remarks is their similarity to official EU discourses on 'European culture' (Shore 1996; 1998). However, unlike European Union officials, Smith concludes that despite these unifying elements any attempt to create a supra-national community in Europe is unlikely to succeed on the social and cultural levels:

> Of course, one can forge supra-national institutions and create economic and political unions, as Bismarck did for the German states. But this frequently cited parallel contains an obvious flaw. Language and historical memories, as well as myths of ethnic descent, united the population of the German states; the same factors divided the peoples of Europe.
>
> (Smith 1992b: 8)

In Smith's opinion, 'national identity' derives from a deep-rooted sense of ethnic community whereas 'European identity' appears as a relatively superficial and ineffectual force: a utopian dream of intellectuals and idealists with little chance of mobilising mass consciousness. Ernest Gellner gives a more subtle twist to this idea, arguing that a sense of national identification, although in historical terms a recent phenomenon, has become intrinsic to the modern subject:

> The idea of a man without a nation seems to impose a strain on the modern imagination . . . A man must have a nationality as he must have a nose and two ears. All this seems obvious, though, alas, it is not true. But that it should have come to seem so very obvious is indeed an aspect, perhaps the very core, of the problem of nationalism. Having a nation is not an inherent attribute of humanity, but it has now come to appear as such.
>
> (Gellner 1983: 6)

European integration and the problem of identity

Smith and Gellner in their different ways highlight the problem confronting EU officials and policy-makers in their attempt to achieve 'ever closer union among the peoples of Europe': how to transform the heterogeneous and traditionally fiercely nationalistic peoples of Europe into *Europeans*? For EU officials, the challenge is to find a European alternative to the axiomatic and hegemonic grip that the nation-state continues to hold over the minds of the peoples of Europe. As Gellner (1983) argues, the focus of political loyalties in modern societies is no longer to a monarch or land or faith but rather to a culture.

This is the dilemma confronting EU officials and politicians today: the Single European Act of 1987 and the Maastricht Treaty of 1992 have laid the economic and legal foundations for what has become in effect, an embryonic 'European state'. As Goldstein (1993: 122–3) described it, this was to be 'the first transnational state of the nuclear era' which, when completed, 'would rank among the legends of world history'. However, if it is a new state, it is a state 'without a European nation, since there is still no European mass media, parties, interest groups (except in business), or public' (Hoffman 1993: 31). Unlike most nation-states, what the EU conspicuously lacks is a common culture around which Europeans can unite. There is no popular 'European consciousness' to rival that of the nation-state or lend support to those economic and legal foundations. Moreover, those cultural elements which give unity and coherence to existing national identities (such as shared language, history, memory, religion) tend to divide rather than unite fellow Europeans. The problem recalls Massimo d'Azeglio's comment following Italian unification in 1870: 'we have made Italy: now we must make Italians'.[6] Despite the massive transfer of regulatory and decision-making powers from the nation-states to the European Union, there has been no corresponding shift in popular sentiment or political loyalty.

Until the 1980s, public support was not a high priority for EU political elites. Their attitude was summed up by Pascal Lamy, Jacques Delors's *chef de cabinet* and powerful political fixer: 'The people weren't ready to agree to integration, so you had to get on without telling them too much about what was happening'.[7] This characteristically *dirigiste* approach was heavily influenced by traditional 'neo-functionalist' theories of integration. These assumed that political and social integration would follow automatically from economic and legal integration, almost as a by-product of the measures required for building the European Economic Community (EEC) and the single market. Over four decades ago, Ernst Haas posed the question of whether political actors in the member states could be 'be persuaded to shift their loyalties, expectations and political activities towards a new centre, whose institutions possess or demand jurisdiction over pre-existing national states' (Haas 1958: 16). The neofunctionalist answer was that the public's loyalty to the emerging European institutions would grow as each successive step towards political union demonstrated the economic benefits to be gained by further integration. This 'instrumental loyalty', so the argument went, would provide sufficient 'permissive consensus' to enable each subsequent step towards ever-closer union to be implemented. Prosperity and the success of the integration process itself would therefore fuel and legitimise further progress towards, and public acceptance of, political unification.

European integration, to date, has been an elite-led, technocratic affair orchestrated primarily by 'a small layer of key politicians and civil servants' with little reference to the 'citizens of Europe' in whose name it justifies its existence (Hoffman 1995: 235). This harsh assessment is not confined to critics and opponents of the European Union. According to the Reflection Group which prepared the 1996 Intergovernmental Conference, 'the Union's principle internal challenge is to reconcile itself with its citizens' and 'ensure that European construction becomes a venture to which its citizens can relate' (Reflection Group 1995: 2, 1). However, it also recognised that public dissatisfaction with the EU has arisen from

a high level of unemployment . . . social rejection and exclusion, the crisis in relations between representatives and those represented . . . the European Union's growing complexity and the lack of information on, and understanding of, its raison d'être . . . [problems which] are receiving no satisfactory response from the Union because of the gaps or shortcomings in its mechanisms.

Seldom has the EU appeared so unpopular or irrelevant to the needs of its citizens. These views were echoed in Jacques Santer's first speech to the European Parliament in Strasbourg as Commission President when he warned that 'the future of the Community can no longer remain the prerogative of a select band of insiders' (Santer 1995: 4). This, however, is precisely how many people perceive the EU. The high rate of voter abstention and declining turnout at successive European elections – which has fallen from over 61 per cent in 1979 to under 50 per cent in 1999 – indicates that electors remain largely indifferent or hostile to the EU (cf. Lynch 1993).[8] This was confirmed by the EU's own 1997 *Eurobarometer* report. Support for EU membership across the Union had plummeted from 73 per cent in 1991 to just 46 per cent, while only 41 per cent of European electors think their country benefits from EU membership (CEC 1997a). This unpopularity arises also, according to Hoffman (1995: 235) from the fact that 'European bureaucrats' have consciously tried 'to bury the controversial issues under a mountain of 300 technical directives and because the parliament, despite its new power . . . continues to appear remote and bogged down in technicalities'.

Identity and legitimacy

Despite four decades of institutional attempts to build Europe at the level of popular consciousness, the 'peoples of Europe' have simply not embraced the 'European idea' in the way that was hoped for or, indeed, predicted by neofunctionalist models of integration. The task confronting the Commission, to coin its own phrase, is how to transform this 'technocrats' Europe' into a popular 'people's Europe'. However, this does not just entail winning more public support for the EU: Rather, the challenge lies in creating a 'European public' in the first place. By far the greatest obstacle to European integration today hinges around the problem of *legitimacy*. The credibility and authority of the European Union's supranational institutions, which include the Commission, Court of Justice and European Central Bank, rests upon their claim to represent the 'European interest' over and above that of the individual member states. This, however, presupposes a transnational European public whose 'general will' arises from common interests that can be represented and championed by these supranational bodies.

The fundamental dilemma for the EU lies in the fact that the 'European public', or *demos*, barely exists as a recognisable category, and hardly at all as a subjective or *self-recognising* body – except perhaps among a small coterie of European politicians, administrators and businesspeople. Four decades after the birth of what some authors proclaim as 'the world's first truly trans-national organisation'[9] the European integration process has conspicuously failed to engender a transnational European public. The essential ingredient that is missing from the European Union is the political identification of the peoples of Europe. For Muttimer (1996: 284–5), the EU's 'central institutions must be granted political legitimacy by the community's population before a true political community can emerge'. As Miguel Herrero de Miñón states (1996: 1), 'the people of Europe are remote from the decision-making process because there is no such thing as a "European people"'. This inevitably raises the question: 'what is this "European interest" that EU institutions were created to serve? Herrero de Miñón's answer (1996: 1) is blunt: 'the lack of "demos" is the main reason for the lack of democracy. And the democratic system without "demos" is just "cratos", power.'

As Graham Leicester (1996) argues, without the critical underpinning of truly transnational democracy the new European constitutional order will fail and the self-denominated political needs and reasons of Europe's institutions will simply become a new version or *'raison d'état'*. The most successful federations of our time invariably have a national body politic; a sense of 'we, the people' – not simply enshrined in the rhetoric of official constitutions, but embedded in the fabric of popular consciousness. Western democracy, based on the Roussonian principle of the 'general will' and the sovereign people, 'requires both empowered representative institutions and a body politic to represent'. As critics point out, 'without this basic reality, representation is an empty concept' (Herrero de Miñón 1996: 2). But creating a European body politic is by no means an easy task. The abortive attempts by the USSR to forge a new kind of 'Soviet Man' through state propaganda and a strong unitary structure are testimony to the fragility of trying to mould a 'demos' out of different nationalities through the prior establishment of state-like institutions. The pioneers of the European Community undoubtedly knew this, but for various reasons (discussed below) the instrumentalist neofunctionalist approach that dominated policies towards furthering European integration for much of the postwar period ignored this important lesson.

Identity and the single market

Significantly too, business leaders and market research analysts now agree that lack of 'fellow feeling' among Europeans is undermining the evolution of a single European market and damaging European competitiveness. In its annual review of consumer trends, the London-based Henley Centre for market research finds that 'European consumers do not feel "European" in a political or legal sense' (Henley Centre 1996b: 70), and that 'the weakness of our collective European identity . . . is both a source and a symptom of a deeper commercial malfunctioning' (Henley Centre 1996a: 10). Moreover, the absence of political and social solidarity 'could well undermine Europe's efforts to remain globally competitive' (Henley Centre 1996a: 23). The reasons behind this assessment are set out very clearly:

much has been built, even in our GATT-enriched world, on artificially repressed labour costs, the most elaborate protectionisms and – unfashionable to recall in these days of neo-liberal hegemony – generations of state subsidy. Even more critically still, the leading economies have, virtually always, as a matter of public policy and social tradition, corralled national demand for national production; in other words, a strong home market has always been present (certainly the case for the USA and Japan). *Our contention is that the absence of a widespread sense of European identity is not merely a disappointment for europhiles and eurofederalists and the technocratic zealots of Maastricht; it actively corrupts the evolution of an ingredient essential to Europe's long-term competitiveness.*

(Henley Centre 1996a: 10)

In short, European financial analysts and corporate strategists have added their voices to the European Commission's clarion cry for the creation of a 'European identity', arguing that a strong integrated home (i.e. European) market is vital to Europe's long-term position in global markets.[10]

Identity and 'culture'

Europe's 'federal destiny', or *vocation fédérale*, as European officials and politicians often call it, is therefore by no means inevitable or assured. Its success will depend upon the EU's ability to acquire democratic legitimacy and authority which, in turn, hinges on its capacity to forge a *popular* sense of belonging and loyalty to EU institutions and ideals (García and Wallace 1993). Indeed, the goal of 'ever-closer Union among the peoples of Europe', enshrined in the 1957 Treaty of Rome and echoed in successive treaties, hinges largely on the European Union's capacity to forge a new sense of 'Europeanness': a collective identity that can transcend exclusively parochial and nationalistic loyalties and lay the foundations for a higher level of consciousness based on allegiance to European, rather than national, institutions and ideals. The key question asked by both EU policy-makers and social scientists, therefore, is whether a 'European identity' and 'European consciousness' could be developed to underpin the integration process and to challenge or even displace the cultural hegemony of nationalism.

'Culture' and 'cultural politics' as analytical and indigenous concepts

The problems are formidable, but can they be overcome? More specifically, what strategies has the Commission devised to promote its vision of an 'ever-closer union' and to inculcate a sense of 'Europeanness' among the peoples of Europe and how have these been translated into policy? How effective have these initiatives been and what sorts of political and ethical issues do they raise? More importantly, how are concepts of 'Europe', 'citizenship', the 'European idea', and the 'peoples of Europe' represented in official EU discourses and what implications does European integration have for the future of the nation-state and nationalism in Europe?

These questions are central to the cultural politics of European integration. The concept of 'culture' used by anthropologists differs substantially from that of political scientists, politicians and EU officials.[11] Indeed, much of the ambiguity surrounding the term culture, as Raymond Williams (1976: 87) observed long ago, is because 'it has now come to be used for important concepts in several distinct intellectual disciplines and in several distinct and incompatible systems of thought' (Williams 1976: 87). A brief review of these definitions may help clarify these different systems of thought.

At least five broad categories of usage for the culture concept can be identified, four of which, I suggest, are of little analytical value and should probably be treated as cultural idioms in need of critical analysis themselves. First, there is the narrow yet hegemonic definition which restricts culture to questions of art, the entertainment industries or the acquisition of learning. This conception – still promoted in the organisational logic of encyclopaedias, newspapers and government ministries – emphasises elite aesthetic forms 'central to the received humanistic canon of "art", music and texts of a "literary" character, as well as scientific achievements, discoveries, inventions and so on' (Turner 1993: 416–17). This is the sense most frequently invoked in European Commission discourses and, perhaps more importantly, typically reified in the committee structures of the Parliament, Council of Ministers and Commission, each of which has its own committees and *rapporteurs* for 'cultural affairs'. According to this 'Eurocentric' conception, culture is conceived primarily in terms of high culture. However, the EU's increasing emphasis on the cultural industries – including sport, entertainment and audio-visual production – means that alongside the traditionally elitist canonical notion of culture as artistic works requiring protection from the normal laws of economics sits a more *laissez-faire* view of culture as a set of commercial industries and commodities. This sometimes results in major contradictions and tensions in policy, as was witnessed in the conflict between the EU and USA over the status of film and television in the last round of World Trade talks (Collins 1994; Shore 1997a).

A second category, less fashionable today, construes culture in terms of acquired learning or 'civilisation': an abstract noun 'which describes a general process of intellectual, spiritual and aesthetic development' (Williams 1976: 90). According to this interpretation, culture is a property or asset that 'cultivated' people have and others do not. To lack culture is tantamount to lacking manners and education. Again, there are echoes of this conception in the way EU politicians evoke the idea of 'European civilisation' in their speeches and writings, and in the invidious comparisons this invites with the rest of the world. A third category is often used by companies seeking to integrate people into a workforce or solve basic problems of management (as in 'company culture'). This construes culture either as 'the "informal concepts attitudes and values" of a workforce' or as 'the formal organisational values and practices imposed by management as a "glue" to hold the workforce together' under what is termed the 'corporate culture' (cf. Wright 1994: 2). As we shall see, this 'organisational culture' approach has been influential also in shaping management and personnel policies in the European Commission as well as in business administration.[12]

A fourth category, often misleadingly defined as *the* anthropological definition, stems from Tyler's (1871) all-encompassing – but analytically useless – notion of culture as 'a particular way of life, whether of a people, a period, a group, or humanity in general' that is informed by a 'common spirit' (Williams 1976: 90). This definition makes it possible to generalise about large configurations of people as belonging to a particular culture ('Japanese culture', 'British culture', 'American culture'), united by shared 'webs of significance' (Geertz 1973: 5) or an underlying symbolic order embedded in the deep structures of language and cognition. Implicit in these approaches is the dubious notion of an 'authentic culture' arising from an *a priori* system of essential meanings; an underlying code or 'grammar' which anthropologists must decipher in order to understand the logic by which cultures work.[13] As Wright (1994: 27) notes, however:

> Anthropologists are critical of their discipline's previous conceptualisations of culture – either as a checklist of surface characteristics of a bounded group, or as a 'deeper' set of shared meanings. Both rely on an idea of 'shared meaning' without asking 'is it actually shared?' to what extent? by whom? how does it come to be shared?

The point, then, is that, rather than assuming 'shared meaning', anthropologists and other critical social scientists increasingly take culture to be a site of struggle and contestation: an ongoing processes of continually negotiated meanin*g*s. According to this conceptualisation culture is not only a disputed *concept* but a disputed *space*, central to which are issues of language and power, and ideology and consciousness. It also emphasises the point that 'culture' is not a distinct entity or domain separate from the social, but a concept which necessarily includes the *content* of social relations as well as the structure of those relations (Goody 1992: 11). Equally, it recognises that 'cultures' are themselves culturally constructed through the very processes that purport to describe and objectify them (Wagner 1981). This approach is exemplified in different ways by many cultural critics. For Turner (1993: 417) culture refers to 'collective forms of social consciousness arising in the context of historical social processes'. For Williams (1981: 13) it is 'the signifying system through which necessarily (though among other means) a social order is communicated, reproduced, experienced and explored'. For Wagner (1981) it is an act of invention through which anthropologists also render visible their own culture. For Wright (1994: 26) it is essentially a 'political process' by which certain discourses, or ways of thinking and acting, are constructed and contested through language and power. The important point recognised by all these authors, however, is that while anthropological definitions of 'culture' may serve analytical purposes, culture is also an *indigenous* category, or folk idiom, and that native perceptions and uses of the concept of 'culture' constitute a fertile area of study. These definitions come closest to the analytical approach adopted in this book. All emphasise that culture is not a separate sphere but 'a dimension of all institutions – economic, social and political' and 'a set of *material* practices which constitute meanings, values and subjectivities' (Jordan and Weedon 1995: 8).

It is important to emphasise, however, that anthropological approaches generally do two things at once. First, they explore indigenous conceptions of culture – in this case, the complex meanings EU policy-makers attribute to the culture concept (notably the 'Eurocentric', 'functionalist' and 'commercial' definitions of culture mentioned above), and their policies and practices towards culture as an agent of 'Europeanisation' and the 'administrative culture' of the institutions they serve. Second, they try to develop analytical concepts of culture through which to study those indigenous conceptions. This second objective necessarily entails a more political approach to cultural issues and the culture concept itself. Treating the 'cultural' aspects of European integration as political provides a theoretical approach to the questions raised above. It also demonstrates that questions of culture are inseparable from questions of power. This fact is often overlooked or deliberately played down in EU discourses on European culture which typically defines the 'cultural sector' in terms of art, heritage, information, education, audio-visual production and sport. However, the intention of this book is not simply to challenge the tendency among EU officials to promote oversimplified, consensual models of culture and identity (see Shore 1993). Rather, it is also to bring a political focus into discussion of 'culture' and, conversely, cultural perspectives into the study of EU politics. In either case, the goal is the same: to set out the contours of a *critical anthropology of European integration* by making cultural politics less marginalised and invisible in studies of the European Union. As Jordan and Weedon (1995: 4) put it:

> Whose culture shall be the official one and whose shall be subordinated? What culture shall be regarded as worthy of display and which shall be hidden? Whose history shall be remembered and whose forgotten? What images of social life shall be projected and which shall be marginalized? What voices shall be heard and which silenced? Who is representing whom and on what basis? THIS IS THE REALM OF CULTURAL POLITICS.

A critical anthropology of European integration also asks how are these images, histories and discourses about Europe made authoritative and what cultural assumptions inform the actions of those who hold the power to define? As Donnan and McFarlane (1989: 6) state:

> Social anthropology is not only interested in understanding the impact of policy on 'the people'; it is also interested in analysing the cultures of the policy professional, in penetrating and uncovering the perceptions and practices of those who seek to make their definitions of the world and its problems stick.

The policy professionals who feature in this study are the European Union's political and administrative elite – particularly the European Commission. Understanding this *classe politique* – and the organisational culture of this supranational institution – is the theme of the second half of this volume. The central concern of Part I, instead, is to understand what 'culture' means for those who inhabit this institutional space. More importantly, it explores the way EU elites have utilised this term in their attempts to extend the integration process into what they call the 'cultural sector' – a vague category defined largely in terms of the arts, 'heritage', media and communications, information, education and sport.[14]

As we shall see, this emphasis on 'culture' represents a major shift in elite approaches to European integration since the 1980s. What is interesting here, however, is the way that EU officials have appropriated core sociological concepts such 'culture', 'identity', 'social cohesion' and 'collective consciousness' as mobilising metaphors for building 'European culture', 'European identity' and 'European consciousness'. The 'problem', according to the European Commission, is that Europeans are not sufficiently aware of their common cultural values and shared European heritage and are inadequately informed about what Community is doing for them. Its 1988 communication on the 'people's Europe' thus concluded that 'action is needed in the cultural sector to *make people more aware of their European identity* in anticipation of the creation of a European cultural area' (CEC 1988b: 37 – my emphasis). Thus, 'stimulating public interest in the European venture' was now officially recognised as a necessary step to elicit 'the direct involvement of the people in their own destiny' (CEC 1988b: 36).

The need for greater EU intervention in the domain of culture was frequently stressed during fieldwork interviews with officials of the European Commission and Parliament. This view was also echoed in numerous EU reports calling for more active policies in the 'cultural sector' – which in EU discourse includes the arts and media, information, education, tourism, sport and heritage (Adonnino 1985; CEC 1988a). Two reasons for this emphasis on culture are typically cited. First, because 'culture' has become a major area of commercial activity, and therefore falls increasingly within the Community's sphere of legal competence over economic and industrial policies. Second, and more significantly, because the notion of culture itself is now recognised as a key dimension of European integration. As a European Parliament report stated, 'the cultural dimension is becoming an increasingly crucial means of giving effect to policies seeking to foster a union of the European peoples founded on the consciousness of sharing a common heritage of ideas and values' (Barzanti 1992: 5).

This statement reflects a view commonly held by EU officials and federalists that the European Union is a 'community-building' enterprise involving a *'rapprochement'* among the peoples of Europe. According to the Commission, it must therefore be conceived as a cultural and psychological process, and thus part of a wider historical project for bringing about social cohesion among fellow Europeans hitherto divided by nationalism and war (Taylor 1983). As the Commission declared, in language echoing Durkheim:

> The success of various symbolic initiatives has demonstrated that Europe's cultural dimension is there in the collective consciousness of its people: their values are a joint cultural asset, characterised by a pluralist humanism based on democracy, justice and liberty. The European Union which is being constructed cannot have economic and social objectives as its only aim. It also involves new kinds of solidarity based on belonging to European culture.
>
> (CEC 1988b: 3)

Identity-formation and 'culture-building' have thus become explicit political objectives in the campaign to promote what EU officials and politicians call *l'idée européene* or 'European idea'. However, this raises the fundamental question, what exactly is 'European culture' and 'European consciousness' and how might these be nurtured and diffused?

Imagining the new Europe: agents of European consciousness

It has become fashionable among academics to describe 'Europe' as a 'fiction' (Pieterse 1991), or 'imagined space' (Said 1978) formed from 'mental maps' (Wallace 1990a: 7), even a 'kingdom of the spirit' (Garton Ash 1989). This metaphor, however, misses a crucial point. Whereas a kingdom is a space that has been conquered and domesticated by a sovereign ruler, in the EU this process of domestication is still occurring – which is one of the reasons why European and national politicians continue to argue over their rival 'visions of Europe'. It seems pertinent, therefore, to ask, *how* is this new Europe being imagined, and whose images prevail?

The answer to both questions lies in part in the analysis of what can be termed the 'agents of European consciousness'. By this term I do not mean simply those institutions and actors at the centre stage of European Union affairs (although they rank among the most important), nor am I concerned with individual consciousness in a psychological sense. Rather, I refer to those forces and objects through which knowledge of the European Union is embodied and communicated as a socio-cultural phenomenon: in other words, *all* those actors, actions, artefacts, bodies, institutions, policies and representations which, singularly or collectively, help to engender awareness and promote acceptance of the 'European idea'. These agents of consciousness range from the abstract and intangible to the concrete and the mundane: from EU institutions and civil servants, the single market, the euro, the metric system for weights and measures, and the proliferation of EC laws and regulations, to educational exchanges, town-twinning, invented Euro-symbols and traditions, European Union historiography, and the harmonisation of European statistics by the Eurostat office. All of these elements contribute in one way or another to the way people perceive and experience Europe in relation to themselves. All contribute to creating the conceptual and symbolic foundations that make it possible to *imagine* the new Europe as a political entity and community, and to conceive of one*self* as part of that community. Just as nationalism is flagged in everyday life in a host of often rather mundane or taken-for-granted factors and sentiments – what Michael Billig (1995) calls 'banal nationalism' – so the agents of European consciousness serve to communicate Europeanism in ways that are frequently ignored or taken for granted, although this process has a long way to go before European institutions become as 'naturalised' and as uncritically accepted as those of the nation-state.

To a large extent these agents of European consciousness are what constitute the European Union. Just as the extraordinary expansion of new books, articles, journals and university courses dealing with the EU, its law institutions and history have created 'European Union studies' as an institutionalised field of study, so European Community institutions and the activities of those associated with them are what effectively produce – and help to reproduce – the European Union as an *idée force*.

'Europeanisation' is the term sometimes used to describe this process. The idea that Europeans can be 'Europeanised' appears contradictory, but the concept is none the less useful for understanding what some authors call the 'colonisation' of Europe by itself (Morley and Robins 1990). Michael Hechter (1975) coined the term 'internal colonialism' to describe the process by which peripheral regions of the British Isles were slowly incorporated in the United Kingdom, both politically and ideologically. A similar term might also be applied to the wider European canvas to describe the process of integration. As Borneman and Fowler (1998: 489) write in a recent anthropological review of the concept, 'Europeanization works as a strategy of self-representation and a device of power'. It is an accelerated process driven largely, but not exclusively, by the organisational and administrative power of the EU, and it 'is fundamentally reorganising territoriality and peoplehood, the two principles of group identification that have shaped modern European order' (1998: 487). That would appear to be its purpose: to reconfigure not only the map of Europe but the terms and processes by which people in Europe perceive themselves and construct their identities. More importantly, Europeanisation is an inherently circular and self-reinforcing process. EU institutions and laws are continually generating their own environments and conditions for expansion:

> Always seen as a means to realize some ill-defined community, the EU is increasingly an end in itself. However, this circularity – the EU as both cause and effect of itself – begs the fundamental question of what it in fact is.
>
> (Borneman and Fowler 1998: 488)

There are several ways of answering this question anthropologically. One of the canons of anthropological research is that part of our understanding of social life must be grounded in the folk model: the 'actors' frame of reference, or the 'natives' point of view'. This insiders' (or 'emic') perspective is usually analysed through more theoretical and analytical outsiders' (or 'etic') perspectives. However, this classical emic/etic distinction is complicated in the case of the EU by two key factors. First, the folk model in question was, generally speaking, extremely theoretically informed – to the extent that EU officials frequently perceived and objectified themselves using models from the social sciences, particularly integration theory. This is a curious exemplar of the way that, for EU officials at least, integration theory itself works as an agent of European consciousness. Second, EU officials and supporters are themselves the key contributors to the growing canon of theoretical literature on European integration and institutions, thus blurring still further the distinction between actors' and observers' model. The contribution of EU personnel to the invention of this new field of 'European Union studies' should not be underestimated. Since the launch of its 'Jean Monnet Project' in 1990 the Commission has created over 1,722 new university teaching projects in 'European integration studies' – including 409 'Jean Monnet Chairs').[15] Its staff and employees have also played a prominent role in shaping the content and agenda of this emergent field of study. An extraordinarily high number of EU officials are themselves prominent writers, academics, pundits and experts within this newly institutionalised domain of knowledge. Equally striking is the large number of publications that have been produced by writers who are connected to the EU institutions either as recipients of EU funding or as current or former employees.[16]

How full-time career civil servants working for an allegedly over-stretched and under-staffed administration find time to be academics as well as administrators and policy professionals is an interesting question. One answer, perhaps, is that the Commission specifically encourages such intellectual activity and deliberately recruits its A-grade staff from people with academic backgrounds (particularly in economics, law and European studies). Indeed, this intellectual profile constitutes a fundamental aspect of the way Commission *fonctionnaires* see themselves and their role as architects of European construction. Consistent with this self-image, the Commission has created its own think-tank of academics – the *Cellule de Prospective* or 'Forward Planning Unit' – whose employees include physicists, theologians, political scientists and environmental experts. It even included social anthropologists, a group of whom were employed during the 1990s to report on the 'internal culture(s)' of the European Commission's various Services and Directorates (which, as noted, indicates the seriousness the Commission now accords to 'culture'). Furthermore, each Directorate-General allocates a significant proportion of its budget to support units of a 'think-tank' type.

The key point, however, is that, as well as being major agents of European consciousness and protagonists in the process of European integration, those on the EU payroll also rank among its public foremost chroniclers and interpreters. That so much of the academic writing on the European Union has been produced by authors who are connected to the EU institutions, networks and relays is itself an illustration of Borneman and Fowler's point that Europeanisation is a 'strategy of self-representation and a device of power'. The important question, however, is, how has this conflation of roles – EU officials as protagonists and analysts of the EU – influenced debates over European integration? As the universities have come to depend increasingly on EU money for research grants and project funding, often dispensed through professionals whose careers have been closely tied to the EU, it would not be unreasonable to assume that 'European Union studies' are not as critical of the EU as might otherwise be the case. As we shall see, the 'Europeanisation' of higher education has been a particular target and objective of EU 'cultural action'. This has prompted one author to comment that the majority of studies on the European Union 'tend to be of an uncritical and even laudatory nature and often delivered in elegiac prose' (Delanty 1995: x).[17] It is for this reason, among others, that European Union Studies might benefit from *critical* anthropological perspectives.

Governing Europe

With its goal of creating 'ever-closer union', the EU seeks to lay the foundations for a unique system of pan-European government that has no precedent in history. Its aim is to create a new kind of post-national political and cultural order that will supersede the nation-state. Notwithstanding the sensitivity that surrounds the term 'federalism' in some quarters, the vision of a future European state based on a federalist order is frequently invoked by EU leaders. Jacques Delors was quite explicit about the exalted role he saw for the Commission in the future government of Europe. Speaking on French television in the run-up to the 1990 Inter governmental Conference (IGC), he declared:

> My objective is that before the end of the Millennium [Europe] should have a true federation. [The Commission should become] a political executive which can define essential common interest . . . responsible before the European Parliament and before the nation-states represented how you will, by the European Council or by a second chamber of national parliaments.[18]

To transform nation-states into federated units of a greater Europe, as many in the Commission desire, requires not only a major constitutional change but more importantly a fundamental shift in political culture and identity that not all member states or their peoples wish to take. From the point of view of EU elites, they must therefore be persuaded and, if argument fails, then other strategies of 'Europeanisation' must be deployed. The issue of changing (or creating) popular consciousness raises a number of fundamental concerns for anthropology and politics. These include, in particular, cultural strategies for nation-building, the mobilisation of bias (Lukes 1975) and the 'manufacture of consent' (Herman and Chomsky 1988); political symbolism (Kertzer 1988) and the relationship between ideology and subjectivity (Foucault 1977; Rose 1992). As Gramsci (1971) observed long ago, the most effective way to ensure political control is to make one's conceptions of the world hegemonic: that is, to set the political and intellectual agenda in such a way that ideology appears as common sense or 'natural', and therefore beyond the domain of political debate.[19]

Even more important is the internalisation of social control. The art of government entails creating regimes of power whose truths are unquestioned largely because they are so internalised that they become part of the fabric of subjectivity and the individual's sense of self, and thereby opaque to their critical consciousness (see Shore and Wright 1997). This is where government as *external* constraint becomes 'self-regulation' or *governance*; a form of power that presupposes (and works upon) the agency of individuals, rather than denying it. Hence, much of the power to shape European consciousness lies in the establishment of new norms (or technologies of normalisation) and 'techniques of the self' (Foucault 1978): those processes by which normative categories are established and internalised. In the case of the Europe Union and the creation of European consciousness, these new normative categories include notions like 'European citizen', a 'good European', a 'European problem', 'common European values', 'European culture' and 'Europeanness' itself. These issues strike at the heart of the question of European identity. Constructing Europe requires the creation of 'Europeans', not simply as an objectified category of EU passport-holders and 'citizens' but, more fundamentally, as a category of *subjectivity*. This transformation of identity and consciousness – or, to use the language of neofunctionalism, 'the process by which actors are persuaded to transfer their loyalties and allegiances' – is crucial to the long-term success of forging the European Union. However, it is also an area where the EU's political weaknesses are most transparent. Part of the reason for this is that the EU has put most of its energy into regulation and eliminating barriers to the single market (which are experienced as external constraints) rather than using other technologies that would become part of the fabric of European subjectivity.

It is important, therefore, to examine those mechanisms and processes – or 'political technologies' – by which certain discourses of Europe are rendered powerful and authoritative while others are marginalised or muted. By political technologies I refer to those configurations of knowledge and power that are mobilised in particular ways in order to shape the way individuals perceive and conduct themselves. As Foucault (1991: 96) noted, statistics, 'meaning the science of the state', provide a good example of how this process works. As instruments of government, the invention of statistical measurements enables whole populations to be subjected (and to subject themselves) to the normalising gaze and classificatory grids of anonymous technicians and policy-makers. As Barry (1993) reminds us, standardising the various systems of measurement (for time, space, quantity, volume and value), in order to unify a political and economic space, has long served as a device for political rule, from the dynastic calendars and currencies of ancient Rome and China to the post-revolutionary French metric system and the 'imperial' weights and measures that served to unify the British empire. Such uniform systems of measurement are an integral to the rationality of modern government – for a population that can be counted and 'known' is also one that can be ruled and controlled more effectively; an idea summed up in what Rose (1991) calls 'governing by numbers'. More importantly, statistics play a key role in creating new classifications of people (from 'home-owners' and 'social classes C1 and C2' to the 'high risk groups', the 'unemployed' and the 'educationally sub-normal') and new types of subjectivities. As Ian Hacking (1991: 194) notes, 'the bureaucracy of statistics imposes not just by creating administrative rulings but by determining classifications within which people must think of themselves and of the actions that are open to them'.

The invention of Euro-statistics

This process can be observed clearly in the European Commission's 'Eurostat office' and the way that its new measurements have created new subjects (and objects) of bureaucracy that serve to enhance the 'reality' and power of the EU. Fifteen years ago the idea of 'European public opinion' barely existed as a recognisable category; today it is cited increasingly to make political statements and influence policy. Thus, the Eurobarometer for June 1992 declares that 'people on average want to speed up the construction of Europe', that '76 per cent of Europeans are for efforts being made to unify Western Europe', that 'EC citizens are very much in favour of the Single Market having a social dimension' and that 'the European public strongly supports the idea of a foreign policy and a common defence/security' (CEC 1992c: i).

What is important here is not simply how one chooses to interpret these statistics or whether or not they 'speak for themselves', but the existence of such statistics in the first place. The creation of new instruments for measuring the attitudes and opinions of 'Community citizens' has deep ramifications for the way Europe is constructed and reflected in the mind's eye of the public. As Hacking demonstrates (1991: 183), statistics exert a powerful influence in creating 'statistical meta-concepts' that form the bedrock of the social construction of reality. They open up all sorts of possibilities for creating new conceptual domains. As instruments in the service of European construction, they have been used to construct and mobilise a host of new 'European' meta-concepts and categories including, 'European opinion', 'European public', 'European consumers' and the 'costs of non-Europe' – the famous phrase coined by the 1986 Cecchini Report in support of the single European market.

In short, these new *Eurobarometer* and *Eurostat* statistics are not only powerful political instruments for creating a knowable, quantifiable and hence more tangible and governable 'European population' and 'European space': rather, they are also powerful moulders of consciousness that furnish the meta-classifications within which identities and subjectivities are formed. These observations help to explain why seemingly abstract and esoteric issues such as 'European identity' and 'European culture' have come to feature so prominently in EU discourses and policies towards building the European Union. Seen in this light, the phrase 'making Europeans more aware of their cultural identity' can be translated as 'transforming the peoples of Europe into European subjects'; that is, subjects who not only recognise themselves as 'European citizens' but who also accept the EU's supranational institutions as a legitimate political authority, thus paving the way for the realisation of a fully fledged European state. This brings us back to the question of cultural politics and the formation of a 'European *nation*-state'. To a large extent, what EU elites are attempting to do in the European Union is not altogether dissimilar from that which national elites achieved through the nation-building strategies that were used to forge European nation-states in the nineteenth century. What lessons, therefore, does nation-state-formation and nationalism have for understanding the European Union and the limits of European integration?

European union and the model of the nation-state

Despite the insistence of EU supporters on the *sui generis* nature of the EU, there are nevertheless some interesting parallels to be drawn between the process of 'European construction' and the rise of the nation-state. According to most of the major theories of nation-state-formation, an essential element in the spread of nationalism – apart from the more obvious agents of socialisation such as mass education and conscription and the rise of modern print capitalism – was the emergence of a strategic cadre of intellectuals and administrators: a new elite composed of the professional, and above all educated, middle classes who were to become the pioneers of 'national' consciousness' (Hobsbawm 1986: 166–71).[20] This is vividly illustrated by Benedict Anderson (1983) in his seminal book *Imagined Communities: Reflections on the Origins and Spread of Nationalism.* Although the book charts the spread of nationalism as a global phenomenon, the section dealing with the role of bureaucrats in the former Spanish colonies of Latin America seems particularly germane to European integration. Here, if anywhere, conditions appeared ideal for a federal political system to emerge, given the shared language, religion and cultural traditions of most of the continent. This, however, did not occur. Instead, a patchwork of colonial nationalisms emerged from Venezuela to Argentina, spread largely by a new class of 'Creole' administrators. What was extraordinary about this process was the way in which the old colonial administrative units and market-zones – which initially generated no significant attachments – gradually came to be conceived as 'fatherlands'. From arbitrary lines and frontiers drawn across a colonial map, these territories became imaginary homelands and *patrias* – a pattern that came to be repeated not only in the Americas but throughout the world as the post-colonial states of Africa, Asia, Indonesia and the Middle East gained independence.

To understand this process, as Anderson argues (1983: 55), 'one has to look at the way administrative organisations create meaning' for those who belong to them and how these political actors diffuse that consciousness through the agent of 'culture'. Anderson suggests that Victor Turner's work is particularly useful for explaining how this process works. For Turner (1967), the 'journey' between time, statuses and places is a key 'meaning-creating experience'. This was exemplified in the past in the modal pilgrimages that Christians, Muslims and Hindus made to Rome, Mecca, Benares or other sacred centres. These journeys became fundamental experiences for binding together otherwise unrelated localities and thereby delineating the outer limits of the old religious communities of the mind. Anderson suggests that the secular equivalent of this process in the emergent post-colonial states were the 'bureaucratic pilgrimages' or career trajectories of the local intelligentsias and Creole administrators. Whatever the merits of this analogy, the point to emphasise is simply that organisations and consciousness exist in a dialectical and often complementary relationship. As Hans Kohn (1994: 162) observed over fifty years ago:

> Nationalism is an *idée-force* which fills man's brain and heart with new thoughts and new sentiments and drives him to translate his consciousness into deeds of organised action . . . Nationalism demands the nation-state: the creation of a nation-state strengthens nationalism. Here, as elsewhere in history, we find a continuous interdependence and interaction.

A similar kind of interdependence between organisation and identity might also be said to characterise the rise of European Union.

The European Commission provides an interesting arena for testing whether this hypothesis about the interdependence between institutions and identity also characterises the rise of the European Union. Indeed, the EU is one of the largest and most important new imagined communities to have emerged in the post-colonial era: an entity staffed by a unique transnational and supposedly 'supra-national' administrative elite. It is surprising, therefore, that there have been so few serious sociological studies to date that have documented or analysed its organisational culture and character (cf. Bramwell 1987; Abélès 1995; Bellier 1995; Wilson 1993). A key question addressed in the second part of this study is whether or not Anderson's work on the cultural origins of nationalism – and the pivotal role played by national intelligentsias – provides a useful model for under-standing the EU and the conditions likely to promote the spread of Europeanism. To put it another way, what role do EU civil servants play in the creation and diffusion of *European* consciousness as a mass ideology? Are the EU institutions in Brussels a crucible for forging a new type of European 'Man'?

Theories of nationalism shed light on European integration in two ways. First, the vanguard role of the intelligentsia in precipitating the rise of nationalism in the colonial territories is certainly relevant to the question of the role that EU officials might play in the rise and spread of 'Europeanism'. Tom Nairn's dictum (1977: 340) that 'the new middle class intelligentsia of nationalism had to invite the masses into history; and the invitation-card had to be written in a language they understood' has profound resonance for EU officials. The criticism that European integration has been an elite-led affair is seen by some EU officials as no bad thing; as one Commission *fonctionnaire* put it, 'someone has to show leader-ship'. Indeed, intellectuals and administrators were often the most vocal and ardent pioneers of nationalism in the colonial territories, just as they are fre-quently at the forefront of contemporary regional nationalist movements. In other words, the establishment of autonomous regional or national institutions and the creation of new categories of officials and professionals (including teachers, linguists, administrators), responsible for upholding and defending local interests, or for broadcasting minority languages, created an important occu-pational niche for these incumbents. More importantly, they have a growing vested interest in furthering nationalist sentiment and culture because they owe their very livelihood to its existence. As Anderson (1983: 107) wrote of the rise of nationalism in Latin America:

> The intelligentsia's vanguard role derived from its bilingual literacy, or rather literacy and bilingualism . . . The expansion of the colonial state which, so to speak, invited 'natives' into schools and offices, and of colonial capitalism which, as it were, excluded them from the boardrooms, meant that to an unprecedented extent the key early spokesmen for colonial nationalism were lonely, bilingual intelligentsias unattached to sturdy local bourgeoisies.

If, as Anderson (1983) and Hobsbawm (1986) argue, the pioneers of 'national' consciousness were drawn from disaffected administrators and the educated middle classes, whose self-awareness and confidence grew with the spread of new forms of mass communication – does the situation in the EU offer any useful comparisons? This time the 'natives' invited into the offices of the new European state are the multilingual EU civil servants, but, while they do tend to become increasingly detached from the authority of national politicians and local bourgeoisies, they are by no means excluded from the boardrooms of modern multinational corporations and institutions. As the EU institutions grow in size and scope, so does the number of full-time, professional Europeans working in and around the new centres of administrative and financial power. Thus, a new class of deterritorialised, transnational political actors is created with a vested interest in furthering the integration project and the formation of a *de facto* European state. Just as the bureaucratisation of post-revolutionary French society under Napoleon helped to transform 'peasants into Frenchmen' (Weber 1979), EU elites hope to transform Greeks, Germans, Danes and French into 'Europeans' – a process which, in theory, starts among those elites themselves.

A second reason why theories of nationalism may help us to understand European integration lies in the importance they attribute to developments in the domain of culture and communications technologies in precipitating the rise of nationalist consciousness. This is where cultural politics and theories of nation-state formation once again provide insight into the process of European integration. The novelty of Anderson's *Imagined Communities* was its attempt to explore the *cultural roots* of nationalism and its argument that the nation-state arose only after certain cultural conditions had been realised. The first of these was the fragmentation of those great medieval empires which had been constructed through a world of written (not spoken) signs. The invention of print capitalism and the spread of vernacular languages were particularly instrumental in breaking the grip of the old sacred-script language of Latin, Umaha Arabic and Mandarin Chinese. As Eugene Kamenka (1973: 5) put it, 'for most of recorded history . . . the nation and the tribe did not command the supreme loyalty and patriotism of civilised man'. What did, instead, were transnational empires made possible by literary languages and inter-tribal religions such as Buddhism, Christianity and Islam. However, linguistic diversity and the demise of these universalistic languages did not only undermine the authority and legitimacy of the old empires; like the Tower of Babel, they also destroyed their unity as 'integrated fields of communication', to use Karl Deutsch's (1966) phrase.

According to Anderson (1983: 47–8) and Hobsbawm (1990: 59–60), these new print languages created the bases for national consciousness in three distinct ways. First, they created communities of intercommunicating elites below Latin and above spoken vernaculars which, if made to coincide with a particular territorial state area and vernacular zone, provided a model for the larger nation-to-be.[21] They also gave languages a fixity which, like the image of antiquity that has become so central to the subjective idea of the nation, made them appear more permanent and eternal than they really were. Furthermore, print capitalism created new languages-of-power which became institutionalised as 'the actual language of modern states *via* public education and other administrative mechanisms' (Hobsbawm 1990: 62). It is significant in this respect that EU documents frequently stress the need for closer co-operation in international affairs using the metaphor 'Europe must speak with one voice', but, if European integration is to succeed, the problems of linguistic diversity will certainly have to be conquered. Unlike the nation-state, the EU has no vernacular and no unifying mass-communications technologies – although, as we shall see, EU policy-makers look hopefully towards the information and audio-visual sectors and to the development of specific cultural policies to fill this communications gap. Second, the Enlightenment rationalism that fuelled nationalism radically undermined the concept of the divine right of kings that had been fundamental to the legitimacy of the old multi-ethnic empires. With its commitment to reason, science, prosperity and liberalism and its unshaken belief in progress and rationality and its tacit (and sometimes overt) assumptions about the superiority of European 'civilisation', the EU has itself come to embody much of the Enlightenment legacy.[22] Third, the old sacred communities were undermined by the secularisation of time: by new, non-religious ways of apprehending the world. If the novel, newspaper, map and museum were the 'agents of modernity' in this process, as Anderson argues, what are the contemporary 'European' equivalents? Hegel's aphorism that newspapers serve modern man(*sic*) as a substitute for morning prayers may be significant to this debate. As Anderson says, this 'mass ceremony' replicated simultaneously by millions of other people for 'whose existence the communicant is confident, but of whose identity he has not the slightest notion' gave birth to one of the hallmarks of modern nations: 'the remarkable confidence of community in anonymity'. If community in anonymity is a hallmark of modern 'nations', it is even more the hallmark of a political community the size of the European Union. Yet the absence of popular feelings of belonging to the 'European construction', like the absence of a sense of common historical experience or shared memory, remains a crucial factor in explaining the difficulty of integrating Europeans.

To sum up, these factors made it possible to *imagine* the nation as a political community: economics, military power and communications technologies laid the cultural foundations for nations to recognise themselves *qua* nations, and for states to govern these new nations; and cultural politics provided the necessary legitimacy. As Jürgen Habermas (1992: 3) argues, nationalism is a 'modern phenomenon of cultural integration' created through historiography and transmitted through 'the channels of modern mass communications'. Gellner (1964: 169) put it more succinctly: 'nationalism is not the awakening of nation-states to self-consciousness; it invents them where previously they did not exist'. At this point the link between 'imagining' the state and nation, cultural politics and the formation of political identities emerges quite clearly. The formation of large-scale, collective social identities – particularly national identities – has direct relevance to the question of European integration. While it is probably true that the major elements in the construction and maintenance of a national identity will typically cover a range of fields, including linguistics, economics, law and history, *consciousness* of that identity arises through the medium of culture and communication. For example, 'English national identity' (or at least one version of it) may be bound up in literature, in a selective reading of national history, and in a host of supposedly 'typical English' institutions such as Parliament, the monarchy, Shakespearian drama, cricket and warm beer. However, these are expressed and understood symbolically; through the symbols of state and nationhood, including the Union Jack, the national anthem, the Royal Family, the BBC, the national football team, the British Museum and the various venues that have been appropriated as representatives of England's national heritage.

The role that symbols play in the articulation and formation of patterns of consciousness and identity is crucial to understanding how Europe is being constructed as a political community. Most of the fundamental categories and concepts pertaining to European integration, like those which give flesh and form to the idea of nationhood, are represented through symbols. It is only through symbols that the meanings and 'reality' of ideas such as 'state', 'nation', 'citizenship' and 'Europe' itself can be rendered tangible and comprehensible. There is still a common tendency in much of the thinking and writing on European integration to dismiss symbols as 'cosmetic' and to argue that they are of secondary importance – or worse, simply window-dressing – in contrast to the eradication of those 'real' barriers to integration which involve legal and economic restrictions on the free movement of capital, goods and labour. Anthropologists would ague that it is a mistake to underestimate the importance of symbols and the role they play in mobilising sentiment and public opinion. Indeed, symbols do much more than this. As Turner (1967), Cohen (1974a), Lukes (1975), Kertzer (1988) and others have argued, political reality is itself symbolically constructed. It is through symbols that people come to know about the structures that unite and divide them. Symbols do not simply represent political reality; they actively create it. As Mary LeCron Foster argues, symbols are the foundation of culture for 'without symbolism *there could be no culture*' (LeCron Foster 1994: 366, my emphasis) The European Commission's attempts to mobilise popular support for the EU by creating a new repertoire of public symbols for the Europe Union are therefore neither insignificant nor ineffective. The significance the European Commission attaches to this form of 'cultural action' was summed up by Fontaine:

Everyone nowadays recognises the sky-blue banner with 12 gold stars symbolising European unification, which we see more and more often flying alongside national flags in front of public buildings. Is there anyone who can fail to be moved on hearing the *Ode to Joy* from Beethoven's Ninth Symphony, which in some quarters is already being put forward as the future anthem of a united Europe? What Community national does not enjoy following the 'European Community' sign in airport arrival halls, and passing through simply by showing the uniform passport adopted in 1985? To the sceptic, of course these symbolic measures may seem purely decorative. But because they strike most people's imaginations, and because they come close to the symbols that embody State sovereignty, they testify to the substantial progress made by an idea which has now been transformed from myth into reality.

(Fontaine 1993: 7–8)

As Fontaine states, they do indeed embody state sovereignty. While these may appear to be pale imitations of the icons and imagery used by nation-states, they are none the less important elements for reconfiguring the way Europe is conceptualised and for forging a European political reality at the level of public consciousness. Whether these various agents of European consciousness can consolidate and expand the European tier of authority and create the conditions for the transfer of popular allegiance from the nation-states to the new European centre, as EU strategists hope, is the key question addressed in the chapters which follow.

Notes

1 Pascal Fontaine was former assistant to Jean Monnet (1973–7) and *chef de cabinet* to the President of the European Parliament (1984–7). At the time of writing, he is professor at the Institut d'Études Politiques in Paris.

2 The distinctions between the terms 'European Economic Community', 'Common Market', 'European Community(ies)' and 'European Union' continue to confuse many people. However, these distinctions have important legal implications. The 'European Union', established by the Maastricht Treaty which came into force on 1 November 1993, modifies and adds new fields of activity to those provided by the treaties establishing the three earlier European Communities – the European Coal and Steel Community, Euratom and the European Economic Community (whose main feature was the Common Market). But the European Union also has specific features and objectives of its own and is founded upon 'three pillars': the (modified) European Communities, a new common foreign and security policy, and co-operation in the fields of justice and home affairs. In a move symbolic of the shift in thinking about the nature and scope of European integration, the Maastricht Treaty changed the name 'European Economic Community' to 'European Community'. However, perhaps the most important distinction lies in the political intent behind these categories. As Mathijsen (1995: 5) states: 'Contrary to the European Communities, the Union has no legal personality.' The European Union therefore 'has political rather than legal significance; indeed, it is the ultimate objective of the European integration, the precise scope of which is, as yet, not determined in detail'.

3 The penultimate draft (8 November 1991) of the Maastricht Treaty contained the following wording for Article A: 'by this Treaty the High Contracting Parties established amongst themselves a Union . . . *this Treaty marks a new stage in a process leading gradually to a Union with a federal goal'*. Article W.2 added to this: 'A conference of representatives of the Governments of the Member States shall be convened in 1996 in the perspective of *strengthening the Federal character of the Union* to examine those provisions of the Treaty which provide for such an amendment' (my emphasis).

4 Adenauer, cited in Bainbridge and Teasdale (1995: 7).

5 For further discussion of these arguments see Smith (1990: 188) and Smith (1991: 174).

6 Cited in Hobsbawm (1983: 267).

7 Cited in Ross (1995: 94).

8 Average turnout was 61.4 per cent in 1979, 59.0 per cent in 1984, 57.2 per cent in 1989, 56.5 per cent in 1994 and less than 50 per cent in 1999 (a figure skewed by compulsory voting in Belgium, Greece and Luxembourg). In Germany, France and Sweden only 45 per cent, 44 per cent and 38 per cent of the electorate bothered to vote in the June 1999 elections. In the UK, which registered the lowest turnout in the EU, this figure was 25 per cent (source, Herrero de Miñón (1996: 10); Martin Walker, *Guardian*, 15 June 1999: 12).

9 D. Muttimer (1989: 101) cited in O'Neill (1996: 128).

10 For interesting comparisons to the EU's nation-building activities, see Mackey's (1997) study of the Canadian government's attempts to re-define Canadian national identity during the 1992 'Canada 125' celebrations.

11 For useful reviews of different anthropological approaches to the culture, see Krismundóttir (1996); Wolf (1994); Wright (1998).

12 See Case (1994) and Chapman (1994) for anthropological critiques of the use of the culture concept in business studies.

13 For a critique of these interpretive approaches, see Asad (1979).

14 These are the fields included within the remit of the European Parliament's 'Cultural Committee' and the Commission's Directorate-General X.

15 DG X (1998) 'Jean Monnet Project' application form, European Integration in University Studies: Vade-Mecum 1999: 2.

16 Notable examples include Bainbridge and Teasdale (1995); Shackleton (1993); Spence (1994a; 1994b); Westlake (1994); Von Donnat; Corbett; Brackeniers; Reif; Vignon and Fassella – to mention but a few. Leading British academics who are also Jean Monnet professors in European Integration Studies include Lodge (1993a; 1993b) – also 'European Woman of the Year' — and Moxon-Browne (1993). Even many of the basic textbooks on European Community law are written by former EU officials, a good example being P. S. Mathijsen (1995), who was a former Director-General with the Commission. Among the most noteworthy former EU employees who have written extensively on the European Union are Emile Noël (former Secretary-General of the Commission) and Pascale Fontaine.

17 Ronald Sultana (1995: 116) makes similar observations concerning studies of the EU and education: 'most of the literature that addresses the subject has been marked by an uncritical acceptance of the goals and processes of European unification, and an approbation of the presumed implications of these for educational practice'. This he attributes to the 'undiscriminating appropriation of Brussels discourse' and pro-European rhetoric.

18 Cited in Grant (1994: 135).

19 The introduction of the euro exemplifies how this process works (see Chapter 4).

20 This is borne out by Hobsbawm's (1986: 167) dictum that 'the progress of schools and universities measures that of nationalism, just as schools and especially universities became its most conscious champions'. Although the total of

university students throughout Europe in 1848 was no more than an estimated 48,000, in the revolutions of that year this tiny but strategic group played a pivotal role (Hobsbawm 1986: 168).

21 As Hobsbawm (1990: 60) states, the 'national language' can even be a minority language so long as that minority has sufficient political influence. In 1789 50 per cent of French people did not speak French, while in Italy at the time of unification (1860) only an estimated 2.5 per cent of the population used the language for everyday purposes.

22 As I have argued elsewhere (Shore 1995: 221), the EU's community-building activities reflect many of the modernist assumptions and aspirations of the Enlightenment project while the postmodernist critique of the Enlightenment legacy has largely been overlooked or ignored by EU policy-makers.

2 Creating the people's Europe: symbols, history and invented traditions

> If a European identity could be established and its elements clearly identified, the institutions of the European community would have a much stronger point of reference from which to gather loyalty from its citizens and build up a much needed legitimacy.
>
> (Soledad Garcia and Wallace 1993: 172)

> Cultural policy forms part of the European enterprise and, in this respect, is an integration factor within an 'ever closer union between the peoples of Europe'.
>
> (CEC 1996a: 102)

The invention of European tradition

As the above quotations indicate, the idea that there exists a common European culture, and that this can be developed to underpin the more technical, legal and economic aspects of the integration process, has come to occupy a strategic place in the thinking of EU policy-makers and supporters. The 1996 European Commission *First Report on the Consideration of Cultural Aspects in European Community Action* summed it up clearly: 'cultural policy must make a contribution to strengthening and to expanding the "European model of society built on a set of values common to all European societies"' (CEC 1996a:102). To these ends, the Commission has expended considerable time and energy in financing seminars, workshops and symposia aimed at outlining the features of what European identity and culture might consist of.[1] However, it is one thing to identify the contours and currents of Europe's shared cultural heritage, quite another to weave this into a new popular narrative for awakening European consciousness by interpolating the masses as 'Europeans'. To echo Tom Nairn's point, it is the masses – not simply European elites, politicians and intellectuals – who must be 'invited into history' before a new collective memory can be engendered and a new historical consciousness created.

This chapter analyses the way in which EU elites, particularly the European Commission, have attempted to tackle the problem of Europe's fragmented polity and absent demos by instilling a sense of shared European history and identity.

History is, of course, central to the imagining of community, for how people experience the past is intrinsic to their perception of the present. It is also fundamental to their conception of *themselves* as subjects and members of a collectivity. As Hobsbawm (1992: 3) wrote of the centrality of history to nationalism;

> historians are to nationalism what poppy-growers in Pakistan are to heroin addicts: we supply the essential raw material for the market. Nations without a past are contradictions in terms. What makes a nation *is* the past, what justifies one nation against others is the past, and historians are the people who produce it.

But as Wright (1985: 148) comments,[2] the centrality of history to nationhood 'inheres in the relationship between historical consciousness and "everyday life", the everyday historical memory that informs a subject's sense of what is "normal, appropriate or possible"'. That 'everyday historical memory', often embedded in an unarticulated concept of the past, is the fabric from which collective social identities are woven – and a sense of 'we' as the product of history is created.

My particular focus is on the construction of 'European history' (or EU historiography), and what one might call, following Hobsbawm and Ranger (1983), the 'invention of European tradition'. Invented traditions, in the strict sense, refer to practices 'which seek to inculcate certain values and norms of behaviour' by implying 'continuity with the past' (1983: 1). However, as Foster reminds us (1991: 241), 'the past' – like social memory – 'is a construction, actively invented and reinvented'. Rather than attempting to answer the question 'what is tradition?', we should therefore analyse its *functions* and ask, 'what does it achieve'? Perhaps the immediate answer is that it endows institutions with legitimacy and authority. As Grew and Yengoyan (1993: 1) contend, 'the essential role of tradition is to define the *present*'. It also functions as a mechanism for defining boundaries of inclusion and exclusion.

Hobsbawm and Ranger (1983: 9) identified three different but overlapping types of invented tradition: first, 'those establishing or symbolising social cohesion or the membership of groups, real or artificial communities' (such as Britain commemorating its war dead on Remembrance Day at the Cenotaph, or Sinn Fein marking the anniversary of the 1916 uprising with its annual Easter Parades, or Irish-Americans celebrating St Patrick's Day); second, 'those establishing or legitimising institutions' (such as the state opening of Parliament); and third, 'those whose main purpose was socialisation, the inculcation of beliefs, value systems and conventions of behaviour' (such as attending Mass or a political rally). While these processes have been closely documented in relation to the formation of nation-states in Europe, 'cohesion', 'legitimacy' and 'socialisation' are, as we shall see, concepts equally integral to understanding the cultural politics of European integration. What follows is an exploration of four key sites where EU elites have attempted to invent Europe at the level of public opinion through the medium of 'culture'. First, in the creation of new symbols to represent Europe; second, in the field of information policy; third, in the attempt to

'Europeanise' higher education through the rewriting of history; and finally, in the identification of 'women' as specific targets for EU culture-building activities. Before turning to address these themes, however, it is necessary to chart the fundamental change in thinking that precipitated the rise of EU 'cultural action'.

EU approaches to culture

The emphasis on 'culture' as an integrative mechanism and possible solution to the riddle of European unification marks a fundamental shift in official EU discourses on integration away from the old assumption that socio-political integration would proceed as a by-product of economic integration and technical harmonisation. This theme is worth elaborating, as it underlies much of the rationale behind attempts to create the European Union and will help to situate the discussion in a wider context.

Although it was traditionally defined as a common market and an association of sovereign states, the architects of the European Union (or European Economic Community as it was originally conceived) nevertheless always harboured a deeper vision of 'union among the peoples of Europe'. [3] Yet despite frequent references to 'peoples of Europe', little attention was paid to the cultural dimensions of European integration (Smith 1992a: 57). The idiosyncratic behaviour of real people was largely ignored by the architects of European unification and appeared to have little connection with the integration process. 'Building Europe' was perceived primarily in terms of dismantling barriers to the free movement of capital, goods, services and labour, and this was a task for economists and lawyers. This perspective reflected the traditional technocratic bias which dominated approaches to European integration from the 1950s to the 1970s, epitomised by the so-called 'neofunctionalist' theory of integration (Haas 1958; George 1985). This theory saw integration as a rational process 'arising from the harnessing of pressures produced by the competing interest groups in society' (Taylor 1983: 4), and from a 'spill-over' effect in which rationalisation and harmonisation in one area would generate pressure for harmonisation and integration in others. Economic integration would therefore lead inexorably towards integration in the political domain (Smith 1983; Taylor 1983).[4]

As the French statesman and arch-federalist Jean Monnet saw it, a European state would emerge through the steady, cumulative effect of small incremental steps (Figure 1). This strategy would also avoid any head-on confrontation with national governments, which would willingly surrender control to the Community, at first because nation-states would not feel threatened by their loss of authority in apparently innocuous spheres of activity, and because of the economic advantages to be gained by joining a larger market. But later, as more areas of control were ceded, individual nation-states would become incapable of independent action until 'one day, the national governments would awaken to find themselves enmeshed in a "spreading web of international activities and agencies" from which they would find it almost impossible to extricate themselves' (George 1985: 20). Jacques Delors dramatically reinforced this scenario in

Figure 1 Jean Monnet, one of the 'founding fathers' of the European Union.
Source: European Commission

a speech to the European Parliament in Strasbourg in 1988. Aware of a possible backlash against the Community, Delors warned EU nations to 'wake up' to the seepage of national sovereignty and predicted that in ten years' time eighty per cent of economic and social decision-making would have passed from national parliaments to Brussels (Usborne 1988). As Wallace describes it:

> This was political institution-building as a strategy: to promote economic integration, in the expectation that social integration would accompany it, that the functions, interests and loyalties of elites – at least – would thus be progressively transferred from each nation-state to the broader institutional-ised community, which would in turn 'lay the foundations' for an eventual political union. It was a process which implied a beginning and an end: from

and beyond the nation-state to the eventual achievement of European union.

(Wallace 1990b: 1)

One criticism of this approach, however, was that it tended to view political integration as a mechanical process; a necessary by-product of economic, legal and technical measures. It also rested on rather simplistic and deterministic assumptions. Foremost among these was the belief that, once supranational political institutions were established, 'the transfer of loyalties from the nation states to the federation would occur naturally' (George 1985: 17). The theory assumed that a number of successful international institutions would 'gradually erode the loyalties of citizens towards national governments and refocus loyalties upon themselves' and that the process would generate 'a socio-psychological community which transcended the nation state' (Taylor 1983: 4; O'Neill 1996). The core assumption, therefore, was that integration was a process with a dynamic of its own, rolling forward by an irresistible historical momentum.

This synopsis of early discourses on European integration provides a useful background for understanding the shift in thinking that occurred during the 1980s, away from deterministic and mechanistic models towards more 'culturalist' approaches. Indeed, most officials in Brussels, when interviewed, accepted that the old neofunctionalist approach was inadequate and that the EU needed to be much more proactive in promoting awareness of European culture and heritage in order to 'involve people in their own destiny'. This was typically backed up by references to Jean Monnet, who was frequently (mis-)quoted as having said towards the end of his life, 'if we were to do it all again we would start with culture'.[5] This conclusion was reinforced dramatically by debates over ratification of the Maastricht Treaty, which was rejected by the people of Denmark in June 1992 and only scraped through a referendum in France a few months later.

The 'people's Europe' campaign

Long before the 1992 Maastricht Treaty, however, the EU had embarked upon various initiatives in the fields of media and information policy to promote integration in the sphere of culture by enhancing what it saw as 'the European identity'. For the Commission, the first significant step towards defining a cultural basis for European unification came in 1973 when leaders of the then nine EC members states signed the 'Declaration on the European Identity'. This anodyne statement proclaimed, *inter alia*, that the nine member states shared 'the same attitudes to life, based on a determination to build a society which measures up to the needs of the individual'; that each wished to ensure that the 'cherished values of their legal, political and moral order are respected'; and that all were determined to defend 'the principles of representative democracy, the rule of law', 'social justice' (the 'ultimate goal of economic progress') and 'respect for human rights' (CEC 1973: 119). A year later at the 1974 summit, the European heads of state agreed to a study into the special rights which could be granted to citizens of the member states as members of the Community. The subsequent 1975 Tinde-mans *Report on European Union* recommended measures for protecting rights of Europeans and a specific policy for forging a 'People's Europe' through 'concrete manifestations of the European solidarity in everyday life' (Fontaine 1991: 6). This was followed in 1983 by the *Solemn Declaration on European Union* signed by EC heads of government in Stuttgart (CEC 1983b), which invited member states to 'promote European awareness and to undertake joint action in various cultural areas' (notably, information, education, audio-visual policy and the arts). This was interpreted by the Commission as giving a green light to pursue cultural initiatives, not for their own sake but 'in order to affirm the awareness of a common cultural heritage as an element in the European identity' (cited in De Witte 1987: 136). The introduction of the first direct elections to the European Assembly gave a boost to this policy, not least because the embarrassingly low turnout at the polls helped to precipitate the first concerted attempt by the Commission to promote what it saw as 'European awareness' among the public.

The emphasis on consciousness-raising as a strategy for bringing Europe 'closer to the citizens' and creating 'Europeans' thus signalled a new departure in EU approaches to the neglected domain of culture (CEC 1992b). These ideas were developed as policy initiatives in several areas, particularly the various EC educa-tion and training programmes and audio-visual policy. The 1984 Television Without Frontiers Directive[6] spelt out clearly the perceived link between European cultural identity and integration:

> Information is a decisive, perhaps the most decisive, factor in European unifi-cation . . . European unification will only be achieved if Europeans want it. Europeans will only want it if there is such a thing as European identity. A European identity will only develop if Europeans are adequately informed. At present, information via the mass media is controlled at national level.
>
> (CEC 1984: 2)

'Information' and the idea of pan-national television were thus singled out as two key agents of European consciousness. A major problem for the Commission at this time, however, was that there was no mention of 'culture' in the treaties; thus the Community had no legal competence or budget for cultural programmes. Technically, there was no such thing as 'EC cultural policy'; only a number of ad hoc 'cultural actions' based on resolutions from the European Parliament and Ministers of Culture. To get round the legal problem of competence, European officials and politicians typically invoked economic reasons for achieving cultural ends (Forrest 1994: 12). This strategy was made explicit by Delors in his first speech as Commission President to the European Parliament in 1985:

> [T]he culture industry will tomorrow be one of the biggest industries, a creator of wealth and jobs. Under the terms of the Treaty we do not have the resource to implement a cultural policy; but we are going to try to tackle it along economic lines . . . We have to build a powerful European culture

industry that will enable us to be in control of both the medium and its content, maintaining our standards of civilization, and encouraging the creative people amongst us.[7]

The Commission was thus operating a *de facto* cultural policy long before the Maastricht Treaty gave it the legal right to do so. Calls for intervention in the cultural sector were reinforced by the disappointingly low turn out in the 1984 European Parliament elections. The European Council meeting shortly afterwards therefore agreed to establish an ad hoc Committee for a People's Europe, whose task was to suggest measures 'to strengthen and promote the Community's identity and its image both for its citizens and for the rest of the world' (Adonnino 1985: 5; CEC 1988b: 1). The Committee, chaired by the Italian MEP Pietro Adonnino, produced two reports the following year. Its recommendations covered topics not strictly confined to the 'cultural sector', including simplifying border-crossing formalities, minting a European coinage, increasing duty-free allowances, providing reciprocal recognition of equivalent diplomas and professional qualifications, and giving rights to those living abroad to participate in local and European elections in their country of residence.

The report stressed, however, that it is 'through action in the areas of culture and communication, which are essential to European identity and the Community's image in the minds of its people, that support for the advancement of Europe can and must be sought' (Adonnino 1985: 21). Several areas perceived to possess popular appeal were identified as sites for promoting the 'European idea'.[8] These included proposals for a Europe-wide 'audio-visual area' with a 'truly European' multilingual television channel ('in order to bring the peoples of Europe closer together') a European Academy of Science (to highlight the achievements of European science and the originality of European civilization in all its wealth and diversity'); and a Euro-lottery whose prize-money would be awarded in Ecu and announced throughout the Community ('to make Europe come alive for the Europeans').[9] The Committee also called for the formation of European sports teams; the transmission of more factual information about Community activities and their significance for European citizens (including 'the historical events which led to the construction of the Community and which inspire its further development in freedom, peace and security and its achievements and potential in the economic and social field' (Adonnino 1985: 21–4)); the inauguration of school exchange programmes and voluntary work camps for young people; and the introduction of a stronger 'European dimension' in education (including 'the preparation and availability of appropriate school books and teaching materials'. These populist, nation-building measures were designed to enhance European consciousness and 'Europeanise' the cultural sector. However, the Committee went further and argued that to transform the European Community into a 'people's Europe' also required a new set of symbols for communicating the principles and values upon which the Community is based. In the Commission words:

symbols play a key role in consciousness-raising but there is also a need to make the European citizen aware of the different elements that go to make up his [*sic*] European identity, of our cultural unity with all its diversity of expression, and of the historical ties which link the nations of Europe.

(CEC 1988b: 9)

In short, ordinary Europeans were seen as lacking sufficient consciousness of their European heritage and identity, and the Commission intended to remedy this. To this end the Committee recommended various 'symbolic measures' for enhancing the Community's profile. Foremost among these was the creation of a new EC emblem and flag – which was hoisted for the first time outside the Commission headquarters in Brussels at a formal ceremony on 29 May 1986. That flag, adopted in June 1985, was taken from the logo of the Council of Europe: a circle of twelve yellow stars set against an azure background (Figure 2). The rationale for this emblem, as the Council of Europe described it,[10] was that:

Twelve was a symbol of perfection and plenitude, associated equally with the apostles, the sons of Jacob, the tables of the Roman legislator, the labours of Hercules, the hours of the day, the months of the year, or the signs of the Zodiac. Lastly, the circular layout denoted union.

The circle of twelve gold stars, as Bainbridge and Teasdale (1995: 189) note, is

Figure 2 The European flag, described as 'the emblem of European unification' and 'a rallying point for all citizens of the European Community'.

Source: European Commission. *Copyright:* Eureka Slide

also a Christian symbol representing 'the Virgin Mary's halo (*Revelation* 12: 1)'. According to the Commission, this was therefore 'the symbol *par excellence* of European identity and European unification' (CEC 1988b: 5). Among the other symbolic vehicles for communicating the 'Europe idea', the Committee also proposed the creation of the harmonised European passport (Figure 3), driving licence and car number-plates and a European anthem, taken from the fourth movement of Beethoven's Ninth Symphony – the 'Ode to Joy' – which the Committee recommended be played at all suitable ceremonies and events (Figure 4). Another suggestion was to create European postage stamps bearing portraits of EC pioneers such as Robert Schuman and Jean Monnet. 'Stamps', as the Report noted, 'if suitably designed, can be appropriate vehicles for drawing attention to ideas and events in the Community'. The Committee therefore invited postal services to 'commemorate particularly important events in Community history, such as the accession of Spain and Portugal' (Adonnino 1985: 29; CEC 1988b: 7). That the prosaic postage stamp should be appropriated as an emblem for promoting the Commission's 'idea of Europe' is of secondary significance: more important is the fact that it also becomes instrumental in the invention of the new category of 'Community history'.

Other 'high-profile initiatives' to boost the Community's image included 'public awareness' campaigns, EC-sponsored sporting competitions and awards, the formation of an 'EC Youth Orchestra' and 'Opera Centre' and 'the conservation and restoration of the Parthenon' (CEC 1992b: 3). Other EC-funded cultural initiatives included the 'European Literature Prize', the 'European Woman of the

Figure 3 The standardised European Passport, adopted in 1985.
Source: European Commission

Figure 4 The 'Ode to Joy' from Beethoven's Ninth Symphony, adopted as the 'anthem of European unification'.

Source: European Commission. *Copyright:* Eureka Slide

Year Award', and over one thousand 'Jean Monnet Awards' to create new university courses and lectureships in European integration studies with the aim of 'Europeanising' university teaching.

The Commission also attempted to re-structure the ritual calendar by creating new celebratory calendrical markers, such as festive 'European Weeks', 'European Culture Months' (to accompany the 'European city of culture' initiative) and a series of 'European years' dedicated to the promotion of certain EC-chosen themes (such as the 'European Year of Cinema', or the 'European Year of the Environment'). It also proposed new Community-wide public holidays commemorating decisive moments in the history of European integration – such as the birthday of Jean Monnet and the date of the signing of the Treaty creating the

European Coal and Steel Community. Thus, 9 May – the anniversary of the Schuman Plan[11] for pooling French and German steel production under a common supranational authority – was officially designated 'Europe Day'. The political aim behind these initiatives was ambitious: to reconfigure the symbolic ordering of time, space, information, education and the media in order to reflect the 'European dimension' and the presence of European Community institutions.

Representations of 'European culture' in EU iconography

Most of these proposals were adopted at the European Council meeting in Milan in June 1985 and have since been implemented. My concern, however, is to analyse not the mechanics of how they were implemented but how we might 'read' these discourses for clues about the rationality underlying EU cultural initiatives and the images of 'European culture' upon which they draw. In short, what kind of Europe is being imagined and constructed through these symbols? Three points in particular are worth noting. First, far from embodying the thinking of a new age in human history, they seem to indicate an altogether more conservative current of nineteenth-century social evolutionist thought prevalent among EU policy-makers and strategists. This invariably portrays the European Parliament and Commission as heroic agents of change, on the side of history, leading Europe forward in search of its *vocation fédérale*. Second, despite claims made by its supporters that the EU is forging a unique political entity that 'transcends' the nation-state and beckons the dawn of a new era of Europeanism, the new Europe is being constructed on much the same symbolic terrain as the old nation-states of the last two centuries. Flags, anthems, passports, trophies, medals and maps (Figure 5) are all icons for evoking the presence of the emergent state, only instead of 'national sovereignty' it is the EU institutions and ideals that are emphasised and endorsed. Like national Remembrance Day in the UK and Israel, or Bastille Day in France, 'Europe Day' is a commemorative ritual designed to forge a European historical memory. As Connerton (1989: 45) observed, the invention of a 'distinctive class of rites which have an explicitly backward-looking and calendrical character' has long been instrumental in nation-state formation. The EU's claim to be 'going beyond' the model of the nation-state is a highly debatable proposition. According to critics such as Galtung (1973) and Nairn (1977: 306–28), the European Union heralds not the *end* of the nation-state but its expansion into what Nairn (1977: 16) has described as a 'super-nation-state founded on European chauvinism.'[12] This point is echoed by Bunyan and others concerned with what is they see as the advance towards an 'authoritarian European state' (Bunyan 1991), and the spread of secretive para-state bodies within the EU, including those set up to deal with illegal immigration (the Schengen Accord) and the policing of terrorism and drugs (the Trevi group).

The creation of a repertoire of new Euro-symbols also raises the interesting question of whether European and national symbol-systems and identities are in fact compatible or antagonistic. The Commission view, spelled out repeatedly in

Figure 5 Europe as a bounded and historically unified entity. The caption reads: 'Europe, an old continent with a rich history, now moving towards union'.

Source: European Commission. *Copyright:* Eureka Slide

interviews with officials, is that people possess multiple identities (local, ethnic, regional, national, religious) and that these tend to be complementary and segmentary, connecting different orders of ascending 'levels' of belonging. This idea, as they were quick to point out, is supported by modern social theorists, including anthropologists. As they saw it, forging an over-arching 'European identity' was simply a matter of grafting a higher collective identity on to and above existing regional or national identities, like so many Russian dolls or Chinese boxes. Different levels of identity would thus be 'contained' within a hierarchy of nesting loyalties. As one of the architects behind the People's Europe campaign described it:

> Our aim was to create some sort of supra-nationality – through European fairs, exhibitions, campaigns and by using audio-visual material. The Olympic Games showed us that 'united we are strong' . . . What we tried to create was a double sense of belonging: being British *and* being European.

Asked about how the Commission envisaged the relationship between an emerging European identity and that of the existing nation-states, he sketched three concentric circles, one inside the other. 'It's like this', he explained, 'these are the regions, this is the nation-state, and this is the European Community.'

What emerged was a diagram depicting three bounded, harmoniously integrated and hierarchical levels of authority and identity. The possibility of conflict between these strata was ruled out of the equation. This assumption – that existing identities can be successfully encapsulated within a wider European identity – seemed to epitomise the Commission's approach to identity-formation. However, this rests on a fundamentally apolitical conception of identities, one that appears to be grounded in the same sorts of consensus models of society that informed the mainstream 'functionalist' school of social science during the 1940s and 1950s.

A third key point about this new repertoire of Euro-symbols is the contradictory way in which they represent Europe's cultural heritage. Typically, this is portrayed as a well-established and static 'object': an organic phenomenon arising naturally from Europe's rich diversity and centuries of shared history (and hence, as something strong, proud, distinctive and unambiguous). At the same time, European culture is portrayed as fragile and vulnerable; something that needs to nurtured and protected from dangerous, even 'contaminating' foreign influences, most notably Japanese technology and American cultural imperialism – expressed most visibly in Hollywood films and popular American television exports like *Dallas* and *Star Trek* (Schlesinger 1991). Fear of 'Americanisation' – *le défi américain* – is a recurring motif in Commission discourse and one that is echoed repeatedly in official EU documents and reports (Baget-Bozzo 1986; Barzanti 1992; Burgelman and Pauwels 1992; Schlesinger 1994b; Shore 1996). For example, Anthony Pragnell's study *Television in Europe* speaks of European anxiety that

> heavy viewing of programmes from other countries (particularly from the United States . . .) would over time erode the culture, values and proper pride in their own traditions of the countries of Europe. The fear is also that an undue use of US material would have a similar effect on that common sense of identity in Western Europe as a whole which already exists to a significant extent and which it is the aim of European institutions to foster.[13]

The Commission's message about culture and identity is therefore contradictory: European culture and identity already exist in the 'collective conscience of its peoples', but bureaucratic intervention is nevertheless needed to 'defend' it from assault and to make Europeans 'more aware' of their cultural identity. On the other hand, this ambiguity is not without its uses. In particular, the 'environmental approach' to culture (culture conceived as a kind of 'endangered species') justifies further intervention into the cultural sector by EU officials, experts and managers. Indeed, the Commission has an entire Directorate-General ('DG X') devoted to 'culture' (including media, information, heritage, sport and the arts). Despite this, the Commission has no official definition of culture to define its remit. Its 1996 report addresses this issue by quoting the tautological definition proffered by another international organisation:

A cultural area is a 'space within which the association of certain cultural features is dominant' (F. Braudel). This approach can be seen again in the definition of Culture formulated at Unesco's world conference on cultural policies: 'culture consists of all distinctive, spiritual and material, intellectual and emotional features which characterise a society or social group'.

(CEC 1996a: 5)

As the Commission notes (CEC 1996a: 5), 'on this basis, the entire European structure, the Treaties themselves and all the texts they have generated may be regarded as cultural expression and works'. This is precisely the point. However, rather than accepting the implications of its own conclusions, the report immediately declares that 'it is not for an institution to define the content of the concept of culture' and therefore what it proposes instead is 'a pragmatic approach' that restricts 'culture' to those Community texts and policies that have 'taken and take cultural matters into account' (CEC 1996a: 5).

EU cultural policy since 1992

By the early 1990s, according to this restricted but 'pragmatic' definition, EU cultural action had resulted in numerous low-key projects based largely on non-binding Council resolutions for which the Commission could find small amounts of money under its own authority.[14] This situation changed dramatically with the 1992 Maastricht Treaty. Among its innovations, this created the category of 'European Citizenship' and, more importantly, brought several new areas within the jurisdiction of the Community, including education, youth, culture, consumer protection and public health. The Maastricht Treaty thus substantially enlarged the EU's sphere of governance, furnishing it with a host of new legal and technical powers to intervene in domains of everyday life hitherto outside of its direct influence. Maastricht also introduced a new 'Culture article' (Article 128) into the Treaties, thereby providing a specific legal basis for Community intervention into the 'cultural field'. Henceforth, EU cultural action would 'be of a permanent nature and become an acknowledged branch of Community activity' (CEC 1996a: 3). Title IX, Article 128 sets out the Community's objectives towards the cultural field, declaring that: 'The Community shall contribute to the flowering of the cultures of the Member States while respecting their national and regional diversity and at the same time bringing the common cultural heritage to the fore.'

The specific areas where cultural co-operation and action are to be developed. include action to improve 'the knowledge and dissemination of the culture and history of the European peoples'; 'conservation and safeguarding of cultural heritage of European significance'; 'non-commercial exchanges' and 'artistic and literary creation'. It ends by declaring that: 'The Community shall take cultural aspects into account in its actions under other provisions of this Treaty' (CEC 1992a: 13).

At first glance, the phrase 'unity in diversity' suggests that EU policy-makers have begun to embrace a more pluralistic and less managerial and *dirigiste* approach to 'culture'. Closer analysis reveals that this is not the case. Anyone familiar with the history of communism will know that 'unity in diversity' – like 'democratic centralism' – is a deliberately ambiguous and ideologically loaded formula that can be interpreted either as a celebration of pluralism and local autonomy or as its antithesis: power to the centre. In this respect, it shares much in common with that other popular post-Maastricht term 'subsidiarity'. As with its concept of 'European identity', for the Commission, 'unity in diversity' meant that Europe's 'mosaic of cultures' were but smaller units in a greater European design. 'European culture' (or 'European civilisation' as many officials and French historians prefer to call it) was therefore an over-arching, encapsulating and transcendent composite of national cultures; a whole greater than the sum of its discordant parts. Once again there are echoes of Durkheimian thinking. Like Durkheim's (1982) concept of society, European culture is construed as a 'super-organic' and *sui generis* object: a moral whole and level of reality with its own class of facts, requiring its own categories of professional analysts and specialists. Like Durkheim's sociology, the European Commission also seems to be obsessed with the idea of creating 'social cohesion' – a concept that is used as repeatedly as it is uncritically in official EU discourse (Pahl 1991).

At another level, however, Article 128 raises the question, how does one celebrate Europe's cultural diversity while at the same time 'bringing the common cultural heritage to the fore'? And whose definition of that 'common cultural heritage' prevails? The view of most officials in DG X was that, to date, EU cultural action had been geared primarily to raising awareness of diversity rather than the more difficult task of identifying cultural unity. Again, this is a misreading of the situation. If national diversity is celebrated, it is always within a context that emphasises the way these national specificities fit into the overall European picture. Thus, as a recent EU pamphlet describes it: 'the city of Venice, the paintings of Rembrandt, the music of Beethoven or the plays of Shakespeare are an integral part of a common cultural heritage and are regarded as common property by the citizens of Europe' (Borchardt 1995: 73). National cultural icons are thus appropriated, re-interpreted and then offered up as indices of a unitary 'European' history. This strategy is what Alonso (1988) calls 'departicularization' – which once again is a tactic well documented in studies of nation-state-formation (Foster 1991: 242).

Information policy as Europe-building tool: the De Clercq Report

A second area where the European Commission has deployed 'cultural action' for Europe-building purposes is in the field of information policy. The 1993 De Clercq Report provides a good example of this. It also highlights the attitude of EU elites towards public opinion. Following the near-disastrous French referendum of September 1992 which resulted in a mere 51.05 per cent of the electorate voting to accept the Treaty, Jacques Delors set up a working group within the

Commission to examine the European Community's communications policy and to suggest ways to improve the EU's flagging image. The group, called the '*Comité des Sages*' ('Committee of Wise Men'), was composed mainly of communications professionals and public relations experts, together with senior Commission staff (including the head of DG X). It was given six months to carry out its investigation into the problem. The report, drawn up by Willy de Clercq, a Belgian MEP and himself a former Commissioner, was completed in March 1993 and approved by the Commission before being unveiled at a Brussels press conference on 31 March.

The report begins by noting that European integration was a 'concept based far more on the will of statesmen than on the will of the people'. It then proceeds to identify the problem: 'There is little feeling of belonging to Europe. European identity has not yet been *engrained in people's minds*' (De Clercq 1993: 2, my emphasis). To achieve this, the report recommends that Europe should be treated as a 'brand product', to be promoted under the slogan 'Together For Europe To The Benefit Of Us All' (De Clercq 1993: 25). It argues that European governments should stop trying to explain the Maastricht Treaty to their publics – because 'treaty texts are far too technical and remote from daily life for people to understand' (De Clercq 1993: 4) – and concentrate instead on presenting the European Union to the public 'as a "good product" with an emphasis on the beneficial effects "for me"' (De Clercq 1993: 13). Taking up the idea of 'positioning' commonly used in advertising ('whereby branded products are clearly described and placed in relationship to their competitors in people's minds'), the report proposes that 'the Commission should be clearly positioned as the guarantor of the well being and quality of life of the citizen of Europe . . . It must be presented with a human face: sympathetic, warm and caring' (De Clercq 1993: 15). It also suggested that the institutions responsible for European construction 'must be brought close to the people, implicitly evoking the maternal, nurturing care of "Europa" for all her children' (De Clercq 1993: 9).

Among its other recommendations, the report advocated 'personalised certificates awarded to all newly-born babies attesting their birth as citizens of the European Union' (1993: 40); a European library and museum (De Clercq 1993: 27); a 'European dimension' to be included in school textbooks and syllabuses; a European 'Order of Merit' which would outrank all other national honours (1993: 34); a new banner for the Commission bearing the motto 'In Uno Plures'; and direct television appeals by the Commission President directed to the women and youth of Europe (1993: 26–33). The Report continues, in a solemn tone:

> This will probably be the first time in European history that a statesman makes a direct appeal to women. These direct appeals must be carefully planned with a view to maximum media coverage. The tone must be warm, friendly and frank (and with humility) acknowledging the growing pains of the past, and frankly appealing for togetherness now in order to realize all our hopes for the future.
>
> (1993: 26)

At the heart of the advice given to President Delors was that the Commission should set up a centralised Office of Communications, similar to those in the United States and Japan, 'to ensure that the Community speaks with one voice, and communication the "right message" to its target audience' (De Clercq 1993: 48). Senior Commission officials genuinely believed that this Report offered a solution to the EU's communications shortcomings. In fact, it had the opposite effect. At the press conference, journalists staged a walkout in protest and the Greek president of the Brussels International Press Association, Costas Verras, publicly accused the Commission of 'behaving like a military junta'.[15] What particularly angered journalists was the Report's assertion that newscasters and reporters themselves should become 'priority target groups' for EU information activities and that broadcasters should be paid to introduce 'the European dimension' into game-shows and soap operas. As the Report argued, improvements in Community audio-visual policy should be made with the aim of persuading reporters about European Union. 'It is crucial to change their opinions first so that they subsequently become enthusiastic supporters of the cause' (De Clercq 1993: 35).

This incident, which occurred as I began fieldwork in Brussels, provides important insight into EU conceptions of, and instrumental strategies for nurturing, European consciousness. What is also significant is the fact that, although the Report received widespread condemnation from the press, the EU Commissioner for Information and Culture, João de Deus Pinheiro, refused to distance himself from it and said that he would be using some of its proposals. While many officials admitted to me in private that the Report's approach was too commercial and 'a bit over the top', none criticised its basic premise of using 'information' as a tool for manufacturing consent.

Europeanisation of mass education and the rewriting of history

A third area where EU officials have sought to invent Europe as a category of thought is education. Many of the Commission's efforts have been deliberately aimed at schools and the 'young Europeans of tomorrow', a policy summed up in the Commission's phrase 'introducing the *European dimension*' into education. To these ends, it also established two major 'framework programmes' for educational exchanges ('SOCRATES') and youth training ('LEONARDO') to which some Ecu 325 million were allocated in 1996 alone.[16] Central to the process of constructing any new political order, however, is the mobilisation of history and memory, particularly among the young. As Gellner (1983) and Hobsbawm (1990) remind us, mass education was one of the foremost technologies for inculcating nationalist consciousness among the peoples of the emergent nation-states. For this reason, the European Commission now emphasises the importance of rewriting history from a European perspective to challenge the nationalist bias of traditional teaching and learning (Brugmans 1987). Through its SOCRATES and Jean Monnet funding programmes, the Commission has actively promoted the teaching of 'European integration' at university level. But, as Nicholas Moussis (1997: 372) laments;

> what the Community has not tackled yet is the education of citizens in schools. History lessons, in particular, taught from the national angle, accentuate the division, the wars and the hatreds among European nations rather than their common cultural heritage. The Ministers of Education should one day agree on a handbook of European history and culture, which could make young Europeans understand that the national cultural particularities, which make up Europe's wealth, are all part of a great European civilization.

This was also the view of many Commissions officials in DG X, many of whom spoke with passion about the necesity for school textbooks and syllabuses written from 'the European perspective' to combat the nationalistic bias in most other education systems. Many also contrasted education in the member states with the uniquely 'Europeanist' education their own children received at the 'European Schools' in Brussels.[17] But what exactly does history look like from 'the European perspective'? The following review of several EU-funded textbooks and videos provides an answer.

Typically, EU historiography represents the last three thousand years of European history as a kind of moral success story: a gradual 'coming together' in the shape of the European Community and its institutions. According to this conception, European history is an evolutionary process that starts with 'prehistory' (where the key stages include Homo Erectus, megalithic civilisation, the Neolithic revolutions and the Bronze Age), before advancing to the age of classical antiquity and beyond. The result is that European identity is portrayed as a kind of moral success story: the end product of a progressive ascent through history – albeit a highly selective history – from ancient Greece and Rome, to the spread of Christianity, the Renaissance and the scientific revolution, the Age of Reason, the Enlightenment, the French Revolution and the triumph of liberal democracy. These key episodes thus become palimpsests for an essential European cultural community: a 'core Europe' whose common bonds lie in its shared heritage, moral ascendancy and cultural continuity. The EU's choice of 'ERASMUS', 'SOCRATES' and 'LEONARDO' as acronyms for its major educational exchange programmes is a minor example of this. Another is the targeting of the Acropolis and Mount Athos as the two largest EU-funded projects within its 'Conservation of Europe's Archaeological Heritage' initiative (CEC 1992b: 4–7).

These themes of cultural continuity, moral ascendancy and 'unity in diversity' are echoed in an essay by Henri Brugmans (former rector of the Collège d'Europe), appropriately entitled: 'Europe: a common civilisation, a destiny, a vocation' (Brugmans 1987: 11). In the same volume, George Pflimlin describes the last three thousand years of European history as *le miracle européen*. Similarly, the historian Hélène Ahrweiler[18] endorses Paul Valéry's claim that there does indeed exist 'an essential Europe':

> All peoples (Valéry says 'races') and all lands which were in turn Romanized,
> Christianized and subjected – at least mentally – to Greek discipline, are
> thoroughly European . . . Everywhere where the names of Caesar, Caius,
> Trajan, and Virgil, everywhere where the names of Aristotle, Plato and Euclid
> have simultaneously held meaning and authority, that is Europe.
>
> (Ahrweiler 1993: 32)

French historians seem to have made a particularly noticeable contribution to
the EU's attempts to rewrite history. This was also a topic of concern for the
Cellule de Prospective, the Commission's internal 'think-tank'. The idea that
European cultural unity is founded upon a shared ancient civilisation is attractive
to the architects of political integration and clearly informs much of their campaigning work. The problem with such a notion, however, is that it reifies an
outdated idea of cultures as fixed, unitary and bounded wholes that is both sociologically naive and politically dangerous. As Pieterse (1991: 5) states, 'what is
being recycled as "European culture" is nineteenth century elite imperial myth
formation' – except that, where once Europe symbolised empire and expansionism, 'the new idea of Europe is about retrenchment: "the Europeanization, not of
the rest of the world, but . . . of Europe itself"' (Susan Sontag, cited in Morley
and Robins 1990: 3). EU politicians and image-makers, however, continue to
draw on 'classical' images in their quest to identify the essential elements of
European culture, and show little sensitivity towards post-colonial criticisms
of Western Orientalism.

Typically, officials justify their attempts to promote the rewriting of history
books to reflect the 'European perspective' on the grounds that this is necessary
to combat the hegemony of nationalist ideology, which they see as the primary
obstacle to European union. The result, however, is that nationalist ideology is
simply replaced by a new ideology of 'Europeanism'. For example, writing in a
recent EU 'information' booklet, Françoise Fontaine (Monnet's former *chef de
cabinet* and Director of the Commission's Information Office in Paris) charts the
progress of the 'European ideal':

> in the nineteenth century, it was an inspiration for poets and romantics, only
> to be distorted by conquerors seeking to justify their lust for power. It did
> not come to full expression in practical form, however, until a handful of
> courageous, visionary statesmen determined to put a stop to the loss of life
> that seemed to be the inevitable outcome of conflicts between nation-states.
>
> (Fontaine 1991: 5)

The true saviours of Europe from the horrors of Nazism, Fascism and military
aggression during the Second World War are thus not the leaders of the
Resistance or the wartime Allies, but Monnet, Spaaks, Schuman, De Gaspari and
Adenauer: these 'visionary statesmen' have become the symbolic guardians and
ancestors of the 'European ideal'. But if Europe symbolises peace and prosperity,
the nation-state itself – and not simply its distortion under authoritarian regimes –

is construed as an agent of conflict and war. To complete this heroic myth of itself, the EU has also produced a series of films and videos for distribution to schools, colleges and local authorities. These include 'Jean Monnet, Father of Europe', 'A European Journey' (a jingoistic potted history of the various stages, achievements and future of European integration); 'The Tree of Europe' (an 'original feature which will make all Europeans aware of the common roots of their past'); and 'After Twenty Centuries', which surveys two thousand years of European history and features Europeans' 'shared experiences at political, intellectual and cultural level' (CEC 1991: 1–5).

Perhaps the most visual illustration of EU historiography is the Commission's award-winning 1995 film *The Passion to be Free*. As the film's narrator declares:

> For all the diversity and conflict in our history we share today, as Europeans, these freedoms and there is an intellectual and cultural unity in Europe that has evolved from this past. It is what gives momentum to the evolution of the European political union. A union that embraces our separate identities and diverse cultures. The story of our European past is infinitely rich in politics, in art, in science, in thought . . . We are not and never were the product of one culture.[19]

The film's message is that, behind the many apparent differences, the unifying element that binds all Europeans is 'the passion to be free'. This 'spirit' was (predictably) 'born in Ancient Greece', carried forward by the Roman and Carolingian Empires and the Renaissance – and epitomised by various great Europeans, from Boccaccio, Donatello, da Vinci and Columbus to Monnet, Kohl and Delors. An organic thread of continuity thus connects the birth of democracy in classical antiquity with the 'new freedoms' brought by the single market. The film ends by quoting Helmut Kohl declaring that 'the future belongs to Federalism'.

Jean-Baptiste Duroselle's (1990) volume, *Europe: A History of Its Peoples*, represents an even more ambitious attempt to reconfigure history. This 416-page *magnum opus* – part textbook, part manifesto – reflects the historiography implicit in EU discourses on culture. Chapter one opens with the image of rape of the Greek goddess 'Europa', and proceeds to discuss the geographical complexity and uniqueness of the 'continent' of Europe. Chapter three describes the Celts and Teutons as the first Indo-Europeans. Chapter four proceeds under the heading 'Classical Antiquity: Greek Wisdom, Roman Grandeur'. Chapter five ('The First Four Centuries AD in the West') is devoted exclusively to the expansion of Christianity. Chapter seven is a lengthy discussion of whether Charlemagne's empire marks the 'beginnings of Europe'. Chapter eight ('Europe Under Siege') opens with a vivid image of banner-waving Saracens on horseback – 'European civilisation' thus being equated unequivocally as Christendom defending itself against the resurgent forces of Islam. The book continues in a similar vein until chapter seventeen ('The Road to European Disaster') which deals with nationalism, chapter eighteen ('Europe Destroys Itself') which covers the period of 1914–45, and finally chapter nineteen, 'Europe's Recovery and Resurgent Hopes', which focuses on the 'makers of Europe' and the 'building of Europe in the face of Gaullism'. The net result is that European history is presented as the story of reason and unity triumphing over disunity and nationalism – the apotheosis of the Enlightenment project, or what Wolf (1982: 5) calls 'history as a genealogy of progress'. It is invariably a selective, sanitised and typically heroic re-reading of the past, one that systematically excludes or ignores the darker side of European modernity such as the legacies of slavery, anti-Semitism, colonialism or imperial conquest. The book's conclusion – that Europe's history has been marked by a 'general if halting growth in compassion, humanity and equality' triumphing over darker 'nationalistic instincts' (Duroselle 1990: 413) – simply confirms this interpretation. European history, it seems, is as much about 'forgetting' as it is about remembering and interpreting past events.

Inventing Euro-woman: the 'Women of Europe Award'

So far we have focused on cultural action creating Europeans without reference to gender differentiation. There is, however, an important gender dimension to EU cultural politics, exemplified most notably in the 'Women of Europe Award'. This recently invented award offers useful insights into the way the Commission's information policy – with its strategic targeting of women – has been translated into practice.

The Women of Europe Award was initiated in 1987 under the auspices of the European Commission, the European Parliament and the European Movement. Its aim is to 'honour a woman from each Member State who, in the previous two years, has helped to increase European integration among the citizens of the European Union'.[20] According to one of its founders, the idea came as a 'brainwave' during a Brussels lunch in 1987 with two Belgian members of the European Movement who had been lamenting the fact that the ancestral heroes of the EU were all 'founding *fathers*'. The plan was to correct this male bias by giving official recognition to women who had made outstanding contributions to 'European construction'. The award is organised as follows. Member states appoint a National Committee composed of representatives from the European Parliament, Commission, national women's organisations, academia and business to produce a shortlist of nominations. This is then voted upon by a national jury composed of this committee and journalists, and a ceremony is held to award the prize – a symbolic silver pendant of clasped hands. From these national winners, one is selected each year by an international jury to hold the title of 'European Woman of the Year'.

The overall Award winner in 1996 was Marit Paulsen, a Swedish trade-union-schooled farmer with ten children who writes essays in praise of integration and campaigns on behalf of the environment. Leaving aside her practical contribution to European integration, the choice of Mrs Paulsen as an archetypal 'European woman' reveals a great deal about the symbolic logic that underlies official thinking about the award. Nominated by the Swedish Commissioner Anita Gradin, and the Swedish MEP Charlotte Cederschiold, Marit Paulsen was born in

Norway in 1939, just as the Second World War had broken out. Her father died early in her childhood, but her widowed mother fell in love with a German man, and Marit grew up with them. According to her biography, her 'childhood quickly taught her how love between two people of different nationalities can bring hatred to the children'.[21] At the age of nine she started work in a local fish factory in the north of Norway. In 1963 she moved to Sweden, working for seven years in an iron ore factory before becoming a farmer, mother of ten children (biological and adopted) and author of seven children's books, five works of fiction and several television and film scripts. We are told that, living in a strongly anti-EU area, 'Marit fights the element of snow and cold and the anti-EU feeling with her burning devotion for the European Union, peace, democracy, the rights of people and animals and the preservation of our beautiful European countryside'.

Marit Paulsen thus epitomes the ideal 'Euro-woman': a down-to-earth 'woman of the people'; a mother figure whose birth and childhood symbolise reconciliation between nations divided by nationalism and war – arguably the strongest, most enduring of the shared emotions that underlie popular pro-Europeanism. She is also a transnational European worker who has taken up permanent residence in another member state; a farmer whose work experience symbolically traverses each of the major areas of common policy (fishing, iron ore and agriculture) that lie at the heart of integration project; a champion of good causes, including closer European integration; a writer and lover of children whose very lifestyle is an embodiment of the traditional Christian virtues associated with 'rural civilisation' (Guizzardi 1976). To quote once again from Paulsen's official biography:

> Marit is the difference between 9 million new EU members in 1995, between a Sweden inside or outside the European Union. With her tremendous fighting spirit and her voluntary and total devotion to the European Union, with her honesty and her down to earth way of discussing and arguing the absolute necessity of entering the European Union for the sake of peace and democracy, she achieved what no money and no amount of sophisticated debates . . . could achieve. She convinced the ordinary person in the street and the farmer in the countryside that the European Union is foremost a project for peace in Europe and, in spite of her own devotion to nature and animals, '*the . . . one question above all other is peace*'. Without peace you have nothing but with peace in Europe you can do wonders.[22]

The presentation ceremony to award Paulsen her title was held during an international conference on 'Women and the Future of Europe' held in Vienna in December 1996. The event is recounted with almost ethnographic detail by Anne McElvoy,[23] one of the journalists invited to attend that conference. Having announced the winner, Mrs Paulsen mounts the podium and informs the audience that 'when building a European home it is unwise to start with the roof'. What this prophetic-sounding statement means is not at all clear, but the Commission's representatives applaud vigorously. As McElvoy notes,

'Institutional Europe has its own meta-language of allegories, euphemisms and omissions'[24]

McElvoy also provides an important critique of the way the European Commission uses statistics to promote the idea of a latent pro-EU public. Prior to this conference, she notes, a questionnaire was circulated in the member states asking the reasons why women in Europe know so little about what the EU is doing for them, and how to correct this. Two of the four categories of reply were designed to imply acceptance of a federal Europe, a third allowed respondents to be 'hesitant but in favour of joining forces against the outside'. The forth permitted one to harbour reservations, but only if one was prepared to be described as 'nationalistic' at the same time. The 17 per cent of women who answered the fourth category were described in the summary as 'in favour of control, order and protection', and 'against sharing and solidarity'. In other words, a Euro-sceptic woman, in the Commission's eyes, is a 'grudging, selfish, small-minded, flag-waving shrew' (McElvoy 1996: 12). The contrast between the virtuous, self-sacrificing Marit Paulsen, who epitomises good 'European values', and the Euro-sceptic female, who symbolises selfishness, individualism and nationalism, could hardly be starker. What we see here in the EU's attempt to arrogate to itself the stereotypical feminine virtues of maternal caring and nurturing is precisely the approach advocated in the De Clercq Report.

Political implications of EU cultural action

From the foregoing discussion, several points can be made concerning the political implications of EU cultural action. First, the 'concrete measures' it prescribes for bringing about the flowering of culture in the frontier-free Europe clearly reflects a bureaucratic, top-down, *dirigiste* and arguably French approach to culture: one that sees 'European culture' largely in terms of *haute culture*, the consciousness of which can somehow be injected into the masses by an enlightened political vanguard with the help of media technologies and communications experts. However, this elitist and instrumental view is increasingly being challenged by more commercial thinking. This is clearly conveyed in the Commission's claim that 'the demand for culture is constantly increasing as a result of progress in education' (CEC 1992b: 7). Significantly, the set-backs arising from the Danish and French referenda of 1992 did not lead the Commission to abandon either its determination or its approach to forging integration. Instead, these led to an intensification of existing strategies and to the adoption of more sophisticated marketing techniques for 'selling' Europe to the public.

Second, the new European 'culture-area' frequently referred to in official EC documents echoes the old culture-area concept in early anthropological writing; the idea of a distinctive, bounded region set apart from others by race, religion, language and habitat. In this case Europe is also conceived as a 'civilisation' set apart from (and above) others by Christianity, science, the Caucasian race and the Indo-European family of languages. Elements of what Gilroy (1987) calls 'cultural racism' are implicit in the discourses and policies of many Western European leaders and EC officials (cf. Thatcher 1988). As Kofman and Sales (1992: 29) argue, this new European identity 'makes invisible the contribution of people of non-European origin to the economic, cultural and social life of Europe, so that non-Europeans are viewed as intruders'. Moreover, the dismantling of internal borders within the frontier-free EC has been matched by the tightening of Europe's external borders and increasingly draconian restrictions and discrimination against immigrants and asylum seekers from 'third countries' (Webber 1991).

Most attempts to define Europe 'from a cultural perspective' are laden with ethnocentric and elitist assumptions about what constitutes Europe's 'cultural' heritage'. Promoting 'European' identity by pitting Europe competitively and hierarchically against its supposed rivals, commercial (as with America and Japan) or conceptual (as with Africa, Asia and Islam), also fuels xenophobia and makes racism more respectable. The easiest way to promote a sense of European identity is to manipulate fears of Europe being invaded by enemy aliens. This is what the Papacy did during the period of the Crusades, what many of Europe's liberal and Christian Democrat governments were able to do with the Cold War and the Soviet threat (cf. Shore 1990: 59–69), and what some claim the right-wing press throughout Europe is doing over the issue of immigrants and 'asylum cheats' (Woollacott 1991). Whipping up a moral panic about fortress Europe besieged by barbarians is one strategy, but as Alibai (1989) points out:

A more sophisticated way, though, is to assert the existence of a shared European ethnic identity, emanating from a common Greco-Roman tradition. This is the current talk of many right wingers who claim that the core culture which runs through the backbone of Europe needs to be nurtured and protected from alien influences.

Third, creating the 'European identity', as depicted in EU discourse, entails a degree of exclusion of the Other. Identity formation, as Evans-Pritchard (1940) pointed out over half a century ago, is essentially a dualistic process involving fission and fusion as new boundaries are created to distinguish categories of 'us' and 'them'. 'European identity' tends to become meaningful only when contrasted to that which is not European. As Europe consolidates and converges, and as the barriers between European nation-states are eliminated, so the boundaries separating Europe from its Third World 'Others' have intensified – and Islam (particularly 'fundamentalism') has replaced communism as the key marker for defining the limits of European civilisation (Hall 1991: 18). The problem with this approach to identity is its absolutism: its failure to recognise cultures as composite and hybrid entities. Culture is not a matter of fixed essences but of labile forms and multiple influences: as Strathern (1992: 2–3) notes, it consists in the limits of what can be thought or brought together from different domains. It is, by definition, heterogeneous, 'impure' and constantly changing. Similarly, identity is always fluid and contextual: it is a process, 'an always open, complex and unfinished game – always under construction . . . It moves into the future by a symbolic detour through the past' (Hall 1991: 18). However much EU architects and purists may balk at the suggestion, American television, Japanese electronics and computer games, Indian and Chinese cuisine, clothes manufactured in South-East Asia and Afro-Caribbean music are all now aspects of everyday European culture.

This chapter has documented the various ways in which the EU has attempted to forge 'European identity' at the level of popular consciousness. As it has shown, imagining the new Europe is an inherently political activity. The EU's encroachment into the hitherto jealously guarded domains of national policy-making is spearheading the Europeanisation of Europe – a process which, as noted, recalls Michael Hechter's notion of 'internal colonialism' (Hechter 1975). The comparison is apposite: just as the nation-state was forged by intellectuals and elites whose goal was to inject nationalist consciousness into the masses (cf. Nairn 1977: 340; Anderson 1983: 106), so European consciousness is being developed and diffused from above by a vanguard of EU politicians, bureaucrats and marketing professionals.

Is this goal of inculcating a more popular sense of European consciousness actually working? So far the EU's new repertoire of invented traditions and 'post-nationalist' symbols appear as pale imitations of nationalist iconography and have failed to win for the EU the title deeds upon which national loyalties and allegiances are claimed, although they have undoubtedly helped to make EU institutions and ideals an increasingly visible and 'concrete' reality in the everyday lives and memories of its citizens (Wilson 1993). However, one cannot deny that these political technologies will be, and are, instrumental devices for instilling European consciousness in the longer term. Obtaining cultural legitimation is a slow and difficult process. One should not forget that, for most nation-states, economic and political unification occurred over decades and often involved coercive state intervention and draconian nation-building technologies. This process also required uniform systems of mass education, conscript armies, taxation, a literate, mobile and anonymous population and, above all, a high degree of cultural homogeneity. As Gellner (1983: 140) put it, 'the cultural branding of its flock' was a *sine qua non* for creating the nation-state. The absence of a shared language,[25] a uniform media and education systems and the 'political roof' of a central state may distinguish the EU from the nineteenth-century nation-state, but they also highlight the obstacles it faces in trying to build the new *Europe sans frontières*. As we shall see, however, invented traditions and cultural action are not the only, or indeed the most effective, ways in which European elites have attempted to promote the 'cultural branding of its flock'.

Notes

1 Cf. Rijksbaron *et al.* (1987). The European Commission's *Cellule de Prospective* has played a major role in this attempt. See, for example Guégen (1994).
2 Cited in Foster (1991: 241).
3 Hence the repeated use of such terminology in the preambles to each successive treaty.

4 For a more exposition of this theory, see Haas (1958), Taylor (1983) and George (1985).

5 This quotation is reiterated by Wistricht (1989: 79). In fact, Monnet said nothing of the kind and this remark is quite out of character with his altogether more technocratic and pragmatic approach to European unification.

6 For analyses of EU audio-visual policy see Collins (1993); Schlesinger (1994a); Shore (1997a).

7 Delors, cited in Collins (1993: 90).

8 For further analysis of these proposals see De Witte (1987) and Shore (1993).

9 This and all subsequent citations are taken from Adonnino (1985: 21–24).

10 Forum, 3/89: 8, cited in Löken (1992: 6).

11 In presenting his proposal to the Consultative Assembly of the Council of Europe three months later, Schuman declared: 'The signatories of the treaty will, with certain guarantees, submit to the authority that they will have set up . . . The Authority . . . will be the first example of an independent supranational insitution' (cited in Bainbridge and Teasdale 1995: 401). See Chapter 5 for discussion of the concept of supranationalism.

12 Alan Milward (1992) goes further. He claims that the EC has not only preserved the nation-states of Europe but also, paradoxically, regenerated them and that the national governments of Western Europe devised the Community precisely in order to enhance their own sovereignty.

13 Cited in Schlesinger (1991: 142).

14 These included, *inter alia*, audio-visual programmes, networking of cultural organisations, the harmonisation of controls on export of cultural goods, restoration projects on symbolic sites of archaeological heritage, and various small schemes to sponsor cultural exchanges, training, business sponsorship of the arts, the translation of important works of European culture, and the admission of young people to museums and cultural events.

15 Cited in Booker and North 1996: 165.

16 Clarke (1996: 107–8).

17 The European schools, of which there are now ten (three in Brussels alone), are funded by the EU. They were created in 1953 specifically for the education of the children of EU officials, who are exempt from paying school fees.

18 Hélène Ahrweiler is Professor of History at the Sorbonne, Paris, and President of the University of Europe, Paris.

19 All quotes taken from '"A Passion to be Free": Revised Commentary Script' (14 March 1995). Dublin: Windmill Lane.

20 Cited in 'Women of Europe Award' leaflet (n.d.), produced by Allison Parry (British President) with the support of the European Commission, Brussels.

21 Cited in 'Marit Paulsen – Women of Europe Award', leaflet (1996).

22 Ibid.

23 McElvoy, a supporter of the EU, is a former deputy editor of the *Spectator* magazine who now writes for the *Independent*.

24 McElvoy (1996: 12).

25 For political reasons, the EU remains firmly committed to linguistic pluralism and the protection of official minority languages. Linguistic assimilation or homogenisation is simply not an option for the EC (see De Witte 1993).

3 Citizenship of the Union: the cultural construction of a European citizen

Citizenship: a revolutionary idea?

On 1 November 1993, the Treaty on European Union (or Maastricht Treaty) finally came into force after suffering numerous setbacks and protracted opposition in many EU member states. On that day every citizen of an EU member state automatically became a 'Citizen of the Union'. The creation of this new legal category of 'European Citizenship' was hailed as one of the major innovations of the Maastricht Treaty, a Treaty which, it was proclaimed, 'marks a new stage in the process of creating an ever closer union among the peoples of Europe' (CEC 1992a: 3). Exactly what 'Citizenship of the Union' means in political or cultural terms, however, is still a matter of debate.

According to most dictionary definitions, a 'citizen' is a 'member of a State',[1] yet EU leaders and supporters insist that the EU is *not* a state in the conventional sense. But can one be a citizen of a 'non-State' and, if so, what does this mean in practice? Given that citizenship and statehood have been closely associated for most of the twentieth century, the creation of 'Union Citizenship' invariably raises the question of whether the EU has now crossed the point of no return in the process of transforming itself into a nation-state writ large. As Closa (1992: 1139) states:

> the defining and primordial element of citizenship is the enjoyment of political rights. In domestic law, the term 'citizen' applies only to persons in possession of *full political rights*. Political rights guarantee the possibility to influence state policy, which is exclusively reserved to nationals.

Citizenship is thus the legal conception of an individual who owes allegiance to, and receives protection from, a state. Furthermore, as Scruton (1982: 63–4) argues, 'international law does not recognise the distinction between citizenship and nationality and regards the first as completely determined by the second'.[2] This raises a further question of whether, in establishing 'European citizenship' as a status in law, the EU has not also created a *de facto* new form of nationality. The fact that the 1957 Treaty of Rome specified union among the 'peoples' of Europe in the plural suggests that it did not originally intend to create anything resembling a supranational notion of sovereignty. Citizenship was to remain, it seemed, the exclusive constitutional prerogative of the member states. However, under the leadership of Delors and spurred on by a more confident and aggressive Commission, the Maastricht Treaty also marked a new stage in the ambitions of EU leaders and their goal of transforming the peoples of Europe into an amalgamated 'European people'. But can there ever be such a thing as a 'European citizenship' in the social or cultural sense? Raymond Aron answered this question in 1974 with a categorical 'no'.[3] By this, he did not rule out the possibility of collective political action across national frontiers, but rather the possibility of a European consciousness leading to feelings of obligation to the European commonwealth as an imagined historical community.[4] The EU's problem, as Habermas (1992: 9) – writing just before the Maastricht Treaty – summed it up, is that 'to date, genuine civil rights do not reach beyond national borders'. Equally important is the fact that democratic processes have also been largely confined within national borders.

Within the European Commission, the invention of European citizenship, like the 'people's Europe' before it, was typically justified as a response to 'a need which was widely felt by public opinion and political circles in Europe', as officials in Brussels put it. However, 'European public opinion' is a problematic and largely rhetorical notion that reflects more a political ideal harboured by EU elites rather than current political reality as perceived by observers outside of Brussels. As the German sociologist M. R. Lepsius summed it up tersely: 'There is no European public opinion'[5] – which explains why the architects of European integration have sought to invent one through the creation of a European citizenry. The absence of a tangible European public has not, of course, prevented the Commission from claiming to speak for, or represent the interest of, the 'people of Europe'. Indeed, European citizenship was frequently portrayed as a measure that enjoyed enthusiastic public support. Once again, a major political act was carried out in the *name* of 'the European public' (and its putative needs) when the primary function of that measure was to *create* the space in which a European public might eventually emerge. And once again, too, the motive behind this measure was the need for cultural legitimacy. Developing the concept of Union citizenship was thus acknowledged as a necessary step for strengthening the EU's 'democratic legitimacy'[6] and for making 'the process of European integration more relevant to the individual citizens by increasing their participation' (CEC 1997c: 6).[7]

However, the introduction of Union Citizenship on 1 November 1993 aroused neither enthusiasm nor anxiety among the newly hailed citizens of Europe, most of whom were either unmoved by or unaware of it. According to Elspeth Guild (1997: 30), there are two possible explanations for this indifference: 'first, everyone knows that citizenship of the Union is not really citizenship at all, but just some fancy words on a piece of paper; and second, if it is more than some fancy words it does not confer on the holder any rights which he or she did not already have'. Taking up these questions as a starting point, this chapter tries to make sense of the concept of 'European citizenship' by analysing its political and cultural significance. Our discussion is framed around three key questions: first what does 'citizenship' mean in a cultural and political sense, and why has this concept acquired such salience in debates about European integration? Second, what are the *consequences* of European citizenship, particularly for those residents of EU member states who are classified as 'non-Europeans'? Third, how feasible is the notion of a 'post-national citizenship' currently being advanced by many social theorists and EU enthusiasts?

To answer the first question it is useful to draw on historical examples of the ways in which citizenship was constructed in earlier times. The following passage from Simon Schama's monumental chronicle of the French Revolution, *Citizens*, provides some interesting insights.

> On September 19, 1783, at around one in the afternoon, to the sound of a drum roll, an enormous taffeta spheroid wobbled its way unsteadily into the sky over the royal palace at Versailles. Sixty feet high, it was painted azure blue and decorated with a golden *fleurs-de-lis*. In a basket-cage suspended from its neck were a sheep named Montauciel (Climb-to-the-sky), a duck and a rooster. When a violent gust of wind made a tear near the top of the balloon, there were some fears for the safety of the barnyard aeronauts. All, however, survived the eight-minute flight . . . Astonishment was not confined to the passengers. As many as 130,000 spectators were said by one account to have witnessed the event . . . an immense crowd congregated on, and in front of, the palace courtyard where a special octagonal platform had been erected for the occasion.
>
> (Schama 1989: 123)

Thus begins Schama's chapter 'The Cultural Construction of a Citizen'. According to Schama, these awe-inspiring *globes airostatiques* were epochal events in several ways. Foremost among these was because they helped to re-order the nature of public spectacle in France – and, in doing so, generated an audience that was hard to contain within the old regime's sense of decorum. As Schama (1989: 124) comments: 'The ascent at Versailles was itself a major breach of court protocol. The palace had been built around the ceremonial control of spectacle though which the mystique of absolutism was preserved and managed.' But with these spectacular displays the official and enclosed science of the Royal Academy made way for the theatrical science of public experiment.

> Instead of being an object of privileged vision – the speciality of Versailles – the balloon was necessarily the visual property of everyone in the crowd. On the ground it was still, to some extend, an aristocratic spectacle; in the air it became democratic.
>
> (Schama 1989: 125)

The closeted and controlled etiquette of Louis XVI's reign was therefore unceremoniously swept aside by a looser and more anarchic kind of public ritual in which it was no longer possible to preserve the hierarchies of court seniority. These spectacles heralded the displacement of the King with a more potent public persona: the inventor. Like tens of thousands of other literate Frenchmen, the Montgolfier brothers – paper manufacturers from south-east France – were amateur scientists, yet the popularity of their invention provoked a public reaction that was unprecedented:

> Thunderously applauded by the crowd, congratulated by the King and Queen, lionised by the Academy, compared incessantly with Christopher Columbus, they approximated more to a new type of citizen-hero: Franklins of the stratosphere. A typical contemporary description of Etienne Mongolfier paints him as the epitome of sober virtues – at once classical-Roman and French-modern: in clothes and manner, the antithesis of the foppish, ornamental courtier.
>
> (Schama 1989: 125)

Schama's vivid description of France on the eve of Revolution is in many respects a cultural analysis of the trajectory of European modernity at the close of the eighteenth century, charting the transition from the old feudal monarchic order to modern mass society based on a new bourgeois, republican and above all 'nationalist' ideal of citizenship. Of course, balloons were not the only spectacle to attract the kind of crowds in which the formal hierarchies of rank and birth were dissolved in the 'collective effervescence' of mass enthusiasm. As Schama points out (1989: 131–2), there were a number of other cultural phenomena during the closing decades of the *ancien régime* in which mass and elite tastes converged, notably boulevard theatre, popular song and the biennial Salon exhibition. But none of these matched the visual power of the *globes airostatiques* as a vehicle for symbolising the new republican ethos.

Some two hundred years later, a public event no less spectacular, and watched by an audience of tens of millions, took place above the skies of Texas as NASA launched into space the veteran seventy-four-year-old astronaut and senator, John Glenn. Just as in eighteenth-century France, the citizen-hero of the nation was raised – literally and metaphorically – above the onlooking crowds thanks to the miracle of modern science. What is interesting about these examples is that they both draw attention to the important relationship between *public spectacle* (or visual representation), the *state*, and changing conceptions (including self-conceptions) of the *citizen*. As I hope to illustrate below, this nexus provides a useful framework for thinking through the concept of European citizenship.

Citizenship: keyword, category of thought, agent of consciousness

Before tracing the development of European citizenship, let us consider first the concept of State citizenship against which it is usually defined. Interestingly, citizenship has become an increasingly important subject for both academics and politicians in recent years. Until the 1980s, as David Held (1991: 19) argues, citizenship was largely ignored by social scientists and the question of 'rights' was dismissed either as an irrelevance or, as many left-wing intellectuals perceived it, as a 'bourgeois sham'. During the 1980s, however, the concept of citizenship underwent a number of revivals and semantic shifts not only in the USA and Britain, but in much of the industrialised world (King 1987). In Britain in particular, its meanings were stretched and inflated in novel ways. For example, in his book *Citizenship* Andrews (1991: 14)[8] describes citizenship as potentially the 'much mooted "Big Idea", that has been missing from left-wing politics' and speculates that it might offer the left 'the possibility of ideological renewal' by providing the basis for 'social cohesion' and a 'new common experience'. Similar ideas were subsequently echoed by the New Labour government of Tony Blair. During the 1980s, however, Conservative politicians in Britain also tried to reclaim the concept as part of their 'culture of enterprise' ideology, by constructing notions of 'active citizenship' and 'Citizen's Charters', the latter of which claimed to offer new consumer 'rights' to customers of the recently privatised utilities.

What is clear from these rival conceptions is that 'citizenship' occupies a contentious political and semantic space. No one definition prevails, although the latter appears increasingly ascendant throughout Europe as neo-liberal models of governance have come to dominate the European economic agenda. As King (1987: 2–3, 165) wrote over a decade ago, 'New Right' theories – which combine traditional liberal values of individualism, limited government and free market forces, with the conservative emphasis on using government to establish a societal order based on social, religious and moral conservatism – have radically undermined the postwar consensus over citizenship and citizens' rights. Two sets of factors help to explain this renewed interest in citizenship. The first concerns processes that are largely external to the nation-state and include globalisation, migration, the spread of communication technologies, increasing transnational connections among people and the creation of international guarantees and the discourse of human rights. All of these have combined to complicate and weaken the link between nation-state and citizenship. The second concerns factors 'internal' to the nation-state. The dismantling of the welfare state, growing centralisation of power, erosion of participatory democracy and the increasing jurisdictional struggle between regional, national and supranational tiers of government have all complicated the relationship between state and civil society.

The point here is that, with the erosion of the traditional bases of legitimacy, 'citizenship' has become increasingly politicised as parties of the left and right, at both national and European levels, have tried to appropriate its 'cultural capital' (Bourdieu 1977). Like the word 'community', citizenship almost always carries positive meanings and has become part of a semantic cluster that includes a host of related political shibboleths such as 'rights', 'empowerment', 'participation', 'democracy' and 'belonging'. To use Raymond Williams's term, citizenship is an example of a 'keyword': that is, not just a term whose meanings are contested or over which ideological struggles are waged, but a site of language within which important social and historical processes occur (Williams 1976: 22). What makes citizenship a particularly interesting keyword is that it 'combines in rather unusual ways the public and social with the individual aspects of political life . . . Individual citizens enjoy entitlements on the basis of a fundamental equality of condition, which is their membership of the community' (Held 1991: 21). Like the term 'community', citizenship is also an egalitarian symbol in that all who possess it enjoy *de jure*, if not *de facto*, equality with respect to corresponding rights and duties (cf. Marshall 1950). More importantly, as was demonstrated during the French Revolution, citizenship entails new ways of thinking and talking about social relations, political structures and the private self. To put it another way, 'citizenship' is a 'category of thought'. As we shall see, it is precisely this dimension that has made citizenship such a salient and symbolically important word in the lexicon of European integration.

Theorising citizenship: social science perspectives

In his now famous 1949 article, 'Citizenship and Social Class', T. H. Marshall, the great British theorist of the welfare state, defined citizenship as a status bestowed on those who are 'full members of a community (1950: 10). The word 'community', however, is misleading. In international law, citizenship defines the rights, privileges and duties an individual possesses by virtue of belonging to a *state* (Guild 1997: 39).[9] The label 'citizen' defines 'an enfranchised inhabitant of a country, as opposed to an alien'.[10] It is not 'membership of a community', but membership of a *state* that therefore marks citizenship in the modern era. This is important to bear in mind when considering the implications of European citizenship.

Leaving aside the legalistic issue of rights, two basic anthropological points are often overlooked in debates about the citizenship. First, as the definition above clearly indicates, citizenship is classificatory device; a way of ordering people in terms of boundaries of inclusion ('insiders') and exclusion ('aliens'). Such classificatory systems invariably function to reinforce the boundaries of state sovereignty. In this respect, citizenship is an identity-marker that simultaneously 'brands' the population that is to be governed whilst reminding individuals of their nationality and the state to which they belong. Second, citizenship therefore functions as an agent of consciousness. It is an ideological construct that not only defines individuals in terms of a particular rationality and set of norms but, more importantly, seeks to infiltrate their subjectivity and consciousness so that they collude, as active and self-conscious agents, in the constitution of themselves as subjects of power.[11] During the French Revolution, for example, the notion of the citizen ('*citoyen!*') acquired a cluster of new meanings associated with ideas of liberty, fraternity and equality. For the first time in history, as Hobsbawm (1986: 80) argues, 'the people' were defined (and came to see themselves) in terms of the 'nation' – a revolutionary concept from which was born the modern idea of nationalism and the era of the nation-states. Much of the key to understanding the momentous events of Revolutionary France, according to Schama, therefore 'turns on the popular eighteenth-century belief that citizenship was, in part, the public expression of an idealised family'. This 'stereotyping of moral relations between the sexes, parent and children, and brother, turns out', he continues, 'to be a significant clue to revolutionary behaviour' (Schama 1989: xv). Ever since 1789, therefore, citizenship has been an important conceptual arm of nation-building and instrument for governing the masses. By contrast, 'European citizenship' – as symbol, as category of thought, and as distinct type of subjectivity – represents a challenge to the hegemonic principles of national sovereignty that has fuelled European modernity.

The key question is, how does this process of identity-formation work? How are people 'interpolated as subjects'? (Althusser 1971). How do they come to see themselves as 'citizens' or members of a political community? The emphasis in this question is very much on the subjective, *experiential* aspect of citizenship, its meanings for social actors and its cultural implications. New states may pass laws or adopt policies that confer citizens' rights and membership on their peoples, but unless individuals internalise these norms and categories the 'citizenship' label will not constitute a meaningful badge of social identity and the nation-building policies will not work. This is precisely the problem the European Union faces in negotiating its relationship with the public. In Joseph Weiler's terms, the EU enjoys 'legal legitimacy' (since national parliaments have agreed to transfer certain domains of sovereignty to the European Community), but it lacks 'social legitimacy'.[12] In this respect, European citizenship might play a role similar to that of the launch of the *globes airostatiques* in pre-revolutionary France: both, in their own way, are rituals of belonging that create their own public.

Just as the idea of citizenship was central to the rise of the nation-state, some writers see 'European citizenship' as the foundation stone for a new kind of post-national politics. According to the sociologist Yasemin Soysal, citizenship rights have increasingly become decoupled from nationality. 'What we have is a trend towards a new model of membership anchored in deterritorialized notions of person rights' (Soysal 1997: 21). This is also Gerard Delanty's (1995) conclusion. In his book *Inventing Europe* Delanty argues that '[s]ince a collective European identity cannot be built on language, religion or nationality without major divisions and conflicts emerging, citizenship may be a possible option'. He therefore calls for a new idea of Europe linked to 'post-national citizenship'; a citizenship unshackled from the state, and based on universal rights and an inclusive multi-culturalism. In his view, this is the only way of going beyond the divisive and exclusivist 'ethno-culturalism' which he sees as inherent both in traditional models of national identity and in current versions of European identity (Delanty 1995: 159).

For other authors, including Antje Wiener (1997) and Charles Tilly, European citizenship is a dynamic process that heralds the end of the nation-state. As Tilly proclaims, 'citizenship grew up as a feature of strong, centralised states, yet today the European Union's form of citizenship attaches its members to an institution that is not a state and may well undermine states as Europe has hitherto known them'.[13] According to this argument, European citizenship is but a further step in the process that leads inexorably to the transcendence of the old order of independent nation-states. This is being replaced, so the argument goes, by a new system of 'multi-level governance' (Marks *et al.* 1996) based on intergovernmental and supranational institutions, political bargains and multi-level actors. What David Marquand (1991) calls the 'irresistible tide of Europeanisation' is thus transforming not only the political geography of Europe but also existing conceptions of peoplehood. For many scholars, what we are witnessing is an emerging 'postmodern' political order that defies categorisation (Sbragia 1993; William Wallace 1996). As William Wallace (1983) once famously portrayed it, the EU's political system is 'less than a federation, more than a regime'. For other writers, including Antje Wiener (1997), it is a 'non-State': an unfinished project or 'hybrid', somewhere between the intergovernmental and the supranational – or a 'network of networks', as Mark Leonard (1998a) describes it.

Tilly, Marquand, Sbragia, Wallace and Wiener share three things in common: first, all hold that the EU's complex system of governance cannot be compared to a state and explicitly reject the argument that the EU is transforming itself into something approximating a nation-state writ large; second, an uncritical assumption that citizenship of the Union is a 'good thing', unquestionably more progressive, cosmopolitan and historically advanced than citizenship of a nation-state (which is characterised as outmoded, chauvinistic and divisive); and third, an implicit assumption that the 'evolution' of European citizenship will somehow match the trajectory of the European Union as it moves towards a federal system. This latter view is consistent with the teleological way in which citizenship has tended to be conceptualised among politicians and social sciences more generally – a tendency that can be traced back to T. H. Marshall himself.[14]

Marshall defined citizenship in holistic terms as a particular kind of 'status' in the community. According to his schema, the evolution of citizenship rights in Britain can be traced historically from civil rights in the eighteenth century to political rights in the nineteenth and social rights in the twentieth. As Welsh (1993: 3) notes, the first category, which was particularly dominant in Enlightenment thinking, entailed an essentially 'negative' conception of rights that granted individuals freedom to pursue their interests without risk of state interference. These included the right to private property, free speech and access to the legal process. However, as Marshall observed, a property right is not a right to own property but a right to acquire it, if you can get it. The extension of voting rights in the nineteenth century thus represented an advance towards 'positive' political rights which, according to Marshall, evolved into entitlements to health care, education and pensions – rights that characterised 'social citizenship' under the welfare state. Following Marshall's schema, citizenship has thus tended to be perceived as a developmental process whose expansion parallels the expansion of the nation-state. As we shall see, a similar 'evolutionary framework' now seems to characterise the way European citizenship is conceptualised.

European citizenship: the idea becomes reality

One striking aspect of 'European citizenship' is its recent origin. Although some elements of citizenship were 'in an incipient stage of development within the framework of Treaty of Rome and the Single European Act' (Closa 1992: 1142), these rights were extremely limited in scope, negative in character, and exercised by only a few. As Welsh (1993: 4) sums it up '[T]hese civil and economic rights – such as free movement, non-discrimination, or the right to appeal to the European Court – were intended primarily to facilitate the completion of the common market'. In 1975 a Commission report had proposed a Passport Union which would harmonise legislation affecting aliens and abolish passport controls within the Community. This latter measure, as Closa (1992: 1150) remarks, had 'a psychological objective of promoting among the citizens a sense of belonging to a single Community rather than being strictly an economic necessity for the market'. The idea of Community citizenship was first mentioned in the 1976 Tindemans Report, but this resulted simply in the creation of a working party to explore ways of extending social rights to EC nationals in other member states (a theme developed at some length, albeit somewhat instrumentally, in the 1985 Adonnino Report). With the introduction of direct elections to the European Parliament in 1979 some additional rudimentary rights were introduced, but these were too weak to generate a coherent notion of Community citizenship. However, a significant shift in language was occurring as terms such as 'Community national' and 'European citizen' began to gain currency to describe those persons subject to the ever-expanding jurisdiction of EC law.

It was only with the 1992 Maastricht Treaty that the vague term 'Community national' became a formal legal concept denoting a status to which rights and benefits of European citizenship may be attached. The background to this measure is significant. The first reported reference to the concept of European citizenship in the framework of debates over political union was in a letter by Felipe Gonzales, the former Spanish Premier – and then only in the context of proposals about tackling Europe's crisis of democratic legitimacy (Closa 1992: 1153). Gonzales's letter to the Office of the European Council proposed that citizenship should be made one of the three 'pillars' of European political union (the other two being EMU and a common foreign and security policy). For its part, the European Commission declared that the concept of European citizenship was central to its objective of strengthening democratic legitimacy, and it 'explicitly noted the exclusion of the "people of Europe" from the economic and neofunctionalist dynamic of the 1992 process' (Closa 1992: 1155).

Two major observations arise from the above points. First, citizenship was clearly promoted as the Spanish Presidency's 'Big Idea' for maintaining momentum towards further integration and for galvanising popular support for the EU. Second, in the final text which emerged at Maastricht, citizenship was listed as one of the political objectives of the Union, and not just a derivative of previous treaties. The member states supported the idea once it was established that Union Citizenship would be 'additional' to – rather than a substitute for –

national citizenship. The legal term for this is '*additionality*'; that is, Union citizenship would not involve a direct relationship between the individual and the Union: rather, it would be supplementary to – and contingent upon – the rights and obligations attached to every national as a citizen of their own member state. Although in theory citizenship rights were to be governed by Community law, in practice the nation-states retain the power to define who is – or is not – a European citizen.

The Maastricht Treaty inserted into the amended Treaty of Rome a new Part Two ('Citizenship of the Union') Article 8. This begins by baldly declaring that 'Citizenship of the Union is hereby established' and that: 'Every person holding the nationality of a Member State shall be a citizen of the Union'.[15] In a tone reminiscent of a Papal Bull, it adds that 'Citizens of the Union shall enjoy the rights conferred by this Treaty and shall be subject to the duties imposed thereby'. The 'rights' referred to by 'this Treaty' are the so-called 'Four Fundamental Freedoms' enshrined in the EC Treaty: namely, the free movement of goods, persons, services and capital. These rights are now attached to EU citizenship, whereas previously they attached exclusively to citizenship of a member state (although for EU subjects this distinction is immaterial). What exactly the *duties* are, Article 8 does not say, nor is there any indication in what direction the provisions may be leading – a point that has prompted criticisms that the governments of Europe have effectively signed a blank cheque for their citizens.

The fact that citizenship of the Union was made obligatory for all member state nationals was itself highly symbolic. Whatever rights may have been conferred by Union citizenship, the right to choose whether to claim it was not an option for those qualifying for it. In fact, the decision to make European citizenship mandatory was taken without reference to the citizen at all. This clearly violated one of the key themes of the Maastricht Treaty itself: the principle that decisions should be taken as closely to the citizen as possible (the principle of 'subsidiarity').

Article 8a grants to every citizen of the Union 'the right to move and reside freely within the territory of any Member State' – subject to various exceptions. In fact, this right to free movement is not as novel or as universal as it appears. The right to move freely across EU borders for economic purposes has long been regarded as fundamental to the creation of a more fluid labour market and has existed ever since the inception of the Common Market. Whereas in the past, this freedom was limited to the 'economically active', the Maastricht Treaty extends this right to include three categories of economically inactive persons: 'pensioners, students and persons with sufficient means that they do not become a burden on the member state's social assistance schemes' (Guild 1997: 35). However, the right to free movement is by no means universal or unlimited. Unemployed persons reliant on state benefits and those deemed unemployable are specifically excluded from the right to free movement under a series of legal provisions designed to 'prevent people of inadequate means becoming a "burden" on the social security systems of the member state where they choose to reside' (Bainbridge and Teasdale 1995: 42 cf. Edye 1997: 70). Article 8a also means that it has become a principle of community law that EU citizens have the right to move freely within a member state. This issue arose in the challenge to a British exclusion order against the Sinn Fein leader, Gerry Adams, but was subsequently withdrawn from the Court of Justice following a settlement (Guild 1997: 35).

Article 8b recognises the right of every citizen 'to vote and to stand as a candidate in election' in the European Parliament and in municipal elections in the member state in which s/he resides. This was intended as a new expression of political citizenship and is often said to be the most significant concession, as there are over four million 'EU nationals' residing in other member states. In the view of the European Commission, this is 'the most noteworthy and visible application of the citizen concept as a way of creating a sense of belonging' (Reflection Group 1995: 21). However, in its *Second Report on Citizenship of the Union* the Commission observes that in municipal elections so far, only one non-national candidate – Silmya Zimmermann, a Dutch citizen resident in Germany – has been elected in her member state of residence (CEC 1997c: 9). Article 8c offers to every citizen of the Union diplomatic or consular protection in the territory of a non-EU country. However, at the time of writing the rules governing this measure had still not been implemented and only in Kuwait following the Iraqi invasion had anything approximating this provision been enacted.

Article 8d gives European citizens the right to petition the European Parliament and appeal to an ombudsman – a measure designed to render EU institutions more open and democratically accountable – but, as the Commission's 1997 report acknowledges (CEC 1997c: 12–14), this right of petition is not particularly new. The remit of the Ombudsman, by contrast, is to investigate instances of alleged maladministration in the activities of the Community institutions (excluding the Court of Justice and Court of First Instance). However, in 1998, a spate of extremely serious charges of alleged nepotism, cronyism and fraud among senior Commission officials (including Commissioners Cresson and Marin) have brought into doubt the effectiveness of the EU's ombudsman system. The problems were highlighted in a recent House of Commons European Scrutiny Committee Report (1999).[16] This concluded that the plans for creating a new 'independent' anti-fraud office drawn up by the Commission and Parliament were flawed by lack of transparency and accountability. The Committee expressed particular concern at its lack of independence from the Commission – the body through which, according to the plan, all proposals for external investigations will have to be made. Thus, the idea of empowering citizens through intermediary bodies – such as an ombudsman or an anti-fraud office – frequently turns out to be stymied in practice by the collusion or conflation between the investigators and the investigated.

To sum up, the concept of Union citizenship has formalised certain existing rights within the Community ambit, introduced some new rights and provided a base for their enlargement (Closa (1992: 1168; Welsh 1993: 7). The final Article, 8e, allows for the European Council to 'adopt provisions to strengthen or to add to the rights laid down in this Part' in future, as the EU's sphere of jurisdiction expands. Thus, the expectation is that Union citizenship will develop in the direction of more inclusive and holistic political and social rights – as the Marshall schema suggested. This is reflected also in the interpretation given to Union citizenship by EU supporters. As Moxon-Browne (1993: 161) proclaims, '[t]he development of EC citizenship will necessarily mirror the EC's development: the full range of privileges and duties attached to citizenship can make sense only in the context of effective transfers of sovereignty from the nation state to the EC's institutions'.

The significance of European citizenship: legal and anthropological considerations

What status should we give to the concept of European citizenship? Here opinion divides sharply between those who proclaim that the new rights it establishes are a major contribution to freedom and democracy (notably the Reflection Group 1995, cf. Moxon-Browne 1993; and Meehan 1993), and those who argue, particularly from a legal perspective, that they amount to very little in practice (Closa 1992; Welsh 1993; Wallace and Smith 1995). For example, Ian Ward's *Critical Introduction to European Law* devotes only a few paragraphs to citizenship and dismisses it as 'a pleasant touch, but of limited practical value' (Ward 1996: 40). Similarly, citizenship receives only three passing references in Mathijsen's (1995) four-hundred-page volume on EU law – hardly the level of attention one would expect for something proclaimed as a 'pillar of the European Union'. Furthermore, as many other commentators point out, most of the rights referred to in the new Articles either already exist or are so narrow that they are of little legal consequence. Thus, many writers conclude that the significance of Union citizenship is 'merely symbolic'.

In my view all of these positions are problematic. There can be little doubt that European citizenship was inserted into the amended EC Treaty as a populist measure to make the Maastricht Treaty more palatable and as an instrument for instilling European consciousness among the masses[17] – an idea encouraged particularly by Jacques Delors. However, to dismiss citizenship as 'merely symbolic' is to miss the point about the importance of symbols as repositories of meaning and agents of consciousness. This point is not lost on Juliette Lodge – herself a former 'European Woman of the Year'. As she correctly argues, the concept of citizenship 'is essentially political' and 'embryonic' (Lodge 1993b: 380). In the words of the 1995 Commission Report for the Reflection Group, its primary function, was to 'heighten the sense of belonging to the Union and enhance its legitimacy' (1995: 19–20). Whether it will achieve this and generate the kind of multiple loyalties common to federal systems, as Lodge (1993b: 380) predicts, is an interesting question.

Four major criticisms are often raised in relation to the Maastricht conception of citizenship.[18] First, the EU concept of citizenship focuses exclusively on rights without outlining a set of corresponding duties. Beyond the rather nebulous notion of duty to be 'loyal' (which must none the less be compatible with the right to freedom of speech) and the more obvious duties concerning voting, taxation and military service, there is little consensus as to what 'duty' might include in the European context. Since classical times the main obligation of citizens (their 'first duty') was not simply to participate actively in the life of the *polis*, but to take up arms when called to its defence. In post-war Europe, the benefits of citizenship in the welfare state were accompanied by the duty to work, to pay taxes and insurance contributions, and to take part in military service. This invariably raises a question concerning what corresponding duties might be imposed on European citizens in future. Might they be required to pay more taxes to the EU? To subsidise transfer payments to develop poorer regions of the Union? To offer service in a new European army or civil defence force? To fight wars for Europe or police disputes in troubled regions such as Kosovo or the Gulf?

Claims that Union citizenship is an 'evolving concept' raise the prospect of these possibilities becoming a reality, particularly given the enthusiasm of some EU leaders for creating a more integrated European defence force. However, despite being what one Commission's booklet calls 'the most potent symbol of the existence of the European Union',[19] the minimalist rights to free movement have so far 'proven to be too thin to generate any corresponding sense of public duty' (Welsh 1993: 8). Moreover, despite the theoretical right to travel and reside freely across the Union, very few Europeans have demonstrated much desire actually to do so. Unlike the United States of America – which is often taken as the model for a future United States of Europe – people in the EU do not regard the continent of Europe as their domestic labour market and are reluctant to cross national frontiers in search of employment – even in those countries where youth unemployment is particularly high (notably in Spain). Indeed, there is less transnational mobility of labour in Europe today than there was two or even three decades ago (Faist 1997: 236). This is borne out in the Commission's own *Eurobarometer* surveys. According to polls conducted in 1996, fewer than one-third of Europeans 'would take a job elsewhere in Europe were they offered one'. Despite the freedom to work and reside in another EU member state, only a tiny number of EU citizens actually do so. For example, OECD figures published in 1994 estimated that in 1990 the foreign population living in the member states amounted to 14 million (out of an EU population of 320 million). Of these, only 5 million were EU citizens residing in other member countries (the rest being *extracommunitari* from non-EC states).[20] Of those 5 million EU citizens resident in another EU country, the highest percentage was found in Belgium (5 per cent), followed by France (2.8 per cent), Germany (2.1 per cent); Ireland (1.8 per cent); UK (1.4 per cent); Italy (0.2 per cent).[21] Once again these figures suggest that the EU goal of creating a transnational political and economic order is hampered by the lack of a transnational European public, or a viable European labour market.

The second major criticism in relation to citizenship is that, despite frequent calls for an official European charter of citizens' rights – going back as far as the 1985 Adonnino Report – it is still unclear whether Union citizenship is meant to codify existing practice or be a catalyst for further integration. Were the new political rights set out in the Maastricht enshrined primarily in order to facilitate free movement of people, goods and services, or to address the deeper problem of Europe's democratic deficit? If the latter, why are EU nationals living in other member states entitled to vote only in European and *municipal* elections rather than national elections? The Commission's reasoning here was that voting in national elections would impinge upon national sovereignty, whereas local election fell within the scope of the general commitment to democracy established in existing treaties. It argued that the local level is where decisions taken by governments most directly affect individuals and concluded that 'Articles 235 and 236 of the Treaty provided enough legal basis for granting voting rights to any citizens from a Member-State, regardless of his residence' (Welsh 1993: 12). But as critics point out, if residence in a Community country is what counts, why should immigrants from non-EU countries be treated differently from immigrants from EU countries?

Third, Union citizenship is criticised for perpetuating the conflation of nationality and citizenship. The very idea of a 'Community national' is a paradox: that is, one can be a Union citizen only by virtue of being a citizen of a member state. The result is that the status of Union citizenship is subordinate to, and wholly dependent upon, the framework of the nation-state. This leads some to ask, do we need 'European citizenship'? The Commission's answer is that the entitlements granted by Union citizenship are 'additional' to those of member state citizenship and in no way compromise national sovereignty. However one interprets this, the result is that decisions about who is, or is not, a European citizen are determined by the existing nationality laws particular to each member state – which inevitably poses problems for the EU's attempts to construct a common European identity. One of the effects of this has been to confirm certain citizenship laws in countries in their chosen mode of 'ethnic nationality' at just the moment when this idea was beginning to be challenged (Cesarani and Fulbrook 1997: 8). This is particularly relevant in the case of Germany, whose citizenship laws date from the 1933 Constitution which privileges the idea *jus sanguis* or citizenship based on the notion of blood ties and ethnic descent (Mandell 1994) – and therefore excludes German-born children of Turkish 'guest-workers' and other minorities.

A final and more widely articulated criticism is that Union citizenship discriminates against non-EU nationals – thereby raising the prospect of an ever-more exclusivist 'Fortress Europe'. By extending voting rights only to member state nationals, the EU is sending an ambiguous message to those residents who are outside the EU parameters. Non-EU nationals effectively become second-class citizens. Their exclusion from the entitlements of European citizenship makes a mockery of the claims about the universality of European Community values. As Welsh notes, we see here echoes of the old exclusivist distinction, embodied in the 1791 French Constitution, between 'active citizens' (those who owned property and who could influence the public domain) and 'passive citizens' (who are seen as contributing very little). These points are worth expanding as they highlight a dimension of the European citizenship debate that is typically sidestepped or ignored in much of the literature.

The social consequences of 'Fortress Europe'

While the European Parliament has been particularly active in championing anti-racism in Europe, one of the charges against the EU is that it has, unintentionally, fuelled xenophobia and racism throughout Europe by creating an economic 'underclass' of foreigners and the unemployed. Central to the EU's goal of creating a single market has been the vision of a *Europe sans frontières*, a territory without internal barriers. For most businesspeople, the prospect of forging the world's largest free-trade area was highly attractive. Politicians, however, many of whom derived electoral support from policies of tighter immigration control and discrimination against non-citizens, were less enthusiastic. EU leaders therefore tried to reassure doubters that everything would be all right, 'provided that what they called "problems" – a term generally stretched to include immigrants and refugees as well as terrorism, international crime and drug-trafficking – were rigidly excluded from the external borders of the community' (Spencer 1990: 30). Thus, as national barriers within Europe have come down, the walls separating the EU from its 'Others' have grown higher (Bunyan 1991; Pieterse 1991; Kofman and Sales 1992). To make matters worse, EU policy statements consistently conflate issues about immigrants, foreigners and border controls with fears about drugs, terrorism and crime. The result of this elision is to lump together immigrants, refugees and asylum-seekers together with drug dealers and terrorists. This category represents all those who show 'disrespect for Europe's frontiers' (Robins 1994: 94), or rather, all those who symbolise disorder and 'matter out of place' (Douglas 1966).

The idea of erecting a *cordon sanitaire* around 'Fortress Europe' therefore came to dominate EU policy-making – culminating in March 1995 in the creation of what has come to be called 'Schengenland',[22] and a host of initiatives designed to fortify Europe's southern and eastern frontiers against illegal immigrants and other species of unwanted alien. 'The liberal commitment to the free movement of peoples within the Community' as Spencer (1990: 30) observes, 'has been counterbalanced by the idea of concentrating and intensifying at external borders all the checks that formerly took place at each frontier'. In case this ring-fence proved insufficient, it was agreed that random internal checks and police surveillance would have to be increased, a prospect that contradicts the EU's claims about giving citizens greater freedom (cf. Bunyan 1991). This point is graphically illustrated in the Commission's 1994 booklet, *Freedom of Movement*. One of its drawings shows a giant policeman surveilling the passing traffic (Figure 6). Below this the text refers to the necessity for 'identity checks' in the 'effort to eliminate international terrorism, drug smuggling and criminality' – a priority which, it says, 'is recognised by citizens' who do not want to see mobility of criminals. Western Europe has thus created, in the words of Jonathan Eyal, 'a set of defences, often imperceptible but much more efficient than the Berlin Wall.

Figure 6 Image from the European Commission's 1994 'Freedom of Movement' booklet.

Author: Bernd Mölke-Tassel

From an airline clerk to a Hungarian border guard, everyone is working to prevent people coming to the West'.[23]

The problem for an open Europe, as Sivanandan (1991: v) put it, 'is how to close it – against immigrants and refugees from the Third World'. Thus, the paradoxical effect of European unification has been an intensification of what Verena Stolcke (1995) calls 'cultural fundamentalism' or Eurocentrism 'a sort of higher xenophobia directed against Muslims and the modern version of the Mongol hordes – east Europeans attempting to escape the economic rubble of communism' (Cesarani and Fulbrook 1997: 3). Immigrants and asylum seekers – particularly women, who tend to occupy more marginal positions in the labour market – have borne the brunt of these increasingly tighter restrictions on entry into the EU. The result has been a new 'boundary' in the shape of a four-fold classification of citizenship status in Europe: 'white citizens, black citizens, legally resident non-citizens ('denizens'), and illegals – including refugees' (Wrench, cited in Kofman and Sales 1992: 31). One perverse manifestation of this 'Fortress Europe' phenomenon is its effects on patterns of migration, including arranged marriages. Morokvasic gives a vivid example of this:

> One of the best-read German newspapers published an interview with Mr. WB, owner of a marriage bureau, in which Mr. WB praises the 'goods' he has on offer for his potential clients, German men: a Polish wife (to be) for only 390DM. The client is free to select four among some 1,500 photos. For each he gets to know as much as her WEIGHT and AGE, sometimes accompanied by attributes like 'super sexy' or 'extremely full bosom'. He can try them out, and even makes another selection of four. If HE is not satisfied SHE goes back to Poland. WB's speciality was South East Asian women but he is now switching to Poles for whom there is a growing demand, especially among retired, divorced and not directly well-off men. No German women would take them – but for Poles they are good enough. Besides, 'Poles are cheaper than Asians both in terms of capital investment and in maintenance: what is a cheap train ticket in comparison to a 5,000DM air ticket from Bangkok or Manila? And whereas a Thai is unprepared for cold German winters – one has to buy her clothes – a Pole brings her own boots and a fur coat. And she is as good in bed and industrious in the kitchen'.[24]

Where once the Cold War division of Europe was marked by barbed wire and minefields, today it seems this has been replaced by a more imperceptible border defined by race, class, gender and nationality, and marked largely by economic factors. The effect has been to transform the border zone between Germany and the Czech Republic into the largest 'red-light district' in Europe. The dark side of European citizenship, then, is its implications for non-EU nationals. European leaders extol the idea of Europe's mosaic of cultures and the transcendence of national borders in a frontier-free Europe. But to achieve these it has created Schengenland and, however unwittingly, invented a new language for articulating European racism. Nowhere is this contradiction between lofty Enlightenment ideals about cultural pluralism and individual freedom and the realities of cultural racism and European intolerance of other cultures more evident that in the case of Europe's gypsy population. Günther Grass (1992: 108) notes with irony: 'They could teach us how meaningless frontiers are: careless of boundaries, Romanies and Sinti are at home all over Europe. They are what we claim to be: born Europeans.' And yet, as Kevin Robins (1994: 95) adds, 'it seems that Europe is afraid of them'. Romanies – together with Jews and Muslims – have borne the brunt of European citizens' prejudice, intolerance and loathing of the alien 'Other' (cf. Allen and Macey 1991). Their very lifestyle – their cross-border mobility – is perceived as sinister, anomolous and threatening to the property-owning citizens of Europe (Okely 1983).

Conclusion: towards a post-national citizenship?

How, then, should we interpret European citizenship? As noted, it was invented by European political elites in order to hail the masses and to address the EU's crisis of legitimacy. From a legal perspective, the Maastricht Treaty has redefined the peoples of Europe as 'European subjects', but this is not the same thing as forging a 'European subjectivity'. The key ingredient or catalyst that appears to be missing from this scenario is, yet again, a coherent sense of identity and European consciousness to invest the legal shell of citizenship with social meaning.

As I have tried to argue, citizenship – together with ultimate legal authority and the power to make international treaties – is one of the defining characteristics of a state. In this respect, European citizenship is not so much a discourse of rights as a discourse of power. It is a political technology for making the EU more visible to its newly constituted subjects so that they see themselves reflected in its largess; a conceptual tool for legitimising a supposedly supranational form of statehood. Its function is to generate a new category of European subjectivity and thereby enable the new European state to communicate directly with its citizens. The question is not whether the EU is an embryonic state, but what kind of state it is becoming. A nation-state writ large? A decentralised federal state? Or something altogether different?

The argument that citizenship is increasingly being disassociated from the nation-state would seem to support the claim that European citizenship represents a latent or embryonic form of nationality. However, comparisons with nation-state-formation are instructive. In the case of both France and the USA, as Hobsbawm (1990) observes, the key condition for granting full citizenship was the acquisition of language skills. Government and governed could thus communicate in a shared tongue. Europe's linguistic pluralism, much as it is celebrated, also poses problems for the nation-building aspirations of EU policy-makers. Some authors perceive in the hazy outlines of a post-national citizenship the citizens' rescue from the oppressive order of nation-states. For example, Gerard Delanty (1995: 161) writes with passion about the need to unshackle citizenship from its association with nationality – thereby liberating the original progressive idea 'that emerged with the French Revolution when citizenship was opposed to the coercive state'. Similarly, William Wallace and Julie Smith (1995: 137) comment with apparent approval on how '[t]he troops of revolutionary France appealed to the "peoples" of Europe, against the states, to raise the banner of popular legitimacy against monarchy and aristocracy'. Their comment that 'Napoleon's armies contained Italians and Germans, Poles and Dutch fighting for a new order against old regimes' seems to resonate with a nostalgic hope that the EU might, somehow, take up this banner against the *ancien régime* of the post-1789 nationalist order.

Clearly, like T. H. Marshall, the drafters of the Maastricht Treaty expected that European citizenship would be developmental, expanding beyond civil and economic rights to include political and social rights – hence Article 8e which leaves space for this possibility. This is why official EU language consistently refers to the 'dynamic' and 'evolutionary' nature of citizenship rights. However, Marshall was writing at a time when the welfare state model was at its peak. By contrast, post-Maastricht Europe has been constructed around the neo-liberal norms of price stability and fiscal rectitude, and the monetarist obsession with 'trickle-down' economics. Indeed, the Maastricht Treaty does not simply embody these principles: as we shall see in the next chapter, it effectively constitutionalises them.

The question is, what might 'social citizenship' entail in a post-welfare, neo-liberal order? Here we encounter another major contradiction in the strategy of those seeking to construct the new Europe. They are trying to graft social rights on to a *laissez-faire* economic framework that is hostile to the Marshall concept of social citizenship – and at a time when the welfare state is visibly being dismantled across Europe. As Marshall and others have noted, there is an historical tension between the free-market conception of citizenship – with its emphasis on individual rights such as the freedom of movement for the economically active – and the conception of social citizenship which is based on a more egalitarian ethos and collective rights. This antagonism is also evident in the Maastricht-inspired view of European citizenship – which critics condemn for being 'both economically and nationally determined' (Ward 1996: 158).

One striking manifestation of the economistic way that European citizenship rights have been articulated is witnessed in the fact that the European Commission's unit responsible for citizenship is located not, as one might expect, in the Social Affairs Directorate (DG V), but in DG XV, the Directorate responsible for the Internal Market. Behind the Commission's current policy of 'getting closer to the citizen' are a host of self-interested political and commercial calculations. Indeed, EU policy-makers now consistently conflate the two domains such that 'consumers' and 'citizens' are increasingly conceived as essentially one and the same thing. A heading in the EU booklet called 'A Citizen's Europe' announces: 'Every citizen a consumer' (Fontaine 1991: 27). The citizen-hero of the new Europe thus appears to be the Euro-consumer. The emphasis on consumption as a defining feature of citizenship opens up an interesting way of analysing the new European state. According to J. G. A Pocock the logic that drives European construction is fundamentally economistic. What is being constructed, he says, is an 'empire of the market'. An economic community based on:

a set of arrangements for ensuring the surrender by states of their power to control the movement of economic forces which exercise the ultimate authority in human affairs. The institutions jointly operated, and/or obeyed, by member states would then not be political institutions bringing about a redistribution of sovereignty, but administrative or entrepreneurial institutions designed to ensure that no sovereign authority can interfere with the omnipotence of a market exercising 'sovereignty' in a metaphorical because non-political sense.[25]

While some might argue that this is a simplification, it does none the less highlight a common pattern among contemporary political systems that is not confined to the EU. What we are witnessing is, effectively, a new form of governmentality developing across the continent and beyond in which the primary basis for political legitimation lies in a government's ability to guarantee, as Terry Turner argues (1995: 18)

their citizens access to commodity consumption on a scale commensurate with their social aspirations. Consumption of commodities has thus supplanted the exercise of the traditional political functions of citizenship as the main mode of the construction – and thus control – of personal identity.

Against the spectre of an 'authoritarian European state' suggested by Bunyan (1991) and other critics of the EU's centralising tendencies, what Pocock, Turner and others propose instead is an altogther more decentred, *laissez-faire* European order in which the political is subordinate to the economic. This captures something of the character of modern systems of government. I suspect it also offers a glimpse of what 'post-national European citizenship' might mean in practice: namely, an identity forged around and through an ideal of the European consumer.

Notes

1 The first definition given in the *Oxford English Dictionary* is 'member of a State or commonwealth, either native or naturalised'.
2 The distinction between citizenship and nationality is analysed in Guild (1997).
3 For a critique of Aron's argument, see Meehan (1993).
4 Habermas (1992) gives a more detailed assessment of these issues.
5 Cited in Habermas (1992: 9). Cf also Robins (1994: 90).
6 Commission Opinion of 21 October 1990 COM (90) 600 Bull EC Supp. 2/ 91:69.
7 Ironically, as Wallace and Smith (1995: 157) note 'the creation of European citizenship, supposed to be a positive aspect of European integration, was one of the main reasons for the "No" vote in the Danish referendum of 2 June 1992'.
8 Evoking T. H. Marshall's dream of a postwar 'citizenship' welfare settlement which could become a 'new common experience' and form the basis for social cohesion, Andrews looks forward to 'a new politics of citizenship which reasserts the language of community and the extension of democracy and offers the

prospect of a more vibrant civil society with more public trust in elected represen-tatives and greater freedom of expression' (1991: 14).

9 As Guild (1997: 33) notes, 'the essence of citizenship remains the constitutional arrangements made for participation by a defined category of individuals in the life of a state'.

10 *Oxford English Dictionary* (1978: 442).

11 As Mathijsen (1995: 7) observes, the Maastricht Treaty not only created new rights and obligations for member states, 'it also directly included their citizens, who thereby became subjects of the Community'.

12 Weiler (1992), cited in Wallace and Smith (1995: 152).

13 Charles Tilly (1998) review of Wiener's book *'European' Citizenship Practice: Building Institutions of a Non-State*, cited on http://www.hcacademic.com/catalyst/W333358X.HTM.

14 See Bulmer and Rees (1997) for an assessment of Marshall and his legacy.

15 All citations are from 'Text in Full of the 'Treaty on European Union', 7 February 1992, *Agence Europe*, Brussels.

16 House of Commons European Scrutiny Committee, Sixth Report, 20 January 1999.

17 This is made explicit in the Commission's 1995 *Report for the Reflection Group*. European citizenship appears in the report under the heading 'Heightening the Sense of Belonging to the Union and Enhancing its Legitimacy'.

18 For an excellent review of these, see Welsh (1993), to whom this chapter is much indebted.

19 CEC (1994) *Freedom of Movement*, Brussels: OOPEC: 3.

20 Cited in Faist 1997: 225.

21 Source: Henley Centre (1996a; 1996b).

22 The 'Schengen Agreement' (named after the small village in Luxembourg where Interior Ministers from France, Germany and the Benelux countries first met in 1985) was based on a series of intergovernmental articles setting out the way in which controls at the common frontiers were to be abolished, but including a number of provisions on sensitive questions such as control of drugs and firearms, transmission of personal data and asylum.

23 Jonathan Eyal, *Guardian*, 15 February 1993, cited in Robins (1994: 95).

24 *Bild*, 9 January 1991, cited in Morokvasic (1992: 69).

25 J. G. A Pocock (1991) 'Deconstructing Europe', *London Review of Books*, 19, 19 December 1991, cited in Robins (1994: 82).

4 Symbolising boundaries: the single currency and the art of European governance

> The art of government is the organisation of idolatry. The bureaucracy consists of functionaries; the aristocracy, of idols; the democracy of idolaters. The populace cannot understand the bureaucracy: it can only worship the national idols.
>
> George Bernard Shaw, *Maxims for Revolutionists.*[1]

> The key political fact is that a single currency will have continent-wide deflationary consequences which cannot be democratically legitimated.
>
> John Gray (1996)[2]

The cultural politics of EMU

On 1 January 1999 the European Union took arguably its boldest step towards integration when eleven member states (all but the UK, Denmark, Sweden and Greece) renounced their sovereignty over monetary policy and adopted the 'euro' as their new common currency. On that date, the euro became a currency in its own right, conversion rates between old currencies and the euro were permanently fixed, dual pricing began in earnest and the European Central Bank in Frankfurt took permanent control over the setting, framing and implementing of the single interest and exchange rate policy for the entire euro currency area. This was the realisation of 'phase 3' of the EU's project for Economic and Monetary Union (EMU), to which most of the member states had committed themselves when they ratified the Maastricht Treaty during 1992–3. By June 2002, the franc, peseta, punt, escudo, deutschmark, drachma, lire and guilder will be withdrawn from circulation leaving only the euro as legal tender. 'Euroland', as the new currency zone is called, embraces over 290 million people and is responsible for one-fifth of the world's economic output and roughly the same share of world trade (20 per cent) as that of the United States. It has transformed the EU into one of the world's most powerful commercial blocs.

Throughout the world, particularly in the City of London, financial dealers and analysts were working overtime to prepare for the anticipated frenzy of activity that would begin when the markets opened. In Brussels, the birth of the euro was marked with an official ceremony designed to attract maximum media attention.

Outside in the courtyard children decked from head to foot in the blue and gold of the European flag began the count down from *dix, neuf, huit* . . . to *un*, and released three thousand balloons into the grey Brussels sky for the benefit of the assembled television cameras.[3] Inside, EU officials, ambassadors and politicians gathered amidst the popping of champagne corks and celebratory toasts to hear minister after minister invoke the historical magnitude of the moment. Carlo Ciampi, for Italy, relieved that the lire had not been excluded from membership, welcomed the fact that 'Italian money is no longer national. Today it becomes European', he added.[4] France's finance Minister Dominique Strauss-Kahn spoke of the dream of Victor Hugo and ended his speech with '*Vive la France en Europe!*' More contentiously, he told reporters that the 'Euro-11' council of finance ministers would rapidly become the 'economic government of Europe'. In the words of Austria's Finance Minister Rudolf Edlinger, 1 January 1999 was 'the dawn of a new era of history'.[5]

As these statements suggest, monetary union has implications that extend far beyond economics. This chapter is not specifically concerned with the economic arguments about EMU. Rather, my aim is to explore the cultural politics of the single currency, particularly the relationship between money, cultural identity and state-formation in Europe. These themes are intimately connected for various reasons, which are addressed below. The control of money has long been associated with national sovereignty and the powers of the state. As the pioneers of the European Community and its more astute leaders have long held, monetary and political union integration are inextricably linked: the more national economies are tied up with each other, the more irresistible closer political integration becomes. However, forging ever closer union through 'irresistible' economic and institutional ties is a strategy riddled with difficulties. EMU aims to create a stable and permanent union, but it could prove to be neither. As we shall see, the optimistic predictions of those who advocate EMU are largely declarations of faith. The single currency is a highly risky venture that requires major changes in the political culture of member states, which not all are ready to make. That the single currency should have achieved such a successful launch in so short a time is in itself a remarkable tribute to the political will of European leaders and the deft behind-the-scenes work of those EU elites engaged in its promotion. But who were the key actors behind the campaign to promote the euro and what arguments did they use? What measures were mobilised to convince people (and the international markets) about the merits of EMU? How were the designs for the new euro coins and banknotes chosen, and what does an anthropological reading of all these themes reveal about the cultural assumptions underlying elite attitudes towards European integration? More importantly, what are its implications of the single currency for changing systems of governance and state-formation in the new Europe? These questions provide the focus for this chapter.

The euro and the 'art of government'

Ever since the idea of a single currency was first advanced in 1949 by the European Movement, European politicians have invested considerable emotional and political capital in the creation of a monetary union, perceiving it to be a critical step on the path to ever closer integration in Europe. They often look to America for their model.[6] The USA is a nation with over 240 million people divided into fifty states; there are no barriers to trade between states and they share just one currency – the dollar – whose strength in the international exchange markets underpins America's diplomatic and political influence in the world. Furthermore, the US dollar, along with Coca-Cola, blue jeans, the hamburger and Uncle Sam, has become a major symbol of American national identity. The vision of a single European market with over 370 million consumers and a single European currency, more powerful than the dollar and strong enough to dominate world interest rates and financial markets, unites politicians from both left and right of the political spectrum – particularly those in Europe who harbour anti-American sentiments.

EMU supporters argue that it will usher in a new era of prosperity, growth and employment built on stable prices, enduring fiscal discipline, lower interest rates and 'enhanced joint monetary sovereignty'.[7] To opponents, however, the single currency is an act of economic folly that will divide Europe, rob nation-states of their sovereignty and submerge national communities in a federation – or worse, a European superstate – which commands little support or democratic legitimacy.[8] Caught between these competing discourses, most people are confused about both the rationale for monetary union and its likely consequences in the political domain.

The rationale underlying EMU is itself part of a cultural and historical discourse that merits closer anthropological analysis – in particular, of its *cultural* and symbolic significance. 'Symbolising boundaries', the title of this chapter, is taken from a book by A. P. Cohen (1986) which explores the various ways in which people construct their identities and social boundaries using symbols of place and locality. Cohen's argument, in brief, is that communities are symbolically constructed. That is, they exist as imagined entities in the eyes of their beholders. It is through symbolic forms and structures that we come to know and identify the boundaries of our own and other societies. The key point, however, is that symbols do not simply *reflect* our political reality: they actively *constitute* it. We do indeed live in a 'forest of symbols' (Turner 1967) and these govern the way we conceptualise not only our social boundaries but also our sense of identity and experience of selfhood. Cohen's argument was directed at the small-scale community, but it does have relevance for the European Union?

Benedict Anderson's (1983) work on nationalism provides useful insights here. Anderson's originality lay in his examination of the conditions that made it possible to think (or 'imagine') the nation: i.e. those agents of consciousness that helped people to reconceptualise themselves as 'nationals' and citizens rather than parochial peasants or subjects within a kingdom. Foremost among the new forms of imagining that first flowered during the eighteenth century were the newspaper and the novel (Anderson 1983: 3). To these were later added other symbolic markers of nationhood, including the map, museum, census, mass education, taxation and national service: all of these cultural forms were instrumental in forging national consciousness. Curiously, Anderson makes no mention of the role of currencies in imagining the nation-state, although these were undoubtedly key agents in the creation of national imaginaries in the twentieth century. The question I wish to answer is, what role will the single currency play in the reconfiguration of national consciousness in the twenty-first century? Will it, as EU policy-makers seem to assume, help lay the foundations for a more popular-based 'European consciousness' to emerge?

The single currency issue also has major implications for national and pan-national governance in Europe. 'Art of government' is a particularly useful concept for unpacking the political significance of the euro because it draws attention to the relationship between discourse and systems of power. As George Bernard Shaw (cited above) suggested, the art of government consists of keeping the population in a state of educated ignorance. Michel Foucault's work on 'political technologies' provides a more theoretical approach for analysing how effective governance is achieved, or, as he put it, how 'regimes or truth' are established.[9] For Foucault, 'political technologies' work by taking what are essentially *political* issues, removing them from the realm of politics and recasting them in the neutral language of science or technology so that they appear as technical/managerial problems to be solved (or rather managed) by technical experts.

As anthropological studies have shown, policy often works by being made to appear 'neutral' and beyond the domain of politics (Shore and Wright 1997). But is this analysis applicable to EMU? How valid is the claim made by euro-sceptics that the single currency is a 'stalking horse' for creating a European state? In so far as EMU has laid the foundations of 'European economic government' and boosted the EU's public profile, the term 'political technology' seems accurate. Indeed, the chief merit claimed for the single currency is precisely that it places economic and monetary policy 'beyond political control' by transferring macro-economic decision-making from national governments to an independent European Central Bank (ECB), a supranational institution modelled on the German Bundesbank whose constitution insulates it from political accountability and whose prime directive is to maintain price stability.[10] The Euro is the most important symbol of European integration and identity to date. It is the European ideal made flesh: a concrete manifestation of the European symbol elevated into a common medium of exchange for the whole continent. More than any other EU cultural initiative, the 'euro in your pocket' will help to transform the EU from a remote set of supranational institutions and abstract macroeconomic principles into a tangible cultural fact at the level of everyday social reality. As François Mitterrand summed it up in 1989, the EU's goal is 'one currency, one culture, one social area, one environment'.[11]

Like European integration, therefore, the euro is as much about 'culture' as it is about economics and law.[12] It is also a key site of contestation between different political interests and ideologies. Despite bold claims about its historical magnitude, there has been relatively little analysis of the constitutional and cultural significance of monetary union. Debates over EMU have been dominated by technical and financial considerations – as though money were simply a unit of commercial value devoid of symbolic meaning: a commodity that 'knows no country' as the old *laissez-faire* adage goes. But as Kenneth Dyson (1994: 3) points out, money 'has an irreducibly Janus-faced nature: an economic and technical face and a cultural and political face'. What interests me is its 'cultural face'. Dyson sums it up neatly:

> Money is political in being a key expression of statehood. States express their sovereignty in issuing and managing their own currency. Hence, banks have a symbolic as well as a technical importance, often expressed in their imposing façades – for instance, those of the Bank of England and the Banque de France. Money is also cultural; it expresses nationhood and identity. Currencies like the French franc, the pound sterling and the US dollar possess an emotional and psychological power. They are 'stores of value' in more than an economic sense, with coins often representing elaborate national mythologies. Correspondingly, a single European currency is evocative of a claim to 'statehood' and 'common culture': a claim that was always bound to be disputed, but a dispute for which EU policy makers – blinkered by the technical economics of EMU and the technocratic policy style of the EC Commission – were unprepared.
>
> (Dyson 1994: 5)

Dyson's point about currencies evoking a claim to statehood and common culture is worth emphasising. The minting of coins and the printing of banknotes have always had a special relationship to the formation of states and the maintenance of state sovereignty – and these, in turn, play a major role in shaping social identity. There is virtually no currency in the world that was not controlled by a nation-state, and no country of significant size that does not control its own currency. Currencies would thus seem to be not only symbolic of state sovereignty but a major determinant of self-government.

At another level, coins and banknotes have traditionally functioned to define the boundaries of kingdoms, empires and nations. The very first coins bore the profile of emperors and kings and symbols of state power, much as they do today. With their images of national figures, monuments and inventions, banknotes and coins are powerful icons and instruments of government that help to render abstract ideas of state and nationhood a daily political reality. But it is not simply that British banknotes carry the image of Queen Elizabeth II and Britannia on one side, or famous national figures such as Charles Dickens, George Stephenson and Florence Nightingale on the other, while the words '*Bank of England*' are emblazoned on both: the important fact is that the pound itself has become symbolically linked with the external image, identity and standing of the British state and the productivity of the nation. Sterling, or, to use a more idiomatic phrase, 'the pound in your pocket', is expressive of national identity as well as providing a quantitative indicator of national economic performance.[13] The same is true of other national currencies, from the Indian rupee and Egyptian dinar to the Japanese yen and the US dollar.

Currencies are thus repositories of meaning as well as vehicles for the expression of cultural identity, particularly national identity. This much is clearly understood by EU political and financial elites, although they tended not to emphasise the point, and typically dismissed fears about loss of identity as scaremongering by nationalists. However, the Commission's own attempts to promote public acceptance of the euro (including balloon and champagne parties and the ceremonial dressing of children in the EU flag) indicate that it clearly accepts the important link between currencies and identity. As Jacques Santer proclaimed:

> The Euro is also a powerful factor in forging a European identity. Countries which share a common currency are countries ready to unite their destinies as part of an integrated community. The Euro will bring citizens closer together, and will provide a physical manifestation of the growing *rapprochement* between European citizens which has been taking place for the past forty years or more.
>
> (Santer 1998: 8)

The deutschmark exemplifies this relationship most clearly. The deep attachment of many Germans to their currency – what Habermas (1992) and others call 'deutschmark nationalism' – has been well noted in the literature and is recognised as a particular problem for EU policy-makers. This is understandable: the deutschmark is the single most enduring symbol of Germany's postwar economic success and it has given Germans something they are proud of and justifiably fearful of surrendering for what may well be the much weaker euro. As one German MEP described it:

> To be German after the war held nothing positive for us. Then we had the reconstruction of Germany and the German economic miracle. Germany's postwar recovery is also the success story of the deutschmark. Other people have their culture and their national history. Germans don't have that. For them, the Mark is a symbolic and emotional issue.

Commission officials agreed that their hardest battle would be to win public acceptance of the euro in Germany. The key campaign message relayed to the German public was thus reassurance that the new currency would be as strong and as stable as the deutschmark.[14]

Part of the political aim behind the euro was therefore to make 'Europe' more tangible and visible to its citizens in the hope that this would spill over into greater popularity and legitimacy for political integration. However, two problems threatened to undermine this venture. The first concerned how international markets would react, the second, public opinion. From the perspective of the

European Commission, the major challenge was therefore cultural: how to 'wean' 'ordinary people' from their attachments to national denominations and convince them of the merits of their new currency. 'The success of the changeover to the single currency', it proclaimed,

> will depend on one condition: the Euro must win full public acceptance. The switch will inevitably upset people's day-to-day habits and will change the ways in which banks and businesses organise their operations. It is therefore essential to keep stressing the many benefits that the single currency will bring.
>
> (CEC 1996a: 21)

The Commission's goal was not simply to allay public anxiety about the change-over to the euro: in the words of Yves-Thibault de Silguy, the European Commissioner responsible for economic and monetary affairs, it was to make citizens 'learn to love their currency'.[15]

Monetary union and state-formation

These factors highlight just some of the reasons why EMU raises wider issues of identity, citizenship and governance in Europe, but more important are the links between economic sovereignty and the state. Federalists and EU supporters outside of Britain, including Helmut Kohl and leading members of the Bundesbank,[16] make no secret of their belief that monetary and political union are inseparable. The fact that most monetary unions throughout history have succeeded only when accompanied by political union supports their arguments.[17] Yet despite so much evidence to the contrary, most politicians in the UK consistently proclaim that EMU membership must be treated as an *economic* matter that has little to do with the creation of a European state.[18] This was confirmed when the Labour government announced to Parliament in October 1997 that it would judge the suitability of UK membership of EMU according to five criteria, all of which were exclusively economic. In the words of Gordon Brown, 'we conclude that the determining factor as to whether Britain joins a single currency is the national economic interest and whether the economic case for doing so is clear and unambiguous'.[19]

As we shall see, government denial of the political and constitutional consequences of EMU was consistent with the conscious attempt by EU elites to 'de-politicise' the single currency, particularly in those member states whose people were considered likely to oppose membership. The reluctance to acknowledge the political ramifications of EMU among British political elites contrasted markedly with the attitude of European political leaders and analysts elsewhere. Kari Impens, speaking for the 'Young European Federalists', put it bluntly: 'moving to a single currency is of course the key step towards a federal Europe'.[20] According to Felipe González, 'the common currency is the greatest relinquishment of sovereignty since the foundation of the European communities'.[21] For Wim

Duisenberg, president of the European Central Bank (ECB), 'EMU is, and always was meant to be, a stepping stone on the way to a united Europe'.[22]

The 'stepping-stone' metaphor once again highlights the 'ratchet-effect' of the integration process: i.e. the 'Monnet method' whereby integration in one policy domain creates the need for integration in others, thus binding member states ever more tightly into the web of EU laws and institutions. Hans Tietmeyer, president of the Bundesbank, spelled this out clearly in 1995 when he told a press conference that: 'A European currency will lead to member nations transferring their sovereignty over financial and wage policies as well as monetary affairs. It is an illusion to think that states can hold onto their autonomy over fiscal policies.'[23] The result, according to Jacques Delors, is that monetary union will not work unless accompanied by 'European economic government'.[24] Unlike Tietmeyer, however, Delors argued that it was now imperative to introduce a counterweight to a central European bank with exclusive authority over monetary policy: EMU demanded a 'political roof'.[25]

EMU thus provides a rationale as well as an instrument for increasing power at the European centre at the expense of its peripheries. Just as the single market requires a single currency, a European Central Bank and uniform economic and monetary policies, so it creates demands for a single European state and legal system to monitor, regulate and govern the new 'Euroland'. Further transfer of powers to the supranational institutions created to manage these new domains of European governance thus become inevitable. This, in turn, is justified constitutionally by the EU's powers – and Treaty imperatives – to take action against anything that obstructs the proper functioning of the single market. Without a currency, a national central bank and control of the domestic money supply, and without the right to borrow, the nation-state can no longer function as independent entity (although critics of this argument contend that economic sovereignty has long been a myth). Conversely, with its single currency, its Central Bank and treaty control over money supply and borrowing, the EU takes on the powers of a sovereign state, albeit a transnational state without a democratic government and unlike anything hitherto created.

An even more controversial aspect of EMU is that it removes economic decision-making from *democratic* control. Independent central banks inevitably raise questions about political accountability even within a nation-state, but critics fear that at the European level — where parliamentary democracy is so underdeveloped – democratic accountability may prove fatally weak. They argue that ceding such powers to unelected central bankers makes a mockery of democracy for, if parliaments no longer control economic policy-making, then at elections people will discover that the representatives they can vote for are not the people who take the decisions. The French Constitutional Council came to similar conclusions in 1992 when it ruled that 'stage three of EMU' meant that 'a State will be deprived of its own competencies in an area in which the fundamental conditions for the exercise of national sovereignty are at issue'.[26]

Another criticism of monetary union is that along with the 'irreversibility' of membership, member states are required, under Article 30 of the ECB Statute, to transfer a large part of their foreign gold reserves. These assets form part of the ultimate guarantee of the currency to European Central Bank control. However, the key factor that is seen by many as a gross violation of national sovereignty is that EMU commits governments to strict budget ceilings, set out in the Maastricht Treaty and enforced by the 'Growth and Stability Pact' of the 1998 Amsterdam Treaty. This places fixed limits on government borrowing and fiscal deficits, and allows governments to be fined if their borrowing exceeds 3 per cent of GDP. EMU members thus no longer have the economic weapons traditionally used to defend a state against unwelcome economic shocks. Their national banks have effectively become regional branches of the ECB, subject to the same principles of neo-liberal economic orthodoxy and political immunity enshrined in Article 3a of the amended EEC Treaty. 'This means', according to Münchau (1999: 21), 'that even large countries, such as Germany and France, have ceased to exist as relevant macroeconomic units. To all intents and purposes, they have become regions'.[27]

The history and politics of EMU

To understand how this situation arose we need to examine first the steps that made EMU possible and second the strategies used to prepare people for the new currency. Although among the EU's most ambitious of objectives, EMU was not mentioned in any of the Treaties until the 1986 Single European Act (SEA). The goal of EMU was first debated in 1969 at a meeting of the (then) six heads of state in The Hague, with 1980 as the proposed target date. That decision led to the 1970 Werner Report which received considerable support from Giscard d'Estaing, Helmut Schmidt and Commission President Roy Jenkins, but the plan received a serious set-back thanks to the oil shock and recession of the 1970s. A less ambitious proposal, but one that nevertheless extended pan-European monetary co-operation, was the European Monetary System (EMS) agreed in 1979. Within this was an agreed Exchange-Rate Mechanism (ERM) that set the parameters by which national currencies could fluctuate against each other. EMU was again taken up in 1985 by Jacques Delors and was mentioned both in the preamble to the SEA and in an amendment to the Treaty of Rome. In 1988 work began on the 'Delors Report' – a highly influential committee composed of the governors of the central banks of the member-states with three independent economists under the chairmanship of Delors. Publication of the Delors Report in April 1989 in turn led to the decision to convene an Intergovernmental Conference (IGC) on EMU. The IGC's conclusions were a key component of the Maastricht Treaty.

The Maastricht Treaty mentions EMU in its preamble (which sets out the general goals of the EU) and refers to it, together with the single market, in Article B, as one of the means by which the Union will 'promote economic and social progress which is balanced and sustainable'. Article 3a of the amended EEC Treaty refers to 'the irrevocable fixing of exchange rates leading to the introduction of a single currency . . . [and] a single monetary policy and exchange-rate policy'. Thus, EMU was effectively 'constitutionalised' by becoming part of the EU's legally binding *aquis communautaire*. The single currency was to be achieved in three stages, as set out the Maastricht Treaty (Articles 102a–109m EEC).

Stage 1. By a decision of the Madrid European Council in June 1989, this began on 1 July 1990 with the removal of exchange controls in eight out of twelve member states (the rest were to follow later). All governments were to adopt measures that would encourage convergence of their economies and join the Exchange-Rate Mechanism. This was designed to 'peg' currencies so that fluctuations occurred only within a band of agreed margins which, for most member states was 2.5 per cent. However, the events of 16 September 1992 ('Black Wednesday'), when Britain and Italy were ignominiously ejected from the ERM, showed that the international markets and currency speculators can play havoc if they sense that some currencies are weak and overvalued.

Stage 2. This began on 1 January 1994, with the newly created European Monetary Institute (EUI) in Frankfurt gradually assuming a co-ordinating role. During this stage member states, except Britain and Denmark who had negotiated opt-out protocols, were to take steps to make their banks independent of government (although it is worth emphasising that Gordon Brown's first act as the new Labour Chancellor in June 1997 was to denationalise the Bank of England, thus preparing the ground for Britain's membership). Before the end of 1998, the Council was supposed to decide, by qualified majority vote, which countries had satisfied the convergence criteria, so that those that qualified could make the transition to the third stage. This occurred on 2 May 1996, when the eleven founder members of Euroland were nominated.

Stage 3. This began on 1 January 1999, with the 'irrevocable fixing' of exchange rates between euros and national denominations. The European Central Bank in Frankfurt (which replaced the EMI) became the sole issuing authority for euro banknotes. In addition to the inauguration of the new currency, stage 3 also entailed the creation of a European System of Central Banks (ESCB) composed of the ECB and representatives from the national central banks.

The Commission's Green Paper on the Practical Arrangement for the Introduction of the Single Currency published in May 1995 set out in detail the 'transition scenario' and the communications campaign that would prepare people for the changeover. This again outlined a 'three-phase approach' for introducing the currency (timetables being a key part of the EU's strategy for sustaining political momentum). Phases One and Two (the naming of those member states deemed eligible for membership and the January 1999 launch) went according to schedule and with a great deal of fanfare. However, the decision by the Commission and EMI about which member states had met the Maastricht convergence criteria was made on political rather than economic grounds. Both Italy and Belgium, for example, had levels of national debt almost double the 60 per cent Maastricht limit. Moreover, most member states had flagrantly massaged their statistics about levels of national debt, spending and borrowing. For example, Italy introduced a one-off 'Euro-tax', described as a 'loan';

Germany sold off land belonging to the state railways, revalued its gold reserves and temporarily cut payments to the social security system, thus affecting an astonishing 10 per cent fall in public investment for the year.[28] The French government, instead, included pension funds from the French telecom giant. Phase Three of the 'transition scenario' was set for 1 January 2002 (called 'E-Day') when the 'definitive changeover to the Euro' begins, euro notes and coins are put into circulation and national currencies are withdrawn. By June 2002, users are expected to be fully prepared and all the technical changes are to be concluded – including the reprogramming of software and machinery, tills and cash dispensers. Henceforward, all money-based transactions (wages, salaries, pensions, bank and balances) will be denominated in euros – Europe's only legal tender.

According to one of its authors, 'the Green Paper's function was to remind governments of their policy commitment and what needs doing [but] the most important thing from the Commission's point of view was to establish a sense of inevitability about the single currency'.[29] By early 1996, this strategy was clearly working: As Anatole Kalesky noted, 'EMU was beginning to acquire an irresistible momentum'.[30] However, whether this reflected support or simply a sense of fatalism about the inevitability of EMU was an open question. The Commission had by no means won the argument – and in Germany, for example, polls consistently indicated that some two-thirds of the population opposed the single currency.

Preparing citizens for the euro: a study in discourse management

During January 1996 the European Commission's campaign for the introduction of the single currency was officially launched; policy documents had been drawn up and circulated for discussion; new opinion polls examining public fears and concerns had been commissioned; a budget for information activities had been agreed; communications strategies were being piloted; the key personnel had just been appointed to oversee the Commission's activities and a bureaucratic infrastructure was being put in place to co-ordinate the various policy initiatives.

However, 1996 was also a difficult time for the Commission. Deepening recession across Europe had provoked waves of industrial unrest in France, Germany, Italy and most other EU countries. This coincided with widespread decline in popular support for further integration. Government attempts to cut budget deficits to qualify for EMU membership under the terms of the Maastricht Treaty were widely blamed for fuelling the recession. To become a founding member of the single currency, member states were required to cut their budget deficit to 3 per cent or below of gross domestic product (GDP), and reduce gross debt to 60 per cent of GDP. However, sluggish tax returns and the high cost of recession-induced social security payments meant that most EU states were well above the Maastricht targets. With the exception of Britain and Denmark, which had negotiated opt-out protocols, most governments were determined to be in the 'first wave' of EMU countries, but the costs of fulfilling the EMU convergence criteria were painful and draconian. In Britain, meeting the Maastricht targets would have required estimated cuts in public spending in the order of £13.5 billion, or else massive tax increases.[31] In Italy, the government's goal was to cut public borrowing by £13.9 billion.[32] In Belgium, the government's three-year austerity programme was so unpopular that its Premier, Jean-Luc Dehaene, obtained special powers to legislate on the budget by decree in order to bypass parliamentary opposition. Dehaene justified this temporary suspension of democracy on the grounds of the critical importance of monetary union to Belgium's future.[33]

Another key factor common to most EU member states in 1996 was the relentlessly rising level of unemployment, ranging from over 22 per cent in Spain to 12.5 per cent in France and over 10 per cent in Germany. By 1997, German unemployment had reached four million, a level not seen since the 1930s and a source of deep consternation not least because even Germany now seemed unlikely to meet the Maastricht convergence criteria. These events, which provided the backdrop to my study, also explain why officials were sometimes guarded in responding to questions about the politics of EMU.

Again, what was striking during fieldwork in Brussels and after was the way EU politicians and officials talked about the single currency. Whereas in Britain (and other member states) EMU was being treated as an essentially technical and legal matter, and therefore best left to lawyers and financial 'experts', for EU policy-makers it was something far grander: the cornerstone of a new kind of supranational political architecture that would lead to the transcendence of the nation-state. Among those closely connected with EMU in Brussels there was a sense of 'history in the making'. The *European* announced that EMU was 'the most audacious project the continent has embarked on in its long history', which would have 'far-reaching practical implications for business and the ordinary citizen, and major constitutional implications for the nation-state'.[34] Helmut Kohl called it 'the most decisive process for this and the next century'.[35] Other commentators went further. For Commissioner De Silguy and for the editor of *Commission en Direct*, the in-house newspaper for EU staff, 'the introduction of the single currency is the most important event since the Second World War' (Bearfield, 1996: 1). Outside of Brussels, however, the peoples of Europe were less aware of the epoch-making nature of EMU. In Denmark, Sweden, Germany and the UK, opposition and anxiety about loss of democratic self-government appeared to be increasing. Making citizens learn to 'love their new currency' was proving to be a formidable challenge.

The measures used to introduce the single currency provide important insight into the way EU elites have tried to control the European political agenda and shape the parameters for thinking about European integration. Central to this strategy was the attempt to 'de-politicise' EMU by presenting it as a 'natural' and 'inevitable' process that would promote 'progress' and 'prosperity'.[36] Above all, the euro had to be presented to the peoples of Europe as a safe and certain venture – something about which all 'expert' opinion was in steadfast agreement. The main arguments used by the Commission were therefore couched in economic terms. The chief benefits of a single currency, it argued, include greater efficiency for the single market; the elimination of transaction costs (estimated to be 0.3 to 0.4 per cent of the Union's gross domestic product); [37] a stimulus to growth and employment; international stability; enhanced 'joint monetary sovereignty' and the creation of 'one of the strongest currencies in the world' (CEC 1996a: 12–15). Officials in the Economics and Finance Directorate insisted that the financial discipline imposed by the Maastricht convergence criteria would create 'competitive disinflation' and a 'virtuous cycle of lower interest rates, market confidence, low inflation and healthy finance' – all based around the principles of budgetary restraint and sound money. This, in turn, would generate investment and growth and stimulate the competitiveness of European industry against its Asian and American rivals. The single currency was therefore presented in reassuringly pragmatic terms as the 'harmonisation' of national currencies into one common currency for the benefit and convenience of all: a necessary step towards completing the single market. Economists and bankers were agreed, it claimed, 'that national monetary autonomy was inconsistent with the Community's objectives of free trade, free capital movements and fixed exchange rates' (CEC 1996a: 8). As one senior official in the Commission's Economics and Financial Affairs Directorate (DG II) summed it up: 'Monetary policy is not a decision for the political arena: it is a technical matter, not an instrument for political involvement.'

These were the arguments officials and politicians used when addressing sceptics in Britain, France and elsewhere uneasy about the constitutional implications of EMU. When pressed, however, or in private, officials admitted that the primary objectives behind EMU were not economic but political and that the single currency was a crucial building block in building a political Union. As the Chairperson of the European Parliament's Monetary Subcommittee, put it, 'the single currency is the *only* policy initiative currently on the agenda for deepening the Union. That is why its implementation is crucial for the development of Europe.'[38].

Another recurring motif in the discourse of Commission officials concerned the importance of 'maintaining the momentum of European integration' and not delaying or deviating from the timetable agreed at Maastricht. The reasons for this insistence, they said, were largely to do with 'psychology'. As one official argued: 'The Maastricht Treaty had been extremely effective in concentrating minds and galvanising member states into action, but if it had to be renegotiated who would believe the new deadline? Who would be constrained by it?' The fear was that, if the EMU project were to fall apart, the ramifications of this would spread far beyond the apparently self-contained question of a single currency. The anxiety among EU pundits and policy-makers was that, if Maastricht were to founder, the whole question of the future of European integration would be in doubt and the EU would face a shattering crisis of identity and direction.

Any delay in launching the single currency might therefore undermine market confidence which would have, according to many MEPs, an unravelling effect on the entire European venture.[39] It therefore became an overriding policy priority to 'talk up' the single currency and allow no room for doubts that it would happen, and on time. 'Confidence', Jacques Santer declared, was 'the key-word for the operation to succeed.' Speaking at the launch of the campaign for the introduction of the euro, he declared that single currency was 'a bearer of hope and should be a spur for our project of integration' and added that it was 'irresponsible to sow doubt' about its introduction.[40]

These arguments reflected a common perception among EU personnel that European unification is essentially a developmental process[41] which must constantly 'move forwards' or else risk backsliding towards 'a Europe of nation-states' and 'a mere common market'. Metaphors of 'health', 'stagnation', 'progress' and 'locomotion' were constantly invoked by informants to express the dangers of what would happen if 'Europe lost its momentum'. Failure to launch the single currency, it was argued, would 'set Europe back a generation'. According to Commission officials, the choice was between 'civilisation or barbarism'. European integration had only one direction: forwards. In this respect, the Commission's ideological stance echoed that of Helmut Kohl: European federation was 'a question of destiny'.[42]

Despite the importance of the relationship between money and identity, few officials were prepared to discuss EMU's cultural and constitutional implications. One policy adviser admitted that this was an acutely sensitive issue and the prerogative of governments only. However, he derided the debate about 'identity' as a 'very artificial and very British' fixation. Another informant in DG II agreed: 'in the rest of Europe the EMU debate is not about *Europe* but about the currency'. The UK was 'peculiar' in this respect. The 'British have a different mindset to other Europeans', was how another (British) respondent explained it: 'ancient prejudices and attachments. It is difficult for them to get a fix on what is happening on this side of the water.'

Elite attitudes towards public opinion

Officials were adamant that Europe cannot be built without the 'active consent of the European citizen' and that the introduction of the new currency would therefore have to be accompanied by a significant 'attitudinal change' among the public. However, what the concepts of 'active consent' and 'European citizen' meant in practice was often vague. Emma Bonnino, EU Commissioner for Consumer Affairs, went some way towards answering these questions. In a letter addressed to the 'European consumer', she declares that 'the single currency can exist only if it is accepted by consumers, who will look upon it as a concrete sign of belonging to the European Union'. The letter continues: 'Our fellow citizens will have to be convinced of the need for a change in currency, and why the change will be in their interest' (Bonnino 1996: 1). These statements about European citizens (constructed as 'consumers'), who 'need to be convinced' about changes that are 'in their interest' suggest an altogether more instrumental approach to that implied by the notions of 'active consent'.

EU officials had gone way beyond *whether* the single currency should be introduced; the question was *how* it would be achieved. According to them, the argument about EMU had been concluded with the ratification of the Maastricht Treaty. The debate was now closed: the euro was a fact and the timetable for its introduction was not negotiable. As if to emphasise the point, the cover of the May 1998 *Infeuro*, the Commission's newsletter, has a map of Europe beneath a caption which reads 'Countdown to the Euro'. The map divides those inside and outside the single currency into two categories: the 'ins' and the 'pre-ins'. The Commission had invented a new word to describe non-EMU members: another example, it seems, of the political use of language that has characterised the integration project.

In October 1995 the Commission launched three information campaigns, termed 'Priority Action Programmes' (PAPs): one for promoting EMU, another called 'Citizens First', and a third for the 1996 IGC called 'Building Europe Together'. This was its first major public information campaign since its ill-fated attempts to explain the Maastricht Treaty to European citizens during the 1992–3 debates over its ratification. The Maastricht debates had made the Commission appear a remote and elitist bureaucracy, out of touch with public opinion and unable to explain its vision of Europe even to its supporters. The Maastricht Treaty itself was incomprehensible even to lawyers, and European elites appeared reluctant and evasive about explaining its implications. This cavalier disregard for public opinion extended even into the European Parliament. As the French social-ist MEP Jean-Pierre Cot commented in 1992, opposing the distribution of copies of the Maastricht Treaty to households in Denmark, 'it is a mistake to let people read the treaty; they will only misunderstand it'.[43]

Fearing another public backlash, EU leaders had undertaken a major revision of their communications policies following harsh criticisms of its lack of professional-ism (Pinheiro 1993). In his inaugural speech as President, Jacques Santer pro-claimed that henceforth, the Commission's priorities would be 'getting closer to the citizen' and promoting more 'openness and transparency'. A 'Europe closer to the citizen' became a popular Commission slogan, used repeatedly by the new Spanish Commissioner for culture, Marcello Oreja. The campaign to introduce the new single currency thus provides an interesting arena for observing how this policy of 'listening to the public' translated into practice.

In December 1995, the European Parliament approved an Ecu 50 million budget for the three PAPs, Ecu 35 million of which would be released pending Parliament's satisfaction that the funds were being properly used. That same month, EU leaders meeting in Madrid agreed to drop the term 'Ecu' and name the new currency-in-waiting the 'euro'.[44] The Commission's next task was to plan its strategy for introducing the euro. In January 1996 it organised a round table meeting in Brussels at which the views of luminaries from the world of economics, politics, consumer associations, the media, marketing professionals – even sports personalities – were invited to discuss strategies for informing the public. For three days the European quarter in Brussels was teaming with dignitaries and delegates, conspicuously sporting conference folders, euro badges and European Parliament passes. At that meeting, a tired and nervous-looking Commissioner De Silguy unveiled before television cameras and the world's press the newly designed logo for the euro. This consisted of a giant old-fashioned hourglass supported on three pillars: at the top of the glass were silver coins denoting the various national currencies; at the bottom, one large shiny golden euro bearing the EU's twelve-star logo (Figure 7). The hourglass logo supposedly symbolised the metamorphosis of the many national currencies into one – a whole greater than the sum of its parts and a process as inevitable and irreversible as sand obeying the law of gravity. According to this image, EMU is like a process of alchemy, transforming base metals into gold.

Figure 7 The hourglass logo used for the launch of the euro.

Source: European Commission

In another emblematic image, a bright euro logo is depicted rising like a star in the eastern sky at the end of a line of national banknotes which stretch into a receding horizon. The old notes are shown marching in line out of darkness into the light created from the shining halo that surrounds the new euro.[45] The conference pack contained a further image of the euro – this time a black-and-white photomontage of a Doric temple constructed out of national banknotes with columns made of coins, at the centre of which is a large Euro 1 coin with a Latin legend *In Unitate Robur* (Strength Through Unity).

To coincide with the launch of the campaign, the Italian Presidency held a cocktail reception at the Musées Royaux d'Art et d'Histoire to formally open a museum exhibition charting the history of money in Europe. 'Time Journey Through Monetary Europe' was designed to show visitors the chronological stages in the evolution of European money, from the production of the first European coins in the Greek city-states and the reorganisation of the Roman Empire on a monetary basis under Augustus, to the monetary systems introduced by Charlemagne and the development of European banking systems in the sixteenth century. This grand tour through monetary Europe culminated in exhibits of nineteenth-century monetary unions, the stock exchange and, finally, modern payment and monetary systems. The message of the exhibition, summed up in the accompanying leaflet, was that 'the European plan for a single currency . . . is the culmination of a long economic and cultural history'. The clockwise direction and circular layout of the exhibition thus reinforced the Commission's theme that 'destination euro' represents the apotheosis of Europe's federal destiny.

In terms of presentation, a variety of strategies were to be used, ranging from leaflets, glossy brochures, newsletters and 'information kits', to conferences, round tables, radio and television broadcasting, videos aimed at informing trade unions and businesses about the benefits the euro will bring to the world of work. As well as the new hourglass logo, a catchy 'jingle' was also created for the launch of the campaign. Other media included the creation of an Internet site; regular transmissions of 'Europe by Satellite'; a travelling exhibition or 'infobus' to meet requests from schools, banks, local authorities and businesses; 'exhibition kits' for those wishing to organise exhibitions on their premises, and teams of trained speakers and celebrities to participate in debates and meetings on the euro in different countries. All of these ideas were set out in detail in an internal DG X paper entitled *Plan operationnel évolutif de communication pour la monnaie unique*. Further proposals included developing trailers for cinemas, 'exploiting the potential of local radio', holding teleconferences, creating 'euro' postage stamps, sponsoring a poster design competition and developing cartoon strips and educational materials for use in primary schools (DG X 1996).

At the time of fieldwork in early 1996, market research teams were piloting some twenty-eight key messages.[46] These ranged from statements of prophecy and political will ('The third state of EMU must and will start on January 1st 1999'; 'The Euro will become a reality. For everyone'; 'A single market needs a single currency'), to proclamations about the benefits of the euro ('The Euro: a symbol for peace and prosperity'; 'The Euro will not divide the European Union in two'; 'The Euro: a democratic choice'; 'price competition is good for consumers. With the Euro you can be sure of it'; 'with the Euro, price stability will be secured'). In general, the messages were designed to reassure consumers that there would be no risks involved in the changeover ('Changing to the Euro will not change your contracts' and 'With the Euro, the value of your savings and pension will remain the same'). Other slogans were aimed specifically at tourists, travellers and businesspeople, for example: 'Euro-travel means change free travel'; 'With the Euro, no more complicated calculations to compare prices in Europe' and 'Can you imagine the USA with fifty currencies?'.

Information versus propaganda?

A striking aspect of the campaign for introducing the euro was the way the Commission tried to position itself in order to play down its own political role. While officials accepted that persuading people to give up their national currencies invariably meant a degree of political intervention, they were wary of the euro being seen as a currency devised by European elites to suit their own purposes. Persuading a sceptical public, it was argued, was a *political* matter and, as such, not the Commission's responsibility but that of national governments. The Commission was therefore anxious to distance itself from the campaign and not to appear too proactive, as this would compromise its 'honest broker' image. Its policy was to adopt a role as non-partisan purveyor of information; a neutral messenger simply acting upon decisions taken elsewhere and set down in the Treaty commitments agreed by heads of government at Maastricht.

To achieve this, the Commission had to abandon the word 'campaign'. According to officials, the Priority Action Programme for the introduction of the euro was not a 'campaign' at all, but an 'information activity'. Furthermore, the Commission was not 'promoting' anything, but merely presenting neutral information. The euro 'did not need promoting' because it already existed; and its foundations rested on sound economic principles, common sense and the provisions of the Maastricht Treaty. The term 'information activity' – which is typical of the Commission's penchant for obtuse jargon – was cited by some officials as evidence of the Commission's more 'objective' approach to information policy as well as its increasingly 'democratic', and 'participatory' stance as far as involving the public in EU affairs. As the Green Paper proclaimed, the 'Euro Priority Action Programme' was 'not about manipulation' but rather 'an essential contribution towards transparency, public education and democratic debate' (CEC 1996a: 72). However, these claims about democracy, empowerment and political neutrality were difficult to sustain. The Commission's persistent use of mass-marketing techniques and advertising professionals and the one-sided nature of the information about the euro being conveyed all suggested that this was a propaganda campaign. Furthermore, most officials continued to call it a 'campaign'. As one official privately admitted, 'Officially it is an "information action", but between you and me, it's a "campaign"'.

However, the distinction between information and propaganda was clearly a touchy issue for interviewees and the ambiguity about the Commission's role within the Campaign seemed to generate a permanent tension. This was vividly illustrated in an interview with two Commission employees working on the 'Euro Priority Action Programme'.[47] I had arranged to meet the head of the Commission's euro campaign, in his office in the Rue de la Loi. Unfortunately, he cancelled at short notice but two of his staff agreed to take his place. The two men – one German, the other French – had been working on the euro campaign for six months and described themselves simply as 'consultants'. Their work experience lay in the private sector communications field, but they were deliberately vague about this. The question, 'what is the aim of the Campaign?' produced a defensive answer:

> The basis of our work is found in the speeches of M. Santer. It is purely information work. The euro doesn't have to be 'promoted': it is not a product but a way of life. The euro is accepted by everybody ... all EU countries will be in the system. The Commission's job is not to persuade but to communicate to people. The people can make up their own minds. We are not trying to impose the euro on them.

When asked directly, 'What particular expertise are you bringing to the job?' they became evasive and replied 'You'll have to ask our employers' and 'I won't speak about my background'. Subsequent questioning indicated that they were professional marketing agents but wished to conceal this because the campaign was not supposed to be about 'selling' the euro. When asked what Commissioner De Silguy had meant when he described the aim of the information action as 'to make people love the Euro', the response was, 'That's not about persuasion, it's about information. Some people are in favour; some against but the majority are still undecided. We have to supply them with the right arguments to help them decide.'

I put it to several officials that most of the information produced for the euro campaign emphasised only the benefits of the single currency and that this could hardly be construed as neutral information. One economist in DG II denied this and claimed that his Directorate was also alerting people to the dangers of a single currency, although he admitted not having seen the materials produced by DG X. Officials in DG X explained that they did plan to address the 'negative' aspects of the single currency, but only when these were raised by the public. In other words, the disadvantages of the single currency would be considered only to refute them. Pushing this question further usually provoked the response that the single currency was a legally binding Treaty commitment that all member states had freely signed up to and that the Commission was therefore simply fulfilling its role as guardian of the Treaties. The head of the Priority Action Programmes was explicit about the need to 'convince' people. He spoke approvingly of the 'discreet visibility' of the 'Benetton effect' ('Benetton doesn't need to advertise its products, it just puts up billboards that people notice and talk about'). 'My job', he added, 'is to render Europe as sexy as a Coca-Cola bottle.' However, campaigning for the euro was 'strictly a matter of information, not propaganda' and had 'nothing to do with winning hearts and minds'.

The interesting question is why, given so much evidence to the contrary, were officials so anxious to deny that their 'Information Actions' were promotional campaigns? If the single currency was so unequivocally beneficial to European citizens, as the Commission claimed, why should it *not* seek to persuade people using marketing techniques? The official reason given was that a Commission-led promotional campaign would violate the principle of subsidiarity whereby decisions should be taken at the lowest level consistent with effective action. However, several 'unofficial' reasons were suggested. First, it was recognised that a campaign seen to be Commission-orchestrated and promoting biased information might backfire. It was largely for this reason that the British government decided in January 1996 to block the Commission from extending its euro campaign to the UK. Second, any admission that the Commission was conducting a propaganda campaign might have provoked a legal challenge because it was exceeding its sphere of competence. Third and more importantly, the European Parliament had expressly forbidden the use of propaganda to promote the euro. Parliament had ruled that information must be seen to be strictly non-partisan or non-party-political and had already withheld funding for the Commission because it was not satisfied that these conditions had been met. Finally, and most importantly of all, under the terms of the Maastricht Treaty, the Commission — together with the EMI — was responsible for judging which member states had met the convergence criteria. Clearly the Commission did not wish to draw attention to what might be seen as a conflict of roles between advocate and ostensibly non-partisan referee.

These considerations prompted the Commission to substitute for the word 'campaign' the more neutral-sounding term, 'information action'. As one German official proclaimed, 'citizens must be convinced of the Euro: our aim is simply to make them aware of its advantages'. But as another informant – and communications professional – admitted, the Commission's traditional patrician approach to public opinion had not changed: 'the view is that the dogs may bark, but the caravan will move forward regardless'. 'Dogs barking', he said, summed up the Commission's view of public opinion.

The term 'information action' – which would therefore appear to be more of a semantic sleight of hand than a genuine change of policy – highlights another important facet of the EU's discourse management strategy. A 'campaign' implies that there is something to argue about; 'information action' not only construes the Commission's role as neutral and non-partisan, it also implicitly casts the single currency as an issue closed to debate, outside the realms of politics. While the Commission still claimed to be 'listening to the public' and engaging in dialogue with European citizens, the single currency was considered a *fait accompli*. The fact that opinion polls showed increasing public disapproval of the single currency was discounted. What the citizen said or thought about it was largely irrelevant to its outcome. In reality, the public had no choice on the matter. Its role was strictly passive: to listen to the arguments and be convinced.

The Commission's claim to be moving beyond 'passive consent' was strictly limited to its own narrow terms of reference. The 'active European citizen' was one who agreed with the Commission's arguments and gave wholehearted consent: a 'good European' who shared the European idea and who had, to echo De Silguy, 'learned to love the Euro'.

Explaining the economics of EMU

Explaining the macroeconomic benefits of EMU was never likely to be an easy task, particularly as its introduction involved considerable economic pain. To meet the Maastricht convergence criteria, governments took drastic measures to reduce inflation, budget deficits and public debt. The result of these deflationary, neo-liberal policies was sweeping cuts in government spending, similar to those carried out by Margaret Thatcher's government in Britain during the 1980s. By December 1995, only Germany and Luxembourg met all of the necessary convergence criteria. The timetable for introducing the euro meant that, for France and Germany – the two key countries concerned – introducing the policies that would achieve the supposedly virtuous economic cycle coincided with world economic recession. The result was a wave of lay-offs, closures and rising levels of unemployment in Germany not witnessed since the early 1930s. A three-week general strike in France brought rioters on to the streets of Paris with slogans and banners blaming the EU.

In interview after interview, however, Commission officials refused to acknowledge any link between EMU and rising unemployment. In their view, the causes of the current economic troubles were not the tough economic measures demanded by the Maastricht Treaty but deeper structural flaws in Europe's economies. These austerity measures were 'the solution, not the problem'; monetary discipline was necessary with or without the single currency. As one of the authors of the Green Paper asserted: 'there is no correlation between cutting public deficits and losing jobs: these structural changes were needed anyway'. This argument was backed by claims that 'all economists agree that high public deficits are harmful' and that a clear consensus existed among European economic experts that the Bundesbank was 'the model for Europe'. The suggestion that some economists disagreed with this assessment typically provoked a lengthy and complicated exegesis demonstrating the objective 'proof' of their argument.

None of the respondents ever questioned or doubted that the European Central Bank should be modelled on the Bundesbank, whose unparalleled success made it the obvious model for the rest of Europe. The argument that this might result not in the 'Europeanisation of Germany' but rather in its obverse, a 'Germanised Europe' (a frequently voiced concern in policy circles outside of Brussels), was regarded as at best outdated and, at worse, racist and therefore politically incorrect and taboo. While some conceded that the Maastricht convergence criteria were not helping the recession, this was blamed not on the austerity measures themselves but on the timetable. The short-term suffering was a necessary medicine for creating the conditions that would bring longer-term prosperity. An economist in DG II summed up the Commission's argument with unflinching certainty:

> We just can't go on supporting current levels of public expenditure. Keynesianism has gone for good. Structural-adjustments have to, and will, occur anyway. It is no use blaming Maastricht for what has to happen anyway. If you go on spending continuously, sooner or later you'll be bankrupt. Underlying all of this are economic realities which are driving the changes.

The 'proof' of this was that 'the countries with the higher levels of spending have the highest levels of unemployment'. Furthermore, Commission predictions showed that the Maastricht financial austerity programme would create 'competitive disinflation' and a 'virtuous cycle of lower interest and inflation rates, market confidence and healthy finance' based on the principles of sound money. EMU would have the 'same impact on the EU economy as the original founding of the EEC: internal rates will fall, confidence and investment will increase and prosperity and employment will follow'.[48]

Off the record, however, this 'expert discourse' about the unassailable economic rationale for EMU was replaced by an altogether different emphasis. One senior official noted the paradox that a former socialist minister (Delors), had instigated a Thatcherite economic programme, while a former Christian Democrat minister (Santer), was trying to rectify the social cohesion problems created as a result of the Maastricht Treaty. Another observed that officials and politicians in Brussels 'want the single currency for *political and strategic reasons* and will distort the economic arguments to an extent' (my emphasis). In her view, the economics of EMU were 'Thatcherite', but 'that was a battle the left lost in 1991' and it would 'just have to learn to live with it'.

Another benefit of EMU, not so frequently articulated, was that it would restrain an over-mighty Germany and prevent a resurgence of German nationalism. As one MEP summed it up, his Germany 'has always lived in peace provided it hasn't had a hegemonic role', but these conditions no longer pertained: Germany now had 'the largest population', the 'biggest army' and the 'dominant economy' in Europe and the Bundesbank was determining European monetary policy. Significantly, these warnings about the latent 'German menace' were made not by a French nationalist or British 'Euro-sceptic', but by Christa Randzio-Plath, a German Social Democrat MEP. Despite the Commission's taboo on the subject, fieldwork confirmed that the 'German question' continues to dominate the attitudes of political elites towards European integration. Moreover, those most preoccupied with strengthening European political integration as a way of domesticating the demons of German nationalism are Germans themselves.

Sovereignty

The argument that transferring economic decision-making from governments to independent central bankers in Frankfurt might be construed as anti-democratic met with a dismissive response. The standard response was that that a European Central Bank would be more democratic than the current arrangement whereby Bundesbank officials exerted a *de facto* control over monetary policy for the rest of Europe. The ECB would give all member states a seat on the board and therefore an equal voice in shaping monetary policy – which would then be constitutionally geared to serving European rather than German national interests. Removing economic management from politicians would be in the best interest of all European citizens because 'politicians always put short-term political self-interest before economic probity'. The ECB would impose a much-needed discipline over national governments, limiting how much they could borrow and spend as a proportion of GDP. This was necessary because 'the public sector's appetite for spending money is insatiable'. Macroeconomic management should therefore be removed from the volatile political arena and relocated in the steady hands of politically neutral bankers whose prime directive is price stability and low inflation.

The constitutional question of sovereignty was dismissed as a peculiarly 'British' obsession. The idea that national governments still exercised economic sovereignty was an 'illusion'. This was emphasised repeatedly by an anecdote about the governor of the Bank of France who had commented that, with reference to interest-rate policy, 'the only economic sovereignty France has today is the time it takes to relay a telephone call from the Bundesbank'. Being 'in' or 'out' of EMU made no difference. Furthermore, giving up control over exchange rates was of little consequence as, so the argument went, competitive devaluation is 'a very blunt and ineffective instrument of economic management' and the short-term advantages they offer are quickly eroded by the inevitable inflation and loss of competitiveness that invariably ensues. As one Commission economist concluded, the EU should follow the example of the United States: 'When California experiences recession they [*sic*] don't devalue, they migrate.'

The US federal system of government often provides a model for the EU. From an economic perspective, however, this comparison is flawed in several respects. There are, of course, much more difficult arguments for Commission advocates to face. Two of these were raised by the Governor of the Bank of England, Eddie George. First, there are 'significant differences between the member countries of the European Union that could cause tensions between them that would be difficult to relieve without the continuing possibility of exchange rate adjustments between the member currencies' (George 1995: 8). However, with the single currency, exchange rates are 'irrevocably fixed', which rules out exchange rate adjustments between member currencies (which have effectively been abolished). According to the Bank of England, there are only two other possible adjustment mechanisms apart from long-term stagnation and unemployment. The first of these is 'migration from areas of high unemployment to areas of lower unemployment'. While this is theoretically possible, the reality is that language and cultural differences are major barriers to cross-frontier migration. This is confirmed by EU statistics which show that less than 5 per cent of the total resident population in EU member countries was foreign, and of these only one-third were from other EU countries (George 1995: 11). In short, unlike Americans, Europeans do not freely migrate across the continent in any significant number – and labour mobility is certainly not on the scale that monetary union in the USA requires.

The second adjustment mechanism is 'larger fiscal transfers from countries with lower unemployment to those where unemployment was higher' (George 1995: 11). This would require huge transfers of resources between states in order to deal with economic 'shocks' or 'disturbances' which affected them unevenly and therefore necessitate a large increase in the EU budget. However, as George warns, not only is there no support for budget increases in any of the EU member states, but 'these adjustment measures could become a source of political as well as economic *dis*harmony within Europe, rather than monetary union acting as something that brings us closer together' (George 1995: 11). This argument is elaborated by Martin Feldstein (1997: 67), who points out that arguments about how large such transfers should be and how the taxes to finance them should be collected 'would exacerbate the more general disagreement that will inevitably arise as the Union seeks to restrict the level and structure of the taxes that individual countries may levy'. For Feldstein the 'notion of a politically independent central bank is contrary to European traditions' (1997: 63), and the effect of relocating economic decision-making to such a body and adopting an inflexible 'one-size-fits-all' monetary policy will inevitably be 'conflict between the country with rising unemployment and the rest of the EU' (1997: 66). Furthermore, 'if EU legislation designed to prevent member-states from competing with each other succeeds, they will collectively become less able to compete with the rest of the world. The result would undoubtedly be pressure for increased EU trade barriers' (1997: 68). In turn, increased protectionism would create serious conflicts with the USA and other trading partners.

These arguments were taken further by Bernard Connolly in his controversial book *The Rotten Heart of Europe,* published in September 1995. According to Connolly, far from being a vehicle for harmonious integration, EMU is a 'dangerous fantasy' and a geopolitical battlefield that will undermine democracy and the rule of law in Europe. His argument centres on the threat EMU poses for democracy. Monetary policy is one of the most important instruments of economic management, yet under EMU it would be wielded behind closed doors and placed beyond parliamentary control. Like all uncontrolled power, he says, it would then be subject to abuse. Connolly also critiques the idea that 'independent' central banks are apolitical guardians of their currency, pointing out that most central banks typically act to defend their own interests against central government, but also in concert with government to increase the state's geopolitical and geo-economic hegemony. His key point, however – which is echoed by other economists – is that EMU could work only if Europe's economies had reached such levels of convergence that monetary union would cease to be necessary. If economies did *not* truly cohere, a single monetary and interest-rate policy for the whole of Europe would place huge strains on the system. Trying to lock member states together via their currencies does not, therefore, forge one nation; 'instead it turns domestic monetary questions into international political conflicts' (Connolly 1995: 392). According to Connolly, Europe's technocratic elite has wilfully misled the public. EMU was really a political tool for preserving the EU's 'corporatist' regulatory state power. Thus:

> The true story of the Exchange Rate Mechanism has been one of duplicity, skulduggery, conflict; of economic harm done to every country in the case interests of the elite; of the distortion of economic logic and the dilution of political accountability.
>
> (Connolly 1995: 378)

What gave these arguments particular weight was the fact that Connolly was the leading official within the European Commission's unit directly responsible for EMU. Following the book's publication, De Silguy suspended Connolly from his post.[49] Among colleagues, his actions were regarded with a mixture of incredulity and accusations of treachery – although colleagues in DG II admitted that the seriousness of his case was undermined by the 'ranting' quality of the book's concluding chapter. However, the following March, similar warnings about EMU generating political instability were echoed by Professor Otmar Issing, a board member of the Bundesbank (Issing 1996a). Most informants condemned these remarks as 'scaremongering'. However, Issing's motives were not to undermine or oppose EMU (although his comments were seized upon by its critics), but rather to get political leaders to support Germany's proposal for a 'stability pact' with automatic fines for EMU members who ran up excessive deficits after January 1999. To these arguments the Commission really had no convincing answers. It therefore tended to avoid them. Thus, the typical response of EU technocratic elites to arguments about the 'weaknesses' of EMU was to argue for the necessity of further transfers of powers to European institutions at the centre. Like a marriage made in heaven, EMU must last for ever because there is no way out. In the words of Hans Tietmeyer (1998: 3), 'monetary union is therefore a monetary community of destiny'. However, formal political unions are no guarantee against conflict or intra-European war. As Feldstein points out (1997: 72), the American Civil War illustrates 'the dangers of a treaty or constitution that has no exits'.

The semiotics of euro banknotes and coins

If currencies are symbols of state sovereignty and cultural identity, another challenge for the Commission concerned the physical appearance of euro banknotes and coins. How were the designs for the new currency selected and what images were deemed most expressive of 'European cultural identity'? and how does one invent a currency from scratch? The selection of the design themes began in 1995 when the European Monetary Institute nominated an advisory group composed of art historians, graphic designers and marketing experts. From the preparatory work of this group, two design themes were selected: 'Ages and Styles of Europe' and a broader theme consisting of 'Abstract/Modern Design'. The features depicted on each of the seven colour-coded euro banknote denominations (euro 5, 10, 20, 50, 100, 200 and 500) were to represent a specific period of Europe's architectural history (Classical, Romanesque, Gothic, Renaissance, Baroque and Rococo, the age of iron and glass architecture, and modern twentieth-century architecture (Figure 8). The abstract/modern theme was to be represented by a design left to the choice of the designer. It was also decided that the European flag should be incorporated into the design of the euro banknotes, as this was 'a universally accepted symbol of Europe'.[50]

On 12 February 1996, a 'design competition' was launched which ran for seven months. Banknote designers nominated by EU central banks were given precise design briefs. An independent committee of experts (the 'jury') subsequently drew up a shortlist of five designs. Meanwhile, some two thousand people were canvassed to gauge public reaction to the draughts. The EMI made its final selection in December 1996 and, following further refinements, the winning designs were ratified in June 1997. While the official criteria for appraisal were 'creativity, aesthetics, style, functionality, likely public perception' and most important of all 'avoidance of any national bias', other criteria are also discernible. The most striking aspect of the euro banknotes, and where they differ from most national currencies, is the conspicuous absence of people, portraits or identifiable places. Instead, the notes present a series of abstract architectural features such as doorways, arches, windows and bridges – none of which are supposed to represent an existing monument. Thus Euro 5 features a classical Roman arch and aqueduct (Figure 9); Euro 10 an archetypal Romanesque church door; Euro 20 a typical gothic church window and bridge, Euro 100 a Baroque façade (Figure 10), and so on up to the Euro 500 banknote, whose design is curiously reminiscent of a typical Brussels office block.

How should we 'read' these designs and what messages, explicit or implicit, do they convey? Several points can be made when we start to 'unpack' the physiognomy of the euro. First, the themes selected are consistent with the 'building Europe' motif, the dominant idiom used by EU elites to describe their project of 'European construction'. Architectural images have frequently been deployed as vehicles for imagining Europe. I suggest this is symptomatic of the modernist assumptions that characterise the way EU policy-makers conceptualise integration and their image of themselves as heirs of the Enlightenment project and architects of the new Europe.[51] Second, the decision not to allow portraits or representations of people and nature (or even existing monuments) is significant. In this respect, the designs are curiously reminiscent of Islamic art, even if the styles are quintessentially 'European'. The bankers' vision of Europe seems to be a landscape of geometric forms without people. However, for the eight Euro coin denominations, each member state was allowed to decorate one side with its own national motif. The other side will carry a common European image; a map of

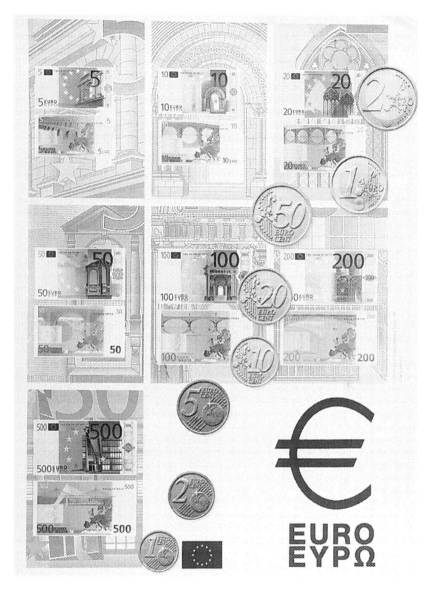

Figure 8 Draft designs for the seven euro banknotes. *Copyright:* European Monetary
Institute, 1997/European Central Bank, 1998

Europe against a background of transverse lines and an EU flag (Figures 11 and
12). The 1, 2 and 5 cent coins emphasise Europe's place in the world; the 10, 20
and 50 present the Union as a gathering of nations; and the Euro 1 and 2 coins
depict a Europe without frontiers. Third, the sequential ordering of the notes,
and the way their ascent in value corresponds to the chronological ascent of

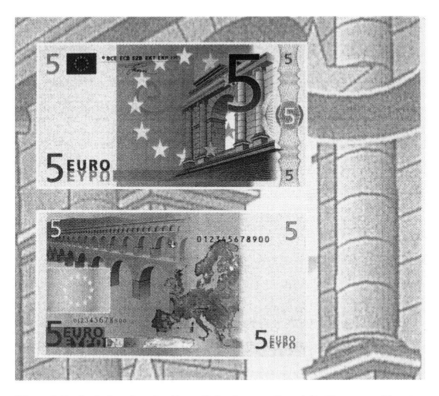

Figure 9 Draft design for the Euro 5 banknote. *Copyright:* European Monetary Institute, 1997/European Central Bank, 1998.

architectural styles and ages, mirrors perfectly the EU's conception of European history as the story of progress – and its teleological notion of Europe's *vocation fédérale*. The architectural heritage theme and the inclusion of the words 'EURO' and 'ΕΥΡΩ' in bold capitals on either sides of each banknote reflect a conscious attempt to endow the currency with a sense of tradition by linking the currency to an imagined classical ancestry. This is exemplified in the official rationale given for the icon used to represent the euro:

> The graphic symbol for the Euro looks like an E with two clearly marked, horizontal lines across it. It was inspired by the Greek letter epsilon, in reference to the cradle of European civilisation and to the first letter of the word 'Europe'. The parallel lines represent the stability of the euro.[52]

Finally, the architectural features selected are themselves highly suggestive. Why the emphasis on bridges, arches, doorways and windows? Why not use illustrations of real buildings, such as St Peter's in Rome, the Uffizi, the Eiffel Tower, the Brandenburg Gate or Westminster Abbey? Apart from the fact that

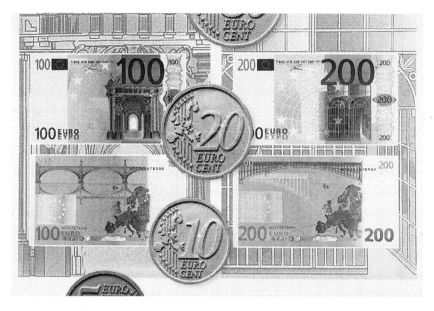

Figure 10 Draft designs for the Euro 100 and Euro 200 banknotes. *Copyright:* European Monetary Institute, 1997/European Central Bank, 1998.

these are irredeemably 'national' sites, it is also worth noting that real buildings are enclosed spaces, fixed, finite and contained. They occupy aestheticised space, but they do not transcend it. By contrast, windows, arches and bridges open up and extend the visual field. They all suggest 'openings' or passageways to another place. For the Euro designers they are thus 'symbols of the spirit of openness and co-operation in the EU'. The bridge (which is situated next to the map of Europe) is also 'a metaphor for communication among the people of Europe'. Similarly, doorways and windows join or 'connect': they also bring in light that illuminates the inside. All these designs symbolise transition, mediation, movement and the promise of a brighter future. Like the Commission's hourglass logo and the 'destination euro' motifs depicting old banknotes marching towards a bright, halo-like Euro on the horizon, the imagery also evokes a religious and millenarian theme.

It would be wrong to over-interpret or read too much significance into these designs. However, it could be argued that most people are not even conscious of the images and portraits that adorn the banknotes they use, so why should the euro designs matter? The Commission and the EMI, by their own actions, provide an answer to these questions. The banknote designs clearly are important, if only in presenting subliminal messages that are flagged continually in the practice of everyday life. As officials acknowledge, the euro is the most important public symbol of European identity to date and is clearly intended to function as an agent of European consciousness. However, it is also a powerful symbol of

Figure 11 Draft designs showing the common face of the eight euro coins. *Copyright*: European Monetary Institute, 1997/European Central Bank, 1998.

the European Central Bank's authority and economic sovereignty within the EU.

This was confirmed by a further twist in the euro story. According to the Bank of England, the UK had preserved the option to include a national feature not just on its coins but on the euro banknotes issued in the UK if it were to participate in EMU.[53] However, on 23 September 1998 the European Central Bank overruled that decision, claiming that this would be inconvenient and confusing and make forgery easier. Wim Duisenberg gave no reason for the change in policy when he reported the decision to the European Parliament and, as commentators noted, the decision itself was taken in secret.[54] However, this decision was widely

Heads or Tails?

In June 1997, the European Council chose the common face of the euro coins at the end of a process entailing a design competition, initial selection by a jury of European personalities, an opinion poll and consultation with consumer associations. Since this date, most of the countries participating in the euro have published their design for the side that is reserved to them. Here we present the national obverses of the countries that have already made their choice.

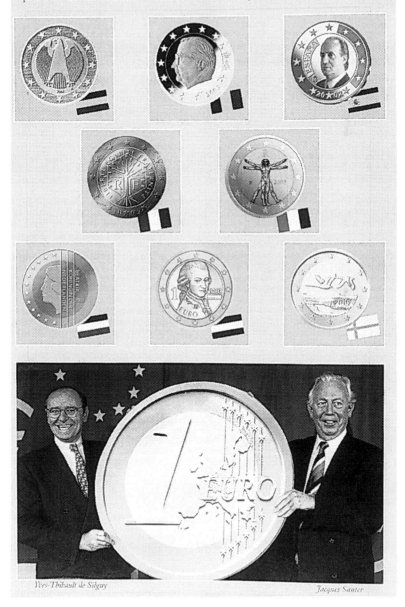

Figure 12 Above: draft designs for some of the national faces of the new euro coins. *Below:* Commissioners De Silguy and Santer unveil the design for the Euro 1 coin.

Source: European Commission, InfoEuro; *Copyright:* European Monetary Institute, 1997/ European Central Bank, 1998

perceived as a demonstration of the ECB's absolute authority and its insensitivity to national feeling. In Britain, the ECB's decision was widely condemned, even by EU supporters. It was also seen as an embarrassment for the Blair government which had been keen to demonstrate its pro-EU credentials. Euro-sceptics and cartoonists had a field day depicting Duisenberg as the faceless, unelected banker determined to erase the Queen's head from Britain's banknotes and 'goose-step' over Britain's national sovereignty and independence.[55]

Conclusions: EMU and political union

The purpose of this chapter was to analyse the cultural and political implications of EMU and to demonstrate why it raises issues of profound symbolic as well as constitutional importance. For EU officials, the single currency was primarily an instrument for 'deepening' the integration process: an economic means to a political end. In their view, monetary union will cement political union which, in turn, will promote European identity: the 'euro in your pocket' being the master symbol that epitomises everything the European Union stands for. In the Commission's presentation of its case to the public, however, these constitutional and cultural considerations were recessive rather than dominant. For EMU to succeed, the financial sector and the public would have had to be convinced of its technical merits and the markets of its certainty – and that required the emphasis to be placed on the economic domain. For the Commission, the key to obtaining public approval for EMU lay in the management of discourse. The campaign to introduce the euro was organised with this in mind. To achieve a climate of confidence and inevitability about the new currency two discursive strategies were deployed. First, the single currency had to be de-politicised and 'naturalised' by presenting it as a 'technical' issue outside of the political realm and a logical evolution of the single market; second, the Commission had to present itself as objective and non-political: a purveyor of facts whose 'information actions' had nothing to do with propaganda or campaigning.

However, the recognition that European citizens still had major doubts about the single currency left officials on the horns of a dilemma: how to 'win' popular support for the euro without using what might be construed as techniques of 'persuasion'. The Commission's answer was a triumph of Cartesian rationalism: EMU, it argued, was 'objectively persuasive' and, given the 'right information', the citizen will reach the same conclusions as the Commission. In short, there exists an objective economic truth about monetary union which stands outside of politics – and if only citizens were properly informed, they too would naturally be convinced. However, the Commission's claim to political neutrality did not stand up to scrutiny. Its reliance on marketing strategies, the careful orchestration of the messages about the benefits of the euro and the one-sided nature of the information given to the public suggested that the Commission was running a propaganda campaign.

The evidence of this chapter contradicts the Commission's claims to have adopted greater 'openness' and 'transparency' in its approach to information policy and public opinion. If, as the Commission insisted, the single currency was inevitable then the citizen had no choice about it; monetary union was not an option, nor was the timetable for its introduction negotiable. What the public thought about the single currency was therefore irrelevant. 'Listening to the public' simply meant using instruments of mass communications to find more effective techniques to persuade people to accept the new currency. Consequently, there was no evidence that European elites had abandoned their reliance on 'permissive consensus' in building Europe – despite the Commission's insistence on the need for obtaining 'active consent' and 'getting closer to the citizen'. Passive and spoken for, the 'European citizen' was largely a rhetorical construction in the discourse of EU elites.

Despite their claims to be presenting 'factual information' and not propaganda, EU officials made no serious attempt to consider the arguments against EMU. Instead, these were left to central bankers and 'euro-sceptics' – whose warnings were then dismissed as politically motivated and 'scaremongering'. The only concern about EMU that official's acknowledged was the public's supposed 'fear of change'. Dissent was thus reduced to a question of 'loss of confidence' or 'lack of information'. In terms of discourse management, intellectual opposition to EMU was therefore denied any foundation by being treated as irrational and based on ignorance.

An interesting question in all this is the extent to which EU officials really did see themselves as non-partisan experts simply 'informing citizens' about the Treaty commitments their governments had signed up to – or was this merely a political posture? Certainly many failed to see, or did not wish to admit, the political role of the Commission in the campaign. As several interviewees responded, 'I leave those political questions to the politicians'. A more generous interpretation is that many officials had genuinely convinced themselves about the 'truth' of their case. Again, however, the fieldwork evidence suggested that the facts on the ground were more complicated than this. What officials were prepared to say 'off the record' was often very different from what they admitted in public. When informants were relaxed, or if the conversation progressed for any length of time, the official justifications for EMU – that it was merely a 'pragmatic' extension of the single market which would bring price stability and boost Europe's competitiveness – gave way to reveal a more passionate bedrock of emotion and ideology. Vivian White cogently demonstrated this in an interview with Xavier Larnaudie-Eiffel, the *chef de cabinet* of Commissioner De Silguy. As White describes it, behind the closed door of his private office Larnaudie-Eiffel abandoned his characteristically phlegmatic pose and let rip, comparing the euro with the building of the great medieval cathedrals. Referring to the Commission, he continued: 'We are the cathedral builders of our age. It should be as solid. We hope it will be as beautiful and we hope it will last as much as the cathedrals. Why not? And it is built a bit in the same spirit with people really feeling that it's worth working for.'[56] According to this logic, the 'macroeconomic architecture' of the single currency – a phrase used by several respondents – acquires an almost religious significance: a temple of late modernity built by visionaries whom history had chosen to unify Europe. Getting the public to share that vision, it seems, has become part of the Commission's new definition of its role.

In his book *Imagined Communities* Benedict Anderson highlighted the importance of stained-glass windows and church reliefs as vehicles of mass communication in medieval Europe. 'While the trans-European Latin-reading clerisy was one essential elements in the structuring of the Christian imagination', he argued, 'the mediation of its conceptions to the illiterate masses, by visual and aural creations, always personal and particular, was no less essential' (Anderson 1983: 29). There are parallels here with EU elites and the euro. Officials hope that the euro will play for the modern European imagination something of the role that Christian iconography played for medieval Europe. By 2002 some 12.7 billion euro banknotes and over seventy billion new coins will be in circulation (European Commission 1997b: 10),[57] communicating the 'Europe idea' to the European laity. With or without its heavy symbolism of bridges and doorways, the euro will act as a powerful agent in shaping people's cognitive orientation. Whether it will succeed in binding European nations together or tearing them apart, however, only time – and events – will tell.

Notes

1 Cited in Stevenson (1974: 817).
2 John Gray, 'A Union that man may put asunder', *Guardian*, 19 February 1996: 9.
3 This image appeared on the front pages of several national newspapers including the *Times* and *Guardian*.
4 Charles Bremner, *The Times*, 1 January 1999: 10.
5 Ibid.
6 Larry Elliot (1993: 61).
7 European Commission (1996a: 12; 1995b: 2).
8 Indicative of this sense of unease, in February 1998 155 German economics professors signed a declaration calling for an 'orderly postponement' (*Financial Times*, 9 February 1998).
9 See Foucault (1978); Rabinow (1984).
10 This principle of central bank independence is enshrined in Article 107 of the Maastricht Treaty which states that the ECB will be independent of 'all other bodies'.
11 Cited in Owen and Dynes (1989: 239).
12 As EU analysts increasingly recognise, issues of culture and identity underpin most of the major problems concerning the future of the European Union (De Witte 1993; Howe 1995).
13 Since the late seventeenth century, the word 'sterling' itself has come to denote something 'of character, principles . . . thoroughly excellent. Capable of standing every test' (*Oxford English Dictionary* (1989): 655).
14 However, this was not the message aimed at German trade unions and business leaders for whom the greater worries were declining exports and loss of jobs due to an over-valued Mark.
15 *Financial Times*, 9 May 1995: 3.
16 Cf. Issing (1996b).
17 This was true of the Austro-German monetary union, which lasted only a decade after 1857, and the Scandinavian effort, which collapsed after 59 years in 1931 (Larry Elliot, *Guardian*, 3 March 1997: 10–11).

18 For example, Sir Leon Brittan argues that 'the European Union has definitely moved away from a federalist vocation' and 'Brussels-based centralisation' thanks to the 'rigorous application of subsidiarity', *Daily Telegraph*, 29 May 1998: 29.

19 *Hansard*, 27 October 1997: cc.583–8.

20 Kari Impens, 'Birth of a Federation?', *New Federalist*, 2 (1996): 13.

21 F. Gonzales, 'Why the Euro will get Europe Working', *The European*, 1–7 June 1998 (cited in http://www.tcog.org/news/euro.html:1).

22 Cited in Jamieson (1998: 23).

23 *Frankfurter Allgemeine Zeitung*, 18 October 1995; also cited in Jamieson 1998: 23 (see the latter for interesting commentaries on Tietmeyer's thesis).

24 *Financial Times*, 13 October 1995: 2.

25 However, whereas the object of Delors's critique was redressing the new powers to be ceded to unelected bankers, Tietmeyer's arguments rested on fears that the new ECB would not be strong enough or sufficiently independent to resist external political pressure in times of economic difficulty. While accepting that 'no one wanted a European superstate', what was needed was 'a corset for a lasting orientation towards stability', ibid.

26 Cited in Ware (1998: 8).

27 Wolfgang Münchau, 'Welcome to the Euro-zone', *Financial Times*, 4 January 1999: 21.

28 John Laughland, *The European*, 16–22 March 1998: 7.

29 Fieldwork interviews, Brussels 1996.

30 *The Times*, 14 March 1996: 29.

31 Burkitt *et al.* (1996: 3).

32 *Independent*, 2 May 1996: 8.

33 *Financial Times*, 11 September 1996: 42.

34 *The European*, 21–7 December 1995: 8.

35 Cited in Ian Traynor, *Guardian*, 20 May 1996: 10.

36 These were the campaign messages proposed in the controversial 1993 De Clercq Report (see Chapter 3).

37 CEC (1995b: 2).

38 Interviews, Christa Randzio-Plath, 1995.

39 These warnings are explicitly conveyed in the 11 December 1995 issue of *EP News*.

40 *Agence Europe*, No. 6652 (ns), 25 January 1996: 1.

41 This idea is also reinforced by neofunctionalist theories of integration (see Chapter 2).

42 Ian Traynor, *Guardian*, 20 March 1996: 10.

43 Noel Malcolm, *Sunday Telegraph* (Books 1), 12 July 1992: ix.

44 This was largely at the insistence of Germany where the name 'Ecu' had acquired negative connotations as a weak currency. The name 'euro' was calculated to offend no one rather than to inspire.

45 This image is contained in the 1997 EU brochure entitled *When Will the 'Euro' Be in Our Pockets?*

46 These occur repeatedly in the Commission's 1995 Green Paper and 1996 pamphlet entitled *Economic and Monetary Union*.

47 Twenty-two fieldwork interviews were carried out with EU officials and politicians directly involved with the EU's campaign for the introduction of the single currency. Since most were given 'off the record' I have tried to preserve anonymity.

48 As Dyson (1994) notes, the 'monetary thesis' (as opposed to 'culmination theory') holds that monetary union, by the normative power of its existence, will create the necessary degree of economic harmony and political integration.

49 Connolly subsequently began an appeal in the Court of First Instance against unfair dismissal.

50 All citations are from the EU website <http://www.ecb.in/emi/press/press05d.htm>.

51 The image and self-image of EU officials are explored further in Chapters 6 and 7.

52 All citations are from the EU WebPages <http://www.europa.eu.int/euro/html-rubrique> 5 November 1998.

53 *Practical Issues Arising from the Introduction of the Euro*, Bank of England, August 1997, cited in Edmonds and Blair (1997: 10).

54 *The Times*, 23 November 1998: 1.

55 *The Sun*, 23 September 1998: 8.

56 Vivian White, 'The Eurocrats. Part 4: Profit from your Euro', BBC Radio 4, June 1996.

57 Cf also *The Times*, 23 September 1998: 1.

Part II

EU civil servants

Introduction

European Commission civil servants: the new Europeans?

> The civil service was one of the great estates of the realm, the 'permanent government', as Anthony Verrier called it. Its senior people exerted a formidable, continuous influence in the highest decision-making bodies in the land. Yet even the more sophisticated citizenry scarcely knew their names, let alone where they came from, what they did, the values they espoused.
>
> (Hennessy 1990: vii)

Introduction: the integration of Europe's elites

Part 1 of this book set out to analyse the various strategies and techniques that EU officials have developed in order to shape public consciousness and promote popular awareness of Europe's 'common cultural heritage'. It explored not only the effectiveness of these nation-building activities but also the rationality underlying the EU's approach to 'culture' as a domain to be developed for building Europe. As we noted, European political elites have increasingly embraced the idea of 'culture' as a possible solution to the EU's problems of legitimacy. However, this new approach does not herald a fundamental shift in thinking. Far from representing a departure from the traditionally technocratic and neofunctionalist solution to integration, the approach of EU elites towards culture has been equally managerialist, positivistic and instrumental. At the root of this lies the belief that 'cultural change' can be engineered from above so as to transform the European Community into a 'community' of Europeans. The project of *construction européenne* seems to combine in equal measure idealism and instrumentalism. 'Ever-closer union' may be the fulfilment of Europe's *vocation fédérale*, but to make the dream become a reality, to coin an EU slogan, a whole battery of technologies have been deployed to Europeanise the masses and to invent Europe as a category of thought. As Timothy Garton Ash (1998: 51) wrote:

> Like no other continent, Europe is obsessed with its own meaning and direction. Idealistic and teleological visions of Europe at once inform, legitimate, and are themselves informed and legitimated by the political development of something now called the European Union. The name 'European Union' is

itself a product of this approach, for a union is what the EU is meant to be, not what it is.

Conflating the normative with the empirical – how things ought to be with how they are – is typical both of the way the EU represents itself and the of way it is represented in many textbooks in the burgeoning field of European integration studies.

A key theme highlighted in the preceding chapters, however, was the tension in reconciling the EU's goal of political union based on the ideal of an emergent 'European people' with its contradictory claims to be encouraging cultural pluralism or 'unity in diversity', and its repeated denials that the centralising trends that are evident in the integration process are leading to the formation of a new European state. As critics point out (Booker and North 1996; Schlesinger 1994a and b; Shore 1998; Wintle 1996), promoting cultural 'Europeanness', while contributing to the 'flowering' of Europe's different national cultures, has sometimes entailed striking intellectual gymnastics.

Part 2 pushes the inquiry further by probing into the 'organisational culture' of EU bureaucracy itself, focusing in particular on questions of administration and practice in the civil service of the European Commission. While Commission officials may not be the most important movers and shapers in the EU's complex policy process, the role of the Commission as policy initiator and guardian of the Treaties places it in an immensely influential and strategic position. The aim of these chapters is to shed light on the composition and character of this institution, especially its internal regime. The argument I wish to develop is that the internal life of the EU's own institutions highlights issues that are indicative of the wider problem of trying to build an ever closer union among the peoples of Europe. If European elites cannot create a coherent 'European culture' and identity in the administrative core and political heartland of the new Europe, what chance is there of forging such an identity among the peoples of Europe at large?

Federalists inside the Commission make little attempt to hide their belief that European consciousness must be nurtured and propogated among the masses if the gains made by the Community are to be consolidated and legitimised, but how do their views of European culture and consciousness square with the patterns of culture and consciousness that are emerging within the EU institutions themselves? Once again, parallels with the formation of new nation-states are instructive. As many theorists of nationalism have noted,[1] the most ardent proponents of nationalism in many emergent, post-colonial nation-states were often the 'creolised' administrators, officials and disaffected intellectuals who had most to gain from independence and nationhood, and the new nation-states they championed were frequently imagined geopolitical spaces constructed from the administrative units of old empires. As Anderson (1983: 127) has argued, national consciousness was spawned on the back of the expansion of the colonial state which, 'invited "natives" into [its] schools and offices'. 'The interlock between particular educational and administrative pilgrimages', he continues:

provided the territorial base for new 'imagined communitites' in which 'natives' could come to see themselves as nationals. To an unprecedented extent the key early spokesmen for colonial nationalism were lonely, bilingual intelligentsias unattached to sturdy local bourgeoisies.

Such comparisons inevitably give rise to the question of whether EU officials might occupy a similar niche or role in an emerging post-national European order. Are they, as a polyglot, deterritorialised intelligentsia, pioneers of European consciousness whose influence as the 'motor of integration' might one day be diffused throughout the Union so that the citizens of Europe come to embrace the EU as their new imaginary homeland?

To date, little substantive work has been carried out on European civil servants that provides answers to these questions. As Edwards and Spence (1997: 1) note, notwithstanding its importance and the controversy that often surrounds it, there is still 'a surprising dearth of academic or other study of the European Commission'. While there has been an explosion of textbooks on European institutions in recent years, many of them written and published by the EU itself, those that do deal with the Commission tend to concentrate primarily on its formal aspects and powers. Typically, these accounts are descriptive and normative, often portraying the Commission's history and role in the integration process in terms of models, neat flow-charts and tidy box-diagrams of the sort once popularly used in systems theory and cybernetics; the EU as it *ought to be*. However, with few notable exceptions, there has been little serious academic analysis of the Commission's complex and messy internal life:[2] its informal practices and relations, how it works on an everyday basis, and the subjective experiences of officials who work for it. Public knowledge about the world of EU officials is therefore confined largely to the uncritical and often self-congratulatory texts produced by the EU itself, or else to media representations which (particularly in Britain) tend to reinforce derogatory stereotypes about meddlesome and faceless 'Eurocrats' determined to centralise power and regulate all areas of national life.

Max Weber once famously described civil servants as 'permanent residents of the house of power', yet remarkably little is known about the residents of Europe's new house of power, or how the Commission functions as a cultural system. Still less is known about the influence EU civil servants exert over the policy process, despite the fact that the concealed influence of administrators on the political process has been a major subject of debate within the social sciences ever since the nineteenth century.[3] Hennessy's observations about the anonymous character and hidden power of senior British civil servants (cited above) apply equally to the European Commission. Like Whitehall, the Commission is run by an 'aristocracy of talent in the shape of an administrative class recruited on the basis of competitive examination' (Hennessy 1990: 5), and, one might add, bound together by legal-rational rules and an ethos of professionalism and independence. And like many closely knit bureaucratic organisations inspired by a political ideal, the Commission – 'the House' as it is referred to colloquially and affectionately by its staff – has developed its own ethos and a strong *esprit de corps*,

both of which play an important role in shaping social relations within the organisation. However, its ambiguous role as a bureaucracy *and* political broker, its
peculiar history and its unusual blend of nationalities with their diverse management styles and traditions have made the Commission a unique form of public
administration. From a creature of modernity that embodied the federalist hopes
and ideals of continental Europe's postwar generation of political leaders, the
Commission has become a hybrid of postmodernity unlike any other civil service
or international organisation.

Part of the uniqueness of the Commission, as we shall see, lies in its extraordinarily complex political, judicial and managerial roles. Together with the European
Court of Justice in Luxembourg, the Commission is reputedly the most 'supranational' of all EU institutions. However, the Commission goes further than this.
Officially, it describes itself not merely as the EU's 'executive body' and 'guardian
of the Treaties' but also as the 'dynamo of European integration', 'defender of
the Community interest' and, on occasions, even the 'conscience of Europe'
(Fontaine 1995: 12). As one official Commission document proclaims:

> The Commission represents the common interest and embodies, to a large
> degree, the personality of the Union. The key theme of the Commission
> under Mr. Jacques Santer is to defend the interest of Europe's citizens. The
> 20 members of the Commission are drawn from the 15 EU countries, but
> each one swears an oath of independence, distancing himself or herself from
> partisan influence from any source.
>
> (CEC 1995a: 7)

These are extraordinary claims for any civil service to make, particularly the suggestion that unelected officials are somehow uniquely placed to 'represent' or
'embody' the interests of European citizens. The statements raise three important
sets of questions. First, what is this 'European interest' that Commission officials
claim to serve? What are the characteristics of this 'European consciousness' that
the Commission believes it embodies, and what status should we give these
claims? Second, who are these officials, where do they come from, how are they
recruited and what are the values they espouse? And to what extent do these
statements, and the discourses in which they are embedded, reflect or influence
the self-image and subjectivity of individuals within the Commission? Third, if it
is the 'dynamo' of the integration process, what makes the Commission work in
practice? Does the Commission provide a model of how fellow Europeans can co-
operate and work together? What sort of 'culture' has it developed within its own
organisation? Is there any evidence of an embryonic 'European consciousness'
developing within this institution? To put it another way, could EU institutions
like the European Commission be the crucible in which a new kind of *Homo
Europaeus* is being forged?

Notes

1 For examples of this kind of 'instrumentalist' approach to theorising nationalism, and the role of the intelligentsia in nation-state-formation, see in particular Anderson (1983); Hobsbawm (1990); Nairn (1977) and Seton-Watson (1977).

2 Among the best of these 'insider' accounts of the European Commission by non-anthropologists are Brigouleix (1986); Grant (1994); Ross (1993; 1995) and Spence (1994a). For anthropological analyses, see Bramwell (1987); Abélès (1996); Abélès, Bellier, and McDonald (1993); Bellier (1995); McDonald (1996).

3 Among the most notable contributors to nineteenth century debates in Britain about the power of bureaucrats were Thomas Carlyle, J. S. Mill and Walter Bagehot.

5 A 'supranational' civil service? The role of the Commission in the integration process

> The Commission operates at the very heart of the European Union. Its role as the source of policy initiatives is unique. . . . The Commission has used its right of initiative to transform the framework provided by the Union's founding treaties into today's integrated structure.
>
> (CEC 1995a: 6)

The 'culture' of the Commission: a problematic category

These final chapters set out to explore more closely the 'organisational culture' of the European Commission in the context of debates about the role that institutions play in shaping consciousness and identity. However, terms like 'culture' or 'political culture' immediately raise problems of definition and focus given the contradictory meanings and uses that surround the culture concept. To speak of *the* culture of the Commission in the singular is also problematic. With over eighteen thousand staff recruited from among fifteen different member states, spread among forty different services and located in twenty-five separate buildings in Brussels alone, many observers would argue that the Commission has created not one but several political cultures with very different management styles and practices. Moreover, the utility of 'political culture' and 'corporate culture' as analytical terms for understanding organisations is highly questionable.[1] Instead, these concepts should be treated as ethnographic data to be analysed rather than as explanatory research tools. What are interesting, from an anthropological perspective, are the various political uses of the culture concept and the way it functions to mobilise and interpolate individuals – or, in this case, to inform and legitimise EU policies.[2]

The concept of 'political culture' in political science dates largely from the 1950s where it was linked with highly questionable models of political development based on structural-functionalist or systems analysis.[3] Typically, it was used as a gloss to describe the sum of political attitudes, dispositions, practices and institutions created by a particular political system: the 'subjective' orientation of people towards politics. This provided data for ethnocentric models from which invidious comparisons could be made ranking the qualities of 'other' political cultures (notably authoritarian and patron – client-based systems), with those of the United States, which invariably emerged as the epitome of the modern, democratic, pluralist and liberal polity (Almond and Verba 1963; Pye and Verba 1965). 'Corporate culture', by contrast, is a term often used in business studies and management theory literature to describe the informal characteristics of a company or organisation. The typical assumption is that these can be identified, isolated, abstracted and cultivated in order to promote 'organisational change' to further the goals of the company. Like theories of integration, both of these approaches tend to be shaped by American behaviourist models of social action and reify culture into a static, object-like entity to be intervened upon and managed. Furthermore, both assume a lack of agency on the part of the individuals, and fail to acknowledge that people are culture-creators as well as consumers and 'subjects' of culture.

To avoid the pitfalls inherent in these approaches, what follows is an anthropological analysis of the culture of the Commission. By this I mean not only an approach based on observations informed by empirical fieldwork,[4] but one that focuses on indigenous rather than analytical uses of the culture concept: on the folk model or 'native's point of view'.[5] Seen in these terms, the 'culture of the Commission' is a category used constantly by Commission staff themselves when describing their institution.[6] Among EU *fonctionnaires*, the natives in question, this term was generally used to refer to the Commission's administration and the various political, behavioural and psychological traits that these administrative and political norms were believed to generate. As an EU folk idiom, therefore, the 'culture of the Commission' usually meant its internal organisation. This included the Commission's personnel and management practices, its origins, ethos and customs, its staffing and recruitment policies, and the general norms and ground rules and implicit assumptions that govern conduct within its various institutions. These elements are vital to the day-to-day running of the Commission and, perhaps more than anything, are what give shape and meaning to its complex inner life. More importantly, from the perspective of EU staff, these institutional norms and practices also constitute the most significant arena within which most EU civil servants experience 'Europe' and 'European construction'. To a large extent, what happens inside the EU's bureaucracy and the kind of society being created there *is* the reality of European integration for its principal political actors.

The 'culture of the Commission' is also a salient category in two other important respects. First, despite the dramatic changes it has undergone since the 1950s (when it was a tightly knit body composed of just a few hundred staff from only six member states), my research found evidence of a strong sense of community and *esprit de corps* among staff – even among new recruits. This sense of belonging was expressed clearly in everyday conversation in the way staff would refer to the Commission as 'the House' – a metaphor typically used by boarding institutions and legislative bodies (such as the US House of Representatives). Staff frequently referred to the 'interests of the House', to 'we in the Commission' and to the 'culture of our institution', all of which suggest a highly developed sense of solidarity and consciousness of kind. Indeed, on several occasions officials expressed their undisguised loyalty and affection for the institution they served. As one veteran French official put it – without a hint of irony or self-consciousness – 'I love this House like I love a woman'. Second, despite their different back-grounds and grades, all staff are employed under the same legal rules and statutes: the Staff Regulations. As we shall see, this extraordinarily detailed, legalistic and Baroque document defines virtually every conceivable right, duty and privilege of an EU official, and is accordingly treated with great reverence, particularly by the staff unions. In short, all EU civil servants are governed by the same statutory rules and obligations. According to both objective and subjective measures, Commission staff thus constitute a discrete and distinctive population.

The Commission's 'organisational culture', its *modus vivendi*, would therefore appear to be a subject of interest both to those professionally involved in Euro-pean construction and to social scientists and political commentators. Contrary to the claim that administration is a 'technical' and managerial concern of minor political significance, my argument is that questions of administration are quintes-sentially about norms of conduct and the art of governance – issues that lie at the heart of European integration. In many respects, the administration of the EU is emblematic of the problems of integration in general. The Commission's organ-isational culture thus provides an excellent site for analysing European construc-tion in action. Given that most organisations tend to recruit in their own image, the way the Commission selects, trains and manages its staff – how it reproduces itself over time – can reveal much about the mechanics and micro-politics of integration. More importantly, most of the major tensions and cleavages in the integration process, particularly those arising from the encounter between intergovernmental and supranational visions of Europe, are played out in the Commission's staffing and management practices.

To contextualise this discussion, however, let us first consider the character of the Commission as a legal entity since these powers and functions are funda-mental to its ethos and identity. They also provide the rationale for virtually everything it does.

Legalism

Three factors must be stressed from the outset in any attempt to analyse the peculiarity of the European Commission as a cultural system: its legalism,[7] the legacy of its supranational aspirations and its wide-ranging yet sometimes contra-dictory functions. The first of these can be briefly stated. The Commission is, first and foremost, a profoundly 'legalistic' institution. Everything it does, all of its external activities as well as internal procedures, must have a legal basis which can be traced back to, or justified in terms of, its Treaties. The Treaties (i.e. the Treaty of Rome and its subsequent revisions and additions) are, in effect, the constitu-tion of the European Union – although these constitute only one part of the *acquis communautaire* or 'Community patrimony', which includes the entire corpus of EU legislation and policies to date, not to mention the legal judgements of the European Court of Justice. This legalism permeates all aspects of the

Commission's work, including its approach to policy, particularly personnel policy and staff-management relations. Anthony Sampson drew attention to this over three decades ago. Lamenting the way that the famous conflict between the Commission and General De Gaulle in the 1960s had compelled the 'Eurocrats' to adopt a 'cautious, depoliticized approach' to European integration – which then laid them open to the charge of being 'bloodless bureaucrats' – he wrote: 'With the rising temper of nationalism, they are increasingly forced back on legalistic attitudes, regarding the Treaty of Rome as the Ark of the Covenant' (Sampson 1968: 68). Peter Ludlow (1991: 95) puts it succinctly: 'the European Community is, for better or for worse, a people of the book' – a fact of which, he notes sardonically, Commissioners and others are not always aware. However, this preoccupation with the law in all the Commission's formal dealings is matched by an informal system of administration governed by a highly particularistic set of norms and practices in which the formal rules and statutes are frequently bent or ignored in favour of more personal, political and 'pragmatic' codes of conduct.[8]

The Commission's legalistic character is also reflected in the central role played by its Legal Service in the Commission's work and in its legal status. As Keohane and Hoffman (1991: 11) note for the EU in general:

> No other international organisation enjoys such reliably effective supremacy of its law over the laws of member governments, with a recognised court of justice to adjudicate disputes. The Community legal process has a dynamic of its own.

This point about the legal process having its own dynamic, to which Keohane and Hoffman pay scant attention, is fundamental to understanding how the integration process works and how the EU's novel system of governance has been established. From a legal and political perspective, the European Community is something of an anomaly that defies easy categorisation. Contrary to the claims that 'subsidiarity' functions as a constitutional check against excessive centralisation,[9] it seems that the EU legal process actively promotes the centralisation of sovereignty and decision-making at European level. Legal integration appears to be following precisely the same kind of neofunctionalist process that Haas predicted would occur in other domains. The 'unsung hero' of European unification, as Burley and Mattli (1993: 41–2) observe, is the European Court of Justice whose 'thirteen judges quietly working in Luxembourg managed to transform the Treaty of Rome . . . into a constitution', thereby laying 'the legal foundation for an integrated European economy and polity'.[10] In Mathijsen's words (1995: 148), 'texts that started out as international treaties have become the "Constitution" of the European Union'.

This constitutionalisation of the EU Treaties is a perfect illustration of the emergence of what Foucault (1991), in a different context, called 'governmentality': the emergence of a new form of governance based on new ideas and technologies for conceptualising and regulating political and economic conduct.

In this case it is not a system of governance derived from the economic rationality of Benthamite liberalism or neo-liberalism.[11] Rather, it is governance based on a legalistic rationality whose primary concern, it seems, is to establish the primacy of European law and Europeanist norms and principles. Moreover, this legalistic governmentality has an in-built, self-reinforcing logic. The Community legal process spawns powerful new bodies such as the European Commission, the European Central Bank and the European Court of Justice; these build on the idea that they alone are uniquely placed to defend the 'European' interest; and their activities then become a catalyst for consolidating and expanding that legal process so that new fields of activity are brought under its control. Thus, institutions that were originally created to 'referee' the Community legal process become the principle advocates and agents for the enlargement of Community law. And as Community law extends itself into new policy fields, so those institutions enlarge the scope of their own powers and control. This is what having 'a dynamic of its own' means in practice: a runaway process of legal integration whose consequences were often unanticipated by its designers. As Mathijsen (1995: 148) concedes, with characteristic understatement, the member states when they ratified the Treaties 'most probably did not, at that time, foresee all the conclusions which the Court has, over the years, drawn from their specific nature'.

Far from being static or monolithic, as Ludlow's and Sampson's Biblical metaphors imply, European Community law is therefore constantly developing and expanding. Through that expansion, the Commission actively contributes to the re-definition and enlargement of its own role and powers. To call the Commission a 'people of the book', is therefore misleading; the 'book' in question is not a finished or bound text: its chapters are still being written, and its narrative and sub-plots become ever more complex with each additional chapter in the saga of integration. Furthermore, Commission officials may appear as its subjects, but they are also its authors and editors; chroniclers of the story of European union as well as its guardians and architects. The Treaties are both the Commission's claim to legitimacy and its most effective instrument for obtaining power. Far from being, as Sampson argued, something the Commission retreats into when it is on the defensive or when its political ambitions are stymied by national politicians, the law has been the Commission's greatest asset and ally. Hence, legalism is itself part of the so-called 'Community method'; it provides a supremely rational, binding and political solution to the problems of European construction.

This legalism also spills over into all other, more seemingly mundane, aspects of the Commission's internal life and is reflected most powerfully in the Commission's internal patois and in-house style of report writing. 'Commission Eurospeak', as one critic described it, is 'a cumbersome melange of bureaucratese and neologisms' (Bramwell 1987: 65). The everyday language of EU officials is replete with technical, legalistic words and concepts – many of them mixed with French terms that go largely untranslated – and hundreds of acronyms that are utterly incomprehensible to all but the initiated few. So vast has been the growth of this new EU lexicon that a number of dictionaries of EU terms have now been published to help the hapless public negotiate their way through this new linguistic maze.

Finally, the Commission's legalism is also reflected in the extraordinarily large number of staff with formal backgrounds in law. Prior to 1990, most of the competitive exams (*'concours'*) for entry into the Commission civil service were open only to candidates with an academic background in either law, politics or economics. As officials from the Council of Ministers summed it up, even in the late 1980s 'the prevailing European view was that the study of law was the path to a post in public administration' (House of Lords 1988: 18). This was confirmed by an informal study 'The Community's Top Management: A Meritocracy in the Making' published by the Commission's *Courrier du Personnel* in October 1987. The ideal *fonctionnaire* was therefore typically a highly trained university graduate with a specialist knowledge in European law, EC institutions and economics: high-flier Oxbridge 'generalists' of the kind preferred by the Whitehall model were simply not required. This meant that candidates with academic backgrounds in subjects ranging from history, archaeology, business studies, sociology and mathematics on the one hand to philosophy, engineering and social work on the other were effectively excluded. Senior Commission officials in its recruitment and personnel division estimated that over half of all A-grade Commission officials were lawyers and economists. While no precise data exist in the public domain to verify or challenge the accuracy of this claim, as a rough calculation it seems plausible. The domination of the Commission by lawyers and economists has undoubtedly shaped its character, style and ethos – and perhaps goes some way to explaining its negative and elitist public image as a bureaucracy composed of technocrats.

'Supranationalism': legal principle, political ideal, or charter for action?

A second feature that makes the Commission unparalleled among international organisations, and one that is also said to characterise the originality of EU governance, is its much-acclaimed status as a 'supranational organ'. From the point of view of EU officials and politicians, the European Commission and European Court of Justice are institutions founded upon the principles of 'supranationalism'. This is a potent yet ambiguous legal term to describe institutions which, within limited areas, have powers and jurisdiction that override or transcend national governments, institutions or boundaries. As Osmañczyk (1990: 884) defines it, supranationalism 'is a form of integration requiring multinational organs having legislative and international legal authorisation in not one but in many states'.

In the context of European integration, 'supranationalism' was a concept endowed with specific meaning by Robert Schuman, the French Foreign Minister who gave his name to the plan that led directly to the creation of the European Coal and Steel Community (ECSC) in 1951. The ECSC was the embodiment of Jean Monnet's plan for regional integration based on the idea of a modest surrender of national sovereignty over certain key commodities, notably coal and steel production. For Monnet and other European federalists, removing these sinews of war from national governments and relocating them under the control of a 'higher', European authority was more than simply a measure of symbolic importance. As O'Neill (1996: 35) puts it, sectoral integration through the ECSC 'suggested a way of integrating Europe by stealth, without directly confronting the interests, offending the national sensibilities or compromising the identity of the existing nation state authorities'. For Schuman, the word 'supranationalism' accurately summed up the novel character, functions and powers of the ECSC's newly created High Authority, and the precursor of the European Commission. Speaking on 10 August 1950 in support of this plan, he told the Council of Europe that

> participating states will be abandoning some degree of sovereignty in favour of a Common Authority and will be accepting a fusion and pooling of powers which are at present being exercised . . . by the governments . . . Thus, the participating nations will in advance accept the notion of submission to the Authority . . . The countries associated in these negotiations have indeed set their feet on a new road. They are convinced that . . . the moment has come for us to attempt for the first time the experiment of a supranational authority which shall not be simply a combination or conciliation of national powers.[12]

This was also the meaning that Winston Churchill gave to the term when he said, in reply to a question in the House of Commons in 1950:

> I would add, to make my answer quite clear to the right hon. and learned Gentleman, that if he asked me, 'Would you agree to a supranational authority which has the power to tell Great Britain not to cut any more coal or make any more steel but to grow tomatoes instead?' I should say, without hesitation, the answer is 'no'.[13]

In its original sense, 'supranationalism' was always an ambiguous and politically contested term. Traditionally, it contained three distinct dimensions. First, it was a legal concept concerning questions of sovereignty and levels of authority; second, for those Europeans who shared Monnet's and Schuman's aspirations, it embodied a federalist political agenda and neofunctionalist assumptions about advancing the integration process through incremental spillover; and third, the concept itself functioned as an instrument for achieving the first two elements. The danger, however, is that these legal and political meanings are often conflated so that the latter is subsumed under the former. The effect of this is to make supranationalism appear as merely a technical and legal term; one that is unproblematic and commonly accepted. Indeed, the idea of 'supranationalism' has become so integral to the way the EU institutions represent themselves – and so essential to their claim to legitimacy and authority – that it has become 'naturalised' and now goes largely unquestioned and unchallenged even by many EU analysts. As one legal commentator observes:

> The originality of the EC governance is typically summarized with the word *supranationalism*, a diffuse notion which has no significance *per se*. As it stands today, the EC's most prominent supranational traits today are its well-developed legal sphere, its decision-making by majority-voting in the Council, the independent expertise found in many of the EC's policy-making processes and institutions and the EC's virtually unlimited jurisdiction. But from the complex relations between these elements arises no essential meaning for the word supranationalism.
>
> (Areilza 1995: 1)

Areilza's last point is crucial, for, in the absence of a more critical approach, essentialist and de-politicised meanings for the concept of supranationalism have prevailed. For those 'Europeans' who follow Monnet's political agenda, this is intentional. As Foucault (1977) notes, power invariably works to disguise the mechanism of its own operation, and redefining a political problem as a legal/technical matter – and therefore 'beyond' political debate – is a powerful way of constructing a hegemonic base for the EC's new system of governmentality. The important point here is that the founding Treaties implied that Community law is not only fundamentally independent of national law but that it ultimately takes precedence over the laws of member states. This principle was subsequently spelled out in a landmark decision by the European Court of Justice (ECJ) as long ago as 1964. 'By contrast with ordinary international treaties', the ECJ declared:

> the EEC Treaty has created its own legal system which, on the entry into force of the Treaty, became an integral part of the legal systems of the Member States and which their courts are bound to apply. By creating a Community of unlimited duration, having its own personality, its own legal capacity and capacity of representation on the international plane and, more particularly, real powers stemming from a limitation of sovereignty or a transfer of powers from the States to the Community, the Member States have [albeit within limited areas] limited their sovereign rights and have thus created a body of law which binds both their nationals and themselves.[14]

Moreover, as that same document declares, 'the transfer by the States from their domestic legal system to the Community legal system of the rights and obligations arising under the Treaty carries with it a permanent limitation of their sovereign rights, against which a subsequent unilateral act incompatible with the concept of the Community cannot prevail'. Community law thus claims to be a higher order of law than the national laws of member states, and therefore takes precedence over any national law deemed to be inconsistent with the Treaty objectives.

As critics point out, defining what is consistent or inconsistent with the object-ives of the Treaty is often a political rather than a judicial matter. In its role as 'interpreter' of the Treaties, the Court's decisions are often manifestly legislative, and not merely judicial, acts (Howe 1992: 14). Lord Patrick Neill (1995: 1), one of Britain's most senior and respected legal experts, draws similar conclusions in his essay on the dangers of 'judicial activism' from an over-zealous European Court. In his view, 'the ECJ has indulged in "creative jurisprudence" on many occasions'. It has also 'frequently adopted strained interpretations of the texts actually agreed by Member States' and introduced 'doctrines and rights of action which cannot be found in those texts' (Neil 1995: 2–3).[15] The point here is simply that the EU has created 'a self-contained system of law derived from the Treaties and the institutions created under them' (Howe 1992: 8). European law and European institutions thus support each other through a self-reinforcing system of bureaucracy and law. This helps to explain why the powers of the EU's institu-tions have advanced continually since the 1950s, even in the so-called 'bad years of Eurosclerosis' when the integration process appeared to have stalled. As Lord Denning summed it up, 'when it comes to matters with a European element, the Treaty is like an incoming tide. It flows into the estuaries and up the rivers. It cannot be held back.'[16]

Significantly, within the Commission and among EU politicians supranational-ism is seldom mentioned by name these days. However, while the word may have fallen into disuse, the idea of supranationalism, as Keohane and Hoffman (1991: 15) argue, remains deeply embedded in the structures of the European Com-munities and in the law they created, such that the concept is now, according to Mathijsen (1995: 8), 'universally accepted and expressed by the words "Com-munity Law"'. In other words, the *acquis communautaire* both enshrines and provides a 'legal bridgehead' for advancing the principle of supranationalism, now disguised by the seemingly more neutral and therefore less contestable term 'Community law'.

A 'supranational' civil service?

For the architects and pioneers of the EU supranationalism represented much more than a legal principle and political ideal, important as these are. Supra-nationalism also embodied the 'Community spirit': a political ideal, a model of post-nationalist government and a style of administration. Jean Monnet, for example, reflecting on the special nature of the European civil service in the 1950s, wrote enthusiastically about the creation of a new kind of *European Man*: 'un nouveau type d'homme [qui] était en train de naître dans les institutions de Luxembourg comme dans un laboratoire . . . c'était l'esprit européen qui était le fruit du travail en commun'.[17] For Monnet, '*Homo Europeaus*', would spring forth, as in Mary Shelley's *Frankenstein*, from the Community's creative laboratory of supranationalism (Figure 13).

Since its creation in the 1950s, the European Commission has thus always aspired to be more than a mere aggregate of its member states' interests or just an

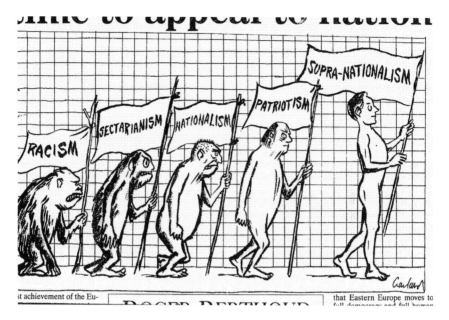

Figure 13 The ascent of Supranational Man according to Garland.
Source: Nicholas Garland, *The Independent*

intergovernmental organisation. It has also long championed the principle that, to fulfil its role properly, its autonomy and independence from governments must be guaranteed. To achieve these ideals, it was deemed essential to create an independent, career civil service whose primary loyalties and allegiances would be to the European Union rather than to its members' countries of origin. This ideal is expressed most visibly in Article 157 of the Treaty of Rome[18] and in the official Staff Regulations. Both of these declare that 'an official shall carry out his duties and conduct himself solely with the interests of the Communities in mind; he shall neither seek nor take instructions from any government, authority, organisation or person outside his institution' (Staff Regulations 1993: 12). Unlike United Nations or NATO staff, therefore, Commission staff are recruited directly by its various institutions and are not seconded by national governments. On taking up a post each member of the European Commission is required to 'give a solemn undertaking' before the Court of Justice in Luxembourg to respect these obligations, and to 'perform their duties in complete independence, in the general interest of the Communities'; and in carrying out those duties, 'neither to seek nor to take instructions from any Government or body'.[19] These obligations apply to all EU civil servants, as set out in the Staff Regulations. Furthermore, any official who breaches these obligations, in the opinion of the Court, can be 'either compulsorily retired . . . or deprived of his right to a pension' (Staff Regulations 1993: 240). Although they are rarely enacted, the Commission's supranational claims can be backed up by legal and bureaucratic sanctions if necessary.

These Statutes reflect not only the idea of creating a civil service independent of politicians and pressure groups but also the conscious attempt in 1958 by the Commission's first, and most vociferously federalist, President, Walter Hallstein, to instil within it a supranational ideology and sense of mission. The original criteria for selection were not simply that Commission staff should have the highest qualities of competence, performance and integrity, but also allegiance to the 'European ideal'. As Virginia Willis (1982: 4) noted in her study of European Community personnel, 'a key additional requirement in the early days was that staff should be devoted Europeans, who by the zeal and commitment to the goal of integration would maintain the momentum of the Commission's progress towards it'. In fact, most of the early generation of British officials who went to Brussels to serve in the Commission were self-selected, much as they are today. As Willis's study concluded (1982: 54), the first generation of EC officials from Britain tended to be 'devoted (to an ideal), different (from their contemporaries at home), discontented (with their lot in the UK), or dutiful (persuaded to go in the public interest)'. Subsequent generations of recruits admit to being motivated by other factors – including the high status, the generous salaries, the enviable conditions of service and the good job security that a post in the Commission brings. However, my research confirmed that a considerable degree of ideological commitment to the 'European idea' persists, even among those newly recruited to the service. As Spence (1994a) argues, 'even after 40 years, the [European] ideal remains and is an integral part of the Commission official's self-perception'. Ideological commitment seems to be a quality still actively sought in recruits – however one might gauge or measure this.

The point to stress here is that, while the idea of the Commission as a crucible for forging a new type of supranational European subjectivity appeared to be something that EU officials were uncomfortable with, this had certainly not been the case in the earlier decades. Officials may no longer invoke references to forging *Homo Europaeus*, or the heady kind of language redolent of the pioneering spirit and optimism of the EU's early founders, but as Spence (1994a: 64) says, 'the collective memory of these halcyon years remains important in the self-perception of Commission staff and contributes strongly to the sense of "we-ness" and singleness of purpose of officials from the original Six'. Significantly, it is in the European Schools, where most of the children of Commission officials are educated, that references to 'laboratories' for forging 'new Europeans' are now most frequently heard. This sense of being 'different' from other Europeans, no longer 'rooted' in one's native homeland, and part of a European vanguard remains a significant part of the Commission's historical *raison d'être* and undoubtedly influences the way EU staff see themselves. One informant, an official with twenty-five years of service in the Commission, summed it up like this:

> We don't necessarily feel that we're 'Europeans', but we do identify with our employer. It's like someone who works for a multinational company: I suppose it's a corporate identity of sorts. We feel a sense of solidarity whenever

the Commission – our employer – is criticised. But remember, people have *chosen* to work here. You shouldn't underestimate the problems of expatriation involved. Most people here do identify with the aims of the Commission. They wouldn't work for it if they didn't ... [though] there is less Euro-idealism in the new generation than in the past.

The idea of supranationalism is embedded in the organisation and ethos of the EU's administration in two further ways. The first concerns what politicians today call the 'tax burden'. Unlike most other Europeans, EU civil servants do not pay taxes to the member state whose citizens they are. Income tax deducted from their Community salaries is paid directly to the Community itself. As foreigners in Brussels, EU officials also enjoy quasi-diplomatic status and numerous financial privileges, including generous relocation grants and expatriate allowances. The significance of this is more political than economic, although EU officials have been described as the most privileged public officials in Europe. This tax arrangement is an important factor that sets EU civil servants apart from their fellow nationals and national states, and makes the Commission unique among public administrations.

The second way supranationalism continues to shape the Commission is in its staffing policy. Unlike other international organisations, such as the United Nations or NATO, Commission staff are recruited directly by its various institutions and are not seconded by national governments. Since its inception, national quotas have been considered anathema to the principles of merit, independence and supranationalism which the Commission espouses. In theory, therefore, there are no national quotas – except at the most senior levels, i.e. 'A1' and 'A2' officials: Commission staff are appointed on the basis of 'quality' and 'competence' following rigorous formal procedures set out in the Regulations. This has become something of an article of faith among official EU spokespersons and managers: the Commission, as I was repeatedly told, 'is not like the UN' (which was a byword for inefficiency, waste and internal conflicts generated by international rivalries and power politics).

However, the gulf between ideals and practice in Commission personnel policy is formidable and, in reality, national quotas undoubtedly do play an important role in recruitment and promotion, especially where posts are considered to be of particular political sensitivity or of importance to national interests. This was summed up colloquially by the often-used expression that such-and-such a post had a 'national flag' on it, or the frequent complaint by staff that their application for promotion was overlooked because the job they sought was earmarked for an official of another nationality. Speaking in private, many officials would cite numerous examples of this in their own particular Directorates. Officially, however, the existence of national quotas is systematically denied. The reason for this is that discrimination on the basis of nationality would be a violation of the Treaties and a contradiction of all that the Commission stands for. As a result, 'national quotas' are something of a taboo subject. Responses from senior managers in the DG IX (Administration) to direct questions about quotas ranged from flat denial ('there are no national quotas: that's all there is to be said on the matter'), to polite refusals to comment on the issue ('I'm sorry, but we don't talk about that'), to admissions, particularly from staff union officials, that national quotas are still very common and a source of tension.

Off the record it was a different story. Many officials gave detailed examples of the way in which calculations about the national composition of different services shape decisions about recruitment and promotion. Britain, Germany and the Netherlands were 'deficit countries', I was told, and their governments had seconded experts to the Commission specifically to work on ways to increase their country's national representation. As one official put it, 'the Commission ties itself up in knots over national quotas. It's time it came clean on this.' But given the prospects for litigation, 'coming clean' does not appear to be an option.

To sum up, supranationalism may no longer feature so prominently in official EU discourse on 'European construction', but it remains embedded and implicit in the deep structures of the EU's organisation. Like the concept of the unsaid or 'covert category' in linguistics, its presence is never far from the surface. More importantly, given the EU's objective of creating a transnational demos, the idea of a future post-national government staffed by supranational cadres provides the Commission with its charter for action and sense of purpose. Without such a supranational leadership – backed by a transnational public – the EU's myth of the future lacks democratic credibility and is unlikely to engage the active participation of the peoples of Europe in this wider polity.

Bureaucracy and political broker: powers and functions of the Commission

The third key characteristic of the Commission is the extraordinarily complex array of functions – executive, administrative, diplomatic, political and legislative – it performs. These are all derived from its responsibility, under Article 155 of the Treaty of Rome, to 'ensure the proper functioning and development of the common market' (CEC 1983a: 238). The Treaties give the Commission three specific powers and duties: to initiate the policy process and act as a 'motor' for European integration; to act as 'guardian of the Treaties' and 'enforcer of Community Law' – if necessary by referring offending member states or institutions to the Court of Justice; and to implement Community policies. Of these, perhaps the most important to the identity and self-image of Commission staff is its role in policy formulation. Articles 155 and 189 of the EEC Treaty confers upon the Commission its 'own power of decision'. This means that, with the Council of Ministers, it can issue acts which are binding for the subjects of Community law within its areas of competence, such as competition policy or the common market (Mathijsen 1995: 73).

More importantly, the Commission enjoys an *exclusive right of initiative* not simply in relation to legislation, but as far as any policies that can be defined as being 'in the general interest of the Communities' (CEC 1983a: 239). The Council of Ministers can normally legislate only on the basis of a proposal submitted to it by the Commission. By submitting drafts for regulations, directives and decisions, the Commission is therefore involved at every stage of the legislative process and bears ultimate political responsibility for all legislative proposals.[20] Furthermore, the Commission's mandate to formulate 'recommendations' and 'opinions' on Treaty issues places it in a powerful position to set strategic goals and shape the political agenda – powers which were exploited very effectively during Jacques Delors's period as president. Within the provisions of the Treaty, therefore, the Commission not only enjoys political independence, it also has enormous scope to define its own tasks and provide its own definition of the powerful yet elusive concept of the 'European interest'. In this key respect, the Treaties clearly provide a strategic resource for promoting the Commission's political ambitions – a fact which also contributes to the legalism described earlier.

Four other functions are worthy of mention. First, Commission officials exercise a management role over the day-to-day operation of those policies where action at the European level has largely replaced that of the nation-state, such as the Common Agricultural Policy, the Common Fisheries Policy and the Common Commercial Policy. Second, they draft and implement the Commission's budget, including the administration of the European Union's substantial Regional Development and Cohesion Fund, Social Fund and Agricultural Guidance and Guarantee Funds. Third, Commission officials are responsible for negotiating on behalf of member states in all bilateral and multilateral agreements to which the European Community is a party, and with international organisations such as the United Nations and the World Trade Organisation. Finally, and in order to be successful in the other tasks, they necessarily perform the role of diplomats and political brokers.

According to Delors, a Commission official therefore has 'six professions': policy innovator, law maker, law enforcer, manager of Community policies, diplomat and political broker.[21] However, it is the first of these – the Commission as policy 'initiator' – which has most influenced the character of the institution. As Ludlow states (1991: 97): 'This function as *animateur* (animator) permeates the whole structure and ethos of the institution . . . [and] is central to the culture of the Commission'. It is also what has fuelled the Commission's often-noted 'sense of mission'. Traditionally, the Commission has always been better at formulating proposals than at implementing or regulating EU law. However, this is changing as the Commission's traditional bias towards policy-drafting gives way to a greater emphasis on management and law enforcement as a result of the new areas of policy that have fallen within its sphere of competence.

Two major points arise from these observations about the Commission's diversity of functions. First, rarely have civil servants been given such complex roles or explicit political power and influence over the decision-making process – even if these powers are shared with the Council of Ministers, Parliament and the Court of Justice. As one official summed it up with measured irony, 'the difference between this organisation and a national civil service is that the Commission is a civil service *with attitude*'. The Commission therefore has a dualistic political identity: as well as being an executive, it was also created to perform a political function and is highly conscious of its political role. 'The Commission is neutral, but that does not mean it is neutered', was how another official explained it. Yet herein lies an important aspect of the problem of the EU's so-called 'democratic deficit': civil servants have no direct or popular mandate to make laws or determine policy. As critics argue, at the heart of the EU there is a serious lack of democratic control or political accountability, while decision-making and policy formation – particularly where ostensibly more 'technical' matters are concerned – are increasingly dominated by committees of unelected bureaucrats. This proliferation of specialised committees and 'scientific' advisory groups and their often secretive mode of operation, summed up by the word 'comitology',[22] is the darker side of the EU's otherwise highly original system of governance. In so far as this brings together national civil servants and obliges them to work together on the basis of co-operation and compromise and in the service of the 'European interest', it is 'supranationalism' of sorts. But this bureaucratic and managerial version of supranationalism is not what was envisaged by the EU's founding fathers.

Second, the Commission's complex functions, its legal status and the ambiguity of its role as political broker and bureaucracy have important implications for the identity and self-image of its staff. This is reflected both in the way that DGs rise and fall in importance in line with the political nature of their responsibilities, the budgets they command and the prestige of their Commissioner, and in the way that senior officials attempt 'to link this internal, bureaucratic power to the enhancement and politicisation of their own service's status' and 'jostle for power' to ensure that their DG leads in the co-ordination of policy areas (Spence 1994a: 90). It is also reflected in debates about the future of the Commission. At the high point of its influence in the late 1980s, with the prestige and optimism it had gained through the single market programme, senior officials and EU enthusiasts were once again speculating openly about the Commission developing into the embryo of a future European government. As Commission President Delors described it in 1988, echoing Walter Hallstein's vision of a transcendent supranational executive for Europe, the Commission had become the 'amorce d'un gouvernement européen'.[23] EU analysts and academics also contributed to this climate of opinion. Peter Ludlow, for example, wrote enthusiastically in 1991 that 'the Commission can become ever more powerful as the thirteenth member of the European Community, with all the advantages that stem from its functions as the custodian of the "European interest". It can and should lead to, but it will not in the immediate future be, the sole government of Europe' (Ludlow 1991: 122). Although this idea received a decisive set-back following the June 1992 Maastricht Treaty referendum in Denmark, that it should have emerged as a serious issue for debate is itself highly significant and indicative of the way the Commission's powers and confidence had grown during the 1980s.

The conclusion that emerges from all this is that, despite frequent references to the Commission's *fonction publique européenne*, many Commission *fonctionnaires* clearly do not see themselves as public servants or mere administrators – a sentiment reinforced, according to some officials themselves, by their distance from European taxpayers and the absence of a self-recognising 'European public' to serve. Instead, many preferred to see themselves in grander political terms as 'policy-makers', 'innovators', 'intellectuals' and 'architects' of the new European order whom the Treaties (and 'history' itself) had proclaimed 'custodians of the European interest'. Contrary to what some EU critics argue, these adjectives used by officials to describe themselves are not so much an expression of 'cognitive dissonance' or the ambitions of a 'power-hungry technocracy' – even though they do reflect the ethos and ideology of 'Europeanism'[24] that has informed the Commission's outlook and orientation since its inception. Rather, they are a logical reflection of its complex, overburdened legal functions and its bias towards policy formulation.[25]

The Commission is thus a creature of the Treaties in several senses. Its character and structure reflect the compromises and contradictions inherent in those Treaties, not only the tensions between the ideals of supranationalism and the politics of intergovernmentalism, but also those between the formal and the informal rules of organisation. The Commission may be a 'people of the book', but the extent to which officials necessarily 'play by the book' is another matter. EU analysts repeatedly speak of the complex 'rules of the game' that govern the policy process at European level – as though 'games theory' analysis and metaphors accurately describe political action and social behaviour within the institutions. However, as we shall see, the internal life of the Commission operates according to cultural norms and ground rules that are often very different from those proclaimed in EU documents or described in the literature. As the next chapters argue, these 'pragmatic' (as opposed to formal) codes and norms are central to understanding the dynamic of integration among European policy elites.

Notes

1 For interesting reviews of the use of the culture concept in organisational studies see Wright (1994); Chapman (1994); Case (1994).
2 The politicisation of 'culture' has emerged as a particularly important theme in recent anthropological writing. For good examples of the scope of this work see Kahn (1995); Turner (1993) and Wright (1998).
3 For a succinct account of the history of the term 'political culture' see Brown (1985); Eatwell (1997).
4 As noted in the Introduction, contemporary anthropological approaches also emphasise the fact that 'culture' is invariably a contested category, the meanings of which are fluid, contingent and unstable.
5 The long-standing epistemological debate about whether one can ever represent the 'native's point of view' is not one I propose to tackle here. For a useful commentary on this issue see Clifford and Marcus (1986).
6 Some analysts would dispute the attribution of the word 'culture' to the Commission in preference for the seemingly more appropriate term 'subculture'. However, the distinction between these categories is not always clear or analytically helpful. Moreover, 'subculture' has tended to be equated with symbolic resistance to perceived subordination among minorities and marginalised groups, and these semantic associations are not appropriate in the case of EU civil servants.
7 By this term 'legalism' I mean more than 'excessive adherence to law or formula', which is the *Oxford English Dictionary* definition. Legalism must also be

understood as a style of thinking, one that is constitutive of a particular 'approach' to governing. In this sense, it is a form of 'governmental rationality' concerned with what Foucault called the 'conduct of conduct' (for a useful analysis of these concepts, see Colin Gordon (1991)).

8 For a detailed discussion of this, see Chapter 7.

9 Definitions of 'subsidiarity' are notoriously vague. As Howe notes (1992: 45), even Lord MacKenzie Stuart, former President of the European Court, 'has condemned the official Treaty definition of the term as "gobbledegook" and considers that it renders a court's task in applying it almost impossible because questions about the relative "effectiveness" of Community or national action are likely to be incapable of judicial resolution'.

10 For an account of this by a former ECJ judge see G. F. Mancini, 'The Making of a Constitution for Europe', *Common Market Law Review*, 26 (1989): 595–614.

11 For a useful analysis of the concepts of government rationality, neo-liberalism and governmentality, see Gordon (1991).

12 Cited in O'Neill (1996: 35).

13 W. S. Churchill in *Hansard Commons*, 27 June 1950, 2147; also cited in Burchfield (1986: 646).

14 European Court of Justice, 1964, Costa *v* ENEL *ECR, Case 6/64*: 585, cited in Harryvan and van der Harst (1997: 145).

15 See also Neill 1995: 57–8. Howe (1992) makes a similar argument. The ECJ's methods of interpretation have 'liberated' the Court to act upon the goals enshrined not only the texts but also in the preambles of successive treaties. This has given it a profoundly political – Howe uses the word 'missionary' – character in pushing forward the European ideal.

16 Lord Dennning MR, in Howe (1992: 8). Howe (1992: 71) notes that Denning has recently amended this passage to read 'European law . . . is now like a tidal wave bringing down our sea walls and flowing inland over our fields and houses – to the dismay of all'.

17 Jean Monnet (1976: 551), cited in Spence (1994a: 63).

18 Article 157 of the EEC Treaty states that members of the Commission shall be 'completely independent in the performance of their duties' and prohibits them from engaging 'in any other occupation, whether gainful or not' (CEC 1983a: 239–40).

19 Members of the Commission also solemnly undertake to 'respect, both during and after my term of office, the obligations arising therefrom, and in particular the duty to behave with integrity and discretion as regards the acceptance, after I have ceased to hold office, of certain appointments or benefits'.

20 It should be noted, however, that although the Commission has the exclusive right of initiative in the legislative process, the Council and Parliament can 'request' it to submit any appropriate proposal. In effect, most EU legislation originates in the Council of Ministers.

21 Delors's remarks are echoed by both Hay (1989: 17) and Spence (1994a: 89).

22 For discussion of the concept of 'comitology', see Chapter 8.

23 Delors, cited in Spence (1994a: 90).

24 For alternative definitions of 'Europeanism' as an ideology, see Scruton (1982: 158); Ludlow (1987: 86–9).

25 Frank Vibert (1995), Director of the European Policy Forum, makes a similar point, arguing that the tasks of the all-purpose, multifunctional Commission should be 'unbundled' to allow it to concentrate more on its neglected managerial functions.

6 The Brussels context: integration and *engrenage* among EU elites

> Little by little the work of the Community will be felt . . . Then the everyday realities will make it possible to form the political union which is the goal of our Community and to establish the United States of Europe . . . For me there has been only one path; only its length is unknown. The unification of Europe, like all peaceful revolutions, takes time.
>
> (Monnet 1978: 346; 367)

Introduction: neofunctionalist theory reconsidered – questions of culture and cognition

The European Commission, often referred to as the European Union's 'civil service', occupies a unique role in the process of 'Europe-building', yet its powers are controversial and contested. Technically a bureaucracy and impartial executive whose 'independence is beyond doubt',[1] and whose function is to defend the 'Community interest', it is also a political power broker and initiator of EU legislation which defines itself as the 'engine of integration', 'custodian of the European idea' and 'conscience of Europe'. The civil servants appointed to administer the areas of policy ceded to Brussels by EU member states are therefore a crucial element in the integration process. Just how crucial their role may be is a question of major theoretical and practical interest.

According to neofunctionalist theories of European integration, these officials should become progressively more 'Europeanist' in orientation and outlook over time and as a result of the process of *engrenage*, or steady 'meshing together' of national civil servants and Commission officials in the various Brussels-based committees and institutions. The semantics of this French term are revealing. In a literal sense, *engrenage* translates into English as 'gears' or 'gearing' and usually refers to links in a chain or cogs in a wheel. As a figure of speech, however, it is used to convey the idea of being 'caught up in the system' (*pris dans l'engrenage*), or a 'spiral' of events over which one has little control.[2] This notion of 'bureaucratic interpenetration', and the image it evokes of individuals becoming snared in the EU's expanding webs and networks, is crucial for understanding the way European integration is conceptualised by EU elites.[3] But *engrenage* is more than simply a decorative metaphor for describing the mechanics of integration; it is an important folk idiom used by EU officials themselves when discussing the cultural and cognitive aspects of integration. It is also an integral concept in the many academic and 'expert' discourses on European political unification, particularly those neofunctionalist approaches that have shaped political thinking about Europe for much of the past three decades.[4] As Bainbridge and Teasdale observe (1995: 132), *engrenage* is a term commonly used in EU parlance 'to describe the practice of involving national civil servants with the work of the Union institutions, notably the Commission'.

Yet for all its significance, *engrenage* remains curiously under-studied and mis-understood.[5] As Juliet Lodge notes, it is sometimes dismissed by critics as a 'tech-nocratic conspiracy to befuddle politicians in the hope of encouraging them to delegate decision-making to civil servants' (Lodge 1993a: 14). This accusation misses the point. The importance of *engrenage* is not whether it functions to deceive politicians or compel them into abdicating powers to EU officials, but rather, its role as a mechanism of institutional and ideological incorporation, or 'agent of European consciousness'. Its 'functions' are to integrate and socialise national subjects into the structures, norms and values of the EU: to draw indi-viduals into the EU's institutional web of meanings in order to change the way they see themselves. *Engrenage* is therefore best understood as a 'political tech-nology' or administrative instrument designed to forge European consciousness and European identity among those policy professionals who operate above the level of the nation-state. In short, it functions as a mechanism to 'Europeanise' national administrative and political elites by socially and symbolically transform-ing them into a cohesive 'supranational' elite that sees itself as distinctly and transcendentally 'European'.

The creation of a specialised coterie of supranational cadres was seen by integra-tion theorists, including Haas (1958), Lindberg (1963), Monnet and Hallstein as a cornerstone of the process of furthering political integration. As Gordon Smith (1983: 248) sums it up:

> no significant degree of integration could take place without the provision of personnel to administer the integrated sectors. And once these officials are appointed they will tend to acquire a loyalty to the organisation rather than to the states of their origin, at least with regard to their won area of work. This development is a first sign of a political will emerging within the supranational organisation.

This, however, is an assumption that has never been empirically tested. Fur-thermore, there is little agreement over what this 'supranational identity' consists of, or how it could be measured. For neofunctionalist theorists, the dynamics of European integration implied a revolutionary transformation in the political iden-tity and conduct of elites at both national and international level. Haas (1958: 16) defined this as 'the process whereby political actors are persuaded to shift their loyalties and expectations towards a new centre, whose institutions possess or demand jurisdiction over pre-existing nation states'. Haas argued that, once created, the new supranational institutions would become the catalyst for a major political and psychological transformation among these key actors. To begin with, nationalism was likely to 'influence and perhaps shape the values and ideology' of officials appointed to staff these new institutions, but thereafter:

> a reverse process of gradually penetrating national ideologies can be supposed to get underway. Decision-makers in the new institutions may resist the effort to have their beliefs and policies dictated by the interested elites, and advance their own prescription. Or the heterogeneity of their origins may compel them to fashion doctrines and develop codes of conduct which represent an amalgamation of various national belief systems or group values ... If permitted to operate for any length of time, the national groups, now compelled to funnel their aspirations through federal institutions, may also be constrained to work within the ideological framework of those organs.
>
> (Haas 1958: 19)

Thus, the process of ideological conversion and the transfer of sovereignty to the level of European elites is complete. According to this theory, the emergence of an ever-expanding network of formal and informal relationships among policy professionals and civil servants would instil the habit of acting and thinking in a 'European way' which, in turn, would have a positive spillover effect on the political psychology of those elites (Webb 1983: 17–18). O'Neill gives a slightly different twist to this theme. As he describes it, the experience of co-operation in policy-making generates a 'sense of professional empathy, understanding and trust that facilitates joint responses to common problems' which leads to 'cognitive change' (O'Neill 1996: 42).

Two observations arise from these statements. First, the idea of *engrenage* as a rational and mechanistic process of institutional development driven by technocratic imperatives is, in essence, a theory of social change not unlike the behaviouristic models that dominated American social sciences during the 1950s, particularly their traditional, positivistic conceptions of what was labelled 'modernisation theory'.[6] Second, in so far as *engrenage* entails a process of psychological reorientation, or deliberate cognitive change, it is equally a model of social engineering. Once again, this is reminiscent of the emphasis that policy-makers and social scientists in the 1950s gave to combating the presumed 'backwardness' of peasant mentality, whose traditional worldview was deemed to be an obstacle to progress and innovation (see Banfield 1958; Foster 1965; Silverman 1968). Beyond this, the theory implicit in the neofunctionalist idea of *engrenage* also raises crucial anthropological questions concerning the way that bureaucracies become repositories of meaning for those who inhabit them and, conversely, how those institutional meanings and identities may come to 'inhabit' those individuals who are *engrenagés* – or enmeshed – within them.

Neofunctionalist theory assumed a causal link between changes in political behaviour and shifts in normative social values. 'Functional spillover' from elite transactions at European level would lead inexorably to 'cultural spillover' which would be sufficiently cumulative and powerful eventually to erode any exclusive sense of national identity and allegiance. As O'Neill (1996: 43) sums it up:

> a cultural osmosis is assumed to be at work in the fabric of these European societies participating in the Community endeavour. And this is a process which will eventually reach beyond those elites who implement it, culminating in the refocusing of popular loyalties away from their traditional attachment to national institutions and the primordial symbols of statehood. The eventual outcome of this process in the neofunctionalist canon is an entirely new European identity.

This approach, which recognises that European institutions are not simply monolithic bureaucratic structures but also 'cultural systems' and powerful agents of socialisation, is consistent with Jean Monnet's emphasis on building institutions as the key to forging European consciousness. As Monnet (1978: 393) summed it up in one of his many oft-quoted aphorisms, 'only institutions grow wiser; they accumulate collective wisdom'. Helen Wallace tacitly endorses this optimistic assumption when she explains that for Monnet and his colleagues it was important to create a framework through which 'the "brightest and the best" ' – or Europe's most 'talented policy engineers' – could be enabled to pioneer new ideas for collective and supranational policies (Wallace 1996: 44). European Community institutions were thus

> the vehicle through which shared European public goods were to be defined and delivered . . . The institutions would focus the interactions of key economic and political elites from the member states and in time create new or successor elites for whom the Community arena would be the preferred and predominant arena.
>
> (Wallace 1996: 43)

EU institutions are frequently portrayed as repositories of wisdom and progress: a 'transmission belt for generating solutions to problems' or 'benign technocracy' designed to enable Europe's 'brightest and the best' to get on with the job of building a supranational system of governance. I would simply note here that these assumptions about the emerging EU state apparatus are manifestly self-congratulatory and simplistic. They also reflect an uncritical and partisan approach to the analysis of modern political institutions that contrasts markedly with the more sober and pessimistic views of critical social scientists in the tradition of Marx and Weber.[7]

None the less, inspired by these beliefs and by the positivistic and teleological framework that has governed orthodox thinking about European integration, many pundits of European integration have blithely predicted the rise of a supra-national European identity within the institutions of the EU. Bramwell, writing in the mid-1980s, commented wryly on this phenomenon. 'There is', he observed, 'a somewhat Pavlovian neo-functionalist model of how such a supra-national unit might become viable; that is, make them work, and they will exist' (Bramwell 1987: 63). The editors of *Policy-making in the European Community* – Britain's most 'committed Europeans' – come in for particular criticism.

> 'Europe' was seen by the British political establishment as something more than the EEC as it was (or is): it represented a kind of cultural saviour, a salvation which could be and would be transmitted in some way not clearly identified or analysed by supra-national governmental institutions. It would 'grow'. Countries would come together, and culture would flow from one to another, like treacle.
>
> (Bramwell 1987: 64)

More importantly, the European Commission clearly identified with the assumptions of neofunctionalist theorists and came to see itself as the principal agent of European integration and European consciousness. These beliefs were reflected not only in the way the concept of 'supranationalism' became incorporated into the Commission's ideology and discourse (where it continues to be a recurring motif in the Commission representation of itself), but also in the way that these claims to supranational status have become part of the self-image and identity of Commission officials. This is a striking phenomenon that raises an interesting theoretical point in the continuing sociological debate about 'agency' and 'structure'. What we see here in this curious symbiosis between neofunctionalist models and identity-formation among EU *fonctionnaires* is not so much evidence of the predictive power of social science theories as an illustration of the ideological power of theory in hailing individuals as subjects or, as Althusser (1971) puts it, 'interpolating subjectivities'. In short, neofunctionalist theory is itself an 'agent of consciousness' that promotes the very changes it purports to analyse objectively. Not surprisingly, therefore, there was a broad consensus of opinion among Commission officials that perhaps 'the main place today where a European identity can be found' was 'here in Brussels in the institutions of the Community'.

The extent to which EU civil servants may therefore be considered 'pioneers' of a new European identity and subjectivity is a question of fundamental importance for the future of Europe. Some authors claim that this process of Europeanisation among elites has already happened among members of the European Parliament – even among those individuals and parties formerly hostile to further integration (Westlake 1994). In an interesting variation on the neofunctionalist idea of *engrenage*, Martin Westlake (1994: 7) contends that the existence of a directly elected European Parliament has created, for the first time, a political elite that is based not in national political institutions but in a supranational institution: in short, a new political class that will press for constitutional reform to extend the powers of the European Parliament as a way of enhancing their own career prospects.

Where Westlake's argument is flawed, however, is in the assumption that MEPs are locked into their Parliamentary careers. In fact, most MEPs' career paths are notoriously mobile and transitory, and many MEPs use their EU experience to find seats in their national parliaments. MEPs also tend to keep their national party ties. However, 'Cotta's law', as Westlake calls it, would seem to be more appropriately applied to understanding the behaviour and orientation of EU civil servants (including Westlake himself) rather than elected MEPs. Even more than elected politicians, these *fonctionnaires* have a powerful vested interest in the advancement of the European Union: having opted for a career in the service of the European Union, their prospects and status, and often their personal identities, become inextricably bound to its fortunes. Fieldwork evidence confirmed this hypothesis. The case of one recently recruited British *fonctionnaire* epitomised the way this process often works. Like many new recruits today, her induction and socialisation into EU norms and practices had begun with a six-month '*stage*' ('traineeship') in the European Parliament, followed by a one-year Master's degree in European Studies at the Collège d'Europe in Bruges. Thus, three key criteria for obtaining a job in the EU were fulfilled: knowledge of its procedures, familiarity with EU discourse and theory, and personal contacts. In her words:

> I suppose neofunctionalist theory is correct. Living and working in the EU does change you. I've certainly become more federalist in my outlook – not as much as some of those who have been here for ages – but I can see the process working on me. It's obvious really; you have a vested interest in promoting the EU because you live here and work for it, so your fortunes become tied up with the fate of the Union. You want it to become more important because you are a part of it. As a Brit you don't like anything too Euro-sceptic that would threaten your livelihood.

Other interviewees endorsed the *engrenage* theory by emphasising what they saw as the positive psychological effects that exposure to the Commission tended to have on temporary national experts ('ENDs') seconded to the Commission on fixed-term contracts. As one specialist in personnel policy described it: 'They find it a wonderfully mind-expanding experience: most who come here want to stay after their secondment has finished. Like the *agents temporaires*, once they get one foot in the door they want to get the rest of their body through.'

This is not, however, a vindication of neofunctionalism, as several major flaws exist in its chain of reasoning. The most fundamental of all is its tendency to conflate transnational elite-formation with an ideal of supranationalism and post-nationalism. A key question is whether the self-interest of an emerging European technical/administrative elite should be equated with the 'European interest' which it claims to embody. Furthermore, is this transfer of allegiance evidence of so-called 'cognitive shift', or simply 'corporate loyalty' of an ephemeral, pragmatic and superficial kind? These questions are easier to address with the benefits of historical hindsight rather than anthropological observation. However, assuming that neofunctionalism is correct in its belief that the loyalties and identities of these political actors can be weaned away from their nation-states and re-focused upon the EU's institutions, what are the social and psychological mechanisms that explain this apparent shift in consciousness? Much has been made of the importance of 'supranational' institutions and the education of elites as the key to fostering *engrenage*, and the need for a truly 'European' civil service to translate this ideal into daily practice, but what kind of administrative regime or 'organisational culture' is developing within these institutions of the European Union? Has the Commission created a 'post-national' civil service commensurate with its supranational ideals? Every new state and empire requires an elite to sustain its vision and ideology. Can 'European Man', as embodied by the archetypal Commission official, play a similar role for Europe as Oxbridge and Milner's Kindergarten did for the British Empire, or the Komsomol Pioneers did for the Soviet Union?

Before addressing these questions, however, we need to ask what the concepts of 'supranationalism', 'cultural spillover' and '*engrenage*' mean in practice, and how they are embodied in the context of life within Brussels, the so-called 'capital of Europe'. Important in this respect is the social and geographical setting in which the Commission is located, and the ways in which EU permanent officials, as expatriates, relate to the wider cultural milieu in which their organisation is situated. The word 'cosmopolitan' was the adjective most frequently used by EU staff when describing what they felt to be the most positive feature of the Commission's organisational culture. By this term, staff generally referred to the 'multilingual' and 'multinational' character of the EU, which they tended to perceive as a cultural 'melting pot' of the different national traditions. This 'emic' perspective – the Commission's self-image, or folk model – has a curious resemblance to ideas about culture and multiculturalism promoted by certain contemporary postcolonial writers. Indeed, one could argue that EU civil servants epitomise the kind of 'deterritorialisation', 'cultural hybridity', 'diasporic identities' and 'transnational connections' that contemporary social theorists often refer to when discussing the transformation of social identities under the conditions of globalisation and postmodernity (Morley and Robins 1995; Hannerz 1996).[8] Or is this the case? How useful is this analytical vocabulary for understanding the specificity of the EU? What role does the institutional habitat play in the formation of identity and consciousness among EU staff, and how important is the 'Brussels factor' in this process?

Brussels, 'capital of Europe'

The main offices are situated in Brussels, two-thirds of which is French-speaking, while the city – classified according to Belgium's federal constitution as one of the country's three autonomous regions – is situated in Flemish Brabant. Brussels is officially a bilingual city and all signposts, billboards or public notices – even traffic fines – are written in both French and Flemish. The Belgian government typically gives a positive spin to the way regionalism has been used to resolve the long-standing linguistic and ethnic cleavages that continue to divide the country. Arriving at Brussels international airport, visitors are immediately assailed with posters announcing that Brussels is not only the 'heart of Europe' but a model of federalism and decentralisation that epitomises the idea of a Europe of the Regions. Throughout the city centre, from Rond Point Schuman to the Grand Place and beyond, a string of new tourist shops have opened to cash in on Brussels's status as the self-styled 'capital of Europe'. These shops – typically sporting names such as 'Euro-temps' or 'Euro-style' – are veritable shrines to EU iconography and paraphernalia (Figure 14). They are devoted exclusively to the sale of 'Euro-souvenirs': umbrellas, baseball caps, sweatshirts, pencil sets, office stationary, alarm clocks, watches, gaudy-coloured school bags and blue Smurfs – all embossed with the EU logo of yellow stars on an azure background (Figure 15). Other souvenirs include car stickers with 'I Love Europe' and 'Europe: My Country'; chocolate 'Euro' coins and miniative European flags for the office desk.[9]

The choice of Brussels and Luxembourg as the administrative centres for the European Community was clearly political. Although other capitals such as Paris or Bonn were arguably better placed to host the new EC offices, few people wanted the larger nations to have this powerful leverage and influence over Europe's fledgling supranational institutions. A trend had also begun with the creation of the Common Market and Euratom, when the European parliamentarians could not agree between Strasbourg and Paris and therefore settled for Brussels as a compromise; the Common Market headquarters, in turn, attracted hordes of diplomats, delegations and pressure groups. During the 1960s, many

Figure 14 One of the many Euro-tourist shops in Brussels.

Figure 15 Examples of the 'Eurostyle' paraphernalia for sale in Brussels Euro-tourist shops.

more big companies, particularly American firms, relocated their headquarters to Brussels. These were followed in 1967 by NATO and SHAPE after their expulsion from France by De Gaulle. Although the city has under a million inhabitants and belongs to one of Europe's smaller countries, as far as the EU is concerned, Brussels has become the *de facto* capital of Europe. Few cities today rival its range of international institutions and agencies. As Watson and Blythe (1995: 14) observe, these act 'as a magnet for governments, business, lobbyists and an eclectic range of interests from all round the world struggling to influence decision-making process that directly affects Europe's 368 million citizens and indirectly millions more around the globe'. This international presence includes:[10]

- over 20,000 EU civil servants (28 per cent of whom are Belgian) and their families
- over 160 embassies (only New York has a greater number of diplomatic missions and diplomats)
- over 90 offices representing regional interests
- 2,000 NGOs, including trade union, business and non-profit associations
- an estimated 10,000 lobbyists and an 800-strong press corps which has overtaken Washington as the largest in the world
- over 2,000 multinational companies
- three 'European' and thirteen international schools
- the seat of the European Council, Committee of the Regions, Economic and Social Committee, Western European Union and Eurocontrol
- Brussels also boasts the world's fourth largest conference industry (behind Paris, London and Geneva)

Despite this heavy international presence, Brussels remains curiously small and provincial, a fact which facilitates the creation of those personal contacts and networks among European elites which are so important to what Middlemas (1995) calls the 'informal politics' of EU policy-making. Anthony Sampson's description of the city, written over thirty years ago, still strikes a hauntingly familiar chord: 'boring and bourgeois', he wrote, 'the centre of the city is a memorial to laissez-faire' (Sampson 1968: 52). Its hub is still the old stock exchange – a building resembling a Baroque cathedral – and the 'Grote Markt', with its Gothic and Baroque guild houses. Its most imposing street was home not to government offices but to the banks which dominate Belgium's industry. According to Sampson, the influence of banking and commerce had created a dour ambience:

> The shops have the faded look of shops in the thirties, and prefer exorbitant profit margins to bigger turnover. The social structure is similarly antique, more suited to the thirties than the sixties. A closed circle of bankers and barons, carefully intermarried, dominate the high social life, cultivating evening dress and gloomy formality: servants are in easy supply. The cultural life is

bleak and self-conscious; most cultural heroes, like Simenon or Jacques Brel, have long since left.

Brussels in the late 1990s is obviously very different from this sombre portrait. The old bourgeois elite has been replaced by more dynamic, professionally oriented, entrepreneurial and party-political elites, and the city has grown substantially richer, thanks in large measure to the EU. As far as Belgium is concerned, Europe is big business. Brussels is still a monument to *laissez faire*, although it has moved with the times. In 1991, the overall economic impact of the EU's presence generated BF 120 billion and created jobs for over 46,000 people (7 per cent of the city's total employment). By 1995 this had increased to 54,000 jobs and an estimated BF 240 billion. The economic benefits are even greater if one adds to this the business given to hotels, shops, restaurants, translators, secretaries, taxi companies, removals firms, security guards, express courier services, construction workers and childminders.

Not surprisingly, the impact of the EU's presence on patterns of everyday life and the social fabric of the city has been dramatic. First, the Europeanisation of Brussels has significantly influenced the language of this officially bilingual French/Flemish city. Increasingly, English is used by residents when speaking with strangers. This is not so much a demonstration of cosmopolitanism as a strategy to avoid taking sides in the internecine conflict between Walloons and Flemings (or, in the eyes of many native Flemish speakers, as a device for resisting the hegemony of the French speakers).

Second, the presence of the EU has had a devastating impact on the infrastructure and architecture of the city. Visitors to Brussels often expect to see an elegant European Union quarter, Europe's equivalent of Washington DC. Instead, they find 'a soulless, administrative district where drab office blocks have replaced the 19th-century town houses, dotted with cranes and building sites' (Buckley 1998: 3). Whereas in other European capitals the wholesale demolition of urban areas (or 'slum clearance' as it was termed) ceased in the late 1970s, in Brussels the bulldozing has continued unabated, erasing whole neighbourhoods of once-elegant nineteenth-century *maison de maître* houses into high-rise monuments of glass and concrete. This lack of planning – or simply bad planning, depending on how one looks at it – has contributed to a dramatic increase in traffic and pollution, and numerous pockets of urban blight. The area most affected – around the Schuman and Leopold station – is known as the 'European quarter'; a mass of high-rise glass and concrete offices dissected by fast and noisy six-lane highways that make travelling on foot at best difficult and unpleasant, and at worst a potentially life-threatening activity (Figure 16). For many local residents (the 'citizens of Europe' hailed by EU documents), this is what the 'Europeanisation' of Brussels has come to mean.[11] From a resident's or pedestrian's perspective, the European quarter is an anti-social environment: an urban space designed for offices and machines where the need for fast and easy access to underground car parks and garages seems to have taken priority over most other concerns. The wealth exhibited in the cars that race down these

Figure 16 The new European Parliament building under construction in the 'European quarter' of Brussels.

inner-city highways (many of them sporting the blue 'EU' diplomatic number plates) is a vivid reminder of the EU's impact as a magnet for financial and political elites.

Along three of these roads (Rue Belliard, Rue de la Loi, Avenue Courtenburg) are located most of the sixty-seven buildings that house the various EU directorates and services. For most of the 1990s, this area resembled a giant building yard, particularly with the construction of the massive espace Leopold, the building designed to house the enlarged EU, which occupied a site larger than London's Canary Wharf. As Erkki Liikanen, EU Commissioner for personnel, administration and buildings, commented after being shown a film shot in the European quarter just after the war: 'I realised then that the war did not destroy the Quartier Leopold. People did.'[12] Annemarie Renard-Deckmyn, deputy director of the Brussels-Europe Liaison Office, was more explicit in identifying the culprits: 'Local people have had to deal with the concretisation of the European idea. People have had to leave their homes because the EU needs offices.'[13] In the spring of 1996, as the new Parliament building was nearing completion, the last resident in the old Gare Luxembourg neighbourhood was forcefully evicted by police, under threat of heavy fines. He had become something of a local *cause célèbre* during the preceding months. However, on the day of his eviction there were no popular protests or demonstrations to mark the occasion – although local press and television reporters had turned up in anticipation. Whether this reflected a sense of powerlessness and fatalism among local residents is debatable: another interpretation is simply that there were no residents left to protest by then.

Vast profits have been made as a result of the enormous building programme and property leasing. According to local estimates, the EU in 1991 was worth 10 per cent of gross domestic product to Belgium[14] and the annual rental of EU offices in Brussels alone earns an estimated BF 110,000 million. Hence, the Belgian government has a major interest in matters relating to EU property and building policies, although the extent of its interest is often concealed. There is also an important political dimension underlying the Belgian authorities' concern with EU buildings and their location. The new European Parliament building (nicknamed the Caprice des Dieux because its semicircular shape resembles that of a famous French soft cheese) was originally disguised as an 'international congress centre' so as not to offend French sensibilities about Strasbourg being the official seat of the European Parliament. Its construction was an important component of the former Belgian Prime Minister Wilfried Martens's strategy to ensure that Brussels was chosen as permanent home for the EU institutions, and to ward off a concerted challenge from Strasbourg for the latter (Buckley 1998: iii).

The new Parliament building was not alone in generating controversy. The enormous pink granite 'Justus Lipsius' building on Rue de la Loi, which houses the Council of Ministers (referred to by EU staff as the 'Bunker' or the 'Kremlin'), took so long to complete that by the time it opened in 1995 it was already too small, having been planned for only twelve member states. The Council subsequently discovered in 1997 that neighbouring land long earmarked for its expansion had been sold without its knowledge to developers by the Belgian state – ironically as part of plans to reduce Belgian's national debt in according with the Maastricht convergence criteria (Buckley 1998).

The office-building and renting boom has generated enormous revenue both for the many local Belgian companies fortunate enough to have won these lucrative contracts and for the Belgian state, which has become the largest and most important local rentier. The greatest speculation surrounds the EU's old Berlaymont headquarters. For years this 1969, thirteen-storey, purpose-built glass-fronted building – shaped like a starfish on stilts – was the most visible and enduring symbol of European unity. Prior to 1991 the building, with its underground car parks, restaurants and duty-free supermarket, was the citadel of the Commission and housed some 3,300 officials. This geographical and physical concentration of Commission personnel undoubtedly helped to generate if not a feeling of '*gemeinschaft*', at least an *esprit de corps* and sense of solidarity among staff sharing the building. However, in 1991 it was hurriedly evacuated when leaking asbestos was decreed a fire and a health hazard. Faced with both a massive bill for repairs and the heavy cost of relocating the evacuees,[15] the Belgian state, which owns the Berlaymont and is the Commission's landlord, at first vigorously rejected the asbestos claims. Even in 1992 senior Belgian government sources accused the Commission of grossly exaggerating the danger to its employees. According to one Belgian official: 'There never was anything wrong with the

Berlaymont. We checked it three times and not once did we find a dangerous concentration of asbestos.'

The struggle waged by the staff unions to get the Commission to take action on the asbestos problem, and the lively public meetings and campaigning this entailed, were important factors contributing towards the growing sense of solidarity and unity among Commission staff. As anthropologists have often pointed out, identity crystallises most sharply in situations of adversity or where there is a perception of risk. In this case, however, the adversaries were not only the Belgian government but the Commission authorities. As one trade union leader explained:

> It took fifteen years of campaigning to get the Commission to evacuate the now-condemned Berlaymont. We finally managed to get a report commissioned by a British firm[16] — only because we had good relations with the Portuguese Commissioner, Cardosa. But we got action only because the asbestos leakage had become so corrosive that the Berlaymont had become a fire hazard. The report showed that, if it caught fire, the whole building would probably collapse in twenty minutes. That report was never made public. It was only when Cardosa asked whether the Commission was prepared to accept legal responsibility if a fire broke out that we finally got a response.

The Belgian state decided to keep the external structure – as a fine example of Belgian modernist architecture – but refused to start renovations until it had firm guarantees that the Commission would move back into the premises when the job was complete. At the time of fieldwork, the Berlaymont had been deserted for over six years, sealed under a white tarpaulin cover, while workers in protective clothing and breathing masks surreptitiously tried to remove its carcinogenic interior. Despite this, the building itself continues to serve as the most recognisable symbol of the EU, and demonstrations and rallies (which in Brussels are almost weekly occurrences) still use it as a focal point for their marches and public protests. The irony of this situation is not lost on local observers and critics: that the EU's most potent icon should be wrapped up like a Christo art-work, concealing the decaying hulk of an abandoned and toxic monolith whose carcinogenic interior has to be hidden from public view while EU and Belgian politicians haggle over the cost of its refurbishment, highlights many of the characteristics of the EU that opponents object to. EU officials were aware of the negative symbolism of the situation and would often joke about it, but the humour was usually tinged with exasperation at the behaviour of the Belgian authorities who had insisted on firm guarantee that the Commission would resume leasing the building prior to any refurbishment. The dispersal and relocation of the Commission's services to new premises scattered around the European quarter and beyond was also sometimes jokingly compared to the collapse of the Tower of Babel, and many staff spoke nostalgically of the 'Berlaymont days' as though the evacuation had marked the end of an era in the history of the Commission. Many also spoke of the way it had affected personal relations and communications between services, rendering the Commission 'more anonymous' on the one hand, yet diversifying the 'corporate cultures' of the different Directorates-General on the other.[17]

The influx of foreigners drawn to Brussels by the magnet of the EU has made this a highly cosmopolitan, multiethnic and polyglot city. The EU's presence has had a significant demographic influence. The proportion of non-Belgians living in the capital has climbed to 28 per cent of the population – roughly half of whom are from non-EU countries (notably Zaire and North Africa). However, despite this heavy influx of foreigners, the population of the city has progressively fallen over recent years, from just over a million in 1977 to approximately a million in the late 1990s. Unlike most other European capitals, it has a surplus of accommodation to rent and to sell. This reflects an interesting demographic phenomenon: as the EU expands, Brussels shrinks, and as the old Bruxellois residents move out to the affluent suburbs and Brabant villages surrounding the city, 'outsiders' move in to colonise the vacated spaces. During the day, the city is choked with traffic and commuters while at weekends large parts of it are deserted. Other parts of the city lie decaying and desolate, having long ago been earmarked for office development that never quite came to fruition.

The 'Brusselsisation' of the EU

The presence of the EU has therefore had a significant impact on the physical fabric and social structure of Brussels, but what impact has Brussels had on the EU and its staff? Was the choice of a small Benelux country beneficial to the goal of forging a more neutral, politically independent, supranational entity? How has the social, political and cultural milieu of Brussels influenced the character and administrative culture of the Commission? These are difficult questions to address, but they have important bearing on the debate about *engrenage*. Two points can be made that provide tentative answers. The first concerns the issue of 'social exclusion' and integration, concepts which have become central themes in recent EU research funding programmes. In this case, however, it is not the marginalisation of peripheral groups in economically deprived regions of Europe but the lack of integration of EU civil servants into Belgian society that is of particular anthropological significance. This theme – the lack of deep, permanent roots or a sense of being integrated into the local society – was constantly echoed in fieldwork conversations with EU staff.

One of the consequences of the EU's growth has been higher rents and higher house prices. The corollary of this has been the creation of a dual economy with completely different prices for the affluent EU *fonctionnaires* and company officials which, in turn, has resulted in the creation of residential enclaves or 'ghettos' of rich diplomats, Eurocrats and foreign businessmen. Even in the late 1960s this pattern was becoming apparent. As Sampson (1968: 53) shrewdly observed: 'Alongside the complacent old Belgian society there has grown up a quite separate one, unrooted and un-Belgian. The Brussels burghers, with their passion for property investments, have zealously prepared for any kind of expansion.' From the 1970s onwards, Brussels therefore witnessed a massive expansion of brand-new apartment blocks and expensive villas built largely to house diplomats and EU officials. Many of these were situated in the well-to-do suburbs to the south and east of the city, or in the communes closest to the EU offices in Etterbeek and Ixelles where signs proclaiming '*appartements à louer*' abound.

Ghettoisation

Acknowledging the dangers of this 'ghettoisation' of foreigners, the Burgomaster of Brussels declared recently: 'It is vital that EU staff become better integrated in Brussels. Rather than living in a Euro-ghetto, we want them to live in harmony with the rest of us'.[18] The problem, however, is that EU staff do live and work in a *de facto* Euro-ghetto; a social and economic world very much set apart from that of ordinary Bruxellois. This is reflected in numerous ways. Their lifestyle is very different from that of local residents: they enjoy diplomatic privileges which make them relatively immune from the hassles faced by most local residents in dealing with the Belgian authorities; their salaries are often two or three times those of people in equivalent jobs in Belgium, and most staff live and work in a very circumscribed area within Brussels. In many respects, therefore, the milieu in which EU officials live is a rarefied habitat significantly detached from everyday life in the city. They are in it, but not of it. Like colonial officers or European diplomats in some Third World countries, their occupation and status places them in a social category outside and above the moral universe of Brussels society.

Significantly, most EU interviewees admitted that their personal contacts with local Belgians were minimal and tended to be confined to financial/bureaucratic or commercial transactions and dealings. Some put this isolation from the host society down to their own lifestyle: long working days spent at the desk in offices situated high above ground level (where the only Belgians one normally encounters are security guards, porters and cleaning staff), followed by weekends spent escaping from Brussels. Many officials, particularly older staff, said that they also had a second home outside of Brussels. For some, air travel was treated in the same way as other people might regard catching a bus or a train. It was not uncommon to find some staff, especially younger, single officials, flying to Milan, London, Paris or Frankfurt each weekend. Equally important for many was a sense of the transitory nature of life in Brussels. Although Brussels is a magnet for large numbers of diplomats, lobbyists, consultants and journalists, most of these people move on after a few years; only the permanent *fonctionnaires* remain. Thus, there is always a friend or colleague's 'farewell do' or 'leaving party' to attend.

However, others attributed their alienation from the host society to the fragmentary and 'unwelcoming' nature of Belgian society itself. Many informants said that coming to live in Brussels for the first time was quite difficult (Danes and Finns were reportedly among those for whom this experience was particularly alienating). Most officials, when interviewed, admitted that they had not found

Brussels or the Brussellois at all friendly or inviting. For many people, the jokes and stereotypes about the Belgian love for dogs and lack of famous personalities notwithstanding, the Brussellois were typically described as 'cold', 'aloof', 'bourgeois', 'indifferent', 'detached', 'closed' and 'snobbish'. Even Belgians make humorous (and not-so-humorous) observations about the perceived lack of any sense of 'public spirit' in the country.[19]

Commission officials in Brussels therefore live and work in what staff themselves call 'something of a rarefied diplomatic bubble', or 'goldfish bowl', where it is reportedly 'very easy to forget that you are living in Belgium' because everyday contact with Belgians is so limited. A recent British recruit summed it up thus:

> It's not like living in a foreign country. You can read English newspapers, they speak English to you in shops, you get Radio Four on the radio and can watch BBC on cable television in the evening. I sometimes wish it were more 'alien'. But when it comes to finding a dentist or going to the local post office, that is always problematic. I find the Belgians difficult to understand.

It is very easy for EU officials to spend their entire waking day focused on EU-related activities, mixing only with fellow EU staff, thinking and talking exclusively about EU matters, and socialising in the bars and restaurants frequented by other members of the technocratic European elite. This tendency towards increasingly insular and institutionalised patterns of socialisation is reinforced by the long hours many officials work, particularly those in the cabinets or in certain high-profile Directorates. But while these factors may help to distance EU officials from ordinary Belgians, they also contribute to forging solidarity and a sense of 'European identity' among fellow Eurocrats.

Dépaysement

If 'ghettoisation' is one factor that promotes integration and *engrenage* among civil servants, a second and perhaps more important factor is the common experience of *dépaysement*, or 'exile'. This was frequently acknowledged by staff themselves. As a senior official explained it:

> There are several factors shaping the European character of the House. Perhaps the most important is *dépaysement*: the fact is that most people who come here have been up-rooted and have had to move away from their home country. They are exiles. Then there is the way that different national traditions tend to rub off on each other. Working in a foreign language is also important. Most people have to work in a language that's not their own, especially if they come from countries other than France or Britain.

EU officials are not 'exiles' in the strict sense of the word, although this is how several informants, especially those with many years of service, described their relationship with their countries of origin. However, their social and material circumstances, and their common experience as 'foreigners' and *fonctionnaires*, undoubtedly promotes rather than discourages what one official called an 'exile mentality': namely, an orientation towards cliquishness and the creation of a strong sense of boundary and difference between 'we' *fonctionnaires* (or 'people of the House') and 'they' ('the Belgians'). Political commentators have some-times described the Commission as the 'thirteenth member state'. Commission officials would often give their own gloss with the joking remark 'we are the Thirteenth Tribe of Europe' – a title which, to extend the metaphor, many sects and millenarian cults have claimed.

It is well known in the sociological and anthropological literature that people who are uprooted or displaced will create new communities and new networks of support among those in similar circumstances – particularly if the host society is not particularly accessible or welcoming, or if it is simply difficult to feel inte-grated into. In many respects, this situation recalls the early debates about 'eth-nicity' among anthropologists concerned with analysing the social consequences of urbanisation in Africa and elsewhere (Cohen 1974b). An interesting observa-tion there was the way in which the new contexts created by migration and urbanisation gave rise to new systems of labelling and identification which, in turn, resulted in new boundaries of inclusion and exclusion. This is not to suggest that EU officials constitute an 'ethnic group' as such.'[20] Rather, it is simply to point out that the rarefied diplomatic habitat within which EU officials dwell, coupled with the social and psychological effects of *dépaysement*, are important contributory elements to the process of *engrenage*, and particularly to the forma-tion of European identity. However, against this it should be noted that, when questioned, most senior staff said that the most enduring social networks outside of work tended to follow along lines of common nationality or language – except of course in families of mixed nationality (of which there were many). Thus, while work-based relationships are extremely transnational, outside of work this appeared to be less evident. As one German official summed it up: 'Young officials and stagiaires tend to mix a lot between nationalities, [but] most officials tend to keep to their own clans once they've settled down here.'

Censorship

A third area where Brussels has had a notable influence over the character of the Commission lies in the realm of censorship and internal politics. The financial importance of the EU to the Belgian state in terms of office building and renting has already been noted. An important consequence of this is the extreme sensitiv-ity with which the Belgian authorities treat anything that might damage the coun-try's reputation or threaten its interests – and the lengths they will go to to protect those interests. A story told by two officials illustrates this succinctly. A former German Director-General who had clashed with his new Commissioner took early retirement, but decided to continue living in Brussels. As a non-EU official he found that, for the first time since living in Belgium, he was now obliged to register as a 'foreigner' at the commune in which he lived (Etterbeek).

The official was shocked at the way he and other foreigners were treated by the authorities. As one informant put it: 'Here was a man earning about BF 450,000 per month, who had lived and worked in Brussels half of his life, being treated as though he were a social security scrounger' and kept waiting by rude officials in a dismal queue in an overcrowded room. The official wrote a short article for the Commission's internal newspaper,[21] recounting his experiences and what it had taught him about the difficulties faced by non-EU residents in Brussels (whose plight, he admitted, he had not been aware of). Following normal practice, the newspaper's editor sent the letter together with a standard note inviting comments from the EU-Brussels liaison committee – the idea being that these would be published alongside the article. After two months the EU-Brussels liaison committee sent back a reply to the letter. In the meantime, however, the former Director-General had written another version of the article, toned down, for the Belgian daily, *Le Soir*. When this was published, the Belgian authorities immediately contacted the office of the President of the Commission to inform Delors of their displeasure. The head of the Directorate-General for Administration (a Belgian) then convoked a full-scale emergency meeting with a representative from Delors's *cabinet*. At the meeting he learned about the second article and the Commission's reply to it. The final copy had already been sent to the printers and the 42,000 newspapers were in the process of being distributed, but the Director-General for Administration was having none of it: all 42,000 copies were subsequently pulped and the editor of the newspaper was officially rebuked for 'causing trouble'.

This story was authenticated by other informants, some of whom spoke scathingly of the 'culture of secrecy' that has developed within the Commission, particularly in areas such as administration and personnel (see Chapter 7). Several younger officials complained about the authoritarian attitudes of more senior officials who, despite calls for greater transparency and democracy, continue to follow practices that are secretive, repressive and draconian. One junior A-grade official complained that his Head of Unit had recently told him, 'You're an A7: your job is not to think, it is to do what you are told'. Another more senior official recounted a meeting with Philippe Petit-Laurent, a former French Deputy Director of Personnel and one of Delors's 'trusted henchmen': 'He banged the table with his fist and shouted at me: "*La Commission est une autorité; les fonctionnaires doivent obéir*".' According to local reputation, Petit-Laurent was the 'political assassin' of the Delors cabinet (a lieutenant of Pascal Lamy, Delors's infamous *chef de cabinet* and political 'fixer') and the man who had 'killed' Richard Hay, the former British Director-General for Administration. The story behind this tale of bureaucratic intrigue was that the post of Director-General of Administration has 'traditionally had a French flag placed over it' – which is Brussels code for a post that is earmarked as being of particular national interest. For some reason, however, this post was occupied by Hay at the time Delors took over as Commission president. By all accounts Hay had fallen out with the Delors *cabinet*: he lacked political skill and was 'too straight and honest', and therefore soon came to be seen as an obstacle to their political goals.[22]

Conclusion: bureaucratic enclavement and the limits of elite integration

There are two major conclusions to be drawn from these stories. First, the incident concerning the former Director-General's encounter with the local authorities highlights the way in which the privileges and immunities of EU officials undoubtedly act to detach them from the conditions of existence of other foreigners and locals in Brussels. The factors that shape the everyday experience of being an EU civil servant in Brussels – *dépaysement*, quasi-diplomatic identity, multilingual work environment, residential segregation, separate schooling for their children, the relative affluence, job security and high status of their position, the continuous exposure to institutional norms and practices – certainly help to foster a strong *esprit de corps* among staff. Together, these elements combine to create a palpable sense of 'European identity' and consciousness among EU officials. However, if *engrenage* is a process that works to 'shift loyalties' and engender sentiments of solidarity among civil servants – to transform them into 'self-actualised' European subjects – it also increases the social and psychological distance between EU officials and citizens in the member states, thereby creating a new kind of core–periphery relationship between Brussels-based elites and the people(s) of Europe. Indeed, from a neofunctionalist perspective, this separation is both necessary and desirable. If the EU institutions are to become a crucible for forging *Homo Europaeus*, as Monnet predicted, and if its staff are to be socialised into the norms and values of 'Europeanness', a measure of isolation, autonomy and immunity from the 'contaminating' influences of parochial nationalism would seem to be essential. Like all neophytes undergoing a *rite de passage*, new EU *fonctionnaires* must first be separated and stripped of their former identities before they can become fully incorporated into their new status and identity. The integration of elites within the EU's institutions therefore necessarily entails certain 'dividing practices' that serve to separate newcomers from their 'mother' country. *Dépaysement* and *engrenage* are therefore key elements in this process that work most effectively to produce the kind of transnational cultural milieu required for the birth of European Man. But this raises another problematic question. If the process of European integration, as its supporters argue, is 'irreversible' and 'irresistible' and has a self-reinforcing 'dynamic of its own', what are the limits of integration at the level of elites? What happens when the integration process passes the point of no return (which many would argue it already has) to produce a new form of transnational governance? While some EU federalists might welcome this as a necessary step forward in Europe's march towards its federal destiny, there is nonetheless the danger of what some organisational analysts call 'bureaucratic encapsulation'. As Griel and Rudy (1984: 261) define it in their study of social cocoons:

> Through encapsulation the organisation attempts to create a situation in which the reality it proffers is the only game in town. Encapsulation creates the setting in which the chief dynamic of the identity transformation

process – intensive interaction with individuals who will conform to the prospective affiliate's emergent senses of self and reality – can take place.

As the next chapter argues, the European Commission is far from being the unified monolithic entity that its external image suggests, and many factors militate against this idea of incorporation and internal cohesion. The 'encapsulation' model therefore does not really fit very well.

The second conclusion to be gleaned from these stories is that the claim that 'Commission officials carry out their duties solely with the interest of the Communities in mind' needs to be questioned more critically. Both the asbestos-in-the-Berlaymont and censorship-of-the-*Courrier-du-Personnel* incidents suggests that the statutory obligation on an official to 'neither seek nor take instructions from any government, authority, organisation or person outside his institution' is undoubtedly compromised by the high-level links and contacts between national authorities and senior Commission staff, a tendency reinforced by the *cabinet* system. However, in both these cases, collusion between the more politicised upper echelons of the Commission and the Belgian authorities may have served to reinforce a sense of solidarity and unity among Commission staff against their political masters, whose 'meddling' in the internal affairs of 'the House' is widely perceived as unwelcome and intrusive. Paradoxically, therefore, the subversion of the Commission's role could be an important catalyst in creating a more aggressive and politicised sense of European identity among EU civil servants.

On the other hand, incidents such as these also tell a different story about European integration that obliges us to rethink some of the conventional models of integration. If neofunctionalist theory is correct in assuming that 'functional spillover' begins with economics and institutional dynamics and ends in 'cognitive change' among strategically placed actors, then other key variables that influence political behaviour and consciousness must also be included in the cultural model. As noted, the EU is not a hermetically sealed 'social cocoon', and its economic and cultural impact on Brussels has been profound (in many respects, the EU has been the saviour of the Belgian state, as Milward (1992) has argued).[23] However, the cultural flows between the EU and Brussels have not simply been one-way. The idea that 'functional spillover' from Brussels to the EU might also occur rarely seems to have been contemplated by those EU theorists and analysts who engage in the discourse of 'supranationalism' (most of whom have totally ignored questions of culture).

The notion that any one national culture might emerge as the dominant culture within the EU institutions is anathema to the vision underlying the idea of supranationalism. According to its self-image, the Commission represents a 'cultural melting pot' where different administrative traditions blend together to produce a unique, yet higher form of organisation. That the Belgian political system might somehow penetrate the EU and change the character of its institutions does symbolic and conceptual violence to the idealist principles upon which the ideology of European integration is founded. This, however, is precisely what the 'Brusselsisation of the EU' argument suggests. EU officials may think of themselves as 'deterritorialised' émigrés and rootless cosmopolitans working for an avowedly post-national political entity, but 'deterritorialisation' in this context necessarily implies 'reterritorialisation' – however shallow those cosmopolitan roots may be in the Brussels soil. In short, EU officials and the institutions they serve occupy a social field that is firmly embedded in its specific local context – and just like any other international organisation (the UN, the OECD, the World Health Organisation, the World Bank), it has come to acquire some of the characteristics of its 'host' country. 'It is symptomatic' wrote the journalist Martin Woollacott, 'that the most effective reputation a senior politician like Dehaene can have in Belgium is that of a "fixer", somebody who can broker the deals between warring factions that are monthly and yearly necessary'. It is equally symptomatic that Jean-Luc Dehaene, the Belgian Prime Minister, was the most favoured candidate to succeed Delors as President of the European Commission, and the one most vociferously promoted by France and Germany.[24] For Woollacott, Belgium's volatile Walloon–Flemish ethnic division, its fragmented federal system of government and its tradition of factionalism, brokerage and political clientelism have 'produced a society in which the quota and the spoils system rule'.[25] Quotas and political clientelism are the antithesis of the Commission's self-image and Jean Monnet's rationalist ideal of a 'United States of Europe' cited at the beginning of this chapter. The question explored in the next chapter is, to what extent has the EU remained loyal to these supranational ideals, and what kind of 'society' has been created within its own interior?

Notes

1　Article 157(2) of the Treaty of Rome states that 'members of the Commission shall, in the general interest of the Communities, be completely independent in the performance of their duties' and that 'they shall neither seek nor take instructions from any Government or from any other body' (CEC 1983a: 239–40). This obligation is repeated in Article 11 of the Staff Regulations (1993: 12).

2　This idea is also conveyed in the idiom '*l'engrenage de la violence*', or 'spiral of violence' (see Collins–Robert *French–English Dictionary – Unabridged* Glasgow: Harper Collins 1993: 299).

3　The shift from technical/mechanistic term to key political metaphor (with implicit theory of social change), and from neofunctionalist theory to the discourse of EU officials maps an important trajectory. Unfortunately, tracing that shift is beyond the scope and competence of the present study.

4　See, for example, the discussion of this in O'Neill (1996).

5　Significantly, *engrenage* receives scant analytical attention in most of the standard textbooks on European integration. For example, although Lodge describes *engrenage* as 'vital' to the integration process, her edited volume devotes only two short paragraphs out of 395 pages to describing its importance.

6　For a useful discussion of this, see O'Neill (1996: 37–49).

7　For useful overviews of critical approaches to the study of modern organisations see, *inter alia*, Czarniawska-Joerges (1992); Roper (1994); Wright (1994); and, of course, Max Weber (1948).

8　As Ulf Hannerz (1996:106) writes, '[T]he concept of the expatriate may be that which we will most readily associate with cosmopolitanism'. However, it is not clear from Hannerz's definition whether EU civil servants fall into the category of 'true cosmopolitans' or 'failed cosmopolitans'. The difference turns on the issue of 'willingness to become involved with the Other' (Hannerz 1996: 103)]. While EU staff may well display 'an intellectual and aesthetic openness toward divergent cultural experiences' and 'a search for contrasts rather than uniformity', it is debatable how far this engagement extends to Belgian culture – or, where it does, how desirable the outcome.

9 These souvenir shops are privately owned and have no formal connection with the EU, to my knowledge. However, the EU does promote organisations that sell 'Euro-style' accessories in the member states (such as 'Relay Europe' in the UK).

10 All data comes from Watson and Blythe (1995).

11 During the early 1990s, a series of 'Stop Euro Brussels' posters appeared around the Schuman area. Organised by the *Comité Extrémist Flamand*, these showed a traditional Brussels church and spire being smashed by a large office in the shape of a enormous boot.

12 Cited in Buckley 1998: iii.

13 Ibid.

14 David Gardner, 'Survey of Belgium', *Financial Times*, 25 June 1991: 33.

15 The estimated bill to the Belgian government for relocating three thousand Eurocrats was £26 million per annum over nine years (Tom Walker, *Times*, 31 August 1992: 6).

16 Commission of the European Communities 'Assessment of Exposure to Asbestos Fibres and Development of Safe Working Methods, Berlaymont Building, Brussels', Interim Report submitted by COWI consult, Consulting Engineers and Planners (March 1990). The report found asbestos particle contamination in the carpets and cabinets running along the windows as well as in the cable shafts and ceilings on several storeys of the building and recommended a detailed programme of maintenance and clean-up work. Significantly, it was not until April 1991 – over a year after the report had been submitted – that the Commission decided to evacuate the building. Since the 1990s, several cases of asbestos-related diseases among staff have emerged and at least one former employee, Albert Borchette, has begun legal proceedings for damages against the Commission.

17 As Bellier (1994) points out, this move also resulted in the Commissioners and their *cabinets* being located in a separate office (the Breydel building) from the main body of the EU civil service, thus adding a very important physical dimension to the symbolic distance that already existed between the Commission's political head and administrative body.

18 François-Xavier de Donnea 'The More the Warier', *The Bulletin*, 31 May 1996: 33.

19 For example, the popular 'Perfect European' postcard on sale in every EU tourist shop – depicting a mélange of national stereotypes – caricatures the typical Belgian as simply absent and 'unavailable'. The image is that of an empty desk and an 'on holiday' notice, while the caption reads 'Available as a Belgian'.

20 According to Cohen's definition (1974a: 97), an ethnic group is fundamentally an *informal* organisation that is not formally recognised by the state, 'has no explicitly stated aims and is not rationally and bureaucratically organised'. However, in so far as 'ethnicity' is a dynamic, political process of boundary-formation which 'provides an array of symbolic strategies for solving most or all of the basic problems of organisational articulation', parallels can be drawn between *engrenage* and ethnicity. Both would appear to be strategies for forging distinctiveness and cultural identity.

21 The *Courrier du Personnel*. This newspaper's tendency to endorse official Commission viewpoints had earned it the nickname 'Pravda' among staff. Attempts by its former editor to follow a livelier and more independent editorial line had resulted, it was said, in his being 'promoted sideways' – a euphemism for 'removed

from his post'. In 1997, this weekly newspaper was re-launched under a new title, *Commission en Direct.*

22 As one informant put it, Hay didn't understand the nature of 'the game' and was something of a 'square peg in a round hole'. He subsequently left the Commission to become head of a Christian college, I was told.

23 This is not to endorse Milward's general thesis. The argument that the European Community rescued the nation-state in Europe can be sustained only if one focuses on European political events prior to the 1980s (which Milward does superbly). Since then, the signing of the Single European Act, the Maastricht and Amsterdam Treaties and the launch of the single currency have profoundly shifted the balance of power between the institutions of EU governance and Europe's nation-states in a way that radically undermines Milward's original argument.

24 In the event, the British government rejected Dehaene's candidature in 1994, primarily to mark its opposition to another overtly federalist Commission. Jacques Santer, the Luxembourg premier, was duly chosen as the 'softer' compromise candidate.

25 Martin Woollacott, 'Murder Most Foul', *Guardian*, 25 April 1998: 20.

7 Transnational, supranational or post-national? The 'organisational culture' of the Commission

Supranationalism and intergovernmentalism reconsidered

One of the most contentious themes in the history of European integration since the 1950s has been the irreconcilable tension between two competing models of the emerging European polity; 'intergovernmentalism' and 'supranationalism'. These terms generally refer to what might be called the 'minimalist' vision of the EU as an association of independent nation-states coming together around limited intergovernmental structures, and a 'maximalist' or federalist vision based on the idea of an evolving European political entity into which nation-states will merge (or 'pool') their sovereignty. Advocates of intergovernmentalism argue for a halt to the advancing tide of Europeanisation and propose an intergovernmental arrangement based on co-operation between independent sovereign states, summed up in De Gaulle's notion of a *Europe des patries*. By contrast, proponents of supranationalism see the increasing transfer of decision-making and regulatory powers to supranational institutions in Brussels as a necessary and desirable 'stage' in the supersession of the nation-state. For them, the EU's transition towards a more federal system of governance, broadly following the model of Switzerland or the United States, is the ultimate goal. This debate reflects perhaps the most fundamental of the ideological and political cleavages that have shaped, and continue to shape, the development of the EU.

The previous chapter began our enquiry into the character of EU institutions by focusing on the wider social and geographical context in which they are located. It argued that *engrenage*, the process by which national civil servants and political actors are encouraged to shift their loyalties towards European institutions and ideals, involves a far more complex set of relationships than most theories of European integration allow for. Its contention was that many of the characteristics of the EU's political culture are, in fact, symptomatic of the wider social and political context in which the EU's institutions are embedded. Contact between the EU agents and nationals is therefore not, as integration theories often assume, a one-way process of socialisation in which peripheral peoples become exposed to the domesticating and civilising influences from the European core. Rather, the Europeanisation of national civil servants has been matched simultaneously by the 'Brusselsisation' of much of the EU's civil service. But what are the consequences of these processes of institution-building, bureaucratisation and inter-cultural communication on the EU's emerging political culture? This chapter explores these questions by analysing the internal regime of the European Commission's civil service, particularly its staffing and management policies and administrative practices. It asks, to what extent has the Commission created within its own institutions an environment conducive to the emergence of a supranational, multicultural and post-national political system? How should we characterise the 'organisational culture' of the European Commission?

A 'cultural melting pot'? The EU's hybrid administration

The conventional view of the Commission, often promoted by officials themselves, depicts the Commission's internal regime as a harmonious yet evolving 'mixture' of French and German civil service traditions. To these, it is argued, the accession of new member states has simply 'added' new management methods and practices, building upon the principles of independence, professionalism and service to Europe that were established from the outset. As Commission staff often portrayed it, these different national administrative traditions have 'rubbed off' on to each other in a complementary and cumulative fashion. Or rather, the *best* features of each national civil service had been synthesised and incorporated within a uniquely 'European' model of public administration – in a similar manner to the idea of 'pooled sovereignty'. According to this Commission folk model, the result of this encounter between different national traditions has been a 'creative synergy' that has produced a unique hybrid of an administrative system. The Commission civil service, it is argued, not only embodies the ideal of an independent European administration standing above the interests of the individual member states, it also functions extremely effectively as a policy-maker and executive – as was demonstrated in its successful handling of the single market programme.

These ideas were typically summed up in the metaphors of 'mixing' and 'blending' used by staff to describe the cosmopolitan character of the Commission – a notion reminiscent of alchemy, or the 'melting pot' rhetoric favoured by many emergent multi-ethnic states. The portrait that the Commission frequently presents of itself is that of a mosaic of different nationalities whose 'unity' is contained within, and expressed through, its cultural 'diversity'. Seen in these terms, the 'organisational culture' of the Commission becomes emblematic of European integration in general: an 'ever-closer union of the peoples of Europe' in miniature, forged within the heartland of the EU's own institutions. Implicit in this portrait are the familiar themes of 'Europeanist ideology' that inform EU cultural policy in general: the Commission's characteristically functionalist model of social cohesion, its uncritical assumptions about harmony and consensus, its belief in the moral superiority of supranationalism as a more 'advanced' system of governance, and its unflinching optimism in 'functional spillover' and the transformative effects of close encounters of the European kind. According to this Europeanist vision, the meeting of different national administrative cultures within the

Commission works in a dialectical fashion to produce a new European synthesis in which they are 'blended' together in relatively uncomplicated yet intrinsically complementary and progressive ways, like so many notes in a musical score. To what extent, then, is this image borne out by facts on the ground?

According to David Spence (1994a: 62), what impedes the realisation of this European ideal is the 'unresolved tension between the aim of supranationalism and the reality of encroaching intergovernmentalism'. This tension, he argues, is embedded in the very structure of the Commission and affects virtually all aspects of its internal life. One manifestation of this is reflected in the word 'Commission' itself. In its more restrictive sense, the Commission refers to that collegiate body of twenty political appointees from the various member states who head and speak for the organisation (the 'College of Commissioners'). On the other hand, the word Commission is also used in a much more generic sense to denote the wider organisation of career civil servants, interpreters and the various administrative units beyond the individual Commissioners and their personal staffs (or *cabinets*). The organisational structure of the Commission can therefore be conceptualised as a two-tiered entity with a political head and a civil service body. However, below this is a third sub-tier composed of seconded or non-statutory staff on the one hand and, on the other, of the various external experts, consultants and companies to whom the Commission has contracted out much of its work (for example, in its aid and development projects, its scientific research programmes or its internal security).

These divisions between statutory and non-statutory staff mirror the wider tension between the 'need for a "European" civil service' and 'the practice of the Member States of seconding or "parachuting" national officials into it' (Spence 1994a: 62–3). However, Spence goes further, arguing that the existence of 'divergent administrative cultures' threatens to destroy the coherence, independence and supranational status of the Commission. My own research corroborates this description but rejects the theory that the Commission's internal problems arise from understaffing and the appointment of non-statutory personnel. The problem of what has recently been portrayed as a dysfunctional organisational 'subculture' within the Commission is not due simply to staff shortages or failure to follow the House rules. On the contrary, I suggest that those rules and administrative norms themselves – and the accepted system of political bargaining and networking – are responsible for creating the Commission's unique political culture. As we shall see, many of its characteristics derive from a chronic lack of accountability and the absence of a coherent personnel policy.

Stepping inside the inner world of the Commission civil service, one undoubtedly discovers a land where supranationalism and intergovernmentalism compete for space, and where international relations can be observed in action. However, tensions in staffing and management are complicated by, and inflected through, other political agendas of a more personal, particularistic and local kind. Debates about nationalism, supranationalism and the 'European interest' are thus played out against a background of political patronage and personal networking, self-interest and elite-formation. In the pages that follow I try to make sense of these divisions between 'formal' and 'informal' systems of administration by analysing more closely the norms and staff attitudes and practices that sustain the Commission's so-called 'bicephalous nature' – and the implications this has for the Commission's claim to 'supranational' status.

Character of the Commission as a public service

As EU staff often remark, no template or precedent exists for creating a *European* civil service, and even within the Commission there is little agreement on what an ideal type of European administration should look like, let alone how it might be developed. None the less, over the forty years of its existence the European Commission has developed into an institution with a style and character of its own quite unlike that of any national civil service. As most EU staff and commentators agree, its age, size, origins, ethos, functions, composition and supranational status have combined to produce an institution without parallel among international organisations.[1]

Age and size

Unlike most national civil services, the European Commission is still a relatively young bureaucracy (barely four dacades old at the beginning of this millennium), and one that has undergone continual change in its role and powers as the European Union has grown. From being a 'policy entrepreneur' for much of the 1980s and early 1990s – when most of its work revolved around formulating legislation to complete the single European market – its role since the 1992 Maastricht Treaty has become increasingly managerial and administrative as it has consolidated those policy areas over which it has acquired jurisdiction (cf. Laffan 1997). The Commission is therefore still engaged in the process of inventing itself and, more than most national civil services, Commission staff are constantly obliged to question their own powers and function. When comparing the Commission to national civil services, officials often describe the latter as more 'traditional' and inflexible in their habits. However, for reasons that are both economic (staff shortage) and political (corporate self-interest and resistance to change by the powerful staff unions), administration and personnel is one area of the Commission that has changed least of all since its creation and consequently has come to reflect characteristics of much older and more conservative bureaucracies.[2] More importantly, being young and having been subjected to continual enlargement, it is also a civil service that has only ever experienced growth; never the kind of cuts or retrenchment that most national civil services have been subjected to. As one Director for Personnel observed, it is a civil service devoid of anything resembling a 'culture of cost-consciousness'.

A second striking feature of the Commission is its size. Contrary to popular stereotypes that depict the Commission as a vast Kafkaesque institution composed of legions of 'faceless bureaucrats', the Commission's administrative apparatus has remained surprisingly small and compact. The total statutory workforce of the EU – including the Parliament, Court of Justice, Court of Auditors, and Council of Ministers – currently numbers only 28,000 staff, some 18,000 of whom work for the European Commission, the largest of all the EU institutions. Of these, one third (or roughly six thousand) are senior 'A-grade' officials involved in policy. Its administrative costs are also relatively small compared with most national civil services, representing only 5.0 per cent of total EU expenditure in 1996, up from just 4 per cent in 1988.[3] It is often pointed out that in terms of staff numbers 'the Commission's policy and executive services are about the same size as the French Ministry of Culture or the Lord Chancellor's Department in the British Civil Service, and smaller than the total staff of the City of Amsterdam or the *Comunidad Autonoma* of Madrid' (Hay 1989: 31).[4] However, unlike the City of Amsterdam or Barcelona, the EU is responsible for an annual budget of some Euro 80 billion, and for initiating and managing a much larger range of policies. Although the Commission has grown dramatically since its inception, when it numbered just a few hundred staff from the then six EEC founder member states, its growth has not been commensurate with either the increasing size of the Union's population or the expansion of its tasks.

The great majority of Commission staff are concentrated in Brussels and Luxembourg, but its research staff, covering everything from physicists to statisticians and numbering over 3,500, are spread over five centres throughout the Union, including Ispra in Italy, Culham in Britain and Geel in Belgium. In addition, the Commission has some twenty-three offices in the various member state capitals and regional centres, including Munich, Milan, Barcelona, Cardiff and Marseilles, as well as over 120 external delegations and sub-offices from Argentina to Zimbabwe.

The supposed army of Brussels 'Eurocrats' is therefore largely a myth. Many officials expressed amusement at public perceptions of the Commission. As one Greek official put it: 'in Greece they think we have large teams of experts working on each area of policy. In reality, whole areas of policy making are overseen by single units – sometimes even by just one individual.' Just how thinly spread the Commission is was summed up by another official:

> I remember when I worked in the Brittan *cabinet*. An MEP raised a question about car insurance policy which required an urgent answer. When we tried to find the unit responsible for the policy we discovered that it was all down to one man – and he was on holiday. Luckily, he hadn't left Brussels and so we were able to get him back. But that incident made me aware of how tight things are here.

Among senior Commission officials there is a certain pride in this institutional leanness. In the words of its former Secretary-General, David Williamson, 'the European Commission is a lean machine'.[5] This metaphor conjures up the ideal qualities of a modern public administration: slim, functional, technical/rational, streamlined, and efficient. One advantage of this small size, frequently cited by officials, is that it has enabled the Commission to develop a close and effective web of personal contacts with national civil servants, politicians, MEPs, pressure groups and lobbyists. According to Keith Middlemas (1995), these contacts are an important ingredient in the creation of what he calls the EU's 'informal' system of governance. As Middlemas agues, the personal nature of ties within the Brussels-based elite has led to the rise of a vibrant 'informal political infra-structure' among the various 'corporate players' involved in the EU political 'game' (Middlemas 1995: xv). For Middlemas, whose theoretical analysis is heavily steeped in the language and assumptions of 'games theory', it is precisely this proliferating system of informal networks based on personal contacts that makes it possible to have an effective and dynamic machinery of power at European level. 'As the competitive symposium extends itself, a sort of interdependence becomes established', he writes:

> Bargaining through networks in a densely structured game reduces friction and produces results for which the formal system may be ill attuned, even on ostensibly formal matters such as easier implementation and enforcement of laws. It allows for wide, flexible participation; it reduces inconsistencies; it gives rise to conventions, rather than formal rules, which can be adapted more easily over time.
>
> (Middlemas 1995: xvi)

Two points emerge from this intriguing thesis. First, that the Commission has remained so small is itself a reflection of the success of *engrenage* and the Commission's ability to 'Europeanise' national civil servants so that they become, consciously or unconsciously, agents and accomplices for promoting EU policies. (Laura Cram (1993) makes a similar point in her essay 'Playing the Tune without Paying the Piper'). Second, the negative side of this dynamic 'informal political infrastructure' that Middlemas and others so enthusiastically endorse is that it also creates conditions that are ideal for encouraging practices of fraud, nepotism and corruption.

The problem of understaffing, however, is not evenly spread across the services. For example, DG IX (personnel), with its 2,600 officials, and DG XII (research), with over 2,000 staff, were described as anything but overstretched. It also tends to be most acute in the more recent sectors or policy areas where the Commission has, for budgetary reasons, been unable to adapt its staffing to meet sudden changes or needs. This problem is compounded by the slow machinery for recruiting new staff and the lack of mobility between different services within the civil service. As one senior official in DG IX commented, 'many staff spend their entire career in the same DG'.[6] As a result, the Commission has been obliged to follow a policy of contracting out much of its work to consultants, companies and various categories of external experts – a practice that has resulted, according to some analysts, in growing incidences of fraud, mismanagement and corruption.

Origins and ethos

Like all bureaucratic institutions, the Commission still carries in its organisational structure the stamp of the ideas and practices that prevailed at the time of its creation. The origins of the Commission can be traced to the High Authority of the European Coal and Steel Community (ECSC), set up in 1952. The Commission is typically perceived as the heir not only to the functional tasks of the High Authority, upon which its own internal structure was modelled, but also to the federalist hopes that prevailed in that era. When the European Economic Community (EEC) and European Atomic Energy Community (Euratom) were created in 1958, each had its own separate Commission. These were subsequently merged into a single organisation in 1967, which became the 'Commission of the European Communities'. Jean Monnet, the first president of the ECSC and a former head of France's powerful state body, the *Commissariat au Plan*, played a decisive role in devising its structure and working methods. The vision of the Commission entertained by Monnet, as noted earlier, was that of a small, tightly knit elite bound together by a strong *esprit de corps*. The idea was to create a vanguard of committed, de-nationalised Europeans who would become effective agents for creating and diffusing the European idea over and above the parochial and sectarian interests of the individual nation-states. Monnet hoped that the supranational institutions in Luxembourg would create an environment conducive to the emergence of a new type of supranational being, or 'European Man'. The idea of an *independent* civil service of permanent officials imbued with its own ethic was thus deemed essential to the task of building this new European order. By the same logic, Monnet rejected the model of delegated or temporary and seconded national civil servants typical of most other international organisations such as NATO, the UN or UNESCO. Perhaps not surprisingly, however, given his own background, Monnet drew on the French civil service as the model for designing this new European civil service.

The rules of the European public service, set out in the Staff Regulations, were therefore designed to guarantee the independence and autonomy of Community officials, as well as to ensure recruitment of individuals of the 'highest quality'. Community officials were also obliged to pledge loyalty to the European Community and promise to uphold and defend its interest above all others. These principles, enshrined in Article 11 of the Staff Regulations, were no doubt designed to give formal expression to the supranational vision as well as to be a catalyst for promoting a supranational consciousness and sense of mission among Commission staff. Whether commitment to the European idea was (or remains) something actively selected for in staff recruitment is an open question. In all probability, recruitment is a consequence of both selection and self-selection (see below). This is essentially what the studies by Willis (1982) and Eichener (1992) concluded:

> The Commission officials' typical motivational structure is quite different from that of the average national government official. The Commission

recruits from people who are highly motivated, risk-oriented, polyglot, cosmopolitan, open-minded and innovative . . . From the beginnings in the 1960s to the present, it has indeed been officials of a special type who chose to leave the relative security of their national administrations to go to Brussels to do there a well-paid but extremely challenging job. These people mutually stabilise their motivational structures with a distinct *esprit de corps*.

(Eichener 1992: 53)

Such claims concerning the psychology of Commission officials are, of course, difficult to verify. Perhaps a more useful approach, therefore, is to analyse what officials actually do and say, and from here track the connections between organisation and ideology and the way these relate to officials' representations of themselves. Much of the Commission's uniqueness derives, as noted, from its unusually complex legal status and powers. Under the EU's founding treaties, the European Commission is not only guardian of the Treaties and initiator of legislation, it is also commonly portrayed as the dynamo or heart of the integration process. In its own words, 'the Commission represents the common interest and embodies, to a large degree the personality of the Union' (CEC 1995a: 7). According to Pascal Fontaine's book *Europe in Ten Lessons*, it is the body that 'represents the interests of Community as a whole' (Fontaine 1995: 12). What this means in practice, however, is seldom specified. Typically, the Commission defines its role as that of an 'honest broker', or impartial referee,[7] 'holding the ring against national rivalries, sectional interests and attempts at unilateralism' (Davignon *et al.* 1995: 78). The notion of a *fonction publique européenne* and the idea of being positioned 'above' national politics have therefore become key themes in structuring the identity and self-image of Commission officials. According to the Staff Regulations, the independence of EU civil servants, particularly from their member states of origin, must be 'beyond doubt'. The Regulations embody the same proclamation of independence, obligation to distance oneself from any external or 'partisan influence', and promise to uphold the Community interest, as the oath sworn by members of the College of Commissioners (CEC 1995a: 7). As a result, as Marc Abélès (1995: 81) observes, the concept of 'European interest' has become a 'floating signifier' that permeates the discourse of EU officials. According to this logic, the Commission and its staff are the embodiment of the supranational political ideal. To quote Abélès:

Ce que fait la spécificité de la Commission, c'est moins son caractère bureaucratique que le fait qu'elle fonctionne en grande partie à une idéel. L'existence d'un dispositif idéel articulé sur la représentation d'une Europe à venire est une donnée fondamentale: ce dispositif est totalement imbriqué dans l'univers de la Commission.

(Abélès 1995: 81)[8]

Many Commission officials thus appear to have internalised the official EU discourses concerning their institutional role and status and have come to see themselves as pioneers of the new European order. Significantly too, the term 'Community interest' has become increasingly elided with that of 'European interest' as though these terms were interchangeable or equivalent. As a result, the Commission has increasingly arrogated to itself the idea that it, alone, 'represents the European interest'. This kind of discourse invariably tends to encourage a sense of mission among staff and encourages them to see themselves as pioneers and architects of the new Europe, as the vanguard of history.

Dominance of French administrative norms and practices

From its inception, the Commission was structured primarily around French (and, to a lesser extent, German) administrative norms and practices. These were fundamentally different to those of the British civil service model where the ideal mandarin was traditionally a high-minded, non-party-political, flexible all-rounder and Oxbridge generalist (Hennessy 1990: 159–60). By contrast, the French administrative model is geared to selecting highly specialised experts and technocrats – lawyers, economists and professional administrators – from the elitist French *grande école* tradition and the Ecole Nationale d'Administration (ENA) where most of the French ruling class have been educated.[9] Other distinguishing characteristics of the French '*grand corps*' model include a 'highly politicised senior management closely linked to the party in power', the powerful *cabinet* system – whereby members of a Commissioner's private office preside over staffing policy in the various services – and the tendency to 'use information as a constituent element of a bureaucratic and political power base' (Spence 1994a: 91). The combination of a formal system composed of 'rigid bureaucratic structures' and rather inflexible legal rules and a pervasive 'informal' system based around personal networks and extremely 'flexible' working methods was also seen by staff as a typically French civil service trait (Spence 1994a: 64).

Another manifestation of the francophone character of the Commission's organisational culture was the dominance of the French language. From the beginning, French was the major working language of administration and management. Not only are meetings of the College of Commissioners held in French, but French remains the official working language of the Secretariat-General. This is the key horizontal service within the Commission whose role, like that of the British Cabinet Office, is to give strategic direction and co-ordination to the work of the other DGs. As a result, 'instructions from the core of the European administration in French imbue the institution with a mentality which looks to French culture and administrative norms as the unstated model of public administration' (Spence 1994a: 64). During fieldwork it was evident that, while French continues to be the dominant language of everyday administration and personnel, English is rapidly displacing it.[10] As a result, an interesting pattern of language-use has emerged. French remains the *lingua franca* of everyday administration and the main language among older staff and within certain DGs (notably the DGs for Development, Agriculture and Administration), while English appears to be ascendant in many others, and particularly among younger recruits.

Alongside these French civil service traditions, the German model, 'more legal-istic and rigid, formed the basis of the European Audit Office, which followed the design of the "*Bundesrechnungshof*" ' (Spence 1994a: 64). This pattern reflected the political weight of the EEC's two leading countries. Just as the Franco-German alliance has traditionally set the agenda for political integration, so these two countries' systems of public administration provided the basic model (at least the formal model)[11] from which the EU civil service has developed. That French, rather than the German, administrative norms and practices predominate – par-ticularly in the areas of personnel and management, the *cabinet* system and the Secretariat-General – is also partly attributable to Emile Nöel, the Commission's first Secretary-General who held this strategic post from 1958 until his retirement in 1987. As Ludlow (1991: 95) states:

> Nöel dominated the administration and was a formidable figure at the political level. His style, however, was very personal, and co-ordination, where it occurred, was effected largely through his own actions and those of his trusted staff members planted throughout the administration.

This pattern of cultivating personal networks within the organisation by planting trusted supporters in key positions was extended even further during the Delors era. This was deeply resented by Commission officials, particularly the staff unions, who claimed that these informal practices undermined the professional-ism and independence of the service. At the time of fieldwork, there was a notice-able backlash of opinion against the Delors 'regime' and the informal administra-tive system that had flourished during his presidency. The general view was that powerful individuals in the Delors *cabinet* had flagrantly abused the formal House procedures to remove those deemed problematic (such as the former Director-General for Personnel, Richard Hay) and to occupy the key posts with 'their people'. 'Delors's people' usually meant trusted French, male, *grand école* high-fliers with close links to the Socialist Party. However, those union officials who railed against these breaches and abuses of the 'House rules' were often identi-fied by colleagues as among the main beneficiaries of the informal system of networks and patronage. An active role in the staff unions[12] or in a Commis-sioner's *cabinet* were often seen as strategies for fast-track promotion for the ambitious *fonctionnaire*. These positions placed one in an ideal position to culti-vate 'friends in high places' – which was widely acknowledged as the 'way to get ahead' in the House.

This juxtaposition of extremely formal rules and high-minded idealism, on the one hand, with heavy reliance on flexible and informal practices, on the other, was one of the most striking features of the Commission's administrative culture. It was also the key characteristic most commonly identified and commented upon by staff themselves. This combination of a formal corporate system that is rigidly bureaucratic and legalistic, counter balanced by everyday practices that are highly fluid, informal and particularistic, was said to be 'typically French'. John Mole echoes this theme in his analysis of the French corporate tradition:

Rules and procedures are rarely broken but they are constantly distorted, manipulated and ignored if they do not serve the purpose for which they were intended . . . Beneath the apparent structure of the organisation there is usually an invigorating sub-culture based on informal networking and characterised by flexibility, scepticism and energy.

(Mole 1992: 19)

This dualism can be observed within the European Commission – a body modelled closely on the French public corporation. Non-French officials with experience in their own national administrations are particularly struck by the hierarchical and political character of the Commission's administration. As one Spanish official summed it up, 'it is a bit like the Mexican army: hierarchical, slow and top-heavy with too many generals and not enough clerical back-up or support'. Another official compared it to the Danish national administration:

When I came here I noticed how French the whole system was. It's more hierarchical and formal. The paper trails are much bigger. Everything I write has to be signed by my Head of Unit, then signed again by his superior, and so on up the ladder. You're not allowed to sign anything in your own name – even a simple letter to a colleague in another unit has to go all the way up and then all the way back down again. We call it the 'Christmas tree' approach. It was not like this in the Danish civil service; I find it very slow and irritating. On the other hand, I enjoy working here more than Denmark. The positive difference is that the work is more stimulating and the environment is much more cosmopolitan and multicultural. Different DGs have different corporate cultures. For example, in DG III I worked in French all the time. Here in DG 1A I work in English 75 per cent of the time. But after a while you stop identifying people as 'nationals'. Perhaps that's because we're all 'bloody foreigners'.

However, other officials rejected the characterisation of the Commission's administrative culture as 'typically French': as one Belgian official put it: 'you British see it as a "French" system. It is not "French", or "German". It is the continental system.' Revealingly, he added: 'They say the Union must be closer to its citizens, but we will never talk the same language as the citizens. Ours is a language of compromise . . . we are creating a new language: a Euro-pidgin language.'

Structure and grading

The Commission is organised into twenty-seven Directorates-General, or 'DGs'. Each of these is known by its name and number, typically referred to by Roman numerals ('DG II – Economic and Financial Affairs', 'DG VIII – Development', DG XX – Financial Control'). In many respects, DGs are analogous to government departments and are often described by EU analysts as 'mini-ministries', each headed by a Director-General under the authority of a particular Commissioner. Staff themselves often used the word 'fiefdoms' to describe the arrangement of DGs and services. DGs in turn are sub-divided into 'directorates' and, below these, individual units, headed by a Director and *Chef de Unite* ('Head of Unit').

In theory each DG broadly corresponds to a distinct policy area. In practice, however, the need to give portfolios to new Commissioners following successive EU enlargements has led to the creation of some rather artificial DGs. It has also resulted in the splitting of existing DGs in ways that have resulted in a confusion of competencies, most notably in the field of external relations, which now spans five separate DGs. This reflects another important feature of the Commission: the extent to which its growth has been conditioned not by rational, long-term planning but by short-term, political considerations, particularly the need to create jobs and provide a balanced spread of posts of adequate seniority to satisfy the member states. In the words of one senior French official:

> The *organigramme* has grown largely to make room for the enlargement states. We've created some useless posts and units as a result, especially in the area of middle-management. DGs XXII, XXIII and XXIV were invented simply so that the new member states could have their own Director-Generals.

In addition to the twenty-seven DGs, there are a number of temporary task forces and special units, as well as five 'horizontal' service departments. Foremost among these are the Secretariat-General, Legal Service, Inspectorate-General, Spokesman's Service, Security and Statistical Offices and Informatics Directorate, most of which are under the direct authority of the Commission President. DGs vary in size from under 120 staff in the smallest such as Credit and Investment (DG XVIII) and Enterprise Policy (DG XXIII) to 894 and 2,600 in the largest, Agriculture (DG IV) and Administration (DG IX) respectively.

By custom, a Director-General and the Commissioner to which he or she is answerable should be of different nationalities, the logic being to prevent national 'clusters' forming as this could conceivably lead to charges of complicity and favouritism. However, this principle is not strictly adhered to. For example, during the Delors III Commission in the early 1990s, both Karel Van Miert, the Commissioner for DG IX (which overseas the staffing policy of the Commission), and its Director-General, Frans de Koster, were Belgians. The general view among staff was that this was a mistake as far as the sensitive issues of recruitment and national quotas were concerned and that having two Belgians in charge of personnel was, in the words of one official, like 'putting Dracula in charge of the blood-donor unit'.

As in every civil service, staff are organised hierarchically according to grade and function, and these status distinctions have an important baring on identity formation. In general, Commission officials were extremely conscious of rank and status, and their conduct towards other staff would shift to reflect this accordingly

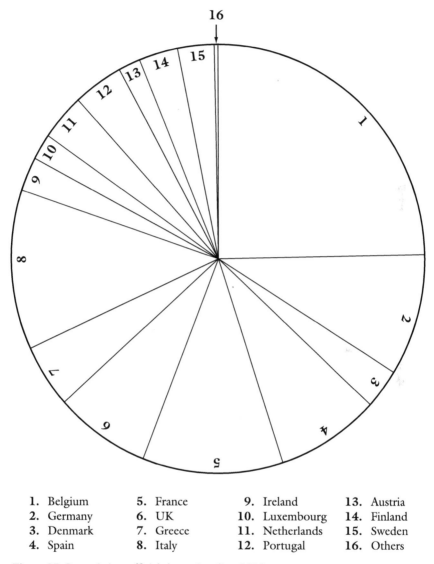

Figure 17 Commission officials by nationality, 1999.
Source: European Commission, DG IX, 1999.

1. Belgium	**5.** France	**9.** Ireland	**13.** Austria
2. Germany	**6.** UK	**10.** Luxembourg	**14.** Finland
3. Denmark	**7.** Greece	**11.** Netherlands	**15.** Sweden
4. Spain	**8.** Italy	**12.** Portugal	**16.** Others

(for example, in patterns of formality, and terms of address). Grading of staff follows the French administrative model, with four discrete bands, labelled with clinical simplicity, A–D (see Tables 1–5). A-grade officials are those, at the top of the hierarchy, responsible for the formulation and management of policy. They are the administrative elite entrusted with what in French is called *conception*, 'a concept that is perhaps best translated as "creative thinking"' (Cini 1996: 116).

Tables 1–4 Commission staff by nationality (%) (*Source*: Spence 1994a; European Commission, DG IX, 1999)

1   Senior A-grade officials

Country	1974	1980	1989	1994	1999
Belgium	13.1	13.5	12.1	12.0	10.7
Germany	18.7	19.0	14.9	13.8	12.0
Denmark	3.8	3.0	2.4	2.9	2.8
Spain			10.1	10.5	10.5
France	18.5	20.2	6.5	16.5	15.0
UK	14.9	14.5	11.7	11.4	10.8
Greece			4.7	5.4	5.3
Italy	18.2	17.4	13.4	13.1	12.3
Ireland	3.9	2.9	3.3	3.4	3.0
Luxembourg	3.1	2.9	1.6	1.0	0.7
Netherlands	6.3	6.0	5.4	5.5	5.0
Portugal			3.9	4.1	3.9
Austria					2.5
Finland					2.4
Sweden					3.0
Others					0.1

2   B-grade officials

Country	1974	1980	1989	1994	1999
Belgium	23.2	27.8	30.0	33.2	31.9
Germany	19.7	16.2	10.5	9.0	7.4
Denmark	2.9	2.5	2.5	2.0	2.1
Spain			9.0	9.1	8.9
France	17.2	16.5	11.4	11.2	9.6
UK	7.3	8.4	6.9	6.8	6.1
Greece			3.4	2.8	3.3
Italy	14.0	13.5	11.4	11.2	10.1
Ireland	1.5	1.2	2.5	2.5	2.6
Luxembourg	5.8	5.3	3.4	2.0	2.0
Netherlands	7.6	7.7	6.2	6.2	5.1
Portugal			2.7	2.8	2.5
Austria					1.9
Finland					3.3
Sweden					2.6
Others					0.3

B-grade officials, by contrast, are technicians, administrators and record keepers, and typically concern themselves with more routine administrative tasks. Secretaries, clerical officers, typists and support staff are classified as C-grade officials. The vast majority (some 80 per cent) of all secretarial staff are women, with the highest percentage being Belgians (1,856 or 39 per cent) and Italians (613 or 13 per cent) followed by French and Germans (roughly 400 or 8 per cent

3   C-grade secretarial staff

Country	1974	1980	1989	1994	1999
Belgium	39.8	39.9	39.0	39.6	38.1
Germany	13.6	11.0	8.1	8.6	8.3
Denmark	2.5	3.2	2.9	2.9	2.4
Spain			5.3	5.4	5.2
France	12.9	12.9	8.1	8.0	8.0
UK	3.3	4.9	4.8	5.6	5.0
Greece			3.3	3.5	3.7
Italy	13.8	15.0	14.7	13.4	12.3
Ireland	1.9	2.1	2.3	2.8	3.1
Luxembourg	7.1	8.2	4.4	3.8	3.0
Netherlands	4.1	3.4	2.5	2.2	2.0
Portugal			2.3	3.6	3.5
Austria					1.0
Finland					2.0
Sweden					1.8
Others					0.2

4   D-grade Commission staff

Country	1974	1980	1989	1994	1999
Belgium	34.6	35.7	36.7	36.4	37.0
Germany	5.5	4.3	1.6	1.0	0.9
Denmark			0.6	0.7	1.0
Spain			3.6	5.4	5.9
France	6.6	3.8	7.0	7.8	6.4
UK	1.7	2.4	1.1	1.0	0.9
Greece			3.3	4.6	4.3
Italy	42.7	43.5	34.6	32.8	29.7
Ireland			0.2	0.2	0.5
Luxembourg	7.2	8.2	6.5	5.3	4.0
Netherlands	1.2	1.2	1.4	1.0	0.9
Portugal			2.5	3.0	4.4
Austria					1.2
Finland					1.2
Sweden					0.9
Others					0.5

each (data from DG IX, 12 February 1996). D-grade staff – some two-thirds of whom are Belgians and Italians (36 per cent and 32 per cent respectively) – are the service workers: drivers, porters (*huissiers*), cleaners and labourers. Translators and interpreters – numbering some 1,700 in total, and referred to collectively as 'LAs' – have a separate system of grading.

Within each grade there are further divisions reflecting distinctions of seniority

Table 5 Full-time Commission officials by nationality, 1999 (*Source:* European Commission, DG IX. Figures do not include staff employed under the 'research' budget or employees in the Official Publications Office)

Country	A-grade	B-grade	C-grade	D-grade	Lang.	Total
Belgium	536	974	1951	283	181	3925
Germany	605	226	429	7	232	1499
Denmark	144	66	123	8	132	73
Spain	526	272	270	45	171	1284
France	752	293	410	49	119	1623
UK	542	187	256	7	195	1187
Greece	269	100	192	33	145	739
Italy	616	309	630	227	187	1969
Ireland	147	80	160	4	19	410
Luxembourg	35	64	155	31	9	294
Netherlands	254	156	101	7	82	600
Portugal	196	75	179	34	129	613
Austria	129	58	53	9	19	268
Finland	120	101	103	9	129	462
Sweden	148	80	91	7	120	446
Others	6	10	9	4	11	40
Total	5025	3051	5112	764	1880	15832

and responsibility. A-grade officials are divided into eight 'rungs' or career levels, from A8s at the bottom (assistant administrators) which is the point of entry of new graduates, to A1s and A2s which are normally (but not necessarily) director-generals and assistant director-generals. A5 and A4 staff are the middle-ranking officials who tend to be the mainstay of the organisation. It is important to note that the normal career path for most officials ends at the A4 rank, the higher posts being political appointments and not subject to the normal statutory provisions. This 'glass ceiling' as some call it, creates a bottleneck that is a major source of frustration among the more ambitious officials. Indeed, the majority of A-grade staff tend to occupy the middle-ranking posts which creates an unusual pyramidal structure compared to that found in most hierarchical organisations. The heavy presence of A-grade officials within the EU civil service further distorts the normal pyramidal pattern. With some six thousand A-grade staff, the administrative cadres constitute roughly one-third of all statutory employees in the Commission – hence the 'Mexican army' anecdote. This extraordinarily high ratio of senior grade officials to technical and secretarial staff (1:3) is another factor that sets the Commission apart from any national civil service. By comparison, the British civil service, which has over 500,000 non-industrial staff, is headed by a small administative elite of some 25,000: a ratio of approximately 1:25.[13]

The Commission is further divided into 'statutory' staff (all those whose posts are covered by the rights and duties set out in the Staff Regulations) and 'non-statutory' (or 'external') staff. This category includes all those seconded national experts ('ENDs') and temporary agents ('ATs') who, like members of the *cabinets*, fall outside of the EU's 'supranational pillar' of administration and are not part of what is termed the 'European public service'. Thus, a certain tension characterises the relationship between statutory and non-statutory staff – the latter being perceived as 'outsiders' and 'not of the House' (Cini 1996: 110). Since the evacuation of the Berlaymont, Commissioners and their *cabinets* have been relocated to the Breydel building, at some distance from the DGs they are meant to oversee. As Bellier (1994) observes, this relocation introduced a psychological as well as physical distance between the Commission's political head and civil service body. This distance also plays a significant role in the alleged loss of control by the political authorities over the administration (see below).

Paper, power and hierarchy

The hierarchical and bureaucratic nature of the administration were among the 'cultural' characteristics most frequently cited by new recruits. These included 'endless signing of letters and memos', 'no sense of urgency', an 'etiquette of deference and formality' with superiors ('even when you get to know people quite closely, they still insist you always use 'vous''); 'rigid procedures that discourage personal initiative', a 'lack of access to information' and the 'annoying habit of people using national and party links to circumvent the system'. Staff were particularly scornful of the House rule by which civil servants of equivalent positions are not allowed to sign letters to each other. As Bramwell (1987) notes, regulations require not only that all correspondence must be 'signed' by superiors but also that at each chain in the transaction the letter must be photocopied and filed – even the photocopyist must sometimes sign a form acknowledging his or her contribution to the paper trail. As one young Dutch official commented, 'it's a very bureaucratic French system'. 'Everything still gets passed around in old folders. But there is now a network of young people who use email to bypass the system. The result is that they can have a document or letter four days before the Director-General gets it.' The costs of this paper mountain are considerable, in psychological as well as in ecological and economic terms. Bramwell (1987: 73) calculated that, in 1981 alone, '29 million photocopies were taken in the main EC building . . . while 126 million pieces of paper were produced in the Berlaymont building in 1982' – and that was when the Commission was half its current size and housed largely in one building. Curiously, this system of multiple photocopying was introduced, Bramwell informs us, not so much for reasons of administrative efficiency but rather as an attempt to prevent the loss of incoming letters and to check outgoing letters as part of an anti-corruption move.

In all bureaucracies, access to information and document retrieval constitute an important basis for power and control. According to Bramwell (1987: 72), however, the customary practice relating to minuting and filing represents one area within the Commission where there is 'an irreconcilable clash of political cultures' and where international rivalry is most blatant. He argues that unlike the civil services of Germany, the Netherlands and Denmark, which were all radically reorganised after the war and now keep files in a centralised filing system in each Ministry, France and Italy did not undergo this process. French civil servants tend to keep their own files on specific subjects and a centralised record-keeping system in the German or British sense is uncommon ('archive' in French referring primarily to a body of printed material, for example printed legislation). A similar system prevails in the Commission. This was also borne out in my interviews with staff, some of whom reported arriving at a new post to find a bare office with just a desk and telephone. Bramwell's explanation for this practice once again emphasises the 'legalism' discussed earlier:

> Because of occasional informality, favouritism and blatant corruption in the early days of the EEC, there was a fixed bias among older civil servants against the idea of retrievable material, lest it be used for court cases against the EEC, and the recent introduction of a thirty-year release rule for Commission records aroused dismay for this reason.
>
> (Bramwell 1987: 73)

Evidence that these practices persist emerged during the recent crisis over BSE, or 'Mad Cow' disease. In December 1996, the European Parliament's Committee of Enquiry into BSE published a scathing report condemning the Commission's and Council's 'negligence' and 'maladministration' in handling the BSE affair. A key target of criticism was the administrative practices of the Commission's Standing Veterinary Committee. 'It is extremely difficult to evaluate the actions of the Standing Veterinary Committee', it wrote:

> as it seems, no minutes are kept of its meetings, other than brief summaries, which have not been forwarded to the present committee of inquiry, despite repeated requests to this effect by its chairman. The sole available information consists of the minutes of meetings drawn up by the Danish delegation.
>
> (Ortega 1996: 11)

Composition

Three things stand out above all others when one considers the inner world of the Commission. First, its multinational and multilingual character. Just stepping into a lift or walking along the corridor or sitting in one of the many staff refectories, one immediately registers the diversity of languages being used – and the curiously agile way in which individuals flit between languages, depending on who has just joined or left the group. Most of the officials whom I encountered spoke at least three languages, sometimes more. This was yet another contributory factor to the sense of solidarity and identity among EU staff and their children, and their sense of 'difference' from those some described dismissively as 'monoglots'. A further aspect of the way EU officials constitute a 'linguistic community' was reflected in the peculiar in-house *argot* or jargon. 'Commission-speak', as

Bramwell (1987: 65) calls it, 'is a cumbersome melange of bureaucratese and French'. This description is accurate. Everyday conversation among EU staff in the canteen, for example, draws on a plethora of Euro-acronyms and neologisms peculiar to the institutions and guaranteed to exclude all but the initiated. Many words and expressions, even fundamental legal concepts such as 'subsidiarity' and '*acquis communautaire*', are barely translatable. Thus, people speak of going '*en mission*' to Strasbourg; of holding a '*tour de table*'; of working for 'EMAC'; or 'IGCs' and 'ENDs'; of problems with an 'AT'; of the difficulties of getting some-one from 'ECHO' to speak to their '*Stagiaire*'; and of their frustrations at being passed over for promotion owing to lack of *piston*, or because of a *sousmarin*.

The second notable feature is the high intellectual and professional calibre of the A-grade staff themselves. They are an impressive group by any standards, often with a clutch of degrees and professional qualifications, and CVs that would put to shame those from more modest backgrounds. In terms of their educational backgrounds, they frequently hail from the most prestigious institutions of their home countries. These include French *Grand Ecole* alumni, British 'Oxbridge' fellows, Italian *Boccone* students and an increasingly large number of 'MA in European Studies' graduates from the *Collège d'Europe* in Bruges and Johns Hopkins University in Bologna. An extraordinarily large number of those I met were also authors and academics who had published on European Union affairs. This also reflected an interesting aspect of the way A-grade civil servants saw themselves: as policy-makers and intellectuals rather than administrators and pub-lic servants.

The third interesting feature is the distribution of nationalities within the Commission. Generally speaking, it has long been accepted that the number of senior (A-grade) posts allocated to each member state should be roughly com-mensurate with the size of its population. Thus Germany, France, Italy and the UK (followed by Spain) are recognised as the EU member states that should have a larger claim on staff resources than their smaller partners like Belgium or Greece. Unlike the World Bank, where voting rights and staff allocations correlate closely with the size of a member-state's contribution to the bank's finances, Monnet's vision of the European civil service emphasised meritocracy and auton-omy.[14] Except at the most senior levels (A3–A1), national quotas are considered anathema and a violation of all that the European idea stands for. However, it is an open secret in Brussels that an informal system of national quotas exists – although legal and political considerations require this to be systematically denied. 'Respecting geographical balance' has therefore become the respectable euphemism for talking about national quotas in staffing.

Despite the evident concern to ensure a more equitable or less 'geographically challenged' distribution of posts, certain marked imbalances persist. Belgians and Italians continue to be heavily over-represented at all levels: for example, in 1996 some 4,300 of the 18,000 statutory staff were Belgians, including 663 A-grades out of a total of 5,969. This compared with 2,887 Italians (835 of whom were A-grades); 2,066 French (950 of whom were A-grades); 1,952 Germans (793 A-grades), and 1,448 from the UK (708 A-grades). Britain, along with Germany and the Netherlands, was one of the foremost 'deficit countries'. Indeed, so serious was this 'deficit' that the British Cabinet Office had seconded an official to compile a report analysing the causes of British under-recruitment. It had also created, several years earlier, a 'European Fast Stream' initiative within Whitehall to improve the take-up rate of British applicants to the EU. Among that seconded official's findings regarding the main obstacles to British recruitment (which included the anti-EU sentiment of the British press, lack of linguistic ability and broad European knowledge), was the observation that British recruits were handicapped by uncertainty about how to lobby or network. 'There is a different ethos and employment culture in the UK and Nordic countries. All candidates should understand the meaning of the word *piston*.' In his words 'excessive modesty is not necessarily regarded as a particularly great virtue here'.

The preponderance of Belgian and Italians in the lower grades is largely attributed to historical factors, primarily the location of the EU in Brussels. Recruiting locally is cheaper and easier – and many locals themselves are second-generation Italians from families that migrated to the mining and industrial areas of Wallonia during the 1950s and 1960s. However, the dominance of Belgians was also attributed to the fact that they had 'leaned to play the system'. As one local Brussellois acknowledged, a job in the EU is the single most sought-after career among Belgian students. According to Cini (1996: 126) the massive over-representation of Belgians in the lower grades 'does not concern national government too much, as these grades have little, if any, influence on policy'. However, as several officials acknowledged, secretaries – like members of a *cabinet* – often exert influence over what their bosses get to see, as well as who gets to see them.

Within DGs the composition of nationalities is normally quite mixed, the policy being to avoid 'national clusters'. However, some units acquire a reputation as strongholds for particular nationalities and regional minorities. As Bramwell (1987: 70–1) noted, certain sub-national groupings were heavily over represented in the Commission. In the case of France, Corsicans and Alsacians prevailed, with Basques and Bretons a long way behind. For Britain, Welshmen (referred to locally as the 'Taffia') were prominent, particularly in the upper reaches, as were Northern Irish. For Italy, Neapolitans were the most important minority.[15]

Recruitment

For most recruits, becoming a *fonctionnaire* is an arduous and lengthy process which requires both stamina and determination and skills in networking and self-promotion. The selection process is based on the *concours* system, the standard mode of entry into the French civil service. Competition for places is extremely tough. For example, in the competition for A7/8-grade recruits launched in June 1993, some 56,000 candidates took the exams for a total of only six hundred places on the 'reserve list'. However, from sitting the first 'pre-selection' test to getting on to the reserve list often takes over two years and even then there is no guarantee of a post. Historically, only half those who pass their exams and get on to the reserve list eventually find a job. Simply holding that *concours* was a major feat of organisation: on the same day, at the same hour, 56,000 candidates were seated in front of their exam scripts in over thirty different venues across Europe, from the Hammersmith Palais in London, to the Heisel stadium in Brussels. Fifteen months later, the six hundred successful candidates who had got on to the reserve list were announced. Most of these candidates can expect to wait anything up to two or three years before they are taken off the reserve list (if at all). In the words of DG IX's Head of Recruitment, 'the process itself is a deterrent. You have to have a lot of patience. But perseverance and determination are qualities we select for.' However, given the pressure for places, that 'determination' some-times leads to other strategies. In March 1998, the entire entrance exam involving over thirty thousand candidates had to be cancelled at a cost of Ecu 1.2 million after evidence of widespread cheating was reported in Rome, Milan and Heisel.[16] Lax and often incompetent exam procedures in Brussels resulted in large number of participants calling friends on their mobile phones from the toilets to find the answers to questions. More importantly, the Commission subsequently launched an internal fraud investigation after evidence showed that questions had been leaked in advance.[17]

Competition is in three stages. The first consists of a pre-selection test based on multiple-choice questions that are marked by an 'optical reader'. These ques-tions are usually of a 'general knowledge' kind, which officials likened to *Trivial Pursuit*, the 'Yuppy' party game popular in Britain during the 1980s. Generally speaking, questions fall into two categories. The first is general knowledge about European culture, science, geography and current affairs, which includes such questions as: 'Who invented the lift?', 'Who wrote *The Marriage of Figaro*?', 'What are the "blue berets"?' and 'When did the Berlin Wall fall?'. The second category is specific knowledge about EC institutions and the history of European integration, including questions about Jean Monnet, the European Court of Justice, the TACIS programme and the Charlemagne Prize. There is even a book that candidates can buy, with advice on how to pass the *concours*, and mock questions to practise and measure one's knowledge of EU affairs (Dupondt 1995). In recent years, however, the Commission has been confronted with increasing doubts about the relevance of these general knowledge tests. There have also been complaints from Nordic member states that the questions on 'European culture' are biased towards a Latin or southern European conception of culture which privileges classical art, literature and mythology but makes little mention of Nordic mythology or arts. There have also been claims of discrimi-nation against British nationals on the grounds that the exams assume knowledge of Latin Law (rather than the UK's legal system based on Common Law), and because of the young age at which people graduate in Britain. For many critics, the *concours* system is thus seen as 'a francophone invention, weighted in favour of the French-style education system' (Mann 1996: 18). It is also criticised on the grounds of gender bias, both in terms of the questions asked (the 'general know-ledge' being allegedly very male-oriented) and in the way answers are marked. The fact that the majority of women applicants fail at the pre-selection test seems to confirm this. Others point out that what it tests for is of little relevance in assessing the abilities and skills needed to be a good civil servant.[18]

Stage two of the *concours* involves a written exam designed to test candidates' language skills and ability to express logical arguments. Those that graduate to the third stage are invited to Brussels for the oral interview, often in two or three official languages, before a 'jury board' composed of three to five officials. Candidates who finally make it on to the reserve list are asked to select three Directorates they would be interested in working for. The most frequently selected DGs tended to be those with the highest external profiles, including foreign affairs, Environment and Development. Once on the reserve list, candidates' CVs are distributed to the DGs and filed for future reference, should a post fall vacant. However, candidates are generally expected to do their own networking and lobbying to get off the reserve list. This inevitably advantages individuals from countries closer to Brussels, those with 'good contacts' inside the Commission and those with the financial means to support themselves until a post becomes vacant – which as noted, may take over a year. Those lacking these advantages who return to their countries to await their call are usually disappointed. Most of the new recruits I interviewed said that they had got their first posts by lobbying Heads of Unit and by cultivating personal contacts. Virtually all agreed that this system encouraged string-pulling and patronage, but accepted this as quite normal, although some candidates (notably from northern European member states) said that the system was culturally biased and discriminatory.

Race and gender

Nationality apart, the Commission does not monitor the 'ethnic' origins of its staff, therefore the composition of the civil service by racial or ethnic background can only be guessed at. The word 'cosmopolitan' was frequently invoked by interviewees when describing the characteristics of the Commission they most liked. However, 'cosmopolitan' in the context of the Commission means 'multinational' rather than multiracial. During six months of fieldwork I saw only two officials (both secretarial staff) who were of black or Asian origin. This is in stark contrast to the heterogeneous population of Brussels and virtually every other European capital. As informants admitted, most officials are white, Caucasian and middle-class, and the representation of ethnic minorities within the EU civil service is not an issue given any weight.

By contrast, the gender balance of staff within the Commission has become an acutely sensitive matter, albeit only relatively recently. The European Council and Commission have long championed the idea of promoting equal opportunities, and Article 119 of the EC Treaty lays down unequivocally the principle that 'men and women should receive equal pay for equal work'. Since the 1970s, the Commission has adopted numerous resolutions, directives and recommendations to ensure that the member states implement this principle in their national legislation, particularly as regards employment in the public sector. In 1984, for example, the Council Recommendation on the Promotion of Positive Action for

Women highlighted the need to 'make efforts in the public sector to promote equal opportunities which might serve as an example'[19] A more recent report goes on to say, 'the implementation of positive actions in the public sector takes on the role of a catalyst in triggering awareness, and as a model for the development of positive action in the private sector'.[20] Overall, the Commission has a ratio of 56 per cent men to 44 per cent women. However, this hides a clear tendency for women to be concentrated in the lower grades. By the mid-1990s, for example, women still accounted for only 13.5 per cent of A-grade staff, some 40 per cent of B-grade administrative assistant posts, yet 80.4 per cent of all C-grade secretarial staff.[21] While officials in 1996 were keen to point out that the number of female directors-general had actually doubled since 1992 – when it launched its second 'Positive Action Programme' the reality was that the increase had been from one to two, out of a total of twenty-four.[22] By June 1996 this figure had risen to three women A1 officials, eight women A2 grades (out of 180) and 149 women A-grades out of a total of 1,255.[23] Bad as they may seem, these figures represent a significant advance on previous years.

Other EU institutions fare no better. By 1996 women still accounted for just 27.3 per cent of MEPs and 17 per cent of A-grade staff in the European Parliament; senior officials in the Council are overwhelmingly male, only 15 per cent of auditing staff are female and there has never been a woman judge at the European Court of Justice.[24] This is naturally a source of embarrassment for EU officials, who are acutely conscious of the inconsistency between their policies on equal opportunities and the EU's own employment record. The usual explanation informants gave for the absence of women in positions of authority was that the Commission's institutional culture discriminated against women: in its recruitment practices (particularly the *concours* system), its old-boy networks, its notions of 'merit' and its working practices: the Commission was clearly perceived as a 'gendered' organisation structured according to male norms.[25] Virtually all agreed that positive discrimination was needed to change that culture. However, the campaign launched in 1995 by the new Finnish Commissioner for Personnel, Erki Liikanen, to increase the number of women A-grade officials to 16 per cent through 'positive action', received a major legal setback in October 1995 when the European Court of Justice's ruling in the 'Kalanke case' found the city of Bremen's 'positive discrimination' policy of automatically giving priority to women to be a violation of equal opportunities.[26]

Salaries and conditions

With salaries set at a level considerably higher than that of similar jobs in most member states, pensions up to 70 per cent of one's last salary on retirement, quasi-diplomatic status and excellent conditions of service, EU officials are reputedly among the most privileged public officials in world. Certainly, the benefits of working for the Commission are considerable. The salary scale for employees, based on a weighted average pay for national civil servants and a formula known as *la Méthodé*, increases annually on the basis of prices and pay rises across Europe. For those recruited from abroad salaries are even higher and non-Belgians receive an additional 17 per cent expatriate allowance. There is also a one-off exemption for VAT on household equipment and cars for employees arriving in Belgium for the first time. At the time of fieldwork an A-grade *fonctionnaire* was earning between BF143,565 and BF412,036 per month (£3,190 to £9,156 at 1995 rates), plus family allowance. At the top of the scale a Commissioner earned around BF500,000 a year. As one seasoned EU analyst and journalist explained: 'With all the various concessions and allowances for officials, most of the tax burden is matched. Therefore the gross figure for salaries is pretty close to an official's take-home pay.' In addition to these high salaries, officials enjoy very generous, indexed-linked pensions, the maximum retirement pension rising to '70 per cent of the final basic salary carried by the last grade in which the official was classified for at least one year'.[27]

The Commission defends these salary levels, arguing that the professional qualifications required of its employees would make them highly paid in other professions. It argues that these high salaries and bonuses are necessary incentives for attracting 'Europe's brightest and best'. Lower down the scale, B and C grade *fonctionnaires* also earn considerably more than their counterparts in national bureaucracies. A newly recruited secretary earned between BF82,000 and BF102,000 (roughly £1,770 to £2,500 per month). The power of the in-house trade unions inside the Commission and their corporatist relationship with the authorities has helped to keep pay scales high. Not surprisingly, pay is a sensitive issue among staff, and many fear (correctly) that some member-state governments would like to see a reduction in EU salaries and privileges. Interestingly, it is the staff unions and their leaders – most of whom are highly politicised – who are the most vociferous defenders of the independence and neutrality of the civil service. As they portray it, the issues of staff pay and conditions are inextricably linked with debates over the Commission's autonomy as a supranational institution. Any proposal to reduce salaries or question working conditions is thus likely to be opposed on the grounds that it will damage the Commission's autonomy or, worse, that it is the thin end of the wedge for bringing about an effective re-nationalisation of the Commission. Protection of salaries and working conditions is therefore closely tied, at least in the perception of the staff unions, with the idea of 'defending the European interest'.

Full details of what an EU official is entitled to, and can expect from a post, are set out in the Staff Regulations. This *magnum opus* of a document, sometimes referred to as the *'fonctionnaires'* Bible', covers every conceivable aspect of staff conditions of service, from rights, obligations, pay scales and career structure to disciplinary measures and pension arrangements. It even details financial compensation arrangements for insurance against accident, occupational disease, from 'total ankylosis of the scapulo-humeral joint' at one end of the scale to 'incurable insanity' at the other (Staff Regulations 1993: 200).[28]

Job security is a key aspect of the employment package and was frequently cited by new recruits as one of the appeals of working in the Commission. Once recruited, it is very hard to be sacked, and demotion is practically unheard of.

Officials serve until they reach the minimum retirement age of sixty (maximum sixty-five). A career in the Commission therefore tends to be a 'job for life'. This is also reflected in the extremely low staff turnover: on average only 250 officials per year leave the Commission service, or just under 1 per cent of the total work force.[29] This extraordinarily low figure undoubtedly reflects the generous pay and conditions of service enjoyed by EU officials. However, the permanence of jobs creates problems for management. As one Head of Unit observed:

> Out here people are well paid and very protected. They tend to take things for granted. They make a fuss about such minor things, like having a reserved parking space. The lifestyle is much more comfortable. The 'gilded cage' problem is true. Promotion prospects are low and there is a bottleneck. Because everyone is so well paid promotion is not so important: it would mean a lot more work for not much more money. The total lack of any carrot or stick leads to a lack of motivation. The problem for a Head of Unit is that staff can't be removed, so they get bypassed. If someone sits and plays computer games all day, you can't do anything.

The 'gilded cage' reference needs explaining as it was a term used frequently by officials. One of the difficulties for staff who become bored or frustrated with their jobs is that those who become accustomed to the high EU salaries and lifestyle find it is difficult to leave. Dissatisfaction and low morale were particularly acute among middle-managers (A-4s), especially those who have reached the top of the career ladder but lack the political support to advance further, those who feel trapped in a dead-end job, or those who, for political reasons, have been moved sideways into unimportant peripheral posts that are, in effect, 'non-jobs' (referred to in Brussels jargon as being sent to the *voie de garage*). These officials were said to be victims of the gilded cage syndrome. The problem was epitomised by a French official who had reached A-4 grade at the age of only forty-seven. Leaning back in his chair in his comfortable, thirteenth-floor office, he admitted to being 'a bit bored' and asked (rhetorically) 'so where do I go from here, and what do I do for the next twenty years?' The suggestion, 'why not apply for a job outside the Commission?' provoked a snort of laughter. 'Where would I find another job', he replied, 'that pays BF35,000 a month for not many hours' work, that allows me to meet interesting people, and that I enjoy? Only managing directors of large companies enjoy comparable pay and privileges, but they have to put in twice the number of hours.'

Under Article 50 of the Staff Regulations (1993: 20), very senior officials may be moved, or 'retired in the interests of the service', but in either case on very generous terms. In general, however, Article 50 was designed as a device for making 'room at the top' for staff from new member states, but it is now seldom invoked. Removing a *fonctionnaire* is usually so difficult that staff tend to be suspended instead, even for disciplinary offences. One reason for this is because of the influence that *cabinets* have over personnel policy. *Cabinet* members often play a gatekeeper role, protecting favoured individuals or interceding on behalf of 'fellow nationals' in seeking promotion. As one German official observed, 'it is theoretically possible [to fire someone] but when I fire someone, I am not firing him, but a nationality . . . The only way to get rid of him is to promote him and "sell" him to someone else.'[30] Another reason is that staff themselves are extremely litigious and have learned to play the system very effectively to their advantage. The Court of First Instance, which came into existence in November 1989, was created largely to cope with the increasing volume of legal cases brought by EU civil servants. As one former Director of Personnel put it, raising his arms in a gesture of despair:

> We still don't sack people who do no work. Disciplinary action is unlikely to produce any results because in most cases the plaintiff arrives at the tribunal with a good lawyer to defend them and the Commission ends up as the accused. There are some very good staff lawyers here in Brussels: I know, because we use them ourselves. Most of the senior managers that I know say it simply isn't worth bothering trying to discipline someone who's lazy.

Many of these problems were identified over two decades earlier in an independent report on reform of the Commission drafted by the Dutch former ECSC Commissioner, Dirk Spierenburg. Among the main failings and 'managerial inadequacies' of the Commission that Spierenburg identified were 'excessive specialisation', 'over-elaborate hierarchies of authority', 'lack of cohesion' between the Commissioners and their services, 'inflexible responses to changing priorities', 'inadequate training' and 'lack of mobility' (Spierenburg 1979: 4–6, 31). The report also identified 'rigged competitions', recruitment 'by devious procedures' and the excessive power of the *cabinets* as key factors contributing to the Commission's loss of cohesion and low staff morale ((Spierenburg 1979: 19, 36). Foremost among the latter were the problems of:

> *Cabinets* 'shielding' Members from their Services, *Chefs de cabinet* usurping the responsibilities of Directors-General, meeting of the *Chefs de cabinet* (and indeed of junior *Cabinet* staff) questioning proposals without consulting the officials responsible for them, interference in appointment procedures with undue weight being given to nationality factors, and so on.
>
> (Spierenburg 1979: 19)

Despite these criticisms, little was done to eradicate these shortcomings. As Ludlow (1991: 81) observed over a decade later: 'The Commission's basic organisational units are much as they were in 1967 and all of the structural weaknesses so clearly identified in 1979 by the Spierenburg report are still there.'

The 'parallel administrative system' and its causes

In theory, all candidates with ambitions to become permanent members of staff in EU institutions must first pass the *concours*. However, many individuals manage to bypass the system, usually by being taken on as *agent temporaires* (consultants, auxiliaries and visiting scientists), as 'detached national experts' on temporary secondment from a national civil service, or as members of a Commissioner's *cabinet*. Once 'inside' the House, these auxiliaries are able to use their positions and political connections (or *'piston'*) to find permanent posts. A system of 'internal' competitions or 'titularisation' exams has, in the past, served to provide the necessary path to permanent status. These entrants are usually referred to in Brussels jargon as *sousmarins* ('submarines'). The presence of so many parachuted political appointees among the higher echelons of the civil service is a source of considerable resentment among permanent staff and is bitterly opposed by the staff unions.

Perhaps the most swingeing indictment of the failure of the Commission's supranational claims comes from David Spence – who is himself a *fonctionnaire* in DG 1A. Spence argues that failure to respect the Statutes and the increasing use of non-statutory staff (especially auxiliaries) has resulted in 'the emergence of an almost parallel administrative regime with its own salary scales, promotion prospects and procedures' (1994a: 65). This parallel system, he suggests, poses a serious threat to the coherence of the Commission's civil service. Many of the problems of mismanagement he identifies supposedly derive from the French civil service tradition. These include a 'highly politicised senior management closely linked to the party in power', the powerful *cabinet* system, and the tendency to 'use information as a constituent element of a bureaucratic and political power base' (1994a: 91). As a result a number of 'dysfunctional' practices have become virtually institutionalised, from nepotism (*'piston'*), and 'parachuting' staff at the top to 'rigged exams' and back-door recruitment methods. As Spence (1994a: 92) declares: 'National quotas and balance, *parachutage*, *sousmarins*, Cabinets, *piston*, seconded national experts, posts reserved for certain nationalities, etc. are all signs of disintegrative seeds lurking in the fruit of apparent integration'.

Like many commentators, Spence blames these 'disintegrative trends' on staff shortages and interfering national governments. It is argued that in response to the need for immediate expertise in the rush towards the single market, the Commission under Delors recruited large numbers of external staff, often on an ad hoc basis, in violation of its formal procedures and high-minded principles of professionalism.[31] The increase in these various new categories of *agents temporaires* has undoubtedly exacerbated the structural cleavage between 'statutory' and 'non-statutory' staff – the latter often being seconded or appointed by national governments. These non-statutory officials are often regarded with suspicion by statutory officials (like Spence) who perceive them as 'outsiders' and speak of their presence as a 'Trojan Horse' that threatens to dilute the supranational composition of the civil service or, worse, to bring about its effective re-nationalisation. By 1992 these non-statutory personnel had increased from a few hundred a decade earlier to 4,651, or 26.7 per cent of the Commission's workforce. However, those officials who complain about the disintegrative trends created by the presence of these floating or temporary staff also recognise their utility. As one official summed it up (himself a former seconded national expert), 'national experts are often better than full-time civil servants. The combination of both creates a symbiosis that enriches the service.'

While Spence's description of the structural divisions and tensions within the Commission is correct, his belief that the causes stem from a combination of staff shortages, contamination by 'outsiders', and meddlesome governments is questionable. My research suggests that while the first two of these explanations are not inaccurate, two other aspect of the Commission's administrative regime were far more important. First, the Commission's excessive legalism and bureaucratisation – and the way staff try to get round these factors; and, second, the conspicuous lack of a coherent 'personnel policy' in the way the Commission manages its staff. Officials were generally scathing about the formal system of administration: it was 'dead' and it didn't work. They also complained that there was no system of human resource management: that, once recruited, you were left to your own devices. As one senior official in DG IX summed it up: 'There is no personnel policy. Or rather, the policy is to have *no* policy. What we have instead are the "Staff Regulations".' This view was endorsed by two former Directors of Personnel and by most of the new recruits that I interviewed. Apart from one brief, five-day induction course (which had been instituted only a few years earlier), most staff said they had received virtually no training, induction, support or guidance. The concepts of 'career development' and 'human resource management' are absent in the Commission. Another senior official, a *cabinet* member with special responsibility for personnel matters, spoke candidly about the problems reconciling 'southern and northern European' styles of management. Practices of 'staff appraisal' or 'performance review', accepted in the Danish, Dutch and British civil services, were 'anathema' in most Mediterranean countries. 'For a Spaniard, the very suggestion of performance appraisal would be considered an insult.'

This was confirmed by other interviewees. Heads of Unit complained about being unable to sanction or discipline bad employees – not only because of the system of national protection via the *cabinet* system but because of the powerful staff unions. Among staff, there was a widespread feeling that promotion prospects had less to do with performance than with political connections,[32] as one former French Director of Personnel put it:

> If you're not Catholic, Socialist, or from the right class it is difficult to make your way here. By 'class' I mean the system of networks. You either have to belong to the Catholic Left, the Socialist Party, come from the Ecole Nationale d'Administration, or be from the Ecole d'Agronomie . . . Under Delors the French got all the best jobs. Before Delors came it was the Italian lobby which held the reins of power – until the death of Nattali. Then the French replaced the Italians. Now we are in a new situation: I'm not sure what it is . . . the networks of influence have changed.[33]

The absence of a proper 'personnel' policy was said to have two consequences: extreme individualism, factionalism and empire-building on the one hand, and disillusionment on the other. This was confirmed in a study by the French polling

agency Cegos, which found a surprisingly high level of disillusion among Commission employees.[34] The attitude towards new staff is that they will either sink or
swim. As one official commented, 'the system favours wide-boys – those who
understand how to play the game'. 'The French', another DG IX official declared,
'are much better than other nationals at promoting their good candidates . . . The
problem is that "survival capacity" is not something you can test for objectively.'
To sum up, the absence of a coherent personnel policy encourages staff to behave
as entrepreneurs and brokers by effectively plotting and calculating their own
career paths and personal networks. The logic of this administrative culture is that
individuals are obliged to act as individualists if they are to survive and 'get on' in
the Commission. A Director-General with almost forty years of service described
it as follows:

> To understand the EU administration you should read the history of the
> Middle Ages. The Commission is not a single or unified body. We have no
> 'boss'. Even Santer is just one colleague among twenty Commissioners. Each
> DG has its own boss; they are like the medieval barons. Departments are very
> independent. The only difference between a Commissioner and a Director-
> General is that we stay longer: they are here for four or five years, but we stay
> for thirty-five years – if we are clever.

Speaking about his own power as former 'baron' in the Personnel directorate he
added thoughtfully:

> What power did I have as Director of Personnel? None. The only power I had
> was my understanding of people; who was connected to whom. If you want
> to remove someone as Director of Personnel you have to know who is pro-
> tecting him and work on his protectors. Hay [a former Director-General of
> Personnel][35] didn't understand how the House worked: who was protected,
> who belonged to which groups. Hay believed in the formal procedures. That
> was his mistake. To survive you need to see where you work and who you
> work with; you need a clientele; you need to know if he's a 'Noèl man' or a
> 'de Koster man'. Yes, there is a French Mafia in the Commission. But there is
> also an English Mafia. You have Mafiosi everywhere, but there are different
> kinds of Mafiosi: there is a gay Mafia; a freemasons' Mafia, an *Opus Dei* Mafia,
> a Socialist and a Communist Mafia. The important thing is that they neutral-
> ise each other – that was my aim when I worked in DG IX. The trick is to find
> out which Mafiosi exist and who belongs to them. Once you recognise these
> networks you can begin to work with them. At the beginning there were only
> about ten of us who were aware of this.

These sentiments were echoed by other senior officials. Those who 'understand
how the House really works' were a small minority of 'players' – veterans from the
'early years' – most of whom combined a high degree of pragmatism with an
extraordinary deep affection for the institution they served. On several occasions,

interviewees spoke passionately about their love for the Commission. As a senior Belgian official declared:

> I love this institution. Once you find your way you realise how interesting it is. It is much more exciting than any national administration. The Commission needs to recruit intelligent people – by that I mean clever and mentally flexible people: we don't need academics; we can't use them: they are too rational: they live in their mind. You need to be irrational: a compromiser. The best compromises are the most irrational ones – look at the European Union, how do you think it has survived all these years?

Networks are therefore central to understanding the way the Commission works in practice. In his view the 'Brits', Danes and Swedes – with their anti-patronage cultures – fail to grasp the networking dynamics of the Commission's internal culture and are not used to the kind of 'institutional slack' found in the Commission. By contrast, the smaller countries are 'much better adapted to appreciating and playing this system because they are more used to compromises. That's why there are so many more senior officials from the smaller countries – they really have a lot of power thanks to the Commission.'

Fraud, mismanagement and corruption

This brings us to the politically sensitive issue of nepotism and corruption in the Commission. On 15 March 1999 a team of five independent auditors and investigators published its long-awaited enquiry into the 'culture' of fraud, irregularities, cronyism and mismanagement[36] that it reported were endemic in the European Commission. The investigation had been triggered by the revelations of Paul Van Buitenen, a middle-ranking official in the Audit division, concerning widespread 'irregularities' in the EU budget. These 'irregularities' – which had prompted the European Parliament and Commission in January 1999 to set up an independent inquiry – included the 'disappearance' of £1.5 million worth of funds from the humanitarian aid office ('ECHO') which the Commission was unable to account for. Subsequent investigations suggested that the Commission was also unable to account for more than £17 billion of European taxpayers' money spent on 'structural' projects as it was not the Commission's practice to keep records.[37] The Committee of Independent Experts report was particularly scathing of the lack of accountability in the Commission. It found that 'undoubted instances of fraud and corruption' which were rife in the administration had 'thus passed "unnoticed"', while Commissioners argued that 'they were not aware of what was happening in their services'. These excuses were clearly inadmissible. In the words of the report: 'Protestations of ignorance on the part of Commissioners concerning problems that were often common knowledge in their services, even up to the highest levels, are tantamount to a loss of control by the political authorities over the Administration that they are supposedly running' (CIE 1999: 137).

This blunt language clearly shocked senior Commission officials who had expected more measured treatment and who had welcomed the inquiry largely in the expectation that it would lay to rest press accusations of fraud and patronage that had been circulating since the previous year. Instead, the auditors revealed that a climate of cover-up, collusion and evasion of accountability pervades the Commission. It concluded, 'it is becoming difficult to find anyone who has even the slightest sense of responsibility. However, that sense of responsibility is essential . . . The temptation to deprive the concept of responsibility of all substance is a dangerous one. The concept is the ultimate manifestation of democracy' (CIE 1999: 144).

While no individual Commissioners were accused of personal dishonesty or illegal gain, the auditors nevertheless detailed a saga of corrupt practices and mismanagement and levelled particularly damning criticisms against Edith Cresson, the French Commissioner responsible for Science, Research and Development. The clearest cases of 'favouritism' were the appointment by Cresson of several associates to well-paid positions in the Commission's research division (DG XII). Most notorious of all was the recruitment by what the report (1999: 124) calls an 'unsolicited application' of a seventy-year-old dentist friend, René Berthelot, to a highly paid post as 'Visiting Scientist' to advise on the EU's Fifth Framework research programme, for which he was manifestly unqualified. During his first twelve-month tenure Berthelot produced no work, yet his contract was renewed for a further six months. The report noted that Berthelot shared a flat in Brussels with Cresson and that virtually all of his expenses-paid 'missions' were to the French town of Châtellerault where Cresson held the post of Mayor until 1997. It was for publishing these same details that Cresson had initiated her legal suit for defamation against the French newspaper *Libération*.

The result of these accounts of fraud, mismanagement and cronyism was the resignation, *en masse*, of the entire Commission and a scandal that plunged the institution into the most traumatic crisis of its forty-two year history. Yet the reaction of senior Commissioners was not, as might be expected, one of humility or contrition but indignation and outrage. At a press conference held on 16 March, the day after the report's release, an angry Jacques Santer declared; 'I am offended'. Neither he nor his fellow Commissioners could accept responsibility for the fraud, irregularities and mismanagement described in the Independent Experts' report: Its 'tone' was 'outrageous', its conclusions were 'perfectly unjustified' and he himself, he noted 'with considerable satisfaction', had been found 'whiter than white'.[38] Clearly failing to comprehend his political disgrace, he then announced that the mass resignations had changed nothing and that he would stay on as 'caretaker' in full power until the end of the year. Significantly, Santer pointed the finger at his predecessor, noting that four of the six cases of abuse identified had their origins in the Delors regime.[39] Edith Cresson, for her part, refused point-blank to accept that she had done anything wrong. Her only expression of contrition was to say: 'Maybe I was a little careless.'[40] When interrogated by MEPs, she retorted, 'are we supposed to work only with people we do not know?'[41] The Labour MEP Michael Tappin, asked her whether she would resign on account of 'the atmosphere of illegality and cronyism which profits the family and friends of your circle?'. Her reply was that she was being hounded only because she had tried 'to do something for Europe', setting up the 'LEONARDO' education and training programmes for young people.[42] She subsequently told France 2 television that she had no need to clear her name since the Commission had been found collectively responsible. To compound this political *hauteur*, Cresson went on to dismiss the charges against her as part of an Anglo-German 'conspiracy' and a 'German-inspired bid to damage France'.[43] What were even more astonishing were reports that many Commission officials agreed that Cresson had been a victim of an 'Anglo-Saxon political crusade' and deplored the way the 'Germans had joined the northerners in a Protestant crusade against the southern culture of state administration'.[44] As Cresson declared, much to the embarrassment of her colleagues, she was 'guilty of no behaviour that is not standard in the French administrative culture'.[45]

Other Commissioners were also investigated and criticised by the auditors: notably, Joâo de Deus Pinheiro, for appointing his brother-in-law to a senior post in his *cabinet* (the appointment of his wife as a 'national expert' was not judged to be irregular); Monika Wulf-Mathies for favouritism in appointing the husband of a close friend as legal adviser in DG XVI, and Manuel Marín, concerning his wife's appointment to a high-grade Commission category B post. However, by far the worst case of corruption was found in the Commission's Security Office, one of the Commission's 'horizontal services' directly responsible to the President. The report paints a picture of a sinister inner world of clientelism and corruption where collusion between the Commission's Security Office (headed by a former head of the French secret services) and the Belgian police was rife. Specific examples of fraud included staff recruitment and the awarding of the EU's biggest security contract to the Belgian company Group 4 Securitas.

> There was a peculiar complicity within the security system and between the Security Office and other circles in the Commission that created a kind of 'regulation-free-zone', where existing laws and regulations were regarded as cumbersome barriers to various forms of arbitrary action rather than as limitations to be respected. The security system appears to have been undermined by a sub-culture which was characterised by personal relationships, a system of 'give-and-take' and a withdrawal from the overall system of control and surveillance. The question must be asked as to how such a sub-culture could develop, exist and prevail in a section of the European civil service without being detected from within, brought to light only when a newspaper published the allegations.
>
> (CIE 1999: 102)

Key features of this 'subculture' included the 'power to offer "small favours" to colleagues in the Commission, such as cancelling police fines for parking offences or drink-driving'; the hiring out of security staff as private chauffeurs and gardeners; and the theft and re-sale of office furniture. The security office had become 'a private club for former police officers from Brussels or the vicinity for whom special recruitment "competitions" were arranged' (1999: 102). Even more alarming is the report's disclosure that the Security Office had even put the Commission's own internal fraud-busting team (UCLAF) under its surveillance during its enquiry into the Security Office. In the words of the report, neither Santer nor his private office 'took any meaningful interest in its functioning. As a result no supervision was exercised and "a state within a state" was allowed to develop' (1999: 105).

The Committee of Independent Experts' report thus delivered a coruscating indictment not only of individual Commissioners but of the entire management and corporate culture of the Commission – with implications for the European project itself. What it exposed was the extraordinary degree to which patronage, fraud and corruption – key features of what Spence terms the 'parallel administrative system' and what Middlemas calls the dynamic 'informal' politics of integration – had become established, even institutionalised, within the Commission. The denial of responsibility by Commissioners merely exemplified the chronic lack of accountability or 'democratic deficit' that characterises the EU.

Equally importantly, both this report and my own research findings highlights the gulf that exists between the Commission's claims about itself ('guardian' of the European interest and so forth), and the behaviour of its officials in practice. The picture it portrays of the Commission's organisational culture is a far cry from Monnet's vision of a supranational elite championing a new model of transnational governance. This evidence also challenges the positivistic assumptions of integration theorists. How, then, should we interpret these findings and what conclusions can we draw about the EU's claim to be forging ever closer union among the peoples of Europe? These questions are addressed in the final chapter.

Notes

1 For an interesting set of perspectives on the Commission see Davignon *et al.* (1995a).

2 Significantly, even Delors, who intervened into virtually every other area of the Commission, refrained from attempts to reform the Commission's internal organisation. The local description of DG IX as the most 'conservative' and 'unreformed' part of the House was one of the reasons I chose to examine the issue of staffing and management more closely during fieldwork in Brussels.

3 CEC, *The Budget of the European Union: How Is Your Money Spent?* Brussels: OOPEC, 1996: 2.

4 This is also roughly the same as the number of clergy in the Church of England.

5 David Williamson, 'The Looking Glass View of Europe', *Financial Times*, 15 December 1994: 25.

6 During fieldwork I met many individuals whose entire career had been spent in DG IX and DG X. Informants reported that mobility between services was often difficult and had only really begun to be encouraged quite recently.

7 As Jacques Santer (1995: 12) declared in a speech to the European Parliament: 'Even a game on a level playing field still needs a referee. This is the role of the Commission, which will be strict in enforcing the rules on abuses of dominant

positions, restrictive practices and State aids.' However, as Ross (1993) has demonstrated, his predecessor, Jacques Delors, was not so even-handed when dealing with French companies.

8 In fact, the Commission's ethos is, as I argue below, largely a product of its bureaucratic character.

9 According to one former Director of Personnel, the majority of French recruits to the Commission today were now 'Enarques', or ENA graduates. This contrasted notably with the pre-1980 period when a job in the Commission carried less kudos among ENA high-fliers. Today, by contrast, there were so many in the Commission that there was now a thriving club for ENA alumni in Brussels with a regular programme of meetings, public seminars and social events.

10 According to the Head of the Translation Service, by 1995 English had overtaken French as the major language as far as the translation of internal documents and official texts was concerned.

11 It is curious that, in most accounts of the origins of the EU's civil service, neither the Italian nor Belgian system of public administration receives much acknowledgement. This may be because their influence has been more discreet, and is perhaps more important when considering the Commission's informal system of administration.

12 The actual size of the different staff unions is something of a mystery, as very few union officials were prepared to divulge this apparently 'sensitive' information to me. As I discovered, the unions are intensely jealous and suspicious of each other and exist in a state of almost permanent opposition. However, intra-union solidarity is most evident where attempts are made to revise the Staff Statutes or reform the method by which salary levels are calculated.

13 *Civil Service Statistics*, London: HMSO, 1995.

14 However, the balance between nationalities in the Commission was initially also based on budget contributions (Cini 1996: 125).

15 My own research was unable to confirm this, although informants agreed that there was some truth in Bramwell's claims.

16 Buckley, *Financial Times*, 24 September 1998.

17 *Independent*, 24 September 1998: 14.

18 These criticisms prompted the Commission to decide that in future candidates will be tested specifically on their knowledge of the history and institutions of the EU and on their command of a second official Union language.

19 *OJ*, L331, 19 December 1984: 34.

20 Com (95) 247 fin. Cited in European Parliament (1996).

21 CEC (1994d: 21).

22 R. Watson, *European Voice*, 25–31 January 1996: 19.

23 European Parliament (1996: 15).

24 Cited in European Parliament (1996); *European Voice* 25–31 January 1996: 18.

25 For analyses of the gender of organisations see Cockburn (1994); Roper (1994).

26 Kalanke *v.* Freie Hansestadt Bemen 17 October 1995 C-450/93. The 'Kalanke case' became a major topic of conversation at the time of fieldwork as officials (and lawyers) heatedly debated the distinction between 'positive discrimination' and 'positive action'.

27 Staff Regulations (1993: 27–28).

28 Incurable insanity is not in the International Classification of Diseases. Why it should be classified as an occupational hazard for civil servants is a mystery.

29 Figures supplied by the Commission's Pensions Unit show that staff turnover, as measured by the annual number in receipt of severance pay, was less than one per cent per annum across all EU institutions during the period 1991–5.

30 Michelmann 1978: 489, cited in Spence 1994a: 69.

31 A good example of this concerned staff recruitment for the recently created

'Committee of the Regions' ('CoR'). In this case, the widespread use of nepotism and political patronage was so blatant that it provoked a series of strikes and protests among EU staff, culminating in a successful case against the CoR in the Court of First Instance.

32 This point emerged also in the evidence collected by the House of Lords Select Committee Report on Staffing in the EU (1988: 112–13).

33 This point has been noted elsewhere. The *Economist* 326 (20 March 1993) recounts a similar incident concerning an official who, recently promoted to Head of Division, brushed aside congratulations from a colleague with a self-deprecating smile saying; 'Besides my qualifications for the job, I'm also French, Socialist, Jewish and a freemason'.

34 Cited in Spence 1994a: 69.

35 Richard Hay was a former British Director-General of DG IX who, I was told, had been 'killed' (i.e. removed) by Delors.

36 For detailed coverage and press reaction to the report see *Independent*, 16 March 1999; *The Times*, 16 March 1999 and *Financial Times*, 16 March 1999.

37 Watts and Gill, *Sunday Business*, 18 October 1998: 1, 5.

38 Smith and Peel, *Financial Times*, 17 March 1999: 2; see also editorial *The Times*, 17 March 1999: 21.

39 Bremner, *The Times*, 17 March 1999: 4.

40 White, *Guardian*, 17 March 1999: 2.

41 Bremner, *The Times*, 16 March 1999: 13.

42 Walker, *Guardian*, 24 February 1999: 13.

43 Tucker, *Financial Times*, 17 March 1999; Bremner and Bell, *The Times*, 17 March 1999: 5.

44 Bremner *The Times*, 17 March 1999: 4; see also *Independent*, 17 March 1999: 2.

45 Bremner, *The Times*, 16 March 1999: 13; this was also confirmed by several interviewees.

8 Conclusion: European construction, democracy and the politics of culture

Administration of the EU: formal versus informal systems

This book set out to explore two key themes in the EU project of 'European construction'. The first concerned the Europeanisation of the masses and the various ways in which the EU has attempted to solve its problem of legitimacy by creating the conditions for the emergence of a European public. The second concerned the politics of elite-formation and the question of whether the EU has developed within its own institutions the embryo of a European identity and consciousness commensurate with its supranational ideals, and to act as a catalyst for diffusing the European idea among the population at large. What conclusions, therefore, can we draw from this study concerning the cultural politics of European Union and the role of the Commission in the integration process?

Let us turn first to the idea of the Commission itself as a supposed exemplar and laboratory for European unification. Like many integration theorists and activists, Jean Monnet, the EU's foremost visionary and eponymous ancestor, placed great emphasis on the transformative role of institutions and elites in building the new European order. His remark, 'rien est possible sans les institutions: rien est possible sans les hommes'[1] still reverberates in the speeches of EU politicians and is quoted repeatedly in the 'information' brochures and videos produced by the Commission.[2] Graham Leicester (1996: 8) summed it up succinctly:

> Instead of an inherited myth about a nation forged in past battles, the Community is based on a 'myth of the future'. It is only in contemplating the eventual goal of federation, or 'ever closer union' as it became in the Treaty of Rome, that the peoples of Europe might discern a vision of their participation in a wider polity.

In many respects, this vision provides a classic example of what anthropologists, echoing Malinowski (1926), term 'myth as a charter for legitimation'. It is a vision still invoked today in the speeches and arguments of EU supporters and European political leaders.

However, as Leicester (1996: 8) states, '[t]he unfulfilled sense of a federal order which informs the treaties without determining their content places a straitjacket around thinking about institutional reform'. It also tends to obscure the reality of what the EU is, with teleological notions about what it ought to be – and what kind of a political entity it might be evolving into. Like the vision of the classless society at the 'end of history' that once inspired intellectuals to uncritical adulation for Soviet communism, the EU's supranational idealism, its evolutionary conception of itself and its sense of European integration as an unfinished project of social and political engineering, all combine to obstruct critical and intellectually honest thinking about its institutional shortcomings.

As the previous chapter demonstrated, this supranational vision and sense of federal mission, which is epitomised in the idea of *construction europeâne* , pervades the ethos and orientation of the Commission and its civil servants. Implicit in the way the Commission represents itself are precisely the same themes of Europeanist ideology that underlie the culture-building practices analysed in the first half of this book. Foremost among these themes are its uncritical assumptions about harmony and consensus, its functionalist model of social cohesion, its belief in the moral superiority of supranationalism as a more 'advanced' system of governance, and its unflinching optimism in 'functional spillover' and the enlightening power of *engrenage*. In this respect, 'European construction' is perhaps the last and possibly the greatest of the Enlightenment grand narratives. It also shares most of the same positivistic, rationalist and Eurocentric assumptions about civilisation, progress and destiny that characterised earlier ones. Conceived within this paradigm, the European Commission, the self-proclaimed 'heart of the integration process' and custodian of the European interest, saw itself as the body that would guide and lead this process to fruition. It might not be a democratic institution, but that did not matter: the priority was to provide Europe with 'leadership' and keep up the momentum towards further integration. Part of the Commission's myth of itself was that within its own organisation, freed from the constraints and hegemonic influence of the nation-state, the meeting of different national administrative cultures would work in a dialectical fashion to produce a new 'European' synthesis; a transnational whole greater than the sum of its national parts. Under the political roof of the EU's institutions, *engrenage* would work to transform national civil servants into a distinctly European public administration: a frontier-free 'people of the book' that would both symbolise and embody the ideals of supranationalism.

The concept of a 'supranational' civil service therefore raises fundamental questions about the nature of the integration process and the role of institutions. The argument of the previous chapter was that the 'gestalt' or 'melting pot' image outlined above is over-simplistic and misleading. Seen close-up and from within, the 'House' presents a very different picture. The inside of the European Commission is a social and symbolic world riven with contradictions, stratagems and political horse-trading of the kind with which games theorists, Kremlinologists and anthropologists are quite familiar. As ethnographic studies of organisations have long shown, beneath the external appearance of order and formality, most bureaucratic organisations tend to develop messy yet thriving informal sectors which follow very different cultural codes and principles (Wolf 1966; Boissevain

1974; Bailey 1971; Gellner and Waterbury 1977; Wright 1994) A key analytical distinction can therefore be drawn between the 'official system', based on legal-rational norms and procedures, a codified morality, and conformity to universalistic principles, and the unofficial or 'pragmatic' system (Bailey 1971) which follows more individualistic, particularistic and idiosyncratic cultural codes and practices. As Wolf (1966) observed long ago, these informal systems based on networks, patronage, instrumental friendships and paternalism are 'interstitial, supplementary and parallel' to the formal structures of an organisation as well as 'parasitical' upon them. According to this analysis, the two systems are not separate or mutually exclusive but complementary and self-reinforcing. The informal system based on networks, patronage and rule-breaking is not an aberration of the formal system: it is its logical outcome.

Theorising the EU: 'government without statehood'

Assuming the increasing involvement of national politicians in this game to be somehow 'educational', some EU supporters took the growing web of EU networks and committees as evidence that a new European political culture was indeed emerging. Many academics, for their part, have also contributed to the belief that from the EU's complex institutions and networks has evolved a fundamentally new type of entity that is transnational, supranational and even 'post-national'. From a constitutional and legal perspective this analysis is possibly correct: the EU is a hybrid of modernity which, as its advocates proclaim, is without parallel in world history. Never before has a group of old nation-states sought to merge their sovereignty in quite the same way to create such a complex new political system As Sbragia (1993: 24) puts it, the EU 'does not fit into any accepted category of governance'. Some writers go further and argue, with John Ruggie (1993: 140), that the EU represents 'nothing less than the emergence of the first truly postmodern international form' (cf. Cooper 1996), and the 'first transnational state of the nuclear era' as Goldstein (1993: 122) calls it. According to Ian Christie (1998: 5), we are witnessing the emergence of a new political system based on a 'highly integrated', 'cosmopolitan', 'transnational administrative elite'.

   According to Ruggie (1993: 140), the difficulty with attempts to theorise the EU is that we lack an adequate vocabulary to describe its evolving architecture.[3] This problem is not confined to the EU. As Etienne Balibar (1991: 16) puts it, 'the state today in Europe is neither national nor supranational, and this ambiguity does not slacken but only grows deeper over time'. Echoing this theme, European leaders have abandoned the old language of states and territories and speak instead of overlapping layers of European economic and political 'spaces' tied together, in the words of Jacques Delors, by the 'Community's spiderlike strategy to organise the architecture of a Greater Europe' (cited in Ruggie 1993: 140). This has inspired some EU supporters to new heights of semantic creativity in their attempt to capture in words the uniqueness of the EU. Wallace, Wallace and Webb (1983) once famously described the EC as 'less than a federation [but] more than a regime', a formula that became something of an orthodoxy for students of European Union studies. More recently, William Wallace has amended this formula. Taking up points raised in the recent literature on 'multi-level governance' (Marks 1993, 1996), Wallace (1996: 439) argues that the EU has evolved into something radically new; what he calls 'Government without statehood'.

Towards a European 'superstate'?

For political anthropologists Wallace's statement invariably invites comparisons with the extensive literature on 'acephalous societies', or what the old anthropological textbooks referred to as 'tribes without rulers'. To apply the notion of 'government without statehood' to the EU is an intriguing thesis, but is it accurate? Is the EU in the process of transforming itself into a state, or has it already effectively become one? While some authors are genuinely keen to stress the complexity of policy-making in the EU and invoke Rosenau's notion of 'governance without government', others use the *sui generis* argument to reject any suggestion that the EU might be developing into a European superstate. The usual argument against this is that any comparisons between the EU and the nation-states it seeks to transcend are meaningless because 'Europe' is an 'unfinished project' whose 'ultimate trajectory is unknowable'. Others sidestep the question altogether by dismissing the question as a sterile debate over 'definitions' and semantics. These attempts at discourse management are as anthropologically interesting as the process of state-formation they seek to conceal.

To most critical observers it seems quite evident that the European Community has acquired most of the characteristics of a state,[4] however much some might wish to deny this. It is an internationally recognised body with the power to negotiate and make international treaties; its laws and Court take precedence over national laws; within large policy areas (those sole competencies covered by the EC) it exercises a monopoly on decision-making and jurisdiction over a defined territory and its population; it has created its own legal category of 'Union Citizenship' and its own currency, the Euro; and it now has an independent European Central Bank empowered to set interest and exchange rates for the entire euro currency zone and the legal authority to fine member states who fail to comply with its 'sound money' policies and strict public spending and borrowing targets. What it does not yet have is a monopoly over the legitimate use of violence, a key criterion in Max Weber's traditional definition of statehood – but then neither did many pre-modern states (Giddens 1985).[5] However, the development of a common European army is, as Romano Prodi declared recently, the 'logical next step' after merging national defence industries.[6] Neither does it have what Gellner (1983) might describe as a monopoly over the 'means of orientation' despite its efforts to 'Europeanise' public opinion and mass education within the member states.

Another key feature of modern states is the ability to control one's external frontiers and the movement of people across national borders. The EU claims these powers for itself as part of the precondition for creating the single market and a 'Europe without frontiers'. There is also increasing pressure on EU member states to bring immigration, law and order – the so-called third 'pillar' of the Union – under the jurisdiction of supranational organisations rather than, as at present, intergovernmental ones. The abolition of internal frontier controls in those countries that have signed up to the Schengen Agreement has resulted in an intensification of police and customs controls at the external frontiers of the Union and a stepping up of Europe-wide policing and surveillance – which is yet another characteristic of modern states. Civil rights activists warn that compulsory ID cards for all residents are a logical step in this process. The assumption of most EU leaders has been that the removal of internal frontiers presents common 'problems' for the Union, and that this requires a '*cordon sanitaire*' to protect EU citizens against external threats from terrorism, drugs and immigration. The Maastricht Treaty has spawned a proliferation of 'informal' groups concerned with European co-operation over law enforcement, customs, policing and immigration. 'This qualitative shift', as Bunyan (1991: 32) wrote:

> cannot be attributed simply to being features of 'supranational' or 'transnational' co-operation. The move from *ad hoc* co-operation to permanent institutions and agencies – to the creation of a European state – is a quite logical development. But this state is different to those of the national states of the EC. The usual tenets of 'liberal democracy' cannot be applied to the new European state. The idea of the 'separation of powers' between the executive, the legislature – backed by an independent civil service – and the judiciary does not apply. This state has been conceived by governments, honed by state officials, and passed back to governments to agree.

Whether the EU's many state-like characteristics amount to a 'state' proper, as Bunyan contends, is a matter of some dispute. Those who reject such claims often adopt the legalistic arguments that the EU cannot be a state because it does not define itself as a state, nor is it recognised as a state in international law. They also argue that the power of the Council of Ministers over decision-making at the European level discounts the European superstate thesis. Neither of these arguments is convincing. The first, because it sounds like the 'Emperor's clothes'; the EU is not what it looks like to outsiders, but rather, what lawyers and EU officials define it to be, from the myopic perspective of international law. As the old hunters' saying goes, 'if it looks like a duck, walks like a duck and quacks like a duck then it probably is a duck'. The second, because it assumes that the Council of Ministers – the most secretive and bureaucratic of EU institutions – has somehow remained separate and aloof from the Brussels machinery of governance and its 'spiderlike' webs of power. In fact, decision-making in the Council of Ministers – whose meetings, like those of the ECB, are held 'behind closed doors' and without minutes – has moved dramatically from the rule of unanimity to that of qualified majority voting.

To those who have followed the history of the EU, none of this should come as any surprise. The process of cumulative integration through functional 'spillover' that was so clearly described by the early theorists of European integration is, *de facto*, laying the foundations of a centralised European state. That is what EU leaders have long aspired to create, and that is what the neofunctionalist strategy – or 'Monnet method' – was designed to achieve. In Brussels and across Europe these facts are readily acknowledged and accepted by political leaders. The narrative of European integration that is told in Germany, Italy and the Benelux countries, for example, is a tale of Europe's rescue from the nation-state[7] and the promise of salvation through the creation of what, it is hoped, will eventually develop into the United States of Europe.[8] On this point Chancellor Helmut Kohl was unequivocal:

> In Maastricht we laid the foundation stone for the completion of the European Union. The European Union Treaty introduces a new and decisive stage in the process of European Union which within a few years will lead to the creation of what the founding fathers of modern Europe dreamed after the last war: the United States of Europe.[9]

In Britain, by contrast, many pro-EU politicians and academics are curiously reticent about acknowledging this and usually try to steer the European debate away from 'dangerous' – or 'theological' – constitutional issues. There is, and has long been, a politics of denial about the EU's federal intent. For reasons of political expediency, those who share the Europeanist vision, or have a vested interest in its promotion, have tried to de-politicise the European question on the grounds that the electorate are not yet ready to accept the EU goal of ever closer union. This, of course, is a dangerous strategy that is likely to backfire when people, to use Delors's phrase, 'wake up to the loss of sovereignty' that their leaders have signed away for them.

This is why the organisational culture of EU institutions, to whom national governments have transferred so many of the powers and functions, assumes such significance. If a transnational federal European state is being created, it is of critical importance to understand its *modus operandi* and, above all, the inner workings, compositions and character of its central institution, the Commission of the European Communities.

Beyond the auditors' report: corruption in the EU

This brings us back to the problem of explaining the internal culture of the Commission. Prior to the mass resignations provoked by the revelations of the Committee of Independent Experts, many EU analysts had enthusiastically praised the EU's proliferating 'informal political system' as part of the secret of the Commission's success in 'orchestrating' European unification (Middlemas 1995). The virtue of the new Brussels political regime was said to reside precisely in the personal networks it had generated and the way it had educated political leaders into accepting the new rules of the European 'game'; namely, by learning the politics of compromise and the diplomatic skills of striking bargains through a complex exchange of political favours and concessions; what Italians call *l'arte d'arrangiarsi*.[10] Douglas Hurd once likened negotiating in the EU, not unfavourably, to playing a game of 'three-dimensional chess'. The metaphor of the 'game' was also used by officials to describe both European integration in general and the inner life of the EU in particular.

How should we interpret these findings concerning the internal culture of the Commission? What explanations can be offered for revelations of endemic nepotism, corruption and mismanagment made by the Committee of Independent Experts, and is this, as some critics claim, much more serious than simply an indictment of the way the EU is managed? Once again, the conclusions one draws vary according to the position of the observer. Many pro-EU observers took comfort in the argument that the causes of corruption lie in the Commission's chronic understaffing and the consequent opportunities this provided for certain dishonest individuals to flout the rules and Statutes. In their view, those rules themselves were blameless: indeed, they were designed precisely to codify good practice and protect civil servants from meddling national governments. The fact that much of the fraud uncovered by the auditors occurred in those areas where the Commission had contracted out its work to private companies and consultants was taken as proof that corrupt practices were not at all 'endemic' within the Commission's own civil service.

While there may be some truth in this argument, the picture it portrays reflects some familiar structural themes about blame and perceptions of risk. According to the Commission's analysis,[11] the dangerous and corrupting influences are invariably 'external' to the permanent civil service. Those who violate the rules are the non-statutory element – the seconded experts and temporary agents; literally, people 'outside the House'. 'Outsiders' thus become scapegoats for most of the Commission's 'dysfunctional' features. Unfortunately, this conclusion is simply not borne out by the empirical evidence. Many of the worse cases of corruption were 'orchestrated' not by auxiliaries and temporary agents outside the service but by permanent staff inside the House; those statutory officials who enjoy all the benefits, job security, and diplomatic protection that is bestowed on those who are career civil servants. In the case of corruption in the EU's humanitarian aid office, as well as corruption in the tourism division, outright fraud was committed by the Heads of Unit themselves. As the report declares, 'the de facto tolerance of irregular employment practices' created 'an institutional culture [that] is unacceptable. The truth is that, if a "system" is in itself inadequate, it invites irregularity' (CIE 1999: 61).

This accusation goes far beyond any suggestion that corruption in the EU is a marginal problem confined to a few individuals. The problem appears to be structural and systemic: a defective administrative regime that actively engenders abuse of employment practices and fraud. It also generates a climate of collusion. The question asked by the Committee of Independent Experts (CIE 1999: 102) was not only how could such a 'culture' (or 'subculture') of corruption develop within the European civil service but how could it have developed 'without being detected from within'?

Evidence suggests that the existence of fraud within the Commission was known about for a long time prior to the report, but for various reasons it was not just 'tolerated' but largely accepted as part of the Commission's *modus vivendi*. There are three reasons for this. First, because giving jobs and awarding contracts to family and friends is not perceived as morally wrong or untoward in a number of EU countries. Second, because an extremely large number of people were and are implicated in the web of collusion created by the 'informal' administrative system. Many senior Commission staff, including its staunchest defenders, owe their own jobs in the Commission to the various 'back-door' methods of recruitment that mushroomed during the Delors period and earlier – and which Delors himself, in the furtherance of his centralist goals, actively encouraged. Roy Denman, an ardent EU supporter, provides damning evidence of this in his 1996 book *Missed Chances: Britain and Europe in the Twentieth Century*. 'When he [Delors] arrived in 1982', Denman observes (1996: 277–8):

> the French had a major influence in the Commission. By the time he left, in 1992, they had a stranglehold. During his time more than half the twenty Directors General were sacked. Several more left, knowing that had they stayed they would have been pushed. In almost all cases, their fault had been to voice reservations about Delors policies or French interests. Where in a key Directorate General the French did not have a senior figure '*Hommes de confiance*' were placed . . . All this meant changing the Commission into a Tammany Hall with a French accent.

In an international organisation, Denman concluded (1996: 278), something like the 'Delors Effect' is 'very difficult to reverse' once it becomes institutionalised.

The third reason why fraud was tolerated was that the Statutes themselves helped to conceal what was going on inside the Commission. Articles 17–19 expressly forbid officials from divulging information about the organisation deemed sensitive or damaging, and thereby function as an official secrets act or 'gagging clause'. Those who might wish to expose irregularities or corruption are dissuaded from doing so by the threat of disciplinary action, or by loyalty to the institution and a desire not to damage its reputation.[12] Indeed, it was only because the Committee of Independent Experts had exempted staff 'from all secrecy obligations imposed on them by Staff Regulations' that they were able to investigate the allegations of fraud (CIE 1999: 10). What is difficult to explain is how German- or Dutch- or UK-trained civil servants as well as many Scandinavian officials could have remained silent when they encountered malpractices and worse. Could it be that loyalty to the institution and the desire not to damage the reputation of the Community – as well as Article 17 – encouraged staff to keep this matter a closed and guarded secret?

The Staff Regulations combined with the absence of accountability – and the increasingly larger sums of money being dispensed under the various Commission-funded programmes – thus created an ideal environment for corruption to flourish. While many staff were aware of what was going on – and some

tried to oppose it[13] many others accepted it because they benefited from it personally. There is a paradox here. Where the 'parallel' administrative system
blocked the work of the service or led to corruption, this was usually blamed on
deviation from the Statutes. Yet where the same parallel system enabled individuals to bypass the bureaucracy in ways that 'get results', this was heralded as
part of the creative 'symbiosis' that makes the Commission so efficient and
dynamic. This attitude tends to characterise the way officials perceive the Commission: a contradictory mixture of admiration for the way it works, yet frustration with the way it fails to work. As one official commented in a knowing way,
'no one who understands the House uses the formal system. It is dead; it doesn't
work.' This ambiguity towards corruption is also found among those policy-
makers and theorists whose writing set the agenda for thinking about European
integration. As Della Porta and Mény (1997: 2) note:

> [E]vidence of the perverse effect of corruption on the functioning of political
> systems in general, and of democratic ones in particular, is not given universal
> credence. The functionalist analysis in the 1960s and 1970s sought to over-
> look moral connotations and value judgements in regard to democracy by
> stressing the beneficial effect which corruption might have on bureaucratic
> stalemate. Just as the school of organisational sociology had shown that, in
> France, the 'stalemate society' functioned thanks to the generalised practice
> of accommodation on the part of its participants, so American functionalists
> laid stress on the advantages of a degree of corruption in socialist or develop-
> ing countries in providing the means of lubricating the machinery that was
> jammed. *Mutatis mutandis*, the argument was applied to Mediterranean
> societies already characterised by traditions of paternalism, clientelism and
> nepotism. Hence the issue was no longer open to doubt: corruption either
> had a function or else was so ingrained that any attempt to eradicate it was
> futile: better to accept it and try to curb its most glaring imperfections.

The point here is that, if corruption has not been treated seriously by organisational sociologists, political scientists and many European governments, it is hardly surprising that it has not been taken very seriously in the EU either. The
attitudes described above mask the problem by refusing to countenance it. Where
the danger of corruption is acknowledged, for example by Spence (1994a), its
causes are framed in terms of a 'dangerous encroachment' into the Commission's
autonomy and supranational status by national governments. Fraud and irregularities are thus interpreted as evidence of the progressive 're-nationalisation' of the
Commission. This interpretation, however, does not square with the facts. The
evidence from my own research suggests that the 'informal' system based on
pragmatic codes and norms – the system that generated so many of the irregularities noted by the auditors – *is* the effective system of administration, and its
existence has little to do with interference from national governments. On the
contrary, it is the Commission's lack of accountability to elected representatives
of national governments and the absence of democratic control that has led to the

development of an informal system based on patronage, cronyism and fraud. This system was tolerated because it functioned; from the point of view of the Brussels elite, it was the oil that made the machinery of bureaucracy work in practice.

This gives a whole new meaning to the term 'supranationalism'. It is not so much a case of the parochial nation-state being superseded by an efficient, legal-rational and politically superior form of governance embodied by the EU technocracy or by a decentralised, transnational democracy. Rather, the new European architecture is based on an altogether more diffuse, anarchic and unaccountable system of power in which no single member state or national culture is dominant or controls the direction of the EU and its machinery. The key players in the European political 'game' are no longer just national governments. They have been joined by a new class of institutional actors at European and sub-national level who have a vested interest in promoting those institutions, and whose commitment to Europe is fuelled also by the pursuit of private goals, careers and ambitions. In this respect, the logic of the nation-state and nationalism is being transcended by the EU and the new subjectivities it is helping to forge. On the positive side, the decentring of the old concept of state sovereignty and the diffuseness of power encourages the search for dialogue and compromise, which EU advocates cite as the key advantage of the emerging EU model of governance. The negative side, however, is that it creates a 'hollow core' at the heart of the EU decision-making process. That, in turn, encourages a system based on fixes, deals and political horse-trading, and a state without democratic accountability.

A 'clash of cultures'?

As I have tried to suggest, the internal administration of the Commission mirrors many of the problems that continue to plague the project of European integration. In this respect, Edith Cresson's claims that she was the victim of an Anglo-German 'conspiracy', and her comment that patronage and nepotism are standard practice in French public administration are particularly indicative of the difficulties of reconciling the cultural norms and practices of different countries. As Castle and Butler put it: 'Brussels has no agreed administrative culture; what is cronyism in one country is legitimate use of patronage in another and such practices have seeped into the hybrid Brussels bureaucracy.'[14]

What was particularly striking in the aftermath of the scandal was the way in which so many commentators, struggling to explain what had gone wrong, suddenly turned to 'culture' for an explanation. Tony Blair spoke of the unacceptable 'culture of complacency and lack of accountability' and called for 'root and branch reform' of the Commission.[15] John Major pledged cross-party support for efforts in 'changing the culture of the Brussels administration'.[16] In the British press and in the European Parliament the Commission's 'dysfunctional' administration – variously described in terms of a 'culture of collusion and secrecy' and 'culture of corruption'[17] – was roundly condemned. 'Culture', it seems, was being used as a blanket term to describe something inexplicable; a phenomenon so general, pervasive and endemic that its causes cannot be readily identified. On the other hand, it was also a recognition of the deep-rooted and possibly ineradicable nature of the problems afflicting the Commission's internal regime. However, some commentators predictably turned to national stereotypes in search of an answer. Charles Bremner was quick to highlight the clash of styles between countries of the Protestant North and Catholic southern Europe 'Sober North beats EU's siesta South' ran one headline in *The Times*.[18] This theme was developed by other political correspondents, some of whom compared the EU to an 'extended Sicilian family' whose social dynamic was built on 'favours, horse-trading and a steady flow of cash'. In the view of one *Times* correspondent, 'Carolingian Europe, represented by the likes of Jacques Delors, Helmut Kohl and François Mitterrand, is giving way to a Europe more concerned with good housekeeping than compelling vision'.[19]

These stereotypes, however, underscore a very real problem that the EU faces in reconciling cultural differences within its own administration. Spence himself acknowledged this when he wrote about the fundamental tension between the 'traditional French administrative methods', on the one hand, and 'the tradition of human resource management common in the Anglo-Saxon tradition, typified by civil service neutrality, the formal absence of nepotism, a high degree of delegation and the principle of sharing information with colleagues', on the other (Spence 1994a: 91). Somewhat presciently, he concluded that 'whether the two can be resolved in a synthesis containing the positive features of both' was 'a moot point' in the light of the problems now looming (Spence 1994a: 91). My research shows that the absence of a coherent personnel and staffing policy – and the formidable obstacles in creating one – makes this problem all the more chronic.

The European Parliament comes of age?

In the wake of the scandal, many observers have interpreted the mass resignation of the Commission as a sign that European democracy has at last 'come of age': that what we were witnessing was an over-mighty executive being called to account and humbled by an invigorated elected assembly, at last fulfilling its role as democratic watchdog. This view was summed up by Pat Cox, an Independent MEP and leader of the European Liberal Group. 'For the Parliament itself', Cox declared (1999: 14), 'this entire debate has represented a coming of age, a new maturity in understanding its democratic rights and in its capacity to empower itself to act in the public interest.' But is this really the case? How much credit can the European Parliament take for acting on behalf of the public interest? The background to the scandal and the auditors' report reveal a number of quite extraordinary facts that casts the relationship between the European Parliament and the Commission in a new and less flattering light.

First, the report not only exposed deep-seated fraud and corruption in the Commission, it also showed that these had been known about by both the European Parliament and the Commission for at least the past four years but had been played down, to the point of a virtual cover-up.[20] Indeed, it was only thanks to the actions of a courageous 'whistleblower', Paul Van Buitenen, a Dutch accountant working in the Commission's internal audit division, that the reluctant Parliament was forced to set up the Committee of Independent Experts, whose conclusions it was then unable to ignore. These events were set in motion after 9 December 1998 when Van Buitenen handed a dossier containing hundreds of censored Commission documents on frauds, scandals and cover-ups to Magda Avoet, a member of the European Parliament's Green Party group. These documents not only detailed 'unbridled cronyism' in the awarding of Commission contracts,[21] they also provided evidence of an alleged 'dirty tricks' campaign designed to stop public inquiries into fraud. Events earlier that year gave further credence to this claim. Michel Fromont, the editor of the Belgian newspaper *La Meuse* – the first publication to reveal widespread fraud in the EU's humanitarian aid budget – was beaten up in his own home by a group of armed men. He was later telephoned and warned to 'lay off the Commission'.[22] Then in September, the influential British magazine *Index on Censorship* appeared with six blank pages, each stamped 'Censored'. These replaced an article on internal corruption in the EU by Hartwig Nathe, a journalist for the German political magazine *Focus*. Explaining her decision to withdraw the article, *Index*'s editor-in-chief, Ursula Owen said, 'such have been the Kafkaesque obfuscations in the EC, and such has been the pressure on the journalist concerned, that Index finally felt unable to expose him to further risk'.[23] By October, other evidence was emerging that the EU had been paying lawyers representing officials under investigation to hound critical journalists.[24] By January, Paul Van Buitenen had been suspended from his post and was facing disciplinary proceedings. The accusation levelled against him by the Commission was that of 'imparting information to unauthorised and non-competent persons'[25]. This raised the legal question of whether the European Parliament, whose role is to assess whether EU money has been properly spent, counts as an 'authorised body'.

The second astonishing revelation was the failure of the European Parliament to take any corrective action. The European Parliament, like the Commission, had received all the information it needed from the Court of Auditors to suggest that financial irregularities and fraud were rife. Refusing to discharge the budget is one of the few powers the Parliament enjoys, but has rarely been used. For four consecutive years the Court of Auditors had refused to grant the Commission a positive 'Statement of Assurance' as to the legality and regularity of the budget accounts. Yet for three years running Parliament had granted a 'discharge' or clearance, despite reports of malpractice and fraud by both the Court of Auditors' and the Commission's Internal Audit division.[26]

It was only in March 1998, when the Auditors reported an unacceptably high percentage of the EU's budget unaccounted for,[27] and with European elections looming the following year, that Parliament finally refused to grant 'discharge' to the Commission for the 1996 budget. This, however, was done reluctantly and only after some opportunistic political manoeuvring. Parliament had set a December deadline for reconsidering the discharge question, approval of which was largely a formality. However, in the interim, with the Cresson scandal and Van Buitenen affair unfolding, tension between the two institutions had mounted. Parliament again refused to discharge the budget. In an ill-advised move on the eve of the sensitive budget discharge vote, Jacques Santer provoked the Parliament with a demand to 'back him or sack him', a strategy that was supported by the Socialists, the largest political group in the EP.[28] After liaising closely with Santer, Pauline Green, the Socialist Group leader, then tabled a motion of censure which, if passed, would have brought down the entire Commission. This was a bluff. Her real purpose, she later disclosed, was to engineer a comprehensive defeat of her own motion in order to vote confidence in the Commission. Sensing this game plan, Pat Cox, leader of the thirty-seven-strong Liberal group, proposed a resolution that stopped short of a full vote of censure and demanded the resignation of only two Socialist Commissioners at the centre of the alleged corruption: Cresson and Marín. Santer then announced that if any individual Commissioner were censured he too would have to resign – thereby detonating the so-called 'nuclear option'. Fearing the likely damage this would cause, particularly to the new single currency, MEPs voted against the call to dismiss Cresson and Marín, and a Socialist motion to set up a 'committee of wise men' to investigate incompetence, negligence and alleged fraud was passed. Green formally withdrew her motion of censure and another censure motion tabled by right-wing MEPs was defeated by 232 votes to 293 against.

I venture this detailed account because it highlights how the narrow politics of administration and accountancy opens up into the wider politics of accountability. It also illustrates an important thesis of this book: namely, the extent to which an *esprit de corps* has been created not simply among members of the same 'House' (the Commission) but also between the EU's different institutions or 'Houses'. Pauline Green announced the vote as a 'kick in the backside for the Commission', but some observers could not help noticing that she was gallantly kissed by Neil Kinnock as the Commissioners filed out of the parliamentary chamber to celebrate.[29] While inter-institutional rivalry no doubt exists, members of the Parliament and the Commission have a shared interest in protecting and defending each other from those 'outside' the EU institutions. Indeed, many Commissioners, including Cresson and Bonino, are themselves former MEPs, and vice versa. Jacques Santer's announcement, immediately after resigning, that he would seek nomination as a Luxembourg MEP simply confirms this. Furthermore, both Commissioners and MEPs have close links to each other via their political affiliations. The 'party list' system for selecting Euro MPs – a system that concentrates power in the hands of party machines – functions extremely effectively as a mechanism through which this *classe politique* perpetuates itself. From a legal perspective, this raises, *inter alia*, the question of whether there can ever be effective accountability of the Commission to the European Parliament, particularly given Parliament's lack of accountability to its electors. As one Parliament official commented in the wake of the Commission fraud scandal, 'MEPs can't really criticise the Commission because Parliament shares the same institutional culture as the Commission. If there is less fraud in the Parliament it is because the EP's budget is smaller.'

Integration among elites: the significance of *engrenage*

The question asked at the outset was whether the EU has succeeded in creating within its own institutions a supranational administrative elite that might one day become a vanguard for furthering European integration. The evidence of corruption presented above might lead one to dismiss such claims as sociologically naive and misplaced. What this research suggests, however, is that EU officials have shifted their loyalties towards the supranational institutions they serve – much as Haas and other integration theorists predicted. In many respects, the history of European political integration is a story of the progressive 'meshing together' of Europe's political and financial elites and their incorporation or socialisation into the institutions, ideology and norms of the EU. Much more than simply an abstract theory of 'cognitive change', *engrenage* clearly does work as a key mechanism in the creation of a new type of 'European' subjectivity. This process also appears to be occurring in the Council of Ministers, the least supranational of EU institutions, particularly among the seconded national civil servants working in its various permanent committees and specialised working groups. As Areilza (1995: 9–10) observes:

> Typically, participants in the numerous COREPER [Committee of Permanent Representatives] and Council sessions develop a certain allegiance to their own group of equals at the EC level. There is an expectation to produce results and to follow certain unwritten club rules, which minimise or diffuse conflict.

The normative pressure on national officials working on the more detailed and technical aspects of EU policy-making is to achieve results by seeking compromise and playing by the 'club rules'. Package deals, trade-offs and bargaining are an accepted part of those rules, and arguably a necessary part of the process of reaching compromise among these middle-ranking national officials. However, this behaviour is reinforced by the fact that voting rules are less important at this level, given the lack of party politics or electoral burdens. And since only unresolved issues are referred back to ministers and diplomats, pressure to reach consensus 'gives these officials full control over the issue and the possibility of not letting diplomats or ministers decide' (Areilza 1995: 20). One of the reasons why national civil servants accept so much of what the Commission proposes, Areilza adds (1995: 20), is that the EU system encourages 'bureaucratic self-empowerment'. They can thus launch initiatives from the EU that would be difficult to propose at home and thereby enlarge their area of influence vis-à-vis other national administrative units. They also benefit from the primacy of Community measures over any national provision. Hence, the acceptance by national civil servants of the transferral of the decision-making level to the European level has a number of compensations. However, as Areilza concludes (1995: 25), the weakening of the member states as decisive actors in the policy process as a result of this 'management paradigm' (or 'managerial supranationalism' via the plethora of committees and advisory bodies) has not strengthened the EU's democratic credentials or political legitimacy.

Comitology: Parkinson's Law or bureaucratic self-empowerment?

With the transfer of powers from the nation-states to Brussels there has been a proliferation of specialised bodies dealing with policy proposals and regulations and, increasingly, much of the detail of Community legislation is formulated by these committees of experts. 'Comitology' has become established EU shorthand for this system of procedures involving committees, made up of national representatives and chaired by the Commission, whereby member states can exercise some control over implementing powers delegated to the Commission.[30] However, as a recent Parliamentary report on the 'delegation of powers to the Commission' noted,

> [W]ho sits on these committees, when they meet, how they work and what they decide is something of a mystery, except to insiders, assiduous Brussels watchers and a few academics and students. Occasionally the existence and activities of a committee will make the headlines. For example, the saga of the ban on British beef in the 1990s drew public attention to the powers of the Standing Veterinary Committee. But the vast majority of the [250 or more] committees operate outside the public gaze.
>
> (House of Lords 1999: 8)

Moreover, as was demonstrated in the case of the Standing Veterinary Committee, these committees often keep no records of their meetings or decisions. The House of Lords report also notes (1999: 6) that, remarkably, 'no list of the number or scope of these committees is publicly available'. Given its complexity and its implications for transparency and democracy, comitology is important and controversial. Moreover, with the entry into force of the Amsterdam Treaty, the comitology system has been extended to areas previously dealt with in the intergovernmental Third Pillar, including asylum, immigration and free movement of persons. All this simply confirms the fears of those who contend that the EU is developing into an increasingly secretive and centralised state.

This is another reason why the relationship between the European Parliament and the other EU institutions is so unsatisfactory. The drama surrounding the resignation of the Commission – and Parliament's failure to monitor it properly or censure it once corruption had been revealed – highlights the degree of 'collusion' that exists between Commissioners and MEPs, particularly those who belong to the same political groupings. On the eve of the crucial censure vote in January 1999, the Socialist Group leader, Pauline Green, was seen dining in one of Brussels's most exclusive restaurants with Jacques Santer and other senior

Commissioners as they worked to find a solution to their shared predicament. MEPs had themselves recently been subject to widespread criticism in the press for having awarded themselves lavish personal office allowances and for various cases involving MEPs fiddling their expenses. The launch of the single currency that month and fears of what censure of the Commission might do to market confidence in the euro added further incentives for MEPs to broker a compromise with the Commission over the issue of censure. There are two ways of interpreting this: as another example of the EU's successful informal political system bringing adversaries together to seek solutions to common problems; or as evidence of a new transnational politics in which the EU elite staff its different institutions has emerged and is now transforming itself, through recognition of collective self-interest, from a 'class in itself' into a 'class for itself', in the classic Marxist sense.[31] For these professional Europeans the EU has indeed displaced the nation-state as the focus of allegiance. Their personal careers and fortunes are inextricably linked to the success of the EU, a point most of them acknowledged. In this sense, EU civil servants are pioneers of 'European consciousness' and 'European identity'. However, with its bureaucratic, legalistic and technocratic character and the thriving 'informal' system of administration, it is not the kind of European identity envisaged by Monnet and Schuman.

The 'Europeanisation' of mass public opinion?

> The state is invisible; it must be personified before it can be seen, symbolised before it can be loved, imagined before it can be conceived.
>
> (Michael Walzer 1967)[32]

According to the Monnet model, supranational *Homo Europaeus* is someone who no longer feels a deep emotional attachment to the nation-state and whose old parochial loyalties and sense of belonging have been re-directed towards Europe. By these criteria, 'European Man' appears to be a species confined largely to EU's web of institutions and the various economic networks and social spaces these have spawned. But how far has this process of 'Europeanisation' been extended beyond Brussels? The attempt by European elites to invent the EU as an imagined community – to render it visible and appealing in the mind's eye of the public – has been central to the cultural politics of European integration. The hope is that this will spill over into the formation of a fully-fledged European public sphere. Imagining Europe is thus an inherently political as well as a cultural enterprise. This 'Europeanisation of Europe' is a process that recalls Hechter's (1975) notion of 'internal colonialism'. The fundamental difference, however, is that where once Europe symbolised 'empire and expansionism, the new idea of Europe is about retrenchment: "the Europeanisation, not of the rest of the world, but . . . of Europe itself"'.[33] Comparisons with internal colonialism are apposite: just as the nation-state was forged by intellectuals and elites whose goal was to inject nationalist consciousness into the masses,[34] so EU officials, politicians and advertising experts are attempting to instil 'European consciousness' among the peoples of Europe. Seen in this perspective, *construction européenne* appears not only as a teleological grand narrative about 'destiny' and 'progress' but also as a project of social engineering reminiscent of Leninism.[35] In either case, 'culture' has provided the idiom through which elites try to galvanise and mould public opinion.

As political leaders recognise, the credibility of the European Union hinges on the development of a more tangible and coherent sense of shared identity among the peoples of Europe whose interests the Union claims to serve. This is crucial for mobilising people, for winning consent and for creating the 'social cohesion' and feelings of belonging that EU leaders say are needed to underpin the legal, economic and monetary aspects of the integration process. It is also crucial for the democratic legitimacy of the EU's largely undemocratic institutions. As García and Wallace (1993: 172) concluded:

> If a European identity could be established and its elements clearly identified, the institutions of the European community would have a much stronger point of reference from which to gather loyalty from its citizens and build up a much needed legitimacy. We have now to evaluate whether this is a realistic expectation and under what circumstances it could be feasible.

The problem is that the European Union is an embryonic state without a nation. This view is tacitly endorsed even by many pro-EU analysts. Europe's 'trans-nationalising elites' might 'eventually cohere into a European ruling class', as Schlesinger (1994b: 41) speculates, but it is an increasingly detached, bureaucratic and remote ruling class as far as citizens in the member states are concerned. It is within this context that the British and German government's recent emphasis on creating a 'people's Europe' begins to make sense. How to translate this populist notion into policy is another matter. Acknowledging the legacy of complacency, elitism and *dirigisme* that has characterised the EU's approach to public opinion represents a start, but the Commission's (CEC 1996a: 3) aim 'to make Europe the business of every citizen' is not backed by a coherent strategy. Certainly, there is 'a lot more Europe today'; as one official put it, the presence of the European Community and its laws is increasingly felt in the everyday lives of Europeans (Wilson 1993). But the goal of inculcating a more popular sense of European consciousness and shifting allegiances from nation-state to European centre still shows little signs of success. The European Commission has invented a new repertoire of 'post-nationalist' symbols, but these are pale imitations of nationalist iconography and have so far failed to win for the EU the title deeds upon which national loyalties and allegiances are claimed. Indeed, the only group over whom the ideology of 'Europeanism' has had a notable influence seems to be EU officials and politicians themselves and certain intellectuals and businesspeople within the member states. Even senior officials within the Commission accept that there is still no such thing as a 'European public' – including staff in its own *Eurobarometer* office, whose Euro-statistics are crucial to the creation of such a public. As one Commission expert on public opinion research put it:

the reason there is no 'European public' is because there is no common language. Okay, you had the same problem in India and the USSR, but these were federal dictatorships. India has over a hundred languages, but only two are dominant. Because there is no common language, there is no common media [and] no public for the democratic debate over European issues. If there is a 'European readership' it is probably centred around the *Financial Times*.

This adds further weight to the concerns of those who suggest that the EU's technocratic elite inhabits a social universe that is very different, and increasingly remote, from that of the so-called 'ordinary citizens' of Europe. The reality of the EU is, as Graham Leicester (1996: 11) writes, 'that actors at the supranational level – governments and officials – in a sense form *a separate community* from those at the national level – citizens of the member states' (my emphasis). Indeed, anecdotal evidence suggests that an increasing number of children of EU officials, educated in the 'European schools' and other European institutions with strong links to the EU, are now returning to find work in the EU and its various 'satellite' bodies.[36]

Leicester's argument (1996: 11) that 'the acceptance of a Europe-wide political culture and community is higher in practice at the level of the political elites than among the constituent peoples or *demoi*' was vividly demonstrated in the way political leaders in France and Germany handled the debate over the single currency. For example, on 23 April 1998, four days before the official announcement of those member-states that had successfully qualified for membership of the euro, two events occurred in Germany that were deeply symbolic of the gulf between German political elites and the German public. Speaking in the Bundestag, both Helmut Kohl for the Christian Democrats and Gerhadt Schröder for the Social Democrats pledged their parties' unswerving determination to make Germany a founder member of the European single currency. Arguments against Economic and Monetary Union were allowed no space. In the vote, Parliament approved the move by 575 for to 35 against and five abstentions. This resounding endorsement was not, however, a reflection of public opinion in Germany. On the same day, an opinion poll for the Association of Bankers reported that over 62 per cent of Germans strongly opposed the single currency and the abolition of the deutschmark.[37] In this instance, as in other areas of European integration, what the public thought was of no consequence. Some commentators call this determination to push ahead regardless of public opinion 'conviction politics' and courageous Euro-idealism. For critics instead, it suggests that *dirigisme* and elitism – or what Delors once described as 'benign despotism' – continues to characterise the way European elites approach the project of European construction.

Repeated warnings about the dangerous rift that has emerged between Europe's institutions and its citizens are also borne out by the EU's own opinion polls. Recent *Eurobarometer* reports, for example, provide grim reading for advocates of ever closer union. Support for EU membership across the Union has plummeted from 72 per cent in 1991 to only 46 per cent – fewer than at any time in the past twenty years – while eight out of ten Europeans admit to being 'not very well informed' or 'not informed at all' about the EU (CEC 1997a). The 1998 *Eurobarometer* report finds that fewer than half of Europeans think their country's membership of the EU is a 'good thing', and only 41 per cent think their country benefits from EU membership (CEC 1998). This decline in support was a response, in part, to anxieties fuelled by the recession in Europe – which has led to a haemorrhaging of the notion that European integration would lead inexorably to ever-strengthening prosperity. But it was also a reaction to the Maastricht Treaty which, as most analysts agree, was an elitist affair in which 'Eurocrats . . . embarked on a new phase of integration for which virtually no enthusiasm and precious little support actually existed' (Graham 1996: 117). Seldom has the EU appeared so unpopular or irrelevant to the needs of its citizens. Forty years of institutionalised attempts to 'build Europe' seem to have had little impact at the level of popular consciousness and the transfer of loyalties from the nation-state to European institutions in Brussels predicted by neofunctionalist integration theories simply has not happened. If the nation-state is 'historically obsolete', as many politicians and social scientists argue, most Europeans nevertheless remain stubbornly wedded to their national identities, against which the notion of a 'European identity' pails into insignificance.

But is this necessarily the case? Could political actors in the member states 'be persuaded to shift their loyalties, expectations and political activities', as Ernst Haas argued over four decades ago, 'towards a new centre, whose institutions possess or demand jurisdiction over pre-existing national states'?[38] The question asked by EU officials and Euro-federalists is what can be done to encourage people to abandon their parochial attachments to the nation-state and to promote feelings of pride and belonging to 'Europe'? As historians remind us, the nation-state is a relatively recent phenomenon: an 'imagined community' whose existence at the level of mass popular consciousness was forged largely through modern communication technologies and state apparatuses. Modern nations were 'invented' using various nation-building strategies, from newspapers, railway networks, mass education, conscript armies and taxation to the standardisation of vernacular language, the mobilisation of myths and symbols, the rewriting of history and the 'invention of tradition'. If these 'political technologies' proved so effective for creating the nation-states in an age of industrialisation, so some argue, why not use them to engineer a European identity appropriate for the post-colonial, post-industrial age? Hobsbawm and Ranger (1983) suggested there was nothing wrong with fledgling states inventing their own traditions and rituals. How else can the Commission achieve its goal of integrating the peoples of Europe, one might ask? After all, the EU is simply copying the tried and tested formula of nation-building that states have followed since the French Revolution. Surely the ends justify the means.

Flaws in the EU's model of identity

Within the European Commission there are many who advocate such an approach, arguing that identities are segmentary and multifold, therefore creating an overarching 'European identity' is simply a matter of 'stimulating awareness' of our shared cultural heritage to form a new pan-national tier of identity and solidarity. Underlying this 'Chinese box' theory of identity-formation are two key assumptions, both of which are deeply flawed. First is the functionalist idea that because social identities are fluid, shifting and contextual and because individuals invariably have multiple identities, they will necessarily fit together harmoniously, like so many nesting Russian dolls, neatly bounded and hierarchically arranged 'in concentric circles which encourage compatible loyalties from the local to the European level' (García and Wallace 1993: 172).[39] The problem with this analysis is that it ignores politics; once identities become politicised (as most national identities do), tiers of loyalty become enmeshed in sensitive issues of power and sovereignty. There is little historical evidence to support the optimistic assumption that national identities in Europe can be peacefully incorporated and subsumed within a greater regional whole. Furthermore, even senior judges accept that the concept of subsidiarity is incoherent and legally unworkable. If nation-state-formation provides a model, one should remember that decades of conflict, state violence, authoritarianism and war were also preconditions for forging national communities.

The second flaw is the assumption that a European identity can be created simply by exploiting existing 'patterns of European culture'.[40] Many writers wax enthusiastically about European 'core values' – which are invariably located in the Graeco-Roman tradition, in Judaeo-Christian ethics, Renaissance humanism and individualism, Enlightenment rationalism and science, traditions of civil rights, democracy, the rule of law and so on. Leaving aside the criticism that these 'core values' are highly selective, elitist and 'Eurocentric' (Said 1978; Amin 1988; Pieterse 1991; Schlesinger 1994a), the problem is that those cultural elements from which existing national identities are constructed (including language, history, religion, myth, memory, folklore and tradition) are precisely those factors that most divide Europeans. EU elites have tried to get round this dilemma by using the slogan 'unity in diversity' as the official formula for discussing European culture(s), and by evoking the old Gestalt idea that 'European culture' is a whole greater than the sum of its parts – and therefore 'naturally' transcendent. The problem, however, is that few people grasp the 'big picture'. Moreover, who defines what constitutes 'European culture' is itself a politically loaded issue that most EU leaders are reluctant to address. There is also a major contradiction between attempts to mobilise public support for further integration by evoking populist rhetoric about a 'people's Europe' and 'citizenship', and the more traditional attempt by many EU leaders to de-politicise the integration process by portraying it as a legal-rational and primarily 'technical' process that has more to do with history, evolution and destiny than with political will.

A further flaw with the EU's 'nation-building' activities is that any instrumental *dirigiste* approach to culture and cultural policy at European level is specifically ruled out by the Maastricht Treaty. Article 128 states that 'responsibility for European cultural co-operation lies with the Member States' and excludes 'any harmonisation of the laws and regulations of the Member States'. The EU's cultural politics therefore violate its own Treaties and run contrary to its celebrated principle of 'subsidiarity' – which is supposed to limit Community intervention in areas which are not its exclusive competence, particularly education and culture. However much EU officials might contest this and argue that there is no 'official' EU cultural policy for creating a unified European culture – just a unified economy and culture-area for the territories comprising Euroland, perhaps – the charge of hypocrisy is no basis upon which to gain the trust of the people it so craves.

Finally, there is the problem of the loss of accountability and democracy that inevitably occurs with the move to larger political units – quite apart from the non-democratic structure and division of powers that has marked the European Community since its creation. As this study indicates, and as most EU analysts accept, decision-making in the EU is extremely undemocratic: the result of covert deals, bargaining and compromises struck between Ministers and their permanent representatives in the Council of Ministers, conducted behind closed doors. The European Parliament is not a legislature, it does not elect a government, and it lacks credibility as the democratic conscience of the Union. As Hobsbawm (1997: 268) argues, it is therefore 'misleading to speak of the "democratic deficit" of the European Union. The EU was explicitly constructed as a nondemocratic (i.e. nonelectoral) basis, and few will seriously argue that it would have got where it is otherwise.' However, the EU's feeble democracy has become an increasing source of embarrassment and ideological discomfort. Before attempting to transfer popular loyalties through cultural politics, the EU should embark upon institutional reforms to set its own house in order. Popular loyalty has to be earned gradually through incremental actions, not 'captured' by manufactured symbols and state-like institutions. To be effective, European flags, anthems, trophies and institutions must be meaningful, and that means they should come after, not before, political legitimacy has been established and accepted by the peoples of Europe.

The question of whether the citizens of Europe actually want the things that Europe's supranational political class is deciding on their behalf should be asked more seriously. EU elites still regard the treaties as an embryonic federal constitution and appear determined, as Leicester (1996) says, to impose a federal order before the peoples of Europe are ready for it. When asked what lessons they drew from surveys revealing large-scale opposition in many states to the introduction of the single currency, EU officials repeatedly stressed that this was because of the public's 'lack of information', 'fear' and 'ignorance', all of which the EU's 'action programmes' and cultural initiatives are designed to tackle. 'Our surveys constantly show that support for Europe is higher the more educated people are', was how one senior official in the Commission's public opinion analysis unit summed it up; the suggestion being that support for the EU reflects levels of intelligence. This patrician-like approach effectively rules out dissent by redefining opposition to further integration as an expression of 'ignorance' or lack of education. This is a good example of how European integration functions as a 'discourse of power' by recasting political issues as purely technical problems to be resolved by 'informing' and 'educating' the citizen. But it again highlights the democratic deficit that characterises (and undermines) the EU's approach to integration.

Surreptitious integration

While many social scientists are sceptical about the European Union's supranational quest to change the cultural bases of political allegiance across the continent, some observers detect signs that this may already be happening, despite the EU's declining popularity and remoteness from the electorate. For David Williamson, recently retired Secretary-General of the EU Commission, this growing attachment to Europe 'as an entity' is also evidenced in the development of new university Master's programmes dealing with European integration studies. 'Where the question [of European identity] is not tinged with sterile political debate', he writes (1998: 6), 'it is evident that people find no difficulty with European Air Traffic Control, Eurovision, the European Cup, Europe versus America at golf.' Yes: but how institutions such as Eurovision and European Air Traffic Control reflect popular attachment to the EU is far from clear.

The argument that a surreptitious process of Europeanisation is occurring in everyday life is given its clearest expression in Mark Leonard's report for the think-tank Demos, *Europe, the search for identity*. 'Beneath the apathy and ignorance of EU citizens', he writes, 'the EU enjoys a powerful latent legitimacy – one that it rarely taps into.'[41]. What is this 'latent legitimacy'? Leonard's answer is delivered with almost poetic gusto:

> Far away from the Europe of regulations and institutions, the fragments of a cultural identity and European life-style are secretly emerging. This surreptitious identity is carefully stored away in holiday snapshots and memories of art, literature, music, buildings and landscape. It has been captured and promoted in institutions and schemes that allow people to experience Europe directly – unmediated by governments and EU institutions. The most visible ones are the ERASMUS exchange programme, the Eurovision Song Contest, Inter-rail and the Channel Tunnel.[42]

Leonard's point is that the EU must be seen to concentrate on its citizens' priorities and on 'concrete examples' of integration rather than grand designs or abstract principles. If EU institutions base their identity on 'this patchwork of sounds, smells, pleasures and problems that make up our lifestyles, it will bring much more legitimacy than any new institutions' (Leonard 1998a: 27). Exactly what is 'European' about these 'sounds', 'smells' or 'pleasures' is an open question (the smell of a Brussels drain or the sound of a passing Eurofighter jet, perhaps?).

Leonard is correct in one thing: EU leaders' fixation with legal and institutional agendas has, until recently at least, blinded them to the process of European integration occurring at the micro-level. Europe has undoubtedly become more homogeneous than it was even a generation ago. Seen from afar, there are many factors that increasingly work to unite Europeans, from demographic trends (the down-swing of the European household; postponement of marriage; increasing divorce rates; increasing percentage of children born outside of marriage) and growing trade between member states ('Europeans consuming Europe' in their choice of food, fashion and holidays) to shared fears about unemployment, AIDS, crime and environmental pollution. These trends, together with the diminishing influence of religion and growing secularisation, suggest that European demographic and cultural patterns are slowly converging even though enthusiasm for further European integration is in decline. The seemingly universal popularity of American brand products throughout Europe suggests that consumption of 'Americana' has also become part of Europe's cultural currency. As one marketing analyst remarked, 'a borderless cultural Europe in terms of music, sport and cinema exists already' (Graham 1996: 119).

This, then, is one of the paradoxes of European integration. While the formal, top-down, EU-led programme of integration has lost momentum, informal 'bottom-up Europeanisation' continues. According to research by the London-based Henley Centre there now exists an identifiable 'cluster of brands, experiences and icons' which create 'a map of shared experience' and thereby 'lend a distinctly European identity to the consumers of Western Europe' (Graham 1996: 121). These icons include 'Eurostar, Le Shuttle, European Football Championships and European Parliament elections; Tin Tin, Asterix and James Bond; Abba, U2 and Julio Iglesias; Steffi Graf, Boris Becker, Claudia Schiffer and Naomi Campbell; Armani, Boss and Chanel; Hugh Grant, Gérard Depardieu, Sophia Loren and Catherine Deneuve; Philips, Danone, Nestlé and Benetton'.[43]

However, the extent to which these consumer icons reflect Europe and 'Europeanisation' rather than 'globalisation' remains an open question. Moreover, with the exception of environmental problems (which, like the nuclear fallout from Chernobyl, are generally perceived to cross national frontiers), most of the common experiences and anxieties cited above do not necessarily generate a greater sense of intra-European unity or solidarity. On the contrary, the worries that unite EU citizens, including fear of more taxes (68 per cent), drugs and crime (65 per cent), losing the national currency (52 per cent) and unemployment (51 per cent),[44] tend to magnify doubts about the EU project and fuel national chauvinism and xenophobia.

Nonetheless, experience of Europe's cultural diversity has become a key dimension of everyday life in myriad ways, from supermarkets and cinemas to fashion and food. People take more foreign holidays, more 'weekend breaks', make more business trips, more phone calls, watch more European television stations than at any time in the past. The level of cross-border flows is unprecedented. Mass sports like football have become increasingly 'Europeanised' at the level both of players and managers and of television coverage. Eric Cantona, Jürgen Klinsman and Luciano Pavarotti have become household names in Britain. Branches of Benetton and Bata now appear in almost every British high street, while Marks and Spencer have opened up shops in Strasbourg and Brussels. Balsamic vinegar, sundried tomatoes, Calamata olives, porcini mushrooms and freshly baked French baguettes are now available in Tesco's and Sainsbury's. But does all this add up to an emerging European identity that can generate legitimacy or support for the EU project?

The danger is to confuse patterns of consumption with processes of identity-formation. People consume products but their cultural meanings vary according to context. The British preference for Indian food or German cars does not lead inexorably to an identification with India or with Germany. English Football fans may worship Eric Cantona or David Ginola but still dislike the French and Italians. The question is, at what point does experience of Europe spill over into 'European consciousness'? Jacques Delors recognised this in his comments about the need to give Europe a 'soul' and in his frequent warnings that people do not fall in love with a market. Evidence from opinion polls suggests that we are still a long way from the kind of European identity he has in mind. Take mobility – one of the key indicators of the success of the European project. According to EU surveys, fewer than one-third of Europeans 'would take a job elsewhere in Europe were they offered one', and, as we have seen, only a negligible percentage of the population of each member state is made up of other EU nationals: 5 per cent in Belgium (the highest), 2.8 per cent in France, 2.1 per cent in Germany and falling to 0.6 per cent in Spain and 0.2 per cent in Italy.[45] The possibility of cross-border mobility has not yet motivated many Europeans to find work and settle abroad. It is all very well to highlight the increase in transnational tourism, but the mass tourist experience is two weeks in a packaged holiday resort or touring party, safely insulated from any real contact with the 'natives'.

Language remains arguably the greatest barrier to further integration (Smith 1992a; Schlesinger 1994b). While EU surveys report growing linguistic dexterity among young Europeans, other surveys give a different picture. Despite the increasing emphasis on language acquisition in schools, relatively few Europeans speak or read foreign languages. A survey of language skills conducted by the Institut für Demoskopie Allensbach in 1994 found that some 52 per cent of all West Germans did not speak or read any foreign language (rising to 72 per cent for East Germans), and 86 per cent never read any foreign literature.[46] Even among the twenty to thirty year age range almost 69 per cent did not speak or read any foreign language. If only 31 per cent of Germans speak English fluently, we can expect even less from countries such as Italy and Spain, which even more than Germany dub television programmes and films. Significant in this respect are the findings of the 1995 NOP survey carried out for the BBC. On the key question 'how European do you feel?', 84 per cent of all British adult respondents answered 'not at all' or 'a little'. Asked 'with which country do you feel you have the most in common?', the top four countries chosen were all English-speaking

(USA 23 per cent; Australia 15 per cent; Canada 14 per cent), while only a small minority picked a continental country (Germany 7 per cent, Spain 5 per cent).[47] What these figures indicate is that, for most Britons, identification with the 'English-speaking' world still far outweighs identification with Britain's European partners. Some EU supporters like Denman (1996: 287) see this as evidence of British 'blindness' towards Europe and the continuing preoccupation with Empire. A more sociological interpretation, however, is that this confirms that the key elements in the formation of political identities continue to be language, a sense of shared history and memory, and kinship.

Towards a post-nationalist political order in Europe?

Mark Leonard's solution to the challenge of 'making Europe more popular', developed in his later book *Rediscovering Europe* (1998b),[48] is to create new narratives or 'mission statements' that will 'grab the popular imagination'; to do for Europe what the narrative of 'liberty, equality, fraternity' did for revolutionary France, or what the idea of 'God's free Englishmen' did for Cromwell's army during the English civil war. Transcending the nation-state and nationalism is simply a matter of joining up the dots between the scattered fragments of European identity, now carefully woven to create a compelling story about our shared European identity. Unfortunately, this leaves unanswered the fundamental question of what the content of these new European narratives should be. To supersede nationalism and create a Europe nation-state at the cultural level is a formidable task which some would say 'is actually impossible'.[49] This may be unduly pessimistic: as I have tried to argue, the creation of a European demos, if it emerges at all, will follow rather than precede the creation of properly constituted democratic institutions. Until that happens, appeals to the 'European interest' are likely to be interpreted as Brussels code for the self-interests of a technocratic EU elite.

One encouraging sign of an emerging democratic culture in Europe that has so far received little attention comes from a most unlikely source: Europe's media. Edith Cresson, shortly before being forced from office, claimed that she was a victim of a conspiracy by the German media, had filed a lawsuit for libel against the French newspaper *Libération*, and had the Guardian European editor to her office to complain that her tormentor in the Belgian press had 'neo-Nazi links'. This was clearly not a German conspiracy. As Martin Walker (1999), a European correspondent for the Guardian notes, what stoked the public and parliamentary disquiet about corruption and fraud within the European bureaucracy was something altogether new. 'What has been happening over the past year of more in Brussels', he writes,

> has been the emergence of a European journalism. A handful of correspondents, based mainly in Brussels and Luxembourg, banded together into a loose alliance to investigate and expose fraud. In a striking example of Euro-solidarity, they agreed to share documents and sources that came their way,

to help each other with research in individual countries, and to back each other up.[50]

While this is an encouraging sign of an incipient transnational democracy, Walker's observation should also be tempered with caution. There are many journalists in Brussels who doubtless knew about, and might have reported earlier, the irregularities that led to the downfall of the Commission. The handful of investigative journalists cited by Walker contrasts starkly with the many correspondents who have grown comfortable in Brussels and whom the Commission often relies upon to act as information relays. For example, much of the Green Paper on preparing public opinion for the single currency, and several of the Commission's propaganda-like 'information' booklets, have been written by journalists accredited to the EU in Brussels. Like *fonctionnaires*, MEPs and officials in the Council of Ministers, they too frequently come to reflect the interests and perspectives of those inside the institutional bubble.

A more philosophical critique of the Europeanist project, however, depends on whether one agrees with the federalist argument that the nation-state is obsolete and a threat to peace, that we have entered a post-nationalist era of history and that supranational institutions like the Commission are more likely to guarantee stability, prosperity, peace and democracy for Europe's citizens. These are highly dubious assumptions. While democratic countries such as Switzerland, Belgium and Canada are frequently cited as exemplars of successful multilingual, multi-ethnic federal states, the fact is that even these liberal parliamentary democracies are being destabilised by threats of secession and ethnic division. Countries where democracy did not exist, such as the former USSR and Yugoslavia, provide more pessimistic reminders that large federal unions are neither necessarily more stable than small nation-states, nor do they offer greater protection to minorities.

Furthermore, the argument that 'nationalism causes war' – which has provided much of the EU's claim to legitimacy as well as its emotional appeal to intellectuals – is simplistic and does little to explain the complex web of interests and motives that lies behind most wars. Jingoism and militarism are not exclusive to nation states or nationalism. As Nairn (1977) described it, nationalism is 'Janus-faced': neither intrinsically progressive nor regressive, it can be simultaneously both forward-looking and liberatory as well as backward-looking and obscurantist. Nationalism is a mobilising force that can be inflected to suit almost any ideological position, from Fascism and communism to anti-colonialism and Buddhism. The claim that European integration and the supersession of the nation-state are promoting peace, cohesion and solidarity among Europeans has some considerable weight in terms of dealing with the uniquely difficult problem of Germany. But elsewhere in Europe, rather than overcoming divisions, one could ask whether integration is actually fuelling ethnic and national conflict. Certainly European unification since the late 1980s has contributed significantly to undermining the old nation-states, and the idea of a 'Europe of the Regions', which the Commission supports, would push this process further. However, the perceived loss of national sovereignty has resulted in claims by many governments that the expansion of the EU has become a threat to nationhood and this has fuelled an upsurge of defensive cultural chauvinism and regressive regional nationalisms throughout Europe.[51] Like decapitating the mythical hydra, the break-up of old nation-states may simply replace them with a plethora of new nationalisms often more xenophobic and ethnically exclusivist than that from which they have seceded.

Finally, whether the Commission's supranational goals are feasible is a question ultimately bound up with the future of the nation-state. For many EU supporters, 'Europe is a project whose time has come', but that 'narrative' depends on whose Europe we are talking about. The evidence of this study suggests that the EU has created not union among 'the peoples' of Europe' but an ever closer union of technical, political and financial elites in Europe. It is not a 'citizen's Europe' by any stretch of the imagination. The EU's narrative about 'irreversible' integration and 'federal destiny' also depends on how one reads history. A more accurate view of history would note that the processes of nation-state formation and nationalism that have been sweeping various parts of the world since the seventeenth century are far from exhausted. As Anderson (1992) argues, the processes of dissolution set in motion by the collapse of the multi-ethnic, multinational, and multilingual empires of the Middle Ages has still not run its course: the emerging 'New World Disorder' will thus be one shaped increasingly by the break-up of old polities into smaller nation-states. If this interpretation of history is correct, then the European Union – like the former USSR – represents but a temporary 'blip' in an otherwise continuous process of dissolution and fragmentation in the age of late nationalism. If that is the case, then talk of Europe's 'federal destiny' is not only a dangerous myth, it is also profoundly anti-historical.

Notes

1 Monnet's philosophy of 'men and institutions' is expressed most clearly in his writings on the European Coal and Steel Community (see especially Monnet (1978: 372–93)).

2 See, for example, the EU's 1995 award-winning video *A Passion to be Free*.

3 Comparisons are sometimes made between the EU and the United States of America, but these work only by playing down fundamental differences of history and culture that characterise their formation. While the EU represents an amalgam of established national states, the USA is essentially a large nation-state.

4 For example, the 1933 Inter-American Convention on Rights and Duties of States declares: 'The state as a person of International Law should possess the following qualifications: (a) a permanent population; (b) a defined territory; (c) government; and (d) the capacity to enter into relations with other states' (Osmañczyk 1990: 871).

5 As Gledhill (1994: 17) observes, the Weberian definition of the state is appropriate only to the modern European nation-state. As Foucault (1991) notes, what distinguishes the modern state from its predecessors is the degree of 'penetration' of everyday life and the extent of surveillance over the population.

6 Prodi's statement was made in an interview to the BBC programme 'On the Record'; see also *Financial Times*, 10 May 1999: 2. Calls for the formation of a European army are not new. As Monnet (1978: 382) reminds us, the Italian

Christian Democrat leader De Gasperi never tired of repeating: 'The European Army is not an end in itself: it is the instrument of a patriotic foreign policy. But European patriotism can develop only in a federal Europe.'

7 Alan Milward's (1992) book *The European Rescue of the Nation-State* provides a cogent analysis of the early history of the EU which inverts this thesis. The interesting question is whether Milward's argument still applies to the EU Maastricht and Amsterdam.

8 On this point Jean Monnet (1978: 401–2) was also adamant: 'Our Countries have become too small for the present-day world . . . The union of European peoples in the United States of Europe is the way to raise their standard of living and preserve peace. It is the great hope and opportunity of our time.'

9 Helmut Kohl, speech delivered at the Bertelsman Forum, Petersburg Hotel, 3 April 1992.

10 Or, 'the art of fixing' (my translation).

11 This argument was also made by Spence (1994a; 1994b).

12 Those who 'break ranks' and disclose information damaging to the reputation of the institution are typically regarded as having 'betrayed' the Community. Bernard Connolly, the British official who was dismissed from his post for writing a book sharply critical of EMU, is a case in point.

13 The local strike organised in 1995 over the way appointments were made to the Committee of the Regions is a good example of the way the unions can, and sometimes do, unite to oppose glaring evidence of cronyism.

14 Castle and Butler, *Independent*, 16 March 1999: 9.

15 *Independent*, 17 March 1999: 8.

16 *Financial Times*, 17 March 1999: 8.

17 Editorial, *The Times*, 16 March 1999: 19.

18 Bremner, *The Times*, 17 March 1999: 6.

19 Boyes, *The Times*, 17 March 1999: 6.

20 Evidence of this had started to emerge in the year prior to the report's publication. In 1998, the European Parliament's budget control commission had demanded that the Director-General for Administration, Stefan Schmidt, be sacked. It accused him of conducting internal inquiries that were so close to a whitewash that his office had 'lost all credibility' (cited in Walker, *Guardian*, 25 September 1998: 3).

21 Commenting on these documents, Alvoet said: 'We see Commission officials setting up private companies to provide paid services to the Commission. We see people hired or given contracts on the basis of family connections to Commission officials, even when they have no relevant experience' (cited in *Guardian*, 10 December 1998: 12).

22 Walker, *Guardian*, 10 December 1998: 18.

23 Cited in Brian MacArthur, *The Times*, 25 September 1998. In the case of Nathe, as MacArthur reported, the two men he exposed had each sued him for £700,000 damages – and their costs were funded by the Commission.

24 For example, Edith Cresson had initiated a law suit against *Libération* for defamation under French law after it reported, correctly, that she had appointed her former dentist friend to co-ordinate the EU's AIDS research. In October, Emma Bonino threatened legal action against the *Financial Times*, a paper much respected in Brussels and broadly supportive of the EU, over an article on alleged fraud (subsequently confirmed) in the EU's humanitarian office. This led researchers at the International Press Association, which speaks for many of the nine hundred journalists accredited to the Commission, to complain that the press was 'being intimidated by the Brussels machine' (Buckley, *Financial Times*, 12 September 1998: 3; Helm, *Daily Telegraph*, 15 October 1998: 22).

25 Ker and Bates, *Guardian*, 5 January 1999: 3.

26 *EP News,* November 1998: 1.
27 The total EU budget in 1998 was Ecu 80 billion. Since 1995 the Auditors had regularly reported errors of up to 5 per cent of the budget. In the past, this was usually blamed on the member states for not controlling the way subsidies had been dispensed.
28 Santer also angered many MEPs by vowing that he and the Commission would remain in place even if the majority of MEPs voted against them. Only a two-thirds majority could shift him, he said (*Guardian,* 14 January 1999: 13).
29 Grey, *Sunday Times,* 17 January 1999: 7.
30 As an English language term, 'comitology' was first used in C. Northcote Parkinson's *Parkinson's Law* (1958). Parkinson used it to refer to the study of committees and how they operate (Bainbridge and Teasdale 1995: 46–8). However, in the context of the EU 'comitology' has a different meaning and is thought to derive more from the word 'comity' (as in 'comity of nations') rather than 'committee' (House of Lords 1999: 5).
31 See Karl Marx, *Poverty of Philosophy* (chapter two, 'Strikes and Combination of Workers').
32 Walzer, cited in Kertzer (1988: 6).
33 Susan Sontag, cited in Morley and Robins (1990: 3).
34 Cf. Nairn (1977: 340); Anderson (1983: 106).
35 Cf. Garton Ash 1998. Vernon Bogdanor (1990: 41–2) also draws attention to this comparison. The EU, he notes, shares much in common with the failed ideals of socialism, both being products of an era which still believed in technological progress, in growth and rationalisation. Both also have a flawed view of human nature, and both suffer from the dead hand of impersonal bureaucracy which tries to direct human vitality into narrow institutional channels.
36 Some of these were the topic of much conversation in the corridors of Brussels, such as the appointment of the son of the Franz de Koster, Director-General for Personnel. A casual glance at the names in the Commission's *Repertoire Téléphonique* gives some indication of the kinship networks among Commission employees. However, a systematic analysis of this phenomenon was beyond the scope of my inquiry.
37 Boyes, *The Times,* 24 April 1998: 16.
38 Haas (1958: 16).
39 For a critique of this theory of identity-formation, see Shore (1993).
40 Smith (1991: 174). In his later work, Smith is far more sceptical about the possibility of pan-European nationalism succeeding.
41 Mark Leonard *Europe: The Search for European Identity,* London: Demos, 1998: 7.
42 Ibid.: 27.
43 Cited in Graham (1996: 120). The table depicting these icons reads 'Europe: our shared experience'.
44 *Eurobarometer* 47: 37.
45 Cited in Henley Centre (1996a: 78–9).
46 Ibid.: 80–1.
47 NOP Survey on Europe carried out for the BBC, May 1995: NOP/43415.
48 This followed an influential Demos pamphlet published the previous year by Leonard proposing the rebranding of Britain. Significantly, *Rediscovering Europe* was sponsored (and commissioned) by Interbrand, Newell and Sorrell, the 'branding and identity consultants'. Equally significantly in terms of the *engrenage* thesis discussed earlier, Mark Leonard is the twenty-four-year-old son of an EU official and was educated at the European School in Uccle, Brussels.
49 Schlesinger (1994a: 324).
50 Walker, *Guardian Weekly,* 14 March 1999: 6.
51 For discussion of the 'European dimension' in the new racism, see Shore (1997c).

Bibliography

Abélès, Marc (1992) *La vie quotidienne au parlement européenne*, Paris: Hachette.

Abélès, Marc (1995) Pour une anthropologie des institutions', *L'Homme*, 135 (July–September): 65–85.

Abélès, Marc (1996) La Communauté européenne: une perspective anthropologique', *Social Anthropology*, 4 (1): 33–45.

Abélès, Marc, Bellier, Irène and McDonald, Marion (1993) '*Approche anthropologique de la Commission Européenne*, Brussels: European Commission.

Adonnino, Pietro (1985) 'A People's Europe: Reports from the Ad Hoc Committee', *Bulletin of the European Communities*, Supplement 7/85, Luxembourg: OOPEC.

Ahrweiler, Hélène (1993) 'Roots and Trends in European Culture', In S. Garcia (ed.), *European Identity and the Search for Legitimacy*, London: Royal Institute of International Affairs.

Alibai, Yasmin (1989) 'Community Whitewash', *Guardian*, 23 January.

Allen, Sheila and Macey, Marie (1991). 'Minorities, Racism and Citizenship: The Impact of the Single European Market', *European Journal of Intercultural Studies*, 2 (2): 5–16.

Almond, G. and Verba, S. (1963) *The Civic Culture: Political Attitudes and Democracy in Five Nations*, Princeton: Princeton University Press.

Alonso, A. M. (1988) 'The Effects of Truth: Re-presentations of the Past and the Imagining of Community' *Journal of Historical Sociology*, 1(1): 33–57.

Althusser, Louis (1971) *Lenin and Philosophy*, London: New Left Books.

Amin, Samir (1988) *Eurocentrism* (trans. Russell Moore), London: Zed Books.

Anderson, Benedict (1983), *Imagined Communities*, London, Verso.

Anderson, Benedict (1992) 'The New World Disorder', *New Left Review*, 193 (May/June): 3–14.

Andrews, Geoff (ed.) (1991) *Citizenship*, London: Lawrence and Wishart.

Ardener Edwin (1971) 'Introduction' in E. Ardener (ed.), *Social Anthropology and Language*, ASA Monograph. London: Tavistock: ix–cii.

Areilza, José de (1995) *Sovereignty or Management? The Dual Character of the EC's Supranationalism – Revisited*, Cambridge, Massachusetts: Harvard Law School, Jean Monnet Working Paper 2/95.

Aron, Raymond (1974) 'Is Multicultural Citizenship Possible?', *Social Research*, 4 (41): 638–56.

Asad, Talal (1979) 'Anthropology and the Analysis of Ideology', *Man*, 14: 607–27.

Baget-Bozzo, G. (1986) *Report on the Information Policy of the European Community*, Doc A-111. Luxembourg: OOPEC.

Bailey, Frederik (ed.) (1971) *Gifts and Poison: The Politics of Reputation*, Oxford: Blackwell.

Bainbridge, Timothy and Teasdale, Anthony (1995) *The Penguin Companion to European Union*, Harmondsworth: Penguin.

Balibar, Etienne (1991) '*Es gibt Keinen Staat in Europea*: Racism and Politics in Europe Today', *New Left Review*, 186: 5–19.

Baldwin, Richard (1994) *Towards an Integrated Europe*, London: Centre for Economic Policy Research.

Banfield, Edward (1958) *The Moral Basis of Backward Society*, New York: Free Press.

Barry, Andrew (1993) 'The European Community and European Government: Harmonization, Mobility and Space', *Economy and Society*, 22 (3): 314–26.

Barzanti, Roberto (1992) *Draft Report on 'New Prospects for Community Cultural Action'*, DOC EN\PR\210\210674. Brussels: European Parliament.

Bearfield, David (1996) Editorial, *Commission en Direct*, 4 (8–14 February).

Bellier, Irène (1994) 'Une Culture de la Commissione européenne? De la rencontre des cultures et du multilingualisme des fonctionnaires', in Y. Mény, P. Muller and J. C. Quermonne *Politiques publiques en Europe*, Paris: L' Harmattan.

Bellier, Irène (1995) 'Moralité, langue et puvoirs dans les institutions européennes', *Social Anthroplogy*, 3(3): 235–50.

Billig, Michael (1995) *Banal Nationalism*, London: Sage.

Bogdanor, Vernon (1990) 'Of Ideals and Institutions: Diversity in Europe?' *Encounter*, 74 (January/February): 39–42.

Boissevain, Jeremy (1974) *Friends of Friends: Networks, Manipulators and Coalitions*, Oxford: Blackwell.

Bonino, Emma (1996), 'Consumers Vital to a Single Currency', *Frontier-free Europe* (Monthly Newsletter of the European Commission), March.

Booker, Christopher and North, Richard (1996) *The Castle of Lies*, London: Duckworth.

Borchardt, Klaus-Dieter (1995) *European Integration: The Origins and Growth of the European Union*, Luxembourg: OOPEC.

Borneman, John and Fowler, Nick (1998) 'Europeanization; *Annual Review of Anthropology*, 26: 487–514.

Bourdieu, Pierre (1977) *Outline of a Theory of Practice*, Cambridge: Cambridge University Press.

Bramwell, A. C. (1987) 'Dans le couloire: The Political Culture of the EEC Commission', *International Journal of Moral and Social Studies*, 2 (1): 63–80.

Brigouleix, Bernard (1986) *Voyage en Eurocratie*, Paris: A. Moreau.

Brown, Archie (1985) 'Political Culture', in A. Kuper and J. Kuper (eds), *The Social Science Encyclopaedia*, London: Macmillan: 609–11.

Brugmans, Henri (1987) 'L'Europe: une civilisation commune, un destin, une vocation' in H. Brugmans (ed), *Europe: Rêve-Aventure-Réalité*, Brussels: Elsevier.

Buckley, Neil (1998) 'Brussels and the EU', *Financial Times: Special Survey, Brussels Region*, 31 March.

Bulmer, Martin and Rees, Anthony (eds) (1997) *Citizenship Today: The Contemporary Relevance of T. H. Marshall*, London: UCL Press.

Bulmer, Simon (1994) 'The Governance of the European Union: A New Internationalist Approach', *Journal of Public Policy*, 13 (4): 351–80.

Bunyan, Tony (1991), 'Towards an Authoritarian European State', *Race and Class* (January), London Institute of Race Relations.

Burchfield, R. W. (1986) *Supplement to the Oxford English Dictionary*, vol. IV, Oxford: Clarendon.

Burgelman, Jean-Claude and Pauwels, Caroline (1992) 'Audiovisual Policy and Cultural Identity in Small European States: The Challenge of a Unified Market', *Media, Culture and Society*, 14: 169–83.

Burkitt, Brian, Whyman, Philip and Baimbridge, Philip (1996) *Economic and Monetary Union: The Issues Labour Must Confront*, London: Labour Euro-Safeguards Campaign Occasional Paper.

Burley, Anne-Marie and Mattli, Walter (1993) 'Europe Before the Court: A Political Theory of Legal Integration' *International Organization*, 47 (1): 41–76.

Case, Peter (1994) 'Tracing the Organisational Culture Debate', *Anthropology in Action*, 1 (2): 9–11.

CEC Commission of the European Communities'; (1973) 'Declaration on the European Identity', Bulletin of the European Communities. 12 (Clause 2501: 118–27.

CEC (1976) 'Tindemans Report on European Union', reprinted in *Bulletin of the European Communities*, Supplement 1/76.

CEC (1983a) *Treaties Establishing the European Communities*, abridged edition, Luxembourg: OOPEC.

CEC (1983b) 'Solemn Declaration on European Union', reprinted in *Bulletin of the European Communities*, 6, 24.

CEC (1984) *Television Without Frontiers: Green Paper on the Establishment of the Common Market for Broadcasting especially for Satellite and Cable*, COM (84) final, Luxembourg: OOPEC.

CEC (1988a) 'The European Community and Culture', *European File*, Brussels: OOPEC.

CEC (1988b) 'A People's Europe: Communication from the Commission to the European Parliament', COM 88 331/final, 7 July, *Bulletin of the European Communities*, Supplement 2, Luxembourg.

CEC (1991) *Films of the European Communities Available for Non-commercial Distribution*, Brussels: DG X.

CEC (1992a) *Treaty on European Union Signed at Maastricht on 7 February*, Luxembourg: OOPEC.

CEC (1992b) *New Prospects for Community Cultural Action*, COM92 149 final, 29 April, Brussels: OOPEC.

CEC (1992c) *Eurobarometer. Public Opinion in the European Community, No. 37*, Brussels: European Commission.

CEC (1994a) *Information, Communication, Openness: Background Report*, ISEC/B25/94, Brussels: European Commission.

CEC (1994b) *A Portrait of Our Europe*, Brussels: OOPEC

CEC (1994c) *Growth, Competitiveness, Employment*, Commission White Paper, Luxembourg: OOPEC.

CEC (1994d) *Women at the European Commission 1984–1994*, Brussels: European Commission.

CEC (1995a), *The European Commission 1995–2000*, DGX, Luxembourg: OOPEC.

CEC (1995b), *Green Paper on the Practical Arrangements for the Introduction of the Single Currency*, COM(95) 333 final, Brussels: OOPEC.

CEC (1995c) *The European Councils: Conclusions of the Presidency 1992–1994*, Brussels: European Commission, DG IX.

CEC (1996a) *First Report on the Consideration of Cultural Aspects in European Community Action*, Brussels: European Commission.

CEC (1996b) *Economic and Monetary Union*, Brussels: OOPEC.

CEC (1996c) *Video Catalogue*, Brussels: OOPEC.

CEC (1997a) *Eurobarometer, Public Opinion in the European Union*, No. 47, Brussels: European Commission.

CEC (1997b) *Talking about the Euro*, Brussels: European Commission.

CEC (1997c) *Second Report from the Commission on Citizenship of the Union*, COM (97) 230 final, Brussels: European Commission.

CEC (1998) *Eurobarometer. Public Opinion in the European Union*, No. 48, Brussels: European Commission.

CEC (1998a) 'European Integration in University Studies: Vade-Mecum 1999', *Jean Monnet Project*, Brussels: DG X.

Cesarani, David and Fulbrook, Mary (1997) 'Introduction', in D. Cesarani and M. Fulbrook (eds), *Citizenship Nationality and Migration in Europe*, London: Routledge.

Chapman, Malcolm (1994) 'Social Anthropology and Business Studies–Mutual Benefit?' *Anthropology in Action*, 1 (2): 12–14.

Christiansen, Thomas (1997) 'Tensions of European Governance: Politicized Bureaucracy and Multiple Accountability in the European Commission', *Journal of European Public Policy*, 4 (1) (March): 73–90.

Christie, Ian (1998) 'Sustaining Europe: A Continent in Search of a Mission', *EuroVisions: New Dimensions of European Integration*, Demos Collection 13: 3–8.

CIE (Committee of Independent Experts) (1999) *First Report on Allegations Regarding Fraud, Mismanagement and Nepotism in the European Commission*, Brussels: European Parliament and Commission of the European Communities.

Cini, Michelle (1996) *The European Commission: Leadership, Organisation and Culture in the EU Administration*, Manchester: Manchester University Press.

Clarke, Paul (1996) *Europe's Money 1996. A Guide to the EU Budget*, London: Catermill.

Clifford, James and Marcus, George (eds) (1986) *Writing Culture: The Poetics and Politics of Ethnography*, Berkley: University of California Press.

Closa, Carlos (1992) 'The Concept of Citizenship in the Treaty on European Union', *Common Market Law Review* 29: 1137–69.

Cockburn, Cynthia (1994) 'Play of Power: Women, Men and Equality Initiatives in a Trade Union', in S. Wright (ed.), *Anthropology of Organisations*, London: Routledge.

Cohen, Abner (1974a) *Two Dimensional Man: An Essay on the Anthropology of Power and Symbolism in Complex Society*, London, Routledge and Kegan Paul.

Cohen, Abner (ed.) (1974b) *Urban Ethnicity*, ASA Monograph. London: Tavistock.

Cohen, Anthony P. (1982a) 'Belonging: The Experience of Culture', in A. P. Cohen (ed.), *Belonging: Identity and Social Organisation in British Rural Cultures*, Manchester: Manchester University Press: 1–20.

Cohen, Anthony P. (1982b) 'A Sense of Time, a Sense of Place: The Meaning of Close Social Association in Whalsay, Scotland', in A. P. Cohen (ed.) *Belonging: Identity and Social Organisation in British Rural Cultures*, Manchester: Manchester University Press.

Cohen, Anthony P. (1986) 'Of Symbols and Boundaries: or, Does Ertie's Greatcoat hold the key?' in A. P. Cohen (ed.), *Symbolising Boundaries: Identity and Diversity in British Cultures*, Manchester: Manchester University Press.

Collins, Richard (1993) *Audiovisual and Broadcasting Policy in the European Community*, London: University of North London Press (European Dossier Series No. 23).

Collins, Richard (1994) 'Unity in Diversity? The European Single Market in Broadcasting and the Audiovisual, 1982–92', *Journal of Common Market Studies*, 32 (1): 89–102.

Connerton, P. (1989) *How Societies Remember*, Cambridge: Cambridge University Press.

Connolly, Bernard (1995) *The Rotten Heart of Europe: The Dirty War for Europe's Money*, London: Faber and Faber.

Cooper, Roger (1996) *The Post-modern State and the World Order*, London: Demos.

Cox, Pat (1999) 'Democratic Accountability the Winner in the EU Crisis,' *Irish Times*, 17 March: 14.

Cram, Laura (1993) 'Calling the Tune Without Paying the Piper? Social Policy Regulation. The Role of the Commission in European Union Social Policy', *Policy and Politics*, 21: 135–46.

Czarniawska-Joerges, Barbara (1992) *Exploring Complex Organisations: A Cultural Perspective*, London: Sage.

Davignon, Etienne, Ersbøll, Niels, Lamers, Karl, Martin, David, Noël, Emile and Vibert, Frank (1995) *What Future for the European Commission?*, Brussels: Philip Morris Institute.

Davignon, Etienne (1995) 'The Challenges that the Commission Must Confront', in E. Davignon, N. Ersbøll, K. Lamers, D. Martin, E. Noël and F. Vibert, *What Future for the European Commission?*, Brussels: Philip Morris Institute: 12–19.

De Clerq, Willy (1993) *Reflection on Information and Communication Policy of the European Community*, Brussels: Commission of the European Communities.

De Silguy, Yves-Thibault (1997) 'Foreword', in N. Moussis, *Acccs to European Union* Genval: Euroconfidential: 1–4.

De Witte, Bruno (1987) 'Building Europe's Image and Identity', in A. Riijksbaron, W. Roobol and M. Weisglas (eds), *Europe From a Cultural Perspective*, The Hague: UPR: 121–31.

De Witte, Bruno (1993) 'Cultural Legitimation: Back to the Language Question', in S. García (ed.), *European Identity and the Search for Legitimacy*, London: Pinter and Royal Institute of International Affairs.

Delanty, Gerard (1995) *Inventing Europe. Idea, Identity, Reality*, London: Macmillan.

Della Porta, Donatella and Mény, Yves (1997) 'Introduction: Democracy and Corruption', in D. Della Porta and Y. Mény (eds), *Democracy and Corruption in Europe*, London: Pinter: 1–6.

Delouche, F. (ed.) (1992) *Histoire de l'Europe*, Paris: Hachette/Brussels: De Boeck.

Demboir, Marie-Bénédicte, 1996 'Harmonization and the Construction of Europe: Variations away from a Musical Theme' *EU Working Paper, Law* No. 96/4, Florence: European University Institute.

Denman, Roy (1996) *Missed Chances: Britain and Europe in the Twentieth Century*, London: Cassell.

Deutsch, Karl (1966) *Nationalism and Social Communication: An Inquiry into the Foundations of Nationality* (2nd ed.). Cambridge, Massachusetts: MIT Press.

DG X (1996) *Plan operationnel evolutif de communication pour la monnaie unique, Brussels: DG X, Actions prioritaires d'information.* Project: 'L'euro, une monnaie pour l'Europe' (May), Brussels, DG X.

Donnan, Hastings and McFarlane, Graham (eds) (1989) *Social Anthropology and Public Policy in Northern Ireland,* Aldershot: Avebury.

Donnan, Hastings and McFarlane, Graham (1997) 'Anthropology and Policy Research: The View from Northern Ireland', in C. Shore and S. Wright (eds), *Anthropology of Policy,* London: Routledge.

Douglas, Mary (1966) *Purity and Danger,* London: Routledge and Kegan Paul.

Dupondt, Jos (ed.) (1995) *250 QCM sur l'Europe et la politique europeéenne,* Brussels: Sindicat des Fonctionaires Européennes (fifth edition).

Durkheim, Emile (1982) *The Rules of Sociological Method,* translated by W. D. Halls, London: Macmillan.

Duroselle, Jean-Baptiste (1990) *Europe: A History of Its Peoples,* London: Viking.

Dyson, Kenneth (1994) *Elusive Union: The Process of Economic and Monetary Union in Europe,* Harlow: Longman.

Eatwell, Roger (1997) 'Introduction: The Importance of the Political Culture Approach', in R. Eatwell (ed.), *European Political Cultures,* London: Routledge.

Edmonds, Timothy and Blair, Christopher (1997) *EMU: a question of economics,* House of Commons Research Paper 97/124, London: House of Commons Library.

Edwards, Geoffrey and Spence, David (1997) 'The Commission in Perspective', in G. Edwards and D. Spence (eds), *The European Commission,* (2nd ed), Harlow: Longman.

Edye, Dave (1997) 'Citizenship in the European Union: The Post-Maastricht Scenario', in Valerie Symes *et al.* (eds), *The Future of Europe: Problems and Issues for the Twenty-first Century,* Oxford: Berg.

Egeberg, Morten (1996) 'Organization and Nationality in the European Commission Services', *Public Administration,* 74 (winter): 721–35.

Eichener, V. (1992) *Social Dumping or Innovative Regulation?,* EUI Working Paper SPS No. 92/28, Fiesole: European University Institute.

Elliot, Larry (1993) 'Towards a Common Currency', in V. Keegan and M. Kettle (eds), The New Europe, London: Guardian Books.

European Parliament (1996) *Implementation of Equal Opportunities for Men and Women in the Civil Service* (Draft Report), PE 217.381, Brussels: European Parliament.

Evans-Pritchard, E. E. (1940) *The Nuer,* Oxford: Oxford University Press.

Faist, Thomas (1997) 'Migration in Contemporary Europe: European Integration, Economic Liberalisation, and Protection', in D. Cesarani and M. Fulbrook (eds), *Citizenship, Nationality and Migration in Europe,* London: Routledge.

Feldstein, Martin (1997) 'EMU and International Conflict', *Foreign Affairs,* 76 (6): 60–73.

Fontaine, Pascal (1991) *A Citizen's Europe,* Luxembourg: OOPEC.

Fontaine, Pascal (1993) *A Citizen's Europe* (2nd ed.), Luxembourg: OOPEC.

Fontaine, Pascal (1995) *Europe in Ten Lessons,* Luxembourg: OOPEC.

Forrest, Alan (1994) 'A New Start for Cultural Action in the European Community: Genesis and Implications of Article 128 of the Treaty on European Union', *Cultural Policy,* 1 (2): 11–20.

Foster, George (1965) 'Peasant Society and the Image of Limited Good', *American Anthropologist,* 67 (2): 293–316.

Foster, Robert (1991) 'Making National Cultures in the Global Ecumen', Annual Review of Anthropology, 20: 235–60.

Foucault, Michel (1977) *Discipline and Punish: The Birth of the Prison*, Harmondsworth: Penguin.

Foucault, Michel (1978) *The History of Sexuality: Volume One*, Harmondsworth: Penguin.

Foucault, Michel (1991) 'Governmentality', in G. Burchell, C. Gordon and P. Miller (eds), *The Foucault Effect: Studies in Governmentality*, London: Harvester Wheatsheaf.

Franklin, Daniel (1993) 'Survey of the European Community', *Economist*, 328 (3 July).

Galtung, Johan (1973) *The European Community: A Superpower in the Making*, London: Allen and Unwin.

García, Soledad and Wallace, Helen (1993) 'Conclusion' in S. García (ed) *European Identity and the Search for Legitimacy*, London: Pinter and Royal Institute of International Affairs.

Garton Ash, Timothy (1989) *The Uses of Adversity*, Harmondsworth: Penguin.

Garton Ash, Timothy (1998) 'Europe's Endangered Liberal Order', *Foreign Affairs*, 77 (2): 51–65.

Geertz, Clifford (1973) *The Interpretation of Cultures*, New York: Basic Books.

Geertz, Clifford (1984) ' "From the native's point of view": On the Nature of Athropological Understanding', in R. Shwerder and R. LeVine (eds), *Culture Theory: Essays on Mind, Self, and Emotion*, Cambridge: Cambridge University Press.

Gellner, Ernest (1964) *Thought and Change*, London: Weidenfeld and Nicolson.

Gellner, Ernest (1983) *Nations and Nationalism*, Oxford: Blackwell.

Gellner, Ernest and Waterbury, John (eds) (1977) *Patrons and Clients*, London: Duckworth.

George, Eddie (1995) *The Economics of Economic and Monetary Union* (text of speech delivered in Luxembourg), London: Bank of England.

George, Stephen (1985) *Politics and Policy in the European Community*, Oxford: Clarendon.

Giddens, Anthony (1985) *The Nation-state and Violence*, Berkeley: University of California Press.

Gilroy, Paul (1987) *There Ain't No Black in the Union Jack*, London: Hutchinson.

Gledhill, John (1994) *Power and its Disguises: Anthropological Perspectives on Politics*, London: Pluto.

Goldstein, Walter (1993) 'Europe After Maastricht', *Foreign Affairs*, 71 (5): 117–32.

Goody, Jack (1992) 'Culture and its Boundaries: A European view', *Social Anthropology*, 1 (1): 9–33.

Gordon, Collin (1991) 'Government Rationality: An Introduction', in G. Burchell, C. Gordon and P. Miller (eds), *The Foucault Effect: Studies in Governmentality*, London: Harvester Wheatsheaf.

Graham, Sarah (1996) 'Britain in Europe: From Today's to Tomorrow's Europe,' in Henley Centre (ed.), *Planning for Social Change 1996/97 – Vol. 1: Shaping Factors*, London: The Henley Centre: 110–22

Gramsci, Antonio (1971) *Selections From Prison Notebooks*, London: Lawrence and Wishart.

Grant, Charles (1994) *Delors: Inside the House that Jacques Built*, London: Nicholas Brealey.

Grass, Günter (1992) 'Losses', *Granta*, 42 ('Krauts').

Grew, Raymond and Yengoyan, Aram (1993) 'Editorial Foreword', *Comparative Studies in Society and History*. 35 (1): 1–2

Griel, A. L. and Rudy, D. R. (1984) 'Social Cocoons: Encapsulation and Identity Transformation Organisations', *Sociological Inquiry*, 54 (3): 260–78.

Guégen, Daniel (ed.) (1994) *En quête d'Europe*, Rennes: Apogee.

Guild, Elspeth (1997) 'The Legal Framework of Citizenship of the European Union', in David Cesarani and Mary Fulbrook (eds), *Citizenship, Nationality, and Migration in Europe*, London: Routledge: 30–54.

Guizzardi, Gustavo (1976) 'The Rural Civilization: Structure of an Ideology for Consent', *Social Compass*, 23 (2/3): 197–220.

Haas, Ernst (1958) *The Uniting of Europe*, Oxford: Oxford University Press.

Habermas, Jürgen (1992) 'Citizenship and National Identity: Some Reflections on the Future of Europe', *Praxis International*, 12 (April): 1–19.

Hacking, Ian (1991) 'How Should We Do the History of Statistics?', in G. Burchell, C. Gordon and P. Miller (eds), *The Foucault Effect: Studies in Governmentality* London, Harvester Wheatsheaf.

Hall, Stuart (1991) 'Europe's Other Self', *Marxism Today*, August: 18–19.

Hall, Stuart (1992) 'The Question of Cultural Identity', in S. Hall, D. Held and T. McGrew (eds), *Modernity and Its Futures*, Cambridge: Polity Press and Open University Press: 273–326.

Handleman, Don (1990) *Models and Mirrors: Towards an Anthropology of Public Events*, Cambridge: Cambridge University Press.

Hannerz, Ulf (1996) *Transnational Connections: Culture, People, Places*, London: Routledge.

Harryvan, A. G. and Van der Harst, J. (eds) (1997) *Documents on European Union*, Basingstoke: Macmillan.

Hay, Richard (1989) *The European Commission and the Administration of the Community*, Luxembourg: OOPEC.

Hechter, Michael (1975) *Internal Colonialism: The Celtic Fringe in British National Development*, London: Routledge and Kegan Paul.

Held, David (1991) 'Between State and Civil Society: Citizenship', in G. Andrews (ed.), *Citizenship*, London: Lawrence and Wishart.

Henley Centre (1996a) *Frontiers: Brand Futures, Consumer Needs and the Pursuit of Successful Planning 95/96*, vol. 1, London: The Henley Centre.

Henley Centre, (1996b) *Frontiers: Planning for Consumer Change in Europe 96/97*, vol. 2, London: The Henley Centre.

Hennessy, Peter (1990) *Whitehall*, London: Fontana.

Herman, E. and Chomsky, N. (eds) (1988) *Manufacturing Consent: The Political Economy of the Mass Media*, New York: Pantheon Books.

Herrero de Miñón, Miguel (1996) 'Europe's Non-existent Body Politic', in M. Herrero de Miñón and G. Leicester, *Europe: A Time For Pragmatism*, London: European Policy Forum: 1–5.

Hersom, Louis (1996) 'Openness and Transparency – Or What', *Commission en Direct*, 5 (15–21 February): 2.

Herzfeld, Michael (1992) *The Social Production of Indifference: Exploring the Symbolic Roots of Western Bureaucracy*, Oxford: Berg.

Heseltine, Michael (1989) *The Challenge of Europe*, London: Weidenfeld & Nicolson.

Hobsbawm, Eric (1983) 'Mass Producing Traditions: Europe, 1870–1914: in E. Hobsbawm and T. Ranger (eds) *The Invention of Tradition*, Cambridge: Cambridge University Press.

Hobsbawm, Eric (1986) [1962] *The Age of Revolution: Europe 1789–1848*, London: Abacus.

Hobsbawm, Eric (1990) *Nations and Nationalism Since 1780*, Cambridge: Cambridge University Press.

Hobsbawm, Eric (1992), 'Ethnicity and Nationalism in Europe Today', *Anthropology Today*, 8 (1): 3–8.

Hobsbawm, Eric and Ranger, Terrence (1983), 'Introduction: Inventing Traditions', in E. Hobsbawm and T. Ranger (eds), *The Invention of Tradition*, Cambridge: Cambridge University Press.

Hobsbawm, Eric (1996) 'The World as It Is Today' (unpublished interview with Thomas Hylland Eriksen, London, 14 March).

Hobsbawm, Eric (1997) 'An Afterword: European Union at the End of the Century', in Jytte KIausen and Louise Tilly (eds), *European Integration in Social and Historical Perspective*, Oxford: Rowman and Littlefield

Hoffman, Stanley (1993), 'Goodbye to a United Europe?', *New York Review of Books*, 27 May: 27–31.

Hoffman, Stanley (1995) *The European Sisyphus: Essays on Europe 1964–1994*, Boulder: Westview.

House of Lords (1988) 'Staffing of Community Institutions': Select Committee on the European Communities, 11th Report (29 March), London: HMSO.

House of Lords (1999) 'Delegation of Powers to the Commission: Reforming Comitology': Select Committee on European Communities Committee, 3rd Report, (2 February), London: The Stationery Office.

Howe, Martin (1992) *Europe and the Constitution after Maastricht*, Oxford: Nelson and Pollard.

Howe, Paul (1995) 'A Community of Europeans: The Requisite Underpinnings', *Journal of Common Market Studies*, 33 (1): 27–46.

Issing, Otmar (1996a) 'One Currency Could Tear Europe Apart', *Sunday Times*, 10 March, Section 3: 5.

Issing, Otmar (1996b) *Europe, Political Union Through Common Money?*, London: Institute of Economic Affairs.

Jamieson, B. (1998) *Britain Free to Choose*, London: Global.

Jordan, Glen and Weedon, Chris (1995) *Cultural Politics: Class, Gender, Race and the Postmodern World*, Oxford: Blackwell.

Jordan, Terry (1973) *The European Culture Area*, London: Harper Row.

Kahn, Joel (1995) *Culture, Multiculture, Postculture*, London: Sage.

Kamenka, Eugene (1973) 'Political Nationalism – the Evolution of the Idea', in E. Kamenka (ed.), *Nationalism: The Nature and Evolution of an Idea*, London: Edward Arnold.

Keohane, Robert and Hoffman, Stanley (1991), 'Institutional Change in Europe in the 1980s', in R. Keohane and S. Hoffman (eds), *The New European Community: Decision-making and Institutional Change*, Oxford: Westview Press.

Kertzer, David (1988) *Ritual, Politics and Power*, New Haven and London: Yale University Press.

King, Desmond (1987) *The New Right: Politics Markets and Citizenship*, London: Macmillan.

Kofman, E. and Sales, R. (1992) 'Towards Fortress Europe?', *Women's Studies International Forum*, 15 (1): 29–39.

Kohn, Hans (1994) [1945] 'Western and Eastern Nationalisms', in J. Hutchinson and A. D. Smith (eds), *Nationalism*, Oxford: Oxford University Press.

Krismundóttir, Sigrídur (1996) 'Culture Theory and the Anthropology of Modern Iceland', *Social Anthropology*, 4 (1): 61–73.

Laffan, Brigid (1997) 'From Policy Entrepreneur to Policy Manager: The Challenge Facing the European Commission', *Journal of European Public Policy*, 4 (3) (September): 422–38.

LeCron Foster, Mary (1994) 'Symbolism: The Foundation of Culture', in T. Ingold (ed.), *Companion Encyclopedia of Anthropology*, London: Routedge.

Leicester, Graham (1996) 'A Pragmatic Approach to the Construction of Europe', in M. Herrero de Miñón and G. Leicester, *Europe: A Time For Pragmatism*, London: European Policy Forum.

Leonard, Mark (1998a) *Europe: The Search for European Identity*, London: Demos.

Leonard, Mark (1998b) *Rediscovering Europe*, London: Demos.

Lindberg, Leon (1963) *The Political Dynamics of European Economic Integration*, Stanford: Stanford University Press.

Lodge, Juliet (1993a) 'EC Policymaking: Institutional Dynamics', in J. Lodge (ed.), *The European Community and the Challenge of the Future*, London: Pinter.

Lodge, Juliet (1993b) 'Towards a Political Union?, in J. Lodge (ed.), *The European Community and the Challenge of the Future*, London: Pinter.

Löken, K. (1992) 'European Identity: What About Us?', *The New Federalist*, 5–6: 6–7.

Ludlow, Peter (1987) 'European Integration' in M. Riff (ed.), *Dictionary of Modern Political Ideologies*, Manchester: Manchester University Press.

Ludlow, Peter (1991) 'The European Commission', in R. Keohane and S. Hoffman (eds), *The New European Community: Decision-making and Institutional Change*, Oxford: Westview Press.

Lukes, Stephen (1975) 'Political Ritual and Social Integration', *Sociology*, 9: 289–308.

Lynch, P. (1993) 'Europe's Post-Maastricht Muddle', *Politics Review*, 3 (2): 2–5.

McDonald, Marion (1996) 'Unity in Diversity: Moralities in the Construction of Europe', *Social Anthropology* 4 (1): 47–60.

McElvoy, Ann (1996) 'Euro-woman Knows her Place', *Daily Telegraph*, 18 November: 12.

Mackey, Eva (1997) 'The Cultural Politics of Populism: Celebrating Canadian National Identity', in C. Shore and S. Wright (eds), Anthropology of Policy, London: Routledge.

Malinowski, Bronislaw (1926) *Myth in Primitive Psychology*, London: Kegan Paul.

Mandell, Ruth (1994) '"Fortress Europe" and the Foreigners Within: Germany's Turks', in V. Goddard, J. Llobera and C. Shore (eds), *The Anthroplogy of Europe: Identities and Boundaries in Conflict*, Oxford: Berg.

Mann, Michael (1996) 'Stiff Test for Budding Eurocrats', *European Voice*, 15–21 Februrary: 18–19.

Marks, Gary (1993) 'Structural Policy and Multilevel Governance in the EC', in A. Cafruny and G. Rosenthal (eds), *The State of the European Community, ii: The Maasricht Debates and Beyond*, Boulder, Colorado: Lynne Riener

Marks, Gary, Hooghe, Liesbet and Blank, Kermit (1996) 'European Integration from the 1980s: State-centric v. Multi-level Governance', *Journal of Common Market Studies*, 34 (3): 341–78.

Marquand, David (1991) 'The Irresistible Tide of Europeanisation', in Stuart Hall and Martin Jacques (eds), *New Times*, London: Lawrence and Wishart

Marshall, T. H. (1950) *Citizenship and Social Class*, Cambridge: Cambridge University Press.

Mathijsen, P. S. R. F. (1995) *A Guide to European Union Law*, London: Sweet and Maxwell.

Meehan, Elizabeth (1993) *Citizenship and the European Union*, London: Sage.

Michelmann, H. (1978) 'Multinational Staffing and Organisational Functioning in the Commission of the EEC', *International Affairs* 32 (2) (spring)

Middlemas, Keith (1995) *Orchestrating Europe: The Informal Politics of European Union 1973–1995*, London: Fontana.

Miller, Vaughne (1994) 'The 1996 Intergovemmental Conference: Background and Preparations', *Research Paper 94/115*, London: House of Commons.

Milward, Alan (1992) *The European Rescue of the Nation-state*, London: Routledge.

Mole, John (1992) *Mind Your Manners: Managing Culture Clash in the Single European Market*, London: Nicholas Brealey.

Monnet, Jean (1976) *Mémoires*, Paris: Rayard (Livre de Poche edition).

Monnet, Jean (1978) *Memoirs*, translated by R. Mayne, London: Collins.

Morokvasic, M. (1992), 'Fortress Europe and Migrant Women', *Feminist Review*, 39: 69–84.

Morley, David and Robins, Kevin (1990) 'No Place like Heimat: Images of Homeland in European Culture', *New Formations*, 12 (winter): 1–24.

Morley, David and Robins, Kevin (1995) *Spaces of Identity: Global Media, Electronic Landscapes and Cultural Boundaries*, London: Routledge.

Morris, Justin and Lodge, Juliet (1993) 'Appendix: The Referendums', in J. Lodge (ed.), *The European Community and the Challenge of the Future*, London: Pinter 386–96.

Moussis, Nicholas (1997) *Access to European Union: Law Economics Policies*, Genval: Euroconfidential.

Moxon-Browne, Edward (1993) 'Social Europe' in J. Lodge (ed.), *The European Community and the Challenge of the Future*, London: Pinter.

Münchau, Walter (1999) 'Welcome to the Euro-zone', *Financial Times*, 4 January 1999: 21.

Muttimer, D. (1989) '1992 and the Political Integration of Europe: Neofunctionalism Reconsidered', *Journal of European Integration* 13 (1).

Muttimer, D. (1996) '1992 and the Political Integration of Europe: Neofunctionalism Reconsidered', in M. O'Neill (ed.), *The Politics of European Integration: A Reader*, London: Routledge.

Nairn, Tom (1977) *The Break-up of Britain*, London: New Left Books.

Neill, Patrick (1995) *The European Court of Justice: A Case Study in Judicial Activism*, (unpublished manuscript, 13 January).

Okely, Judith (1983) *The Traveller Gypsies*, Cambridge: Cambridge University Press.

O'Neill, Michael (ed.) (1996) *The Politics of European Integration: A Reader*, London: Routledge.

Oostlandcr, Arie (1993) *Draft Report on the Information and Communication Policy of the European Community*, DOC-EN\PR\227\227207, Brussels: European Parliament.

Ortega, Manuel (1996) *Results of the Investigation of the Temporary Committee of*

Inquiry into BSE, European Parliament, 16 December 1996, Doc EN\PR\313\313955, Brussels: European Parliament.

Osmańczyk, Edmund (1990) *Encyclopedia of the United Nations and International Relations*, New York: Taylor and Francis.

Owen, Richard and Dynes, Michael (1989) *The Times Guide to 1992*, London: Times Books.

Pahl, Ray (1991) 'The Search for Social Cohesion: From Durkheim to the European Commission', *Archives Européens de Sociologie*, XXXII: 345–60.

Pflimlin, P. (1987) 'Preface' in H. Brugmans *et al.* (eds), *Europe: rêve-aventure-réalité*, Brussels: Elsevier.

Pieterse, J. N. (1991) 'Fictions of Europe', *Race and Class*, 32 (3): 3–10.

Pinheiro, J. (1993) *The Commission's Information and Communication Policy*, Brussels: OOPEC.

Pringle, Rosemary (1994) 'Office Affairs', in S. Wright (ed.), *Anthropology of Organisations*, London: Routledge.

Pye, Lucien and Verba, Sydney (1965) *Political Culture and Political Development*, Princeton: Princeton University Press.

Rabinow, Paul (1984) *The Foucault Reader*, Harmondsworth: Penguin.

Ramsay, A. (1997) *Eurojargon: A Dictionary of European Union Acronyms, Abbreviations and Sobriquets*, Bruton: Capital Planning Information.

Reflection Group (1995) *Commission Report for the Reflection Group*, Luxembourg: OOPEC.

Riijksbaron, A. Roobol, W. and Weisglas, M. (eds) (1987) *Europe from a Cultural Perspective*, The Hague: UPR.

Robins, Kevin (1994) 'The Politics of Silence: The Meaning of Community and the Uses of Media in the New Europe', *New Formations*, 21: 80–101.

Roper, Michael (1994) *Masculinity and the British Organization Man Since 1945*, Oxford, Oxford University Press.

Rose, Nikolas (1991) 'Governing By Numbers: Figuring Out Society', *Accounting Organisation and Society*, 15 (7): 673–92.

Rose, Nikolas (1992) 'Towards a Critical Sociology of Freedom', Inaugural lecture, 5 May, London: Goldsmiths College.

Ross, George (1993) 'Sliding into Industrial Policy: Inside the European Commission', *French Politics and Society*, 11 (1): 20;–44.

Ross, George (1995) *Jacques Delors and European Integration*, Cambridge: Polity Press.

Ruane, Joseph (1994) 'Nationalism and European Community Integration: The Republic of Ireland', in V. Goddard, J. Llobera and C. Shore (eds), *The Anthropology of Europe: Identities and Boundaries in Conflict*, Oxford: Berg.

Ruggie, John (1993) 'Territoriality and Beyond: Problematizing Modernity in International Relations', *International Organisations*, 47 (1): 137–74.

Said, Edward (1978) *Orientalism*, Harmondsworth: Penguin.

Sampson, Anthony (1968) *The New Europeans: A Guide to the Workings, Institutions, and Character of Contemporary Western Europe*, London: Panther.

Santer, Jacques (1995) 'Address to the European Parliament on the Occasion of the Investiture Debate of the new Commission Strasbourg 17 January 1995', *Bulletin of the European Union*, 1/95, Luxembourg: OOPEC: 5–18.

Santer, Jacques (1998) 'The Euro, Instrumental in Forging a European Identity', *InfoEuro*, 8 (May): 1.

Sbragia, A. (1993) 'The European Community: A Balancing Act', *Publius*, 23 (summer): 23–38.

Schäffner, Christina (1996) 'Building a European House? Or at Two Speeds into a Dead End? Metaphors in the Debate on the United Europe', in A. Musolff, C. Schäffner and M. Townson (eds), *Conceiving of Europe – Diversity in Unity*, Dartmouth: Aldershot.

Schama, Simon (1989) *Citizens: A Chronicle of the French Revolution*, Harmondsworth: Penguin.

Schilling, Theodor (1995) 'Subsidiarity as a Rule and a Principle, or: Taking Subsidiarity Seriously', *Harvard Jean Monnet Working Paper 10/95*, Cambridge Massachusetts: Harvard Law School.

Schlesinger, Philip (1991) *Media, State and Nation: Political Violence and Collective Identities*, London: Sage.

Schlesinger, Philip (1994a) 'Europeanness: A New Cultural Battlefield?', in J. Hutchinson and A. D. Smith (eds), *Nationalism*, Oxford: Oxford University Press: 316–25.

Schlesinger, Philip (1994b) 'Europe Through a Glass Darkly', *Daedalus*, 125 (2) (Spring): 25–52.

Scruton, Roger (1982) *A Dictionary of Political Thought*, London: Pan.

Seton-Watson, Hugh (1977) *Nations and Nationalism: An Enquiry into the Origins of Nations and the Politics of Nationalism*, Boulder: Westview Press.

Seton-Watson, Hugh (1985) 'What is Europe, Where is Europe?', *Encounter*, LXV (2) (July/August): 9–17.

Shackleton, Michael (1993) The Budget of the EC: Structure and Process', in J. Lodge (ed.), *The European Community and the Challenge of the Future*, London: Pinter.

Shore, Cris (1990) *Italian Communism: An Anthropological Perspective*, London: Pluto Press.

Shore, Cris (1993) Inventing the "People's Europe": Critical Perspectives on European Community Cultural Policy', *Man: Journal of the Royal Anthropological Institute*: 28 4 (December): 779–800.

Shore, Cris (1995) 'Usurpers or Pioneers? EC Bureaucrats and the Question of "European Consciousness"', in A. P. Cohen and N. Rapport (eds), *Questions of Consciousness*, London: Routledge.

Shore, Cris (1996) 'Transcending the Nation-state? The European Commission and the (Re)-discovery of Europe', *Journal of Historical Sociology*, 9 (4) (December): 473–96.

Shore, Cris (1997a) 'Governing Europe: European Union Audiovisual Policy and the Politics of Identity', in Cris Shore and Sue Wright (eds), *Anthropology of Policy: Critical Perspectives on Governance and Power*, London: Routledge.

Shore, Cris (1997b) 'Metaphors of Europe: Integration and the Politics of Language', in S. Nugent and C. Shore (eds), *Anthroplogy and Cultural Studies*, London: Pluto Press: 126–59.

Shore, Cris (1997c) 'Ethnicity, Xenophobia and the Boundaries of Europe', *International Journal on Minority and Group Rights*, 4 (3/4): 247–62.

Shore, Cris (1998) 'Creating Europeans: The Politicisation of "Culture" in the European Union', *Anthropology in Action*, 5 (3): 11–17.

Shore, Cris and Black, Annabel (1994) '"Citizens' Europe" and the Construction of European Identity', in V. Goddard, J. Llobera and C. Shore (eds), *The Anthropology of Europe: Identities and Boundaries in Conflict*, Oxford: Berg.

Shore, Cris and Wright, Susan (1997) 'Policy: A New Field of Anthropology', in C. Shore and S. Wright (eds), *Anthropology of Policy*, London: Routledge.

Silverman, Sydel (1968) 'Agricultural Organisation, Social Structure, and Values in Italy: Amoral Familism Reconsidered', *Amercian Anthropologist*, 70: 1–20.

Sivanandan, A. (1991) 'Editorial', *Race and Class* 32 (3): v–vi.

Smith, Anthony D. (1990) 'Towards a Global Culture?', *Theory, Culture and Society*, 7 (2–3): 171–92.

Smith, Anthony D. (1991) *National Identity*, Harmondsworth: Penguin.

Smith, Anthony (1992a) 'National Identity and the Idea of European Unity', *International Affairs*, 68 (1): 55–76.

Smith, Anthony (1992b) 'Europe versus the Nation?' *The New Federalist*, 5–6: 8–9.

Smith, Anthony D. (1993) 'A Europe of Nations – or the Nation of Europe?', *Journal of Peace Research*, 30 (2): 129–35.

Smith, Anthony D. (1995) *Nations and Nationalism in a Global Era*, Cambridge: Policy.

Smith, Gordon (1983) *Politics in Western Europe: A Comparative Analysis*, Aldershot: Gower.

Soysal, Yasemin (1997) 'Changing Citizenship in Europe: Remarks on Postnational Membership and the National State' in D. Cesarini and M. Fulbrook (eds), *Citizenship, Nationality and Migration in Europe*, London: Routledge.

Spence, David (1994a) 'Staff and Personnel Policy in the Commission', in G. Edwards and D. Spence (eds), *The European Commission*, Harlow: Longman: 62–94.

Spence, David (1994b) 'Structure, Function and Procedures in the European Commission', in G. Edwards and D. Spence (eds), *The European Commission*, Harlow: Longman.

Spencer, Michael (1990) *1992 and All That: Civil liberties in the Balance*, London: Civil Liberties Trust.

Spierenburg, Dirk (1979) *Proposals for Reform of the Commission of the European Communities and its Services*, Brussels: European Commission.

Staff Regulations (1993), *Regulations of the Rules Applicable to Officials and Other Servants of the European Communities*, Luxembourg: OOPEC.

Stevenson, Burton (1974) *Stevenson's Book of Quotations: Classical and Modern*, London: Cassell (tenth edition).

Stolcke, Verena (1995) 'Talking Culture: New Boundaries, New Rhetorics of Exclusion in Europe', *Current Anthropology*, 36 (1): 1–24.

Strathern, Marylin (1992) *Reproducing the Future*, Manchester: Manchester University Press.

Street, Brian (1993) 'Culture is a Verb: Anthropological Aspects of Language and Cultural Process', in D. Graddol, L. Thompson and M. Byram (eds), *Language and Culture*, Clevedon, Avon: British Association for Applied Linguistics in association with Multilingual Matters.

Sultana, Ronald (1995) 'A Uniting Europe, a Dividing Education? Euro-centrism and the Curriculum', *International Studies in Sociology of Education*, 5 (2): 115–44.

Taylor, Paul (1983) *The Limits of European Integration*, London: Croom Helm.

Thatcher, Margaret (1988) *Text of Speech Given by the Prime Minister on Europe in Bruges, Belgium*, London: Prime Minister's Office.

Tietmeyer, Hans (1988) 'Political Consequences of Monetary Union', text of speech delivered to the Social Congress of the Commission of Bishops' Conferences of the

European Community', Brussels, 20 February (translated by the British Management Data Foundation).

Turner, Terrence (1993) 'Anthropology and Multiculturalism: What is Anthropology that Multiculturalists Should Be Mindful of It?', *Cultural Anthropology*, 84: 411–29.

Turner, Terrence (1995) Reply to Stolcke, *Current Anthropology*, 36 (1) (February): 16 –18.

Turner, Victor (1967) *The Forest of Symbols*, Ithaca, New York: Cornell University Press.

Tyler, Edward (1871) *Primitive Culture*, New York: Harper.

Usborne, David (1988) 'EC Nations Warned to "Wake Up" to Loss of Sovereign Power', *Independent*, 7 July.

Vibert, Frank (1995) 'The Case for "Unbundling" the Commission', in Etienne Davignon *et al.*, *What Future for the European Commission?*, Brussels: Philip Morris Institute for Public Policy Research:

Wallace, Helen (1996) 'Politics and Policy in the EU: The Challenge of Governance', in H. and W. Wallace (eds), Policy-making in the European Union (3rd ed.), Oxford: Oxford University Press.

Wallace, William (1983) 'Less than a Federation, More than a Regime: The Community as a Political System', in H. Wallace *et al.*, (eds), *Policy-making in the European Community*, Chichester: John Wiley.

Wallace, William (1990a) *The Transformation of Western Europe*, London: Pinter.

Wallace, William (1990b), 'Introduction', in Wallace (ed.) *The Dynamics of European Integration*, London: Pinter.

Wallace, William (1996) 'Government without Statehood: The Unstable Equilibrium', in H. and W. Wallace (eds), *Policy-making in the European Union*, Oxford: Oxford University Press.

Wallace, William and Smith, Julie (1995) 'Democracy or Technocracy? European Integration and the Problem of Popular Consent', *West European Politics* 18 (3): 137–57.

Wallace, Helen, Wallace, William, and Webb, Carol (eds) (1983) *Policy-making in the European Community*, Chichester: John Wiley and Sons.

Walzer, Michael (1967) 'On the Role of Symbolism in Political Thought', *Political Science Quarterley*, 82: 191–205.

Ward, Ian (1996) *A Critical Introduction to European Law*, London: Butterworths

Ware, Richard (1998) *EMU: The Constitutional Implications*, House of Commons Research Paper 98/78, London: House of Commons.

Wagner, Roy (1981) *The Invention of Culture*, Chicago: University of Chicago Press.

Watson, Roy and Blythe, Derek (1995) 'City at the Heart of Europe', *The Newcomer: An Introduction to Life in Belgium*, Brussels: Ackroyd.

Webb, Carol (1983) 'Theoretical Perspectives and Problems', in H. Wallace, W. Wallace and C. Webb (eds), *Policy-making in the European Community*, Chichester: John Wiley and Sons.

Webber, Frances (1991) 'From Ethnocentrism to Euro-racism', Race and Class, 32 (3): 11–18.

Weber, Eugene (1979) *Peasants into Frenchmen: The Modernisation of Rural France, 1870–1914*, London: Chatto and Windus.

Weber, Max (1948), in H. Gerth and C. Wright Mills (eds), *From Max Weber*, London.

Weiler, J. H. H. (1992) 'After Maastricht: Community Legitimacy in Post-1992 Europe', in William James Adams (ed.), *Singular Europe*, University of Michigan Press.

Welsh, Jennifer M. (1993) *A Peoples' Europe? European Citizenship and European Identity*, EUI Working Paper ECS No. 93/2, Florence: European University Institute.

Westlake, Martin (1994) *Britain's Emerging Euro-elite? The British in the European Parliament 1979–1992*, Aldershot: Dartmouth.

Wiener, Antje (1997) *'European' Citizenship Practice: Building Institutions of a Non-state*, Boulder: WestviewPress.

Williams, Raymond (1976) *Keywords*, London: Fontana.

Williams, Raymond (1981) *Culture*, Glasgow: Fontana.

Williamson, David (1994) 'The Looking Glass View of Europe', *Financial Times*, 15 December.

Williamson, David (1998) *European Identity: Premature Brussels Baby or Lusty Infant?*, Bath: European Research Institute, University of Bath: Occasional Paper No. 10.

Willis, Virginia (1982) *Britons in Brussels*, London: PSI.

Wilson, Tom (1993) 'An Anthropology of the European Community', in E. Smith and T. Wilson (eds), *Cultural Change and the New Europe*, London: Westview Press.

Wintle, Michael (1996) 'Cultural Identity in Europe: Shared Experience', in M. Wintle (ed.), *Culture and Identity in Europe*, Aldershot: Avebury.

Wistricht, Ernst (1989) *After 1992: The United States of Europe*, London: Routledge.

Wolf, Eric (1966) 'Kinship, Friendship and Patron-client Relationships in Complex Societies', in M. Banton (ed.), *The Social Anthroplogy of Complex Societies*, London: Tavistock.

Wolf, Eric (1982) *Europe and the People Without History*, Berkeley: University of California Press.

Wolf, Eric (1994) 'Perilous Ideas: Race, Culture, People', *Current Anthropology*, 35 (4): 1–12.

Woollacott, Martin (1991), 'Cry of a Lost Community', *Guardian*, 15 November.

Wright, P. (1985) *On Living in an Old Country: The National Past in Contemporary Britain*, London: Verso.

Wright, Susan (1994) '"Culture" in Anthropology and Organisational Studies', in S. Wright (ed.), *Anthropology of Organisations*, London: Routledge.

Wright, Susan (1998) 'The Politicization of Culture', *Anthropology Today*, 14 (1) (February): 7–15.

Index